Between Faith and Belief

SUNY series in Theology and Continental Thought

Douglas L. Donkel, editor

Between Faith and Belief

Toward a Contemporary Phenomenology
of Religious Life

JOERI SCHRIJVERS

Published by State University of New York Press, Albany

© 2016 State University of New York

All rights reserved

Printed in the United States of America

No part of this book may be used or reproduced in any manner whatsoever without written permission. No part of this book may be stored in a retrieval system or transmitted in any form or by any means including electronic, electrostatic, magnetic tape, mechanical, photocopying, recording, or otherwise without the prior permission in writing of the publisher.

For information, contact State University of New York Press, Albany, NY
www.sunypress.edu

Production, Eileen Nizer
Marketing, Michael Campochiaro

Library of Congress Cataloging-in-Publication Data

Names: Schrijvers, Joeri.
Title: Between faith and belief : toward a contemporary phenomenology of religious life / Joeri Schrijvers.
Description: Albany : State University of New York Press, 2016. | Series: SUNY series in theology and Continental thought | Includes bibliographical references and index.
Identifiers: LCCN 2015016595 | ISBN 9781438460215 (hardcover : alk. paper) | ISBN 9781438460222 (paperback : alk. paper) | ISBN 9781438460239 (e-book)
Subjects: LCSH: Religious life. | Philosophy and religion.
Classification: LCC BL624 .B4644 2016 | DDC 200—dc23
LC record available at http://lccn.loc.gov/2015016595

10 9 8 7 6 5 4 3 2 1

Contents

Acknowledgments ix

Introduction xi

General Introduction: Toward A Contemporary Phenomenology of
Religious Life: Contours and Contexts 1
    The Many Faces of Atheism Today 1
    "Against the Return of Religion: A Critique of the
        Religious Origins of our Political Concepts":
        Jean-Luc Nancy and Peter Sloterdijk 4
    "A Universalizing Faith at the Origin of the Social Bond:
        Postsecularism As a Secularizing Task": Ludwig Binswanger 5
    "A Recognition of the Elementary Faith Underlying the
        Secularizing Task": John D. Caputo 11
    Conclusion: Toward A Contemporary Phenomenology of
        Religious Life 21

Part 1: Without

Chapter 1: Anarchistic Tendencies in Contemporary Philosophy:
Reiner Schürmann and the Hubris of Philosophy 29
    "What is to be done at the end of metaphysics?" 29
    Heideggerian Anarchy 30
    Levinasian Anarchy 38
    Derridean Anarchy 41
    Conclusion: In Praise of Everydayness 43

Chapter 2: What Comes after Christianity? Jean-Luc Nancy's
Deconstruction of Christianity   47
   The End of Metaphysics and the Deconstruction of Christianity   47
   Thinking the World: Between Heidegger and Levinas   50
   The Deconstruction of Christianity   52
   Nancy's Exegesis of the Resurrection Story: *Noli me Tangere*
      and the Faith in Sense   69
   Deconstructing Nancy with Derrida   72
   Conclusion: What Comes after Christianity?   79

Chapter 3: Exercises in Religion I: Peter Sloterdijk and the
Matrix of Monotheism   83
   How to Change Your Life: An Ontological Self-Help Group   84
   Once Again: Violence and Metaphysics   88
   The De-suprematicization of the World: The Matrix of
      Monotheism   90
   An Exhausted Matrix?   94
   Conclusion: Sloterdijk and "The Legitimacy of Postmodernity"   97

Chapter 4: Exercises in Religion II. Living with Exhaustion   101
   Modernity and the Emergence into History   103
   Postmodern Life: Ascetic, Aesthetic, and Athletic Religion   110
   Life, and Nothing but Life: The Liberation from the Matrix?   115
   Changing Codes   119
   Conclusion: Deconstructing Christianity?   122

Conclusion to Part 1   125

Part 2: Between

Chapter 5: In Defense of Deconstruction. John D. Caputo and
His Critics   133
   How (Not) to Do Away With "The With"?   136
   Religion without Religion versus Religion with Religion   142
   Mind the Gap! Of Unconditionals and Their Condition   151
   Conclusion: Begging to Differ   161

Chapter 6: Between Faith and Belief: Derrida versus Caputo   165
   The Event of Religion   165
   Prayers, Tears, and Gnashing of Teeth: On Attempting to
      be an Atheist   169

Derrida as Natural Metaphysician: The Pervertibility of Pure Faith	174
The Aporia, and the Great Unknown: God	178
Conclusion: Between Faith and Belief	181

Chapter 7: Between Strong and Weak Theology: Of a Sacred Anarchy in Caputo and Marion — 185
- A Christian Reversal of Values — 185
- A Sacred Anarchy, or the Authority of Authorities — 189
- From Caputo to Marion: Abandoned to Love? — 193
- Conclusion: Between Phenomenology and Theology — 204

Conclusion to Part 2 — 209
- *Facere Veritatem:* The Primacy of Bad Conscience — 209
- Not Yet Rid of God? Of a Religion Not Quite without Religion — 215

Part 3: Within

Chapter 8: Ludwig Binswanger's Phenomenology of Love — 223
- Greetings from Being — 225
- Phenomenology of Love — 233
- Toward an Ontology Incarnate: The Fullness of Being — 237
- Conclusion: Faith in Love — 242

Chapter 9: The "Ends" of Love: Friendship, Death, and Care — 245
- Heidegger and Binswanger — 245
- The "Unfolding" of Love in the World: Toward a *Liebende Sorge* — 249
- Love, Language, and Community — 255
- Phenomenology of Friendship—The Death of Friends and Lovers — 259
- The Self between Love and World — 264
- Conclusion: Loving Life and Living Love — 273

Chapter 10: From Love to Life (and Back Again) — 275
- The Knowledge of Love — 275
- Body and World: Onward and Upward — 278
- The Art of a Difficult Existence: Binswanger's *Ibsen* — 279
- Binswanger, Art, and the Phenomenology of Religious Life — 284
- Conclusion: From a Finite Life to the Infinity of Love — 287

Conclusion to Part 3 — 291

General Conclusion	293
Phenomenology of Religious Life	293
A Phenomenology of *Religious Life*	303
Notes	317
Bibliography	365
Index	375

Acknowledgments

Chapter 1, "Anarchistic Tendencies in Contemporary Philosophy," on the thought of Reiner Schürmann, has appeared in *Research in Phenomenology* 37 (Brill, 2007) 417–439. Chapter 2, "What Comes after Christianity?" has been published earlier in *Research in Phenomenology* 39 (Brill, 2009) 266–291 and has been expanded here and complemented by my chapter, reproduced with permission of the publishers, "Jean-Luc Nancy's Deconstruction of Christianity," in *Between Philosophy and Theology*, edited by Lieven Boeve and Christophe Brabant (Farnham: Ashgate, 2010), pp. 43–62. Copyright © 2010. Chapters 3 and 4 on Peter Sloterdijk are republished here, extended and revised, with permission of the publisher, from my Dutch monograph *In het licht van de eindigheid. Het einde van de metafysica en de deconstructie van het christendom* (Antwerpen-Apeldoorn: Garant, 2013), pp. 225–260. Chapter 5 as well as the general conclusion contain some sections of my "Marion, Levinas, and Heidegger on the Question Concerning Ontotheology," which appeared in *Continental Philosophical Review* 43 (2010) 207–239, reprinted with kind permission from Springer Science+Business Media. Chapters 5 to 7 are an extended version of a chapter on Caputo that appeared in my *In het licht van de eindigheid*, pp. 155–189, reprinted here with permission from the publisher. Chapter 7 contains elements of my essay on Marion in Willie Van der Merwe and W. Stoker (eds.), *Looking Beyond? Shifting Views of Transcendence in Philosophy, Theology, Art, and Politics* (London: Brill-Rodopi, 2012), pp. 157–172.

    I would like to thank Professor William Desmond, who was so kind to read earlier versions of this work, and Professor Willie van der Merwe for enabling me to complete this book in proper fashion at the VU University Amsterdam. A word of gratitude to Professor Lieven Boeve and my other colleagues of the research group "Theology in A Postmodern Context" at the Faculty of Theology and Religious Studies (KU Leuven), especially Dr. Justin Sands, Dr. Patrick Cooper, and Drs. Bradford Manderfield for the hospitality with which they have greeted my work. Thanks to Nancy, Doug, Eileen, and Laura at SUNY Press for the opportunity to publish in this great series. Finally, a special thanks to Sarah Mina C, my wife, for the cover art.

Introduction

Between Faith and Belief. Toward A Contemporary Phenomenology of Religious Life is, in its own way, a long response to Reiner Schürmann's question "What is to be done at the end of metaphysics?" once "being" is unhinged from God. Each chapter corresponds to an author under discussion and in effect delineates what is to be done "after" metaphysics in general and what might be the fate of religion and transcendence in our secular world. The question of metaphysics, which is considered here as the question concerning ontotheology, can be seen as a question of hubris. It is the hubris of the human being pretending to come up with a 'transcendental signifier' that totalizes and unifies human existence (or even 'being/s in general') in its entirety and so provides existence with an *arche* and *telos* from which there seems no escape.

This book primarily wants to communicate its enthrallment with Binswanger's thinking of love's presencing. It wants to move out of sterile debates of endless deconstructions, of a certain all too certain phenomenology. The main thesis of the book is that, with a great many of contemporary thinkers (traditions are important), we should stand up and not think of this world, its finitude, and its politics as *mere* world, *mere* finitude, *mere* politics, *mere* tradition, and *mere* capitalism. Something transcends all this, and we know not what. This difference, we think, between faith and belief, between finitude and *mere* finitude, is all a contemporary and secular phenomenology of religious life seeks to install.

The General Introduction to this book offers the contours and contexts necessary to understand the contemporary debate around the remainder of God and Christianity "after" metaphysics as well as the state of continental philosophy "after" deconstruction by aligning the significant voices of these debates alongside one another.

Between Faith and Belief is divided in three parts, each of which can be read separately. The General Introduction provides an overview of the current debates on the religious (or not) strand of deconstruction and phenomenology. The main thesis of this book is drawn from my previous work, *Ontotheological Turnings?* (Albany: State University of New York Press, 2011), which surmised already that metaphysics and its "ontotheological constitution" (Heidegger) are inevitable. This book proceeds from this conclusion by enquiring phenomenologically into the "how" of ontotheology and by asking how (not) to comport ourselves to the inevitability of ontotheological thinking. Part 1, "Without," considers some figures of what one might call the "avant-garde" of contemporary thought—Jean-Luc Nancy, Peter Sloterdijk, and the late Reiner Schürmann—who all, in one way or another, want to do away with the Christian tradition or at least try to think "after" and "without" Christianity. Its title is an indication of the attempts of these authors to "overcome" not only the metaphysical tradition but also the Christian heritage that carried this metaphysics. The conclusion of Part 1 argues that such a rupture is simply too bold to be true and argues for the necessity of tradition through mediations and small steps of change, evolution rather than revolution: Christianity will be part of the change and the evolution rather than just put aside.

Part 2, "Between," considers the spiritual inclinations of Jacques Derrida's deconstruction. It does this by staging the debate between John D. Caputo and Martin Hägglund, who has argued that there is no such strand in Derrida, and between Caputo and Jean-Luc Marion's recent theological writings on love. Just as much as the first part tries to show that one cannot do "without" metaphysics or Christianity, the second part of this book argues that, in similar ways, one cannot have a "religion without religion," as Caputo famously defines the religious strand of Derrida's deconstruction. This book, furthermore, derives its title not only from a greeting that Jean-Luc Nancy imparted in my copy of one of his works, but foremost from the fact that the faith without belief that Caputo and Nancy are seeking shows itself to be phenomenologically impossible. One attains such faith only from the various beliefs, and it is, inversely, never certain whether such an "originary faith" is entirely without the beliefs from which it arose in the first place. Hence this position: between faith and belief.

The conclusion of Part 2 leads us into a discussion of the subtitle of this work, a contemporary phenomenology of religious life, a term we take rather loosely from Martin Heidegger. This conclusion extends and promotes certain "religious" features of Derrida's thought, most notably the fact that, for him and for us, the question of finitude has not led us to thinking that all this finitude is just that, *mere* finitude: something else is going on in our dealings with one another; something is at stake that just cannot be reduced to a nihilistic "anything goes." I will show that Caputo would actually be very close to Derrida (and to Levinas) when arguing that one can never reduce the politics (of hospitalities, of Christianities, etc.) to *just that*, to just politics: for within the troubles one has to be hospitable to all the others and the small preferences one has for this singular other rather than another other, there is a responsibility to reinvent the conditions of the possibility of such politics constantly. It is this responsibility that, for Derrida, moves in other ways than those of being. This is what he takes from Levinas and what Caputo takes from both of these thinkers. However, Derrida will move away from Levinas when arguing that these constant revisions and reinventions of our responsibilities are not regulated by whatever ideal one can imagine: there is no way of proving and guaranteeing that a new form of responsibility will be better than the previous one. If there is hope in Derrida, it is that this reinvention of responsibility will be "less bad" than other forms of responsibility. In reality, there is no regulative ideal—there *is* no such thing as the least bad form of hospitality—but there *is* something like an inclination or ontological tendency, if you will, to rephrase, reiterate, and reinvent our ways and manners of being responsible for all.

It is here that Caputo quietly moves away from Derrida and embraces Levinas in order to dodge these very empirical conditions into which we are lodged. Caputo's *dream* of God (which is a sort of imaginary variation of what all of the traditions used to "call God") is, as Hägglund rightly points out, still plagued by seeing in this "God" (who does not "exist" but "insists," as Caputo has it) some sort of totalizing instance that keeps the balance between what is conditional and what is unconditional firmly in check. Caputo aligns himself with Levinas so as to make sure that "the tears unseen by the civil servant" (Levinas) are at least seen by God.

In this regard, Part 3, "Within," presents Ludwig Binswanger's phenomenology of love, one of the first and most radical criticisms of Heidegger's *Being and Time*. Here, phenomenology shows itself at its most affirmative and constructive. With Binswanger, I develop a phenomenology of our being bent, or turned, to one another through the sheer presence of love—what I will call an ontological "salutation" present in being—and will distance ourselves from both deconstruction and Heidegger. Martin Hägglund, for instance, in his insistence on Derrida's atheism, at times also misreads him (and certainly his reading of Levinas) and might be mistaken when concluding that the deconstructing of all ideas of salvation leads one to a place "without" religion. Derrida's *salut sans salvation* will therefore here be expanded with Binswanger's vision of such a greeting, of an originary *coram*, where all, in an "intersubjective curvature" otherwise than Levinasian, are turned to all.

It is from this place that Part 3 speaks: a phenomenological stance on the "togetherness" of all beings ontologically shot through with love—a being "enticed" by, "oriented," and bent toward otherness. This stance here does not proceed from a theological bias, but it is not hostile to religious matters either. On the contrary, it is because of philosophical modesty that the question of the infinite, of transcendence, and of God will need to remain open. It is for this reason that this work searches for a philosophical and phenomenological sense of incarnation and develops, with Binswanger, an ontology incarnate, an ontology that does not shy away from all things ontic and empirical, or, in Nancy's and Caputo's terms, a phenomenology that seeks a sense and a faith *from within* our concrete beliefs. If meaning and sense incarnate only in and through our very concrete dealings with one another, then this work may serve as a much-needed correction to anti-incarnational strands in contemporary philosophy. Such a position is inaugurated by Levinas, where no "instance" of the Other ever coincides with, let alone embraces, a very particular other, but is perpetuated by Derrida, where not one "presence" is to be encountered phenomenologically and all presence is dismissed as a metaphysics of presence. Binswanger's phenomenology of love offers a different approach: here the meeting with the ontic other, although it cannot contain the infinity and borderlessness of love, can conserve and hold onto the (infinite) meaning arising out of the encounter with the concrete other, the very ontic you whom I love.

This phenomenological part spills over into the General Conclusion, which summarizes the main threads of our analyses and tries to launch pathways for this quite secular phenomenology of religious life by giving some ontological relief to Binswanger's view of humanity as "the conversation of all with all." Thinking "after" metaphysics, then, primarily means to come to terms with the fact that it is impossible to have such totalizations or hegemonies over the "entirety of beings." It also means to arrive at a philosophical and phenomenological modesty that is triggered not only by a "fundamental uncertainty" once existence remains without "a whence and a whither" (Heidegger). If metaphysics is withering away in its concomitant strive for certainty, unity, and conceptual mastery over beings, then, Schürmann states, one should develop a phenomenology in tune with an anarchic presencing of persons and things, a sheer happening of world without origins (*arche*) or paradises lost, or a *telos* to attain in one or the other utopian eschatology.

What is to be done when one is always between faith and belief? Rather than desperately attempting to rid ourselves of onto-theologies or religions, one needs to give an account of the "compulsion" of metaphysical phantasms. If metaphysics and ontotheology come naturally to us, as Schürmann states, then it is not so much that "religion without religion" haunts the concrete religions but the other way around: "religion without religion" remains stuck in the religions it wants to overcome or otherwise do away with. For instance, when Caputo mentions the lifelong doubts of Mother Teresa about her religion, he adds that this was a crisis of her beliefs with *no injury* to her faith. But such a shelter, an immunization of faith from belief, might not be given: for example, it forbids thinking of a genuine loss of faith—which nonetheless seems to be happening today to many of us who have become indifferent to all things transcending or escaping our finite lives.

To turn the "deconstruction of Christianity" into a contemporary "phenomenology of religious life," one needs to take into account that contemporary deconstructions of Christianity, such as Nancy's, speak of the end of a religion, and of everything that concerns such an ending, now that the metaphysical Signification erected in the West through the unity that Christianity gathered around itself and its highest being are fading away. Nancy aims to attend to the arising of sense as a surprise, as that which ruptures its stifling into a stable and "fully present" signification. What Nancy explores formally and indeed rather technically is in a way retrieved by Sloterdijk materially. Sloterdijk speaks of the "exhaustion of metaphysics" and religion and seeks to attend to those practices that have taken the place of religion in contemporary society, such as sports and excessive consumption. Religion (and Christianity specifically) for him has been outnumbered and outplaced—in a sense—by other practices that deliver sense and meaning to the lives of our contemporaries.

A contemporary deconstruction of Christianity cannot help but take note of the sheer indifference of our contemporaries toward the question of religion (if not an indifference to the other through inequality and to the world through the ecological crisis). Atheism's anti-religiosity seems to have given way to an a-religiosity. This is also why Marion's phenomenology of love, where love is the be-all and end-all of our encounter with world, can be accused of confusing such an indifference with a hatred toward God (so interpreting it immediately in a religious register). One might say that if there is too much of a religious horizon present in Marion and Caputo, there is too little of such a horizon at work in Sloterdijk and Nancy. Sloterdijk's account of the "exhaustion of the matrix of monotheism" leaves us in a world where the religious transgressions are entirely taken over by athletics and art, and both of these play entirely in the "extension of the domain of the struggle" (Michel Houellebecq), where the option for the poor or the marginalized is turned into a commodity just as well and will be maintained for as long as there is a market available for such an option.

Sloterdijk's description of the end of metaphysics is an accurate one, but one that in the end again resorts too easily to the apocalyptism that can also be detected in Nancy's works. One needs to gather from these chapters that the horizon of life is not exhausted by the horizon of religion. Love and life know of a futurity that outwits, in a sense, the tradition. For, even if one cannot do "without" metaphysics, religion, and tradition (as especially the chapter on Nancy shows), this ought not to lead to a dictatorship of tradition over the lives we are living today.

Yet the fact that there is no such dictatorship does not mean that there would be no place left for religion once being is unhinged from God, once we all are secular. Sloterdijk's search for a politics adequate to our time, a politics that (like Derrida's) would conceive of an authority without power (or at least a power without sovereignty), is to be applauded. Yet Sloterdijk seems to decide too quickly that, with regard to such a rephrasing of authority, Christianity and religion no longer have anything to say. However, many of Sloterdijk's ideas themselves take Christian principles as their condition of possibility (a fact that Nancy too seems to disregard).

The most important result of this book, however, is the inclusion of Binswanger's work into the contemporary debate in Part 3. Binswanger seems to have anticipated the empirical-transcendental phenomenology called for by contemporary phenomenologists and at times even comes close to what Derrida called "a quasi-transcendental dizziness," where it is in effect such a back and forth between the empirical and the transcendental, between the very ontic you—Binswanger mentions the kiss, the embrace, and the handshake—and the meaning of "beings," that makes for the origin of meaning and our encounter with things (in short: with presences).

Binswanger's aim is to come to a full-fledged transcendental and ontological account of the sense of sense, which is, for him, love. In a very classical manner, Binswanger aims in effect for the condition of possibility of the concrete happening of love. This condition of possibility Binswanger finds in the salutation and greeting that is being, in the "intersubjective curvature" that makes that there is no meaning and no love for one alone: even the most solipsistic of solipsisms makes sense if and only if its sense can be communicated *to* the other (through which solipsism is thoroughly senseless). It is such a salutation, a "to you," a vocative without Levinas's hyperbolic accusative, that Binswanger perceives as the ontological condition of possibility of us being turned to one another.

For Binswanger, in effect, it might be argued that at times one must abandon love in order to be and to exist in the world properly (although, because of Binswanger's curious dialectic, the world "has to be" this lack of love and overcome it in the least bad way possible). In this way, one can encounter in his work a dizziness and double passage similar to the one Derrida mentioned. Binswanger would agree with Nancy and Schürmann that this world of ours is not guided by or headed to one or the other divinity and is nothing more than "a sheer happening of world." He would, however, not agree with the view of these authors that it is a "mere passing" of world that we witness. For it is in and through love that one encounters, embraces, and holds on to a sense that surpasses the endless finitude of things. It is through love that we live and laugh and exist in the world and marvel at the spring of meaning, at the "*unausdeutbare Deutbarkeit der Dinge*," as Von Hoffmansthal has it. Philosophy may very well wonder about wonder, but it begins in love. The principle of philosophy, Derrida once wrote, is not philosophy, not the hubris of metaphysical systems, but the modesty and the frailty of us being turned to one another. The principle of philosophy, if there need be any, Derrida says, is a kiss, a touch with brute and mute matter: one can in effect have doubts about anything except the doubt itself, but one, similarly, cannot not touch the other and things.

For in Binswanger, one finds an empirical-transcendental phenomenology centered around the question of love, self, and world, starting from this very ontic you whom I love up to a question about being, and about the being of love: after all, it *is* rather wonderful that we all are interested *in* one another, always and everywhere.

General Introduction: Toward A Contemporary Phenomenology of Religious Life

Contours and Contexts

The Many Faces of Atheism Today

Both faith and atheism today are undergoing a transformation of sorts. It seems that both theism and atheism are in need of some sort of rethinking, lest atheism remain "difficult" and "parasitic" or "ascetic," "pragmatic," or "therapeutic."[1] According to Christopher Watkin, to be an atheist is "difficult" precisely because it is "imitative" and "parasitic" of the old religious days (if not daze), and what is needed today is a thinking that is "post"-theological, "beyond" theology as a sort of "overcoming" of theology. For Martin Hägglund, atheism admits of at least three versions, a "melancholic," "pragmatic," and "therapeutic." The first is close to Watkin's "parasitic" atheism as a sort of nostalgia and mourning "after" the death of God; the second is "pragmatic" in that it admits that some sort of unscathed, auto-immune, and indemnified necessary illusion is needed precisely to account for our commitments to the world. Hägglund's atheism, then, is a "therapeutic one in that it seeks to "treat the religious desire for fullness" and to show that mortal and finite being *lives* precisely as a lacking in being—finitude—that is not desirable to overcome.

For my part, and I think that Watkin and Hägglund would agree, the dominant form of atheism today is the parasitic and melancholic version: we have not yet arrived at post-theological thinking. My position—and I part ways with Watkin and Hägglund here—is that this is to the detriment of theology just as well: there seems to be no theology today that can be deemed trustworthy, and postsecular theologies seem only to assist in their own incredulity as long as they speak only to the ones already belonging to the flock. *Le croire pour le voir* ("one has to have faith in order to see"), as Marion writes, is not the solution: rather, it is part of the problem.

The norm and criterion for such rethinking of a/theism can be none other than our existence in the world, which, from the outset, is a shared existence—there is no existence that is not received. This work, then, is written somewhat in praise of secularization, as the academics of the day go a long way with what has been termed as the "postsecular" and so perhaps are led astray. This is why I ultimately propose a minimalistic universalism of sorts. This minimalistic universalism seeks to be an extension of what Levinas regarded to be the main feature of ethical responsibility, namely that responsibility falls to one despite oneself and is in no way a matter of choice. But this feature can be applied to the most important facts of our lives, namely birth, death, love, faith perhaps, but most definitely to our thrownness in existence and life as well. Across cultures and particular beliefs, these seem to be what we share in common. Yet all of these are, obviously, lived and experienced differently among different cultures and among individuals. This is why this universalism only ever is a minimal one.

A new version of secularism is needed. This secularism would know the limits of the objective and neutral ambitions of Enlightened thinking but would not, for that matter, abandon at least the ambition of some sort of neutrality—it is not always the case that supporters of one or the other religion have the better vantage point toward their religious practice. This is why Peter Sloterdijk, whom we encounter later in this work, adheres to a theory of religion "without zeal," that is, without too much participant observation and/or emotion. Yet the minimalistic universalism portrayed here is not dismissive of religion and Christianity either, for the simple reason that a large part of the world's population is in effect religious. The *philosophical* debate on whether or not there is a "religious structure to our existence in the world"—a quasi a priori (if I may say so) and therefore universal one—seems justified and indeed quite timely.

This work then seeks to contribute to some of the most pressing ongoing debates in contemporary thinking and society. Its aim, though, is rather modest: it seeks to introduce and comment on these debates rather than give an in-depth, specific, and specialized reading of all the authors who are presented here. One of the authors who figures prominently in this work is John D. Caputo. On the one hand, I interpret Caputo's work as describing somewhat the default position of many of our contemporaries:

although there be might be in effect some sort of religious structuring to existence in the world—whether we call it "passion," "love," "greeting," or even "survival"—the ways in which this structure has been institutionalized, if not commodified, have given us plenty of reasons to be wary about just such institutions. This is, I think, the core of Caputo's "religion without religion." On the other hand, Caputo contributes considerably to the ongoing debates. He has, for instance, commented at length, and at times perhaps somewhat *inhospitably*, to the questions raised by Hägglund and recently by Aaron Simmons and Stephen Minister.[2] Although later I portray these dialogues in greater detail, it is important to note from the outset that, for Caputo, both the "atheist" Hägglund and the "theists" Simmons and Minister present us with an "abridged form of deconstruction" and postmodern *thinking*: the former wants us to do entirely "without religion," the latter want us to do "with religion"; the former wants too little of religion, the latter two simply too much. Be that as it may, Caputo should be commended for his willingness to dialogue with these younger scholars seeking their way: all too often today, academic debate is reduced to a sterile piling up of publications that nobody really seems to read and that at any rate do not function as vectors for a contemporary debate or catalysts for thinking.

The stakes of such a secular minimalistic universalism are well summed up somewhere late in Michael Naas's intriguing reading of Derrida's *Foi et savoir*—a book, by the way, only minimally referred to by Caputo and maximally, if I can say so, by Hägglund. Here is what Naas writes, commenting on the following phrase of Caputo's *Deconstruction in a Nutshell*: "The whole point of a deconstructive, postcritical, postsecularizing analysis of what is called reason—that is, the point of a New Enlightenment—would be to show the extent to which reason is woven from the very fabric of faith."[3] But Naas comments:

> I would agree with this claim, so long as "the postsecular" is meant to suggest here not a postsecular return to religion but a critique of the religious origins of our political concepts, as well as an acceptance of the universalizing faith at the origin of the social bond, that is, so long as postsecularism remains both a secularizing task to be accomplished and a recognition of the elementary faith that makes this task possible.[4]

This nicely summarizes what this work sets out to do. Let us comment on this task, which we consider the task of this work as well.

"Against the Return of Religion: A Critique of the Religious Origins of our Political Concepts": Jean-Luc Nancy and Peter Sloterdijk

The chapters on Nancy and Sloterdijk may show our agreement with the fact that what is returning today is not "religion," and certainly not the institutionalized form of "religion with religion." I take Naas's phrasing as reminiscent of Karl Löwith's famous adage that what he witnessed, in his days, was a secularization and translation of a great many of Christian concepts: Heidegger's emphasis on guilt, in this regard, would be nothing but a secular translation of the Christian emphasis on sin. Today, however, what seems to be happening is not an ongoing secular translation of this or that concept, but rather the bankruptcy of any attempt to translate Christianity properly in terms of contemporary cultures. This is a point with which even some theologians, "postsecularizing" as they are, would agree. This work, however, disagrees with their (re)solution to this aporia—an agreeing to disagree that also recurs in the chapter on Marion: it is not because one cannot "secularize" properly that all that one can do is postsecularize; that is, it is not because there is no secular, neutral, and objective reason that the only *option* one has is to "sacralize" and "sanctify" the non-neutral presuppositions one contingently is "thrown into." If one does so, it will be argued, one lapses into a sort of postmodern fideism in which one indeed needs faithful eyes to see the reasons of faith and hope. This is what I would call the "apathetic pluralism" of our days, in which one culture or language game dares not to criticize the presuppositions and non-neutrality of other cultures and language games because, well, such presuppositions is all we have. Postsecularism in this regard does not only leap into fideism but also in a sort of particularism in which one's own presuppositions are valued if not more than at least as good as any other.

On the other hand, one should be attentive to the "religious origins" of our political concepts. It is Derrida who made us aware of just how much "theological heritage" there is in our thinking of sovereignty, for instance, in which the ruler can nicely (but also hypocritically) make an exception for him- or herself. This is why there is a surprising link between ontotheology and ideology, a link that was already perceived, as I will show, by Reiner Schürmann, whose thought is presented in the next chapter. Apart from this, this work repeatedly points to the debate between Löwith and Hans Blumenberg, a debate that is nicely rehearsed by Nancy and Sloterdijk. Blumenberg's "correction" of Löwith is as follows: no matter how hard one attempts to secularize and translate Christian concepts into a more suitable contemporary vocabulary, there will inevitably and eventually come a moment when the "old religious answer" no longer meets the needs of the contemporary situation. This is the moment, according to Sloterdijk, for instance, when religious answers, even if translated or recontextualized, will no longer be heard simply because these religious teachings can no longer understand or even address the questions that the contemporary situation poses. One need only think here of the allergic reaction of a great many religious traditions against homosexuality and same-sex marriages.

"A Universalizing Faith at the Origin of the Social Bond: Postsecularism As a Secularizing Task": Ludwig Binswanger

One should note, first, the active formulations: at the end of metaphysics, what is to be done—to refer to Schürmann—is a seculariz*ing* and a universaliz*ing*. These tasks have been no more completed than ontotheology has been overcome at a simple command. It is for this reason that this work turns to the thought of Jean-Luc Nancy, whose work is one of the most remarkable attempts to rethink the social bond and the question of community today. Nancy's logic is one of sharing, a rephrasing of being-with and of *Miteinandersein* in a world that is nothing but world. Nancy's deconstruction of Christianity, then, is first a secular translation of the "otherworld theory"—all that one thought about the highest and supreme being was *really* about our existing in the world—only then to become a rethinking of community from out of a sort of "Christianity without Christianity," a Christianity that dissolves from within while opening up a situation in which classic Christianity no longer has anything to contribute. It is understandable that Nancy turns to Christianity, perhaps the greatest dream of community that humanity has ever seen. The Eucharist, for instance, imagines a community of all with all: sinners and saints, the dead and the living, the slaves and the free, men and women, Greeks and Jews, Jews and Palestinians. . . . The deconstruction of this *communio* is what for Nancy will amount to the sharing of a world of all with all, a sharing in a sense that is always and already there, though never fully present: the sharing of sense, then, is all there is to the world. The dream of such a *communio* has to give space to the reality of this *cum*: our being together in our world.

It is a lot, but not enough. One might say that I have found in the works of Ludwig Binswanger that which I could not find in Nancy: a full-fledged account of community—in and through the ontic description of my lover's embrace—all the way up to an ontological and metaphysical account of the greeting in being or even that *is* being. Binswanger is here for plenty of reasons. First, he is a regretfully neglected author who has gone a long way in thinking a presence or presencing that is not immediately to be considered a metaphysics of presence: the reexamining of deconstruction so urgently needed is done in this chapter through comparisons of Binswanger with Nancy and Derrida. Second, Binswanger seems to be a predecessor of a main current in contemporary phenomenology: he was in fact "rewriting *Sein und Zeit*" long before Nancy called for it. Love, for Binswanger, is what we now would call a quasi-transcendental, as it is nowhere else than in its intertwining of this very ontic you whom I love and the ontological dream and idea that issue from it, the community of a love of all for all, although this idea is also what ultimately conditions the possibility of every ontic encounter (and pertains to "being" rather than being limited to the concrete empirical embrace of beings). This idea is examined as an "ontology incarnate": it is the very phenomenon of our greeting one another, of saluting, perhaps of being offended if someone did not greet us, that puts Binswanger on track of his phenomenology of love. With this salutation in being, then, Binswanger again is ahead of more contemporary thinkers such as Levinas, Nancy, and even Derrida. Before turning to this ontological greeting, however, let us have a look at the seculariz*ing* aspects of Binswanger's thought. What is remarkable here is that this secularism is not dismissive of religion; it tends neither to exclude nor to regionalize it (as the heralds of the old Enlightenment supposedly have done), but rather tries to include a religious stance within an ontology of love. Binswanger provides our minimalistic universalism with a much-needed framework or substructure on which a religious superstructure could easily arise or graft itself, even though religion (and Christianity in particular), it seems, is not necessary for Binswanger to develop the ontology of love. Love, for Binswanger, is separate from (Heideggerian) care, although it does not leave the latter untouched or unscathed: it rather subverts and uplifts care from within so as to turn it away from itself and attune it to the loving "togetherness" that rages through being. Through such upliftment, then, one might say that the two lovers—one never loves alone—get acquainted with at least the possibility of infinity *within* the finite plane that we deem to be ours. Binswanger's thought of love is not only an ontology, it is also an "ontology incarnate," which, as I said, has considerable advantages over current debates over incarnation in deconstruction. Whereas the empirical-transcendental nature of deconstruction is such, for instance, that the idea of Justice *is* nowhere else than in the diverse and different empirical instantiations of the various accounts of justice—the Law needs laws—but stipulates simultaneously that none of the latter can incarnate the Idea and the Law once and for all (properly: make it fully present), Binswanger proposes a different intertwining of the *eidos* and the *Faktum* altogether: although it is surely true that the *Faktum*, my love for this very ontic you here, cannot *contain* the *eidos* of an infinity in which all greet all, it is nevertheless possible that the *Faktum* can *conserve* something of the idea of an infinite love: the love of my lover, for instance, would not be "love" if we both did not wish this love to last forever. It would be through love, then, that this finitude that marks us can first encounter and then conserve something of the possibility of infinite love.

This is where Binswanger differs considerably from, say, the Protestant trait of postmodernism, where no "instance" of the Other ever coincides with, let alone embraces, a very particular other—think here already of the third party. Binswanger here differs from Caputo as well, who at times and especially for a Christian thinker is downright *anti*-incarnational: no single name could ever contain, let alone conserve, the names "to come." "This thing of love," then, as a transcendental, universal aspiration of the human being, which, most often, is concretized in empirical existence, has a considerable advantage over the aporetic deconstructionist ideas of "justice" and "hospitality," which never *actually* seem to happen or, if there is any such concretion, are only concretized badly, all too badly. The transcendence of love, then, would point us to the possibility of love descending and coming toward this finite realm of ours, rather than, in Jean Wahl's classic terms, the postmodern version of a trans*as*cendence of an Other who only ever points us to other Others or a trans*des*cendance, where the Other is always and already within me and orienting me to the Others sharing this finite plane.

Yet Binswanger speaks not of God. In fact, he avoids in an admirably secular way naming the divine—although the experience of love is to be considered a "grace." Binswanger, in ways similar to Marion, raises the stake of transcendentality to include, start with even, love: it is my very ontic lover who provides the passageway to the ontological encounter and enticing of all beings toward all other beings. Binswanger thus outlines an ontological *coram*: a being-with-of-all-beings-with-all-beings. In a sense, Binswanger corrects Aristotle (in a similar way as Augustine): though it might be true that "all men desire knowledge," it is perhaps even more true that all men and women desire to be loved: there has been, is, and will be no one who has not desired to be loved. So love concerns us universally, transcendentally, and ontologically. Yet one does not love alone (just as, as we will hear Levinas say, "the explanation of a thought can only happen among two": even the most solipsistic one of our thoughts makes sense if and only if it can be understood by an Other). The "experience" of love thus implies and is dependent on this very ontic you whom I love. Yet this lover, my lover, never exhausts the idea of love—this is, as we will see, what makes Binswanger differ from "a metaphysics of presence"—simply because this experience of love is as contingent as anything else in this empirical existence in the world: I could equally love, or have loved, someone else. But, in turn, this discrepancy between these empirical kisses, embraces, and greetings and the ontological encounter (or togetherness) is precisely what makes us "imagine"—Binswanger uses *Ein-bildung*, also denoting something like "imprinting," "marking," "educating," or stamping us with ("the with")—this ontology conditioning the very possibility of finite and empirical love in the first place.

This ontology incarnate of the greeting would be Binswanger's version of the universaliz*ing* faith at the origin of the social bond. For love entails some sort of faith in and affirmation of the fullness of being, a fullness only experienced with this ontic you, though. This, however, does not necessarily make this affirmation merely subjective: the passage through the transcendental precisely insinuates that this affirmation would come to us from out of "the things themselves," namely that it is the reality of our love down here which is aligned to and in agreement with the way "being as such" is constituted. It is therefore the thing of love itself that makes us want to affirm being and existence. In and through love, what is glimpsed is not that being is "unjust" (a certain Derrida) or "evil" (Levinas) but rather that it is better to be than not to be, or, at the very least, that being is "not all too bad."

Binswanger does not speak of God. Instead, he shows himself as a modern thinker wary of modern times: he seems to agree that "religion" is rightly banned from the public sphere but equally laments the modern thinkers' tendency to reduce religion to ethics or some other all too universal and all too transcendental trait, out of touch with being-in-the-world as it is. Binswanger equally, with a remarkable foresight—he is writing in the early 1940s—exposes modernity's tendency to veer into sheer individualism and nihilism: his account of Max Frisch's analysis of the ego that only ever desires its own self at the expense of all others as diabolical is quite remarkable. Let us have a look, then, at Binswanger's conception of religion and Christianity. Recall that what I am seeking in and retrieving from Binswanger is a secularism that does not *exclude* something like faith, as this is perhaps the least bad way to proceed in a world where "secularism" still remains truthful to the current "state of affairs." But for faith and religion, too, it is perhaps better to deal with a secular context, instead of assuming that the option of faith is as viable as any other now that secular reason is exposed as non-neutral, and instead of including itself in a pluralistic and relativistic set of propositions that are equal only because all of these would be non-neutral.

I begin by exploring Binswanger's account of why and how the Christian religion is always and already in the vicinity of the presencing of love. Already in the preface of the *Grundformen*, Binswanger affirms, quoting Feuerbach, that "for the human being, truthfully understood, the way towards the Godhead is always open."[5] Later Binswanger will speak of the "essential closeness" of the loving encounter and the encounter with God but insists that it is one thing to see in the "you" so loved an image and likeness of God and something else entirely to stick to a phenomenological analysis in which the lovers encounter, in and through their ontic love and the "seeking that is the human being's *Sehnsucht*," the idea of infinite of "youness" in general.[6] Binswanger clearly affirms that his is a strictly phenomenological and anthropological analysis: even though one, through the detour of a theological anthropology of Kierkegaard and the likes, could come up with similar results as this phenomenology does, namely that the human being would only become human and lovable once it exposes itself to God, Binswanger agrees with Heidegger here and states that it is "Heidegger's great philosophical act to have found a measure for the self" that is no longer "religious" but solely ontological.[7] In short, Binswanger's phenomenology of love no longer takes "the detour through God" but remains with "the detour through world," where human beings dwell, meet, and actually love one another, although he admits that describing this phenomenologically and anthropologically is "even more difficult" than it would be if one would stick to a theological analysis in which, for instance, the idea of infinity and its presence and incarnation in finitude could be more or less taken for granted.

Notwithstanding this secular stance, Binswanger is equally convinced that one has not understood love, and the passageway from finitude to infinity that love entails, if one does not take into account the "essential religious trait": the human being might turn into a loving self without the ontic presence of a certain you and succeed in loving solely on the basis of invoking a transcendent You—one might need to think of priests, monks, and nuns here. Binswanger's phenomenology, however, does not understand the human being in the light of God but rather the other way around. All of this, in effect, does not turn love into a "religious phenomenon" even though it will show the human being in its "basic religious trait."[8] Binswanger is very keen here to rule out both the all too dogmatic intrusion of the Christian faith into the (worldly) phenomenon of love and the all too dogmatically ruling out of this faith in the name of a certain secular reason.

But why precisely this secular stance then? Because a certain idea of God has been expelled from our being-in-the-world, and Binswanger very much takes into account what I would call the modern *muteness of being*, where, "after" metaphysics, beings no longer, at least no longer immediately, speak of God and of the divine. The secular world, for Binswanger, is one that has to deal with an "*akosmisich, entgöttert, entethisierten* world which has become, because of this, all the more scientific, political, and technological."[9] But whence this *chance* and this *possibility* of love, then, in the "loveless century"[10] that is his? If we are to understand this, it is best to compare two important quotes of the *Grundformen*:

> once the realization of the sense of Dasein is no longer possible in and through its relation to God, the human being experiences an uncanny poverty, an immense limitation as to its claims, yes even a sort of shrinking of its being. The problem of the human being needs a new solution. If we can no longer look for it in "the transcendent" or the eternal realm, then we will need to seek in the temporal and finite realm, in being and time, in being-in-the-world therefore. Yet in these realms alone not all accounts are settled. There remains a residue that does not befit finitude, the *yearning* [*Sehnsucht*] beyond the worldly finitude of Dasein for unification with infinite and eternal being. This is, as we know, only possible as a *contradiction or counterword* [*Widerspruch*] to finitude. The name of this yearning is, today still: *love*.[11]

Modern Dasein, if I might say so, already knows of a "there" without being, a "Da" that does not dissolve and is not satisfied with its fall and thrownness in a world. This is what Binswanger later beautifully describes as follows:

> In Christian anthropology, [. . .] the human being was oriented towards God as to its ground [. . .]. For a secularized anthropology, which does no longer understand the human being from out of God but merely from out of the human being itself, this solution is hard to swallow, yet the problem remains. When we seriously consider the question of the being of the self, [that is] of the truth of its appearing, then we will soon see [that] this Dasein somewhat "knows" about the ground of being, if only because it queries [*fragt*] for such a ground.[12]

The details of these quotes are to be considered later, but what should be noted here is Binswanger's phrasing that although the theological solution to the question of the sense of being is now gone, the *problem* precisely is what remains and shows itself in (and as) *Sehnsucht*, a yearning, a not-knowing what to seek and to do, an ignorance as to the point of it all, or, as Heidegger has it, a "fundamental uncertainty with regard to being."[13] It is this sense of a being-the-there—*das Sein des Da*—that *exists* uncomfortably and uncannily in a now atheological and mute being that is Binswanger's secular starting point and that his phenomenology of love seeks to answer, for it is my lover who will *answer* my question as to the point and sense of being—Binswanger's famous phrases in this regard: *Die Frage-Antwortspiel des Dasein mit sich Selbst* and "the conversation that humanity has with itself." One does not have to await any "grand" answer anymore, and my lover, too, will not put an end to philosophical and theological questioning once and for all, but she will *orient* these questions from out of the sole experience that alleviates the yearning: love. Nothing can really be answered and settled once and for all, except that the thing that will always remain is the speaking of beings about being(s), the speaking of one Dasein to another Dasein and the awareness that this speaking, possibly, is conditioned by and done "in the name of love."

In a sense, Binswanger here is close to the other Heideggerian who figures in this work, Reiner Schürmann. Schürmann, a priest who left the priesthood, is interested neither in love nor in religion but does depict the event of world intriguingly as "a mere coming to pass" in which the sense of being is nowhere else than in the historical figures whom being takes—Heidegger's different "epochs" of being—and in the speaking of beings about beings. If Schürmann asks what is to be done after metaphysics both politically and metaphysically, Binswanger asks what to do—and how to exist intersubjectively with, love—after modernity. What this work takes from both of these thinkers, though, is that one first needs to come to terms with the questions of finitude and historicity before jumping toward any infinity whatsoever.

"A Recognition of the Elementary Faith Underlying the Secularizing Task": John D. Caputo

It is clear that for Binswanger such elementary faith is a faith in love, initiated through my love for my lover and her love for me, an intersubjectivity most properly portrayed in the phenomenon of the greeting. Yet both Caputo and his counterpart, Hägglund, have a thing or two to add when it comes to such an elementary affirmation. Hägglund's atheism, however, is of a peculiar kind: he simply tries to acknowledge—and he is to be commended for that—"the double bind of mortal being" where "the positive can never be released from the negative."[14] This is, in fact, one of Hägglund's main points: amid this "infinite finitude" of ours, infinite because it goes all the way up and all the way down, there is not a single instance that would be exempt or immune for this double bind, where the good can always turn toward the bad and the ugly (and vice versa). In Derridean terms: there is no signified that would be immune or able to indemnify itself against intrusion from its reverse side—not the Other, not God, not "religion without religion" for that matter.

This does not mean, though, that Hägglund's notion of "survival" precludes any affirmation of finitude or of Derrida's "originary yes." For Derrida, however, Hägglund argues, this "yes," this affirmation, is not one that welcomes dreams and hopes for a Justice and Hospitality "to come." Rather, it is an affirmation that always and already has taken place—we would simply not *live* if this affirmation had not already been pronounced or had this decision not already been taken: "whatever we do, we have always already said "yes" to the coming of the future."[15]

All of this may seem a bit abstract, but in the background of this discussion, where to put the "yes"—already (Hägglund) or "to come" (Caputo's *"oui, oui, viens"*)—is an important discussion between Levinas and Derrida. According to Hägglund, Derrida argues against Levinas's all too neat distinction between ethics and politics. Levinas, in effect, seems to indicate at times that the others—the third party (politics)—nicely stand in line and wait until my dealings with this singular Other "without context" are finished, that is, when the good or ethical element has happened. For Derrida, then, there would be no way to distinguish once and for all between ethics and politics in such a way. This means that there would not be an ethical moment that would be exempt and safe from the messiness of politics, so that, ethically if not ontologically, justice and injustice happen *at the same time*. If the third, then, does not give us time to pause, then indeed all other moments than the political one, be they "religious" (Caputo), "poetical" (Richard Kearney), or "ethical" (Levinas), seem to be suspended. For Hägglund, Derrida's affirmation would be "merely" the affirmation of a "yes" already in place as soon as one goes out the door or hits the "snooze" button in the morning. Everything, in a sense, has already been decided at the very moment I decide to affirm another finite day. "*Les ouis sont toujours déjà venus.*"

Caputo, on the other hand, locates the stakes and (perhaps) the referent of such a *"oui, oui, viens"* a bit higher. In fact, in both his responses to the "theists" and to the "atheists" (Simmons, Minister, and Hägglund, respectively) as well as his response to Kevin Hart, who wonders whether this "religion without religion" is not simply (yet) another version of an Enlightened query so as to distinguish between the (ontological) "genus" and the (ontic) "species" of religion,[16] Caputo points to what he thinks is an underlying distinction supporting and justifying his idea of a "religion without religion," namely between faith (*foi*) and belief (*croyance*)—a distinction that recurs, in a slightly different way, in Jean-Luc Nancy. In and through the institutionalized versions of religions and their beliefs, Caputo thinks, rages a more originary faith in "what is going on" in these religions "with" religion, in what "they are about," a faith in the event that they try to name, no matter how improperly. "Religion without religion" can be but a second-order discourse, a specter and a ghost of the "settled" religions. This faith then affirms, to put it in colloquial terms, what "keeps us going," directs us toward our futures, makes us settle for one or the other belief even though we know that these beliefs do not completely answer for this faith that remains blissfully ignorant about the last ultimate stakes of life, its prayers, and its tears. All of this seems to explain Caputo's philosophical approach to religion—prior to his *The Weakness of God*—it is an inquiry into what religions are really about, an inquiry as to the condition of possibility of the event that transpires in these "religions with religion." "Religion without religion" is what transpires in these institutions (and what will haunt them if they tend to forget): a desperate seeking and questioning of the human being of its existence and its being, its hopes and desires, its prayer perhaps for something other than mere finitude amid all finitude.

Caputo's recent account of the "lifelong doubts" of Mother Teresa is illuminating in this respect:

> When I speak of [. . .] *foi*, not *croyance*, [I speak of] a deep faith I have in the course of things, in the future, in others [. . .] in the joy of life, in love, etc. [. . .] I was delighted to read of Mother Teresa's life-long doubts [because] I think what she is confessing is important. Suppose Mother Teresa decided to change her beliefs? There would not be the least reason for her to give up her faith, on the work she did, or on our faith in her.[17]

Caputo later adds, significantly: "she suffered a blow to her *croyance* with *no injury* to her *foi*."[18] A lot of the questions that this work asks regarding the venture of "religion without religion" are present here: first, would not, as I will show in the chapter on Nancy, this distinction between *foi* and *croyance* be one of those "utterly deconstructable distinctions" Hägglund mentions in his reply to Caputo?[19] Is, second, Caputo's speculative remark on "changing one's beliefs" really possible; that is, can one really jump from one belief to the other, from one "with" to the next? And if so, is a sort of ironic stance, which Caputo à la Rorty regularly invokes, the only thing that would explain this? Is it, third, really the case that one is always and already, because of a fundamental contingency and historicity, at a certain critical distance from one's beliefs, without the "with," as it were?[20] Fourth, is this distance really the "weak force" of "God knows what" that Caputo thinks it to be? What if this neo-vitalism of Caputo, and its concomitant "elemental," "immemorial," and "promissory powers," is *as metaphysical as* the "with" Caputo wants to do away, well, with? For would not such a weak force be present always and everywhere, that is, come close to some sort of permanent presence that cannot only not be forgotten—"impossible to forget"—but also does not admit of the change and the historicity that Caputo nonetheless advocates?[21]

In short, I suggest that Caputo has not sufficiently taken into account the "with," whether it would be an "X" with religion, with identity, with sovereignty, and so forth. Here is the question that is not, or at least is too little, present in Caputo and his contemporary respondents: *what with the "with"?* This means: what if the "with" (religion, identity . . .) is always and already constituted ontotheologically? What if no distance at all, whether ironic or critical, would in the last resort be possible and certainly not in a non-ontotheological manner? What if a religion without religion simply would be impossible, not only because it would be only a second-order discourse and "parasitic" of the first order—as Caputo claims—but also because there is no way to do without the "with"? "X without X" simply does not explain the presence (and the violence) of the "with." This is what my *Ontotheological Turnings?* was already pointing to (though in other authors) and what we encounter here as the "natural metaphysician in us," which Schürmann addresses and which would make "ontotheology," or "X with X" if you like, somewhat like an obsessive-compulsive disorder, for which there would be no therapy as of yet.

To be sure, at times Caputo comes close to addressing this logic of the "with" and its tendency to enclose truth in assertions, stable signifiers, and whatnot. "Religion with religion [. . .] will always turn out to be *somebody's* religion, meaning *ours*, because *we* are the ones who were lucky enough ('grace') to be standing in the right place at the right time" when God supposedly revealed Godself.[22] Caputo does not show how, precisely, a "religion without religion" would be possible (why would it not just lapse into a new "with"?), nor does he show and explain to us *why* "religion with religion" is always violently metaphysical (if this is not a tautology): why and how does one leave the "with" in a sufficient manner?

The "with" haunts the "without" perhaps more than the "without" would haunt the "with." This is what one can gather from the fact that pretty much the same questions can be addressed to Caputo and Hägglund. Michael Naas, for instance, advances against Hägglund that, even though beliefs, faiths, and "religion with religion" might be phantasms and, as such, illusory foundations to be exposed (as Hägglund does), one should ask rather why such phenomena have had such a hold on us, "why metaphysics, has, so to speak, lived on so long, why religious conceptions of God and salvation have had such an enduring history" *and continue to do so?*[23] This question returns first in the chapter on Schürmann, with the "natural metaphysician in us" and the concomitant "hegemonic phantasms" from which we can never flee.

This is also why Hägglund's and Caputo's respective positions are closer than one would expect: Just as when one can ask Caputo why his "religion without religion" would not be able to suffer *any injury* and would remain *safe* when it comes to "religion with religion," so one can ask Hägglund why and how he thinks his radical atheism would be unscathed and immune even from the phantasms of religion? Would not a negative answer to these questions—the pure "without religion" as well as a pure "atheism" is impossible—indicate already that both of these authors still desire somewhat of a pure position sheltered precisely from all "impure" ontotheologies?

I, for one, would love to be an atheist. But the combination of the verb and the noun, it seems, runs into problems: that's somewhat the point of this work. It does remain a phenomenology of "religious" *life*, however, because it wants to remain close to the minimalism that a contemporary metaphysics seems to demand: it will not turn the phenomenon of love in an overarching, exemplary "experience" that would deliver once and for all the meaning of all other experiences. This is also why, after metaphysics, one should be wary of invoking any "overarching aspiration," be it "religious or prophetic" or "radically atheistic."[24] For such a strategy, seeking an aspiration that would be permanently present in the works of one Jacques Derrida, for example, would tie the name "Derrida" to just one thought, (re)turning these works to a/his *corpus* if you like. The strategy of deconstruction is however multiple, explaining why one day one thinks such and such and another day something else entirely, explaining therefore why one at times adheres to a "religion *with* religion," with all its phantasmatic and compulsive misfortunes, and at another time is haunted by a "religion" that seeks a stance outside determinate religion and quests for a spirituality attuned to the signs of the times. This is what makes one reluctant to subscribe to Caputo's "weak force" raging through being and turning being into a "moment," as it were, of being's way toward the good (whether or not capitalized). On this point, one might be inclined to repeat Marion's lament over Heidegger's *Es gibt* and direct it to Caputo: namely, it risks turning this "it gives," through a "metaphysical regression," into an "indeterminate power [. . .] to the point where it would appear an ontic agent."[25]

A similar "logocentrism" and a similar "logic" might, however, be present in Hägglund's book. This is, in fact, what Caputo advances against Hägglund: a constant "abridging" of deconstruction to make it fit into the straitjacket of a certain atheism.[26] One might wonder indeed whether the concept of "survival" needs to be used to describe the weal and the woe of our lives, if this were to imply that both "theists" and "inauthentic atheists" (if one may risk the concept) would not know that a great share of their lives is just about "survival." For Hägglund, in effect, the time of life would be nothing but a self-centered *conatus essendi* that relentlessly exposes and is relentlessly exposed to the coming of a threatening future, whereas for Levinas for instance such a persevering in being is split open right at the start, with birth if you like, where being shows itself as something "received," "given" or as something in which we are "thrown" or that has been "handed down" to us before an ego even appears. In this regard, one might repeat Jean-Luc Nancy's complaint toward Heidegger's *Being and Time* and state that, just as "it is too contemptuous to represent humanity to oneself as though the immense majority of our peers [. . .] passed their lives [. . .] misunderstanding [. . .] the intractable real that is dying,"[27] it is similarly too depreciatory both to think that most of us spend our lives unaware of the self-centeredness of our own survival (and that it is "deconstruction" that is needed to retrieve precisely this) and to think that "theists" and their autoimmune deities would be incapable of accounting for the promises and the threats that would be mortal being.

Yet Hägglund's "logic" can be pointed to in multiple ways. For instance, that which Hägglund advances against the autoimmune supreme beings of the religious traditions is that, for Derrida's deconstruction, these religions would share a "common denominator," which is such that all religions, no matter which ones precisely, and even less where (at what point in history) or by whom (which authors precisely), "posit the messianic as a promise of timeless peace."[28] Although Hägglund is right to point to Derrida's "Faith and Knowledge" here, stating in effect that "every religion" involves a "horizon of redemption, of the restoration of the unscathed,"[29] it is far from Derrida and deconstruction, however, to posit a "common denominator," an essence underlying the diverse conceptualizations of religion as well as an "overarching aspiration" that would ask the same question about the same problem over and over.[30] The point of a certain deconstruction is and was precisely that such an essence, and the notion of commonality that underlies it, is always and already rendered inoperative. It is here that a certain deconstruction of Hägglund's "logic" would begin. In this respect, the sheer abundance of the formula "thinking X *against* X" is to be noted as well as his preferred phrase "taking issue with (this or that)."[31] What, and that is what this work does, would happen if one thought "against" such an "against"? It would be, surprisingly, to turn to the later Derrida, who advised Nancy to think *with* and *alongside* the Christian and philosophical tradition rather than against it or to pretend to be able to think without this tradition. In short, Derrida's advice to Nancy—a "salut without salvation"—is reminding Nancy of the Promethean trait of his deconstruction of Christianity, whereas, in fact, Derrida points out that this deconstruction is rather somewhat like a modern Munchausen: at the very moment it thinks it is reading this tradition against the tradition, it is all the more sinking and seeking within this very tradition.[32] This is, if you like, Derrida's explanation of why both theists—God is (this or that)—and atheists—God is not and certainly not (this or that)—have a hard time today. Let us listen to these important words of Derrida:

> Just as it is neither enough to present oneself as a Christian nor to "believe" [. . .] in order to hold forth a language that is "authentically" Christian, likewise it is not enough *not* to "believe" or believe oneself [. . .] *non*-Christian in order to utter a discourse, speak a language, and even inhabit one's body while remaining safely sheltered from all Christianity. This is not about being free of harm, safe, and saved, seeking one's salvation outside of [or: immunity from, JS] Christianity. *These values would still be Christian ones*.[33]

It is as if the "*Il n'y a pas de hors-texte*" has come to mean: there is nothing outside Christianity. Alas for the atheist, perhaps, there is no shelter from Christianity. The theist and the atheist alike are dealing with, and have to deal with, the debris of a Christian culture that is opening not onto a postsecular, quasi-relativistic world of different kinds of faith with a bit of reason, but rather onto a culture that is *no longer* Christian but is *not yet* non-Christian. This is why Derrida deems the deconstruction of

Christianity, of a certain Christian flesh, necessary as much as impossible: it is what happens when one thinks in a not quite *non-Christian* culture. One therefore might legitimately wonder whether Hägglund's attempt to insulate all attempts at immunization and indemnifications—a "radical" atheism safely sheltered from religion—would not be, in Derrida's very terms, a hyperbolic version of a certain Christianity, an "unavowed theology" perhaps or even a "theology of atheism."[34] It might be that Nietzsche was wrong, then: it is not nihilism that will be an uncanny guest in the centuries to come, but it is Christianity rather (although nihilism might have issued from it).

To be sure, an "elementary faith" and "affirmation" are needed inasmuch as they are necessitated through such a culture in transition. But this faith and this consent, for Derrida, are consenting with the "irreducible plurality of bodies [. . .] that cannot be gathered in a divine, Christic body that would be in some way one and common."[35] This consent, therefore, would be a "different yes" to the happening and event of world and implies "an altogether different provenance of the same 'yes'—by essence always addressed to a 'you.'"[36]

This faith and this affirmation are not the faith or the beliefs one finds in extant religions (although they surely are present there as well). This "elementary" faith, rather, is close to the "intersubjective curvature" in being that Levinas mentioned at the closing of *Totality and Infinity*: the fact, if not facticity, that it takes two (or more) for there to be any sense, signification at all. It is no coincidence that the quotes of Derrida that I just mentioned end with an address, by essence, to you, to others in general. "In the beginning," then, it seems is the salutation, an elemental and originary *coram* that does not decide for or against religion even when it is the "milieu of the religious" (Naas) where "religion begins"—the "second source" of religion. Where and how does religion begin?

"Religion kicks in," Caputo writes, when we focus on something other than ourselves and "in response to something that has swept us away."[37] Whereas Caputo insists on the joy accompanying this experience, if only because it initiates the thought that, after all, there might be something greater than ourselves, it seems more fair to stick to Derrida and insist on a shame overwhelming and embarrassing us and that makes us step back— the "first source" of religion. Derrida mentions the retreating of Plutarch's Bellérophon before a woman indecently imposing herself. Bellérophon steps back in shame for her shamelessness, feeling inhibited by God knows what. Derrida comments: "this movement of shame, this reticence, this inhibition, this retreat is [. . .] like the immunizing drive, the protection of the immune, of the sacred [. . .] that is the very origin of the religious, of religious scruple."[38] This drive is, of course, threatened from within: it comes too late, for Bellérophon has *already* seen the indecency before retreating and stepping back. The reticence and the religious scruple have, if you like, a peculiar form of *Nachträglichkeit*.

One is reminded of the famous example of Derrida, right at the beginning of *The Animal That Therefore I Am*, feeling shame before his cat watching him when he was coming out of the shower. And of the shame for this shame that came afterward, for why indeed feel shame: what was there to hide, immunize, or shelter from the cat's gaze? Nothing, perhaps: nothing is safe when nothing can be saved. To this example, if we may, I would like to add my own: while visiting Auschwitz some years ago, all of a sudden it started to rain heavily. I, and the group of which I was a part, immediately ran toward the camp buildings to seek, yes, shelter. How does one find shelter in Auschwitz? Is it not simply inappropriate to seek shelter in Auschwitz? But then again, would it have been appropriate to just stand in the rain? Would that not have been an inappropriate romanticizing of the experience, a sort of all too Christian and untimely expiation and atonement? I was ashamed for my shelter as much as I would have been ashamed for not seeking shelter. The question, too, has a religious ring: I was ashamed for what happened there and felt the need to pray. But how does one pray to God in Auschwitz? Would it be appropriate even to pray to the Christian God there, for we all know that Christianity at least in part was responsible for what happened there? This soon became a "prayer without prayer," if you like, without anyone to pray to, without salvation indeed. A stammering and a cry *for* you, the murdered. Religion, I have come to think afterward, begins when one is at a loss for words, religious words, when the words of the "religions" are *lacking* and when this lack is not something that can be overcome. *Religio*: "*scruple*, hesitation, indecision, reticence (hence modesty, respect, *restraint* before that which should remain sacred."[39]

This is at least an indication of what "the salut without salvation" might have meant for Derrida. The radical atheist will be happy. After "religion with religion," there remains something of a "religious scruple." The theist will be happy too, for a little while at least. The deconstruction of Christianity necessitates the overcoming of the simple theism-atheism distinction, and their respective rather propositional truths, by finding the common ground from which both theists and atheists can welcome and greet one another and think together.

Fortunately, on such a faithful salutation to the other, the later Derrida had quite a lot to say and perhaps a bit more than "the faith in the mutable"[40] that Hägglund seems to prescribe. However, Hägglund's analysis of this "salut without salvation" is worth considering—and one should keep in mind just as well that if Derrida salutes Nancy at the end of *On Touching* with just such a salutation it is because, for Derrida, there is still *too much* of a theological echo of salvation present in Nancy. For Hägglund, then, Derrida "deconstructs the religious idea of salvation" by proposing "as irreconcilable the notion of *salut* as greeting or salutation to the other from every *salut* as salvation (in the sense of the safe)."[41] Hägglund proceeds: "moreover, [Derrida] proposes to question the very desire for salvation: 'to consider the greeting or salutation of the other, of what comes, as irreducible and heterogeneous to any seeking of *salut* as salvation.' "[42] This secular and mundane greeting—safely sheltered from the sacred or the religious?— for Derrida, would be, still according to Hägglund, "pronounced 'at the moment of encounter or separation, at the moment of parting or meeting again, and each time it is [. . .] a 'salut' at the coming of what comes.' Thus, the greeting *salut* signifies an experience of temporal survival: it is addressed to a mortal other that is coming or going."[43]

This calls for a few remarks. First, if Derrida reproaches Nancy for retaining too much of "salvation" *in* the "salut," would this not mean that the distinction between *salut* and salvation, however "irreconcilable" they are, cannot always be properly made and would perhaps be impossible— truly aporetic and abyssal?[44] Is not the fact that Derrida admits that their relation is "neither one of exteriority nor one of simple opposition or contradiction"[45] reason enough to think that one cannot have the one without the other? It is to such a *Verflechtung* that is neither a (logical) opposition nor a (theological) incarnation that this work tries to point: neither "with" nor "without" religion, if you like. Also, and granted the ambition to come to such a secular greeting or a *salut* almost without salvation, what should be admitted just as well is that, for Derrida, every coming of the other would still need to be considered as a greeting or salutation even if the "salut" could be deconstructed along Hägglund's lines. For, even if one concedes a "non-ethical opening of ethics,"[46] this opening remains constituted by an originary *coram*, by a tending toward otherness and toward the other.

This would mean that one could align somewhat Derrida, Levinas, Nancy, and Binswanger on precisely this point: prior to the religious address that is prayer (*à Dieu*), the address that is ethics (presupposing that the other is good and "respects"[47] me), the address that is nonethical (the other might just as well be a bad other that does not "respect" me), there would be an *ontological* salutation in being, through which all beings, eventually, are turned toward all beings. This ontology, the greeting present in everything we say, do, and think, is again an ontology incarnate: it is attested to in the "coming and the going," in the *Wink* we give to the other, in the discomfort felt when someone does not greet us, and so forth. This, then, is an "intersubjective gesture" that is not yet ethical: one does not greet oneself, and neither can one greet on one's own. The greeting, then, attests to the impossibility of solipsism that we see Nancy describing so beautifully, where the *ego cogito* can only be truly alone if it is understood by the other (through which not even the *cogito* is alone, obviously), just like Derrida's notion of the secret only makes sense because the secret is always and already shared (and thus turned into less of a secret).

Conclusion: Toward A Contemporary Phenomenology of Religious Life

I, for one, would love to be a believer. But the combination of the verb and the noun, of love and belief, respectively, runs, it seems, into problems. This is what partly explains the attraction of Caputo's "religion without religion," aiming for the event that is going on in the extant religious traditions. These traditions matter, for Caputo, not for what they say and believe but rather for what they are about. The event, then, exceeds the names given to it in this or that tradition. If Caputo, to use Nancy's distinction, tries to make sense of what is going on in the significations of these religious traditions—to the point of forgetting the phantasm of the "with"—then this explains the wariness of believers toward Caputo's thought: they would need to admit in effect that the truth of their tradition does not lie within their tradition, that therefore their tradition is not the entire truth. This corresponds nicely with the deconstruction of Christianity that Nancy is proposing: it is willing to consider the very fact that one or the other tradition can in effect disappear and self-de(con)struct—something that "believers" and theologians of all varieties cannot do.

It is such a relativization that this work claims as its own and that is why it goes along with Caputo considerably: it might indeed be love that forces us to take some distance from certain all too rigid beliefs, and it might indeed be a lack of love that causes the rigidity of certain beliefs and traditions. Yet Caputo seems to downplay what we have called "the phantasm of the with" above. One should move beyond Caputo, as it were, and take into account both the with and the without and explain how, in the rhythm that is life, one can be an atheist one day and a believer the next. It is not to side with either the apologetics of our days (Simmons, Gschwandtner[48]) or with the atheists (Hägglund), but rather to understand why both positions can attract and fascinate contemporary scholars today.

A *contemporary phenomenology of religious life*, then. Every word in the title is equally important. It is contemporary in that it seeks to aim at a deconstruction of Christianity, interpreted as the attempt to make sense of the heritage and the remains of a certain Christian metaphysics in the West. It is religious, or even spiritual, in that even though it is sympathetic toward thinkers such as Hägglund, and the thought of a radical finitude, it believes that a radical finitude is not hostile per se toward religious questions. Perhaps quite to the contrary, the thought that everything comes to pass, indeed the thought of world as a "mere coming to pass," as Schürmann puts it, makes the sense of the religious even more pressing: how can religion align itself with this finite thought of world once all jumping to an afterworld, outside of being and time, has become impossible? It is a question of life, then, in that it seeks to erect a modest question of the living being in general[49] over and against contemporary attempts such as Marion's to turn love into the example par excellence, in which the meaning of being would once and for all be decided. It is a phenomenology, finally, not only in that all the authors I discuss here are steeped in the phenomenological tradition but also in that it seeks to reassess, albeit in an entirely secular manner, what one could call the basic religious posture, namely an *exodus* out of the everyday world; a second moment of *conversion*, conceived of here as the arrival of insight; and a third moment of *mission*, conceived of here as the simple sharing of insight with others.[50]

Let me give just the example of Heidegger here (who, however, has not always led by example). Heidegger's existential analytic in *Being and Time* was, for all that, a way to cope with the end of metaphysics (although this, as such, had not been its topic already) by returning philosophy, in a way, to its original stance, namely a meditation on what it is for a being, in this case (and in each case) my being-there, to be in the world. Dasein, for Heidegger, is thrown into a particular, historical world. The way this world "worlds," moreover, changes over history. In this regard, it is no surprise that Heidegger, writing in the *interbellum* as he was, proclaimed anxiety as the basic mood of the human being.[51]

Yet, for our purposes here, it is important to recall that for Heidegger, it is not sufficient to marvel at being-in-the-world, for our very being-in-the-world is most often precisely the end of marvel and wonder. Being-in-the-world is constituted by our commerce with other beings in the world.

"First and foremost," Heidegger often writes, Dasein is absorbed in its world. The usual characteristics of the world are such that Dasein is assured of its place in the world and with itself. The world, and the certainty one receives through one's preoccupations within the world, serve as some sort of comfort and in any case as a "tranquillization." This "tranquillization"[52]—being-in-the-world in effect functions as a kind of drug—occurs in a particular way: it is so obviously an everyday affair that it usually goes unnoticed. Heidegger speaks of a Dasein "led astray" by its own condition, for "it could be that the "'who' of everyday Dasein" just is not" what this Dasein in each case can and has to be.[53] Most often, Dasein turns away from itself through turning to others: it will check, for instance, the status update of the others on Facebook over and over. Everyday Dasein thus checks "what the others are doing" and will, consequently, do exactly as all the others are doing. In its everyday mode, Dasein "stands in subjection to others. It itself is not; its being has been taken away by the others. Dasein's everyday possibilities are for the others to dispose of as they please."[54] This is what Heidegger calls the "averageness" of everyday Dasein. For what exactly does everyday Dasein do? Heidegger portrays three modes of such everydayness: everyday Dasein is talkative (it talks like the others and echoes what "they" have said); it is curious (always on the lookout for the next talk of the town) and its talk always remains ambiguous (what one talks about is understood only so and so; it is all opinion and no knowledge—think of Twitter here). It is important to note that these modes are not immediately derogatory, but rather span the three ecstasies of time in which each Dasein is always thrown: one reads and talks about everything that everyone else *has read* (the past); one is reading what everyone else is reading (the present); and one is curious about the next thing that one *will have* to read and talk about (the future). And, what is more, the present will entirely determine and inform the future: "everyone also knows already how to talk about what has to happen first—about what is not yet up for discussion but 'really' must be done."[55] It is this that, for Heidegger, makes the future entirely predictable and controllable and constitutes therefore the end of wonder about being.

Despite all appearances, Heidegger stresses that this is not a moralizing interpretation of being-in-the-world: even though the *illustrierte Zeitung* (one of Heidegger's infamous aversions), magazines, and "hypes" (in which one present phenomenon governs the appearance of all other future phenomena) are part and parcel of the lives and times of "the They," Heidegger's message is *not* to avoid these altogether. There is no hubris in Heidegger here: as if one particular Dasein could eradicate all averageness permanently. In effect, *Being and Time* would be a hubristic and moralizing endeavor had Heidegger argued that the liberation of Dasein from everydayness were indeed permanent. In that case, one would have a Dasein quietly overseeing and depreciating the other Dasein's averageness—very much like a transcendental subject standing apart and overseeing all of its empirical experiences. However, Heidegger's point is exactly the opposite, for such an "everyday way in which things have been interpreted is one into which Dasein has grown in the first instance, with *never* a possibility of extrication."[56]

Yet an escape and *exodus* out of this sedation of being-in-the-world, out of what "They" prescribe for our being, *is* and *remains* possible. This exodus, then, can be seen as a *temporary* awakening out of the tranquilizing effects of everyday being-in-the-world. For everyday Dasein in the end might know nothing else than the life that it leads as prescribed by others and interpret its averageness as the necessary way of life. Everydayness may in effect grant being-in-the-world some security and certainty and confer upon it improperly the illusion of stability and permanence. The averageness of being-in-the-world is such that the false certainties one acquires there take the form of unquestioned and perhaps necessary mode of being. These preoccupations-within-the-world in effect confer upon this world, and its traditions and habits, some sort of coagulation, such that nothing other than these traditions and habits can any longer be imagined. The thought that something else is *possible* as well never really arises: in everyday Dasein, actuality reigns over possibility, and what is contingent will appear as if it is necessary.

Only rarely, then, and without any reason or cause being given for this, Dasein awakens from its (self-chosen?) slumber and tranquilization. This happens, as is well known, in anxiety. For anxious Dasein, the comfort and certainty of everydayness *disappears* only to make appear the nullity and nothingness of one's being-in-the-world. Heidegger writes:

> That which anxiety is anxious about is being-in-the-world itself. In anxiety what is environmentally ready-to-hand sinks away, and so, in general, do entities within-the-world. The "world" can offer nothing more, and neither can the Dasein-with of others. Anxiety thus takes away from Dasein the possibility of understanding itself, as it falls, in terms of the "world" and the way things have been publicly interpreted. Anxiety throws Dasein back upon [. . .] its authentic potentiality-for-being-in-the-world.[57]

It is when nothing actual makes sense any more that everything becomes possible for Dasein. Anxiety alleviates, in a sense, the weight of the world only to show and make appear my being as a being-in-the-world precisely. This is why anxiety individualizes Dasein: it shows that, for all that, I am and will have to be in the world. It shows my being to itself as an ordeal and as a task, because now I will have to mediate between the actuality of the ordeal and the possibilities accompanying the task.

It is, however, barely noticed that this task—the "possibility of taking action"[58]—and of making decisions in general and in one's ownmost way, more often than not, *fails*. This would mean that it is *inauthentic* to think that there is such a thing as pure authenticity. If anything, then, this is something like a *positive failure*: authenticity would be the decision *not to decide* on the others or the self *once and for all*.[59]

This is the marvel and wonder about being that *Being and Time* sought to retrieve: when the world no longer appears, all that nevertheless appears is precisely that there is nothing other than world. It is to such a *conversion* or introspection at least that anxiety seems to point: angst reveals that there is nothing to be revealed. Being-in-the-world only ever shows itself to show that there is nothing-than-world precisely. Simultaneously, this "revelation" indicates that being-there is a task that, while pertaining to all of us, pertains first and foremost to me, and only me: I cannot *not* be the span between my birth and my death (and suicide would change nothing about this). Dasein *owes* it to itself and to others to be its being. Finally, anxiety and death make clear that, more often than not, Dasein shies away from this task and this ordeal. "Authenticity," then, does not mean that one no longer flees from everydayness, but rather to be aware of this flight as such, or, as François Raffoul has it, authenticity means dealing authentically with one's inauthenticity.[60] This is what is revealed through anxiety over one's finitude, namely that the tranquilization and comforting securities with which one usually flees from one's finitude are in themselves only an illusion once seen in the perspective of the finite time into which Dasein is thrown. This is why this "conversion" for Heidegger is also a liberation of sorts: even though fleeing from one's mortality is inevitable, and necessary perhaps, the "enlightenment" brought about by facing one's finitude is precisely the ability to see that what first appeared as necessary is contingent, to realize that what first seemed coagulated and clotted—a tradition for instance—can always be revived and animated again from out of the permanent destabilization that is finitude.

The moment of mission in Heidegger is multiple. Most often it is a matter of awakening the Dasein in the other. Dasein therefore may not be confused with the human being as such. Dasein, rather, is the *phenomenological gaze* that faces the finitude of all beings and turns this finitude into the paradigm of life. Finite Dasein is instructed, by the ever-present possibility of its death, about what will happen to it anyway and what it will have to face nevertheless: "giving itself up."[61] It is this forsaking of the self's tenaciousness and its clinging to false forms of certainty that Dasein, properly, intends to share with others. In and through anxiety and the readiness for finitude it entails, Dasein in effect "frees itself for its world":[62] it will no longer be (permanently) absorbed by the world and will no longer be satisfied with doing as all the other are doing. This liberation opens for Dasein the possibility "to let the others who are with it 'be' in their ownmost potentiality-for-being [. . .] it can become the 'conscience' of others."[63] Dasein can enact and incarnate the call from which the others can awaken.

To and for what exactly each Dasein decides itself "remains in darkness."[64] Far from Heidegger to moralize and give guidelines here! Not only because the risk of failure is immense—for one does not know, one never knows: *on ne sait pas. Il faut essayer*—but also because the decision falls to each Dasein individually: "*only* the resolution itself can give the answer."[65] Each Dasein will have to make up its mind separately about how to live in a world without manual.

Part 1

Without

1

Anarchistic Tendencies in Continental Philosophy

Reiner Schürmann and the Hubris of Philosophy

"What is to be done at the end of metaphysics?"

"What is to be done at the end of metaphysics?" It is Reiner Schürmann's question, and it is one that deserves to be posed. For, if indeed we would agree with Schürmann and Heidegger that the collapse of metaphysics and its addictive afterworlds is "of immediate historical concern to us,"[1] the question of action, attitudes, and comportment toward such a collapse seems all the more urgent.

It is to the latter question that Schürmann has contributed considerably. Reginald Lilly, the translator of Schürmann's *Des Hégémonies brisées*, for instance notes that

> the connection between the existential analytic and the history of being as onto-theology has never been made clear by Heidegger or his commentators. [I]t is precisely such a connection that Schürmann means to make in basing his topology on an analytic of ultimates. [This] analytic promises to give us those elements, structures, and dynamics that are fundamental to human existence and are presumed by any history of philosophy.[2]

It would be unfair, however, to see Schürmann as but one more "Heideggerian" or, as I show below, "deconstructionist." To be sure, his interpretation of Heidegger is intriguing and often innovating: one need only think of his efforts "to read Heidegger backward" without regard for the fashionable distinction between the early Heidegger and its mystical and mythical sequel or of his interpretation of Heidegger's work on Nietzsche, which, as Schürmann convincingly shows, "speak *formally* of Nietzsche, but *materially* about technology."³

And yet Schürmann pushes one to look beyond Heidegger, and perhaps indeed to "consequences more extreme than Heidegger would wish."⁴ It remains to be considered whether Schürmann actually succeeded in showing the fundamental unity of thinking, acting, and being, but in Schürmann finally the tragic condition of the human being is given a voice in contemporary philosophy. In effect, Schürmann might even have the strongest case to date to take the existential character of metaphysical questions into account.

In its simplest form, we all know or at least have a pre-understanding of our tragic condition, for the "point of departure" of the analytic of ultimates "is the knowledge from which no one escapes and which escapes no one, even if the natural metaphysician in each of us closes his eyes to it [. . .]: the knowledge that we arrive by our birth and go to our death."⁵

In addition to the "practical" and existential character of metaphysics' most intimate questions, this chapter addresses the import of Schürmann's notion of "the natural metaphysician in each of us," for the question that seems to divide Derrida and Schürmann seems to hinge on precisely this issue of a metaphysics that comes naturally to us. Finally, this chapter, in relating Schürmann not only to Heidegger but also to Levinas and Derrida, pays attention to the new understanding of philosophy that seems to emerge from Schürmann's work which is due precisely to its "practical" starting point.

Heideggerian Anarchy

The title of this section, which may surprise the "Heideggerians," is not mine but Schürmann's.⁶ This section addresses Schürmann's *temporalizing of the ontological difference*, turning it into a temporal and therefore an-archic difference, and conveys the practical import of it.

The "Practical a Priori"

The existential character of metaphysical questions comes to the fore in Schürmann's beautiful contradictory notion of "the practical a priori." If Lilly's statement that only the analytic of ultimates of *Broken Hegemonies* shows the connection between Heidegger's history of being and some form of existential analytic, the "practical a priori" of *Heidegger on Being and Acting* can serve as a hermeneutic key to bring the profound continuity between Schürmann's two major works to light. In this sense, my effort here is a sort of "reading Schürmann backward." This will allow me to interpret Schürmann's nuanced stance on the question of overcoming metaphysics and to correct some of the views on his œuvre that have emerged in secondary literature, as for instance in Vahabzadeh's entirely metaphysical characterization of the 1982 work as "bearing the stamp of a flourishing life, an effect of natality [. . .] while *Broken Hegemonies* certainly comes from a life pulled toward death."[7]

If one of the main theses of *Broken Hegemonies* is that all of the major metaphysical systems (mainly, Plotinus, Cicero and Augustine, and modern philosophy) have arisen from the ultimate analytic of natality and mortality, in that all of these systems are subjected to a sort of natural drive to maximize or overdetermine one phenomenal region over others—according to Schürmannn, the main mode of procedure of metaphysics is to focus on the phenomenon of fabrication, those things that are manmade—then this native and natural tendency toward generalization, universalization, and "de-phenomenologisation" inevitably gives birth to its "other," namely the pull and pressure of finitude. For the phenomenological and singular encounter with finite beings in and through our finite comprehension of those beings resists precisely such a "fantasmic" maximization under the rule of one overarching and hegemonic phenomenon (whether it be the One, nature, or the modern *cogito*). It is death, as the one and only singularization to come, that throws the hubris of these philosophies, rendering reason of all beings, back on its "humble condition,"[8] the lives and deaths that you and I will have to lead.[9] The ontology of natality, that is, of the natural metaphysician in us, inevitably gives way to its parasitical other in the return of the denied,[10] namely the contingency and historicity of time as that which will lead us to our deaths.[11]

It is true that *Broken Hegemonies* offers an elaborate discussion of the historical moments of such metaphysical madness that was perhaps lacking at the time of his Heidegger book. Nevertheless, the main theses of the first-mentioned book are present in the latter book as well—which already makes it impossible to consider it solely as "stamped by a flourishing life." Both what Schürmann will later, with Arendt, name as the ontological traits of mortality and natality figure in his earlier book as well. Take, for instance, the trait of mortality. Commenting on the lineage from Ancient philosophy, the Nietzschean overturning thereof, and its connection with our (post) modern technological era, Schürmann writes that for "the [technological] manipulable to inherit the prestige of the ancient Good, the representation of an ideal hierarchy *must have contained its fatal agent within itself ever since its conception.*"[12]

Not only does metaphysics therefore write, so to say, its own testament, as if its birth certificate were at the same time its hour of death, but, even in Schürmann's *Heidegger*, the dawn of metaphysics originates in the human being's natural—should I say: compulsive?—behavior. Indeed, even the Heidegger book intimates the natural origins of metaphysics, for metaphysics results from a "need for an archaeo-teleocratic origin," the "want of a hold" on our epoch, and is therefore perhaps nothing more than a "self-incurred illusion of perfect presence."[13] It is this need and this want that, according to Schürmann, account for the tragic condition of human beings and force them to, on the one hand, posit in one way or another a grand narrative while, on the other, being forced to hear the demand of that which such metaphysical narratives precisely deny, namely finitude and mortality, that is, time. If one of the aims of *Broken Hegemonies* was to show how metaphysical positions are rooted in everyday experience, one can find thus the appeal to experience in Schürmann's anarchy book as well.

Such a priority of praxis and everyday experience crystallizes in what Schürmann coins as "the practical a priori." With this notion Schürmann espouses what seems to be an extraordinary everyday banality, namely, that "to understand authentic temporality, it is necessary to 'exist authentically'; to think being as letting phenomena be, one must oneself 'let all things be,' to follow the play without why of presencing, it is necessary to 'live without why.' "[14] In short, "a mode of thinking is made dependent on a mode of living."[15] Schürmann shows that such a practical a priori is present in both the early and the later Heidegger.[16] For reasons of space, I limit Schürmann's argument to Heidegger's *Being and Time*. Schürmann asks: "what is it that conceals the transcendence of Dasein?" and answers thus: "A certain way of behaving, a certain attitudinal way of being in the world—inauthenticity," adding that in "*Being and Time*, the classical ontologies [. . .] spring precisely from inauthentic existence" and he concludes that all this "indicates first and foremost that the retrieval proper of the being question is bound to fail unless it is preceded by what [Heidegger] then calls an existentiell modification"—"First comes an appropriation of existentiell possibilities, then existential ontology."[17] The later Heidegger, Schürmann argues, will move away from the individual implications that *Being and Time* still could admit and will espouse the public and political dimension of the practical a priori: *Eigentlichtkeit* or authenticity is substituted for "*Ereignis*" and, yes, "*Volk*."

One must note that the practical a priori is, for Schürmann, a method rather than an empirical stance: it is the path that may lead "from a way of living to a way of thinking." It is to avoid "the 'methodical' errancy" of metaphysics, which substitutes the contingency of time for the consolations of the eternal or the permanent presence of consciousness and forgets about its humble and historical origins, and which therefore is accompanied by "a methodical retrenchment of life or of praxis" to the point that one can, as angels supposedly once did, "speak from mind to mind."[18]

Such a priority of praxis is by no means absent from contemporary continental philosophy: it is for instance to be found in the phenomenology of the other of Emmanuel Levinas and in the phenomenology of givenness of Jean-Luc Marion. For both authors, the response to the appeal (whether it be from God or givenness) lies phenomenologically prior to the appeal: it is only in and through men's and women's responses that the appeal appears. It matters little that, for Marion, the responsiveness of human being is broadened to entail more than the (Levinasian) human face. It matters that in both cases a certain mode of comportment accompanies the act of thinking, whether it be, for Marion, the abandoning of oneself to whatever gives itself, or the ethical bearing witness to the other in Levinas.[19] Levinas's analysis of "enjoyment" in *Totality and Infinity* definitely shows that such a "practical a priori" is accompanied by an attentiveness to life.[20]

Though all these thinkers would therefore agree that such a practical a priori does not consist of an ontic, determinate and individual act, but rather of an ontological and transcendental attunement—from Heidegger's *Stimmung* or mood—they diverge as to that which is capable of uttering such an appeal.[21]

The Event and the Phenomenology of Presencing

For Schürmann, this appeal is obviously Heideggerian in nature: it is to the presencing of being that the human being is to correspond. Schürmann's phenomenology of presencing presents a temporalized version of Heidegger's ontological difference. According to Schürmann, "Heidegger's entire effort consists in recovering [. . .] that broader sense of being as coming into presence (*Anwesung*) or presencing (*Anwesen*)."[22] At this point, it is necessary to consider Schürmann's interpretation of Heideggerian anti-humanism: for the history of being to appear as ontotheology, it is necessary that all reference from being to human beings (as a privileged relation) disappears. To think being as time, it is no longer necessary to think human temporality, that is, the human being as time.[23] In this sense, Heidegger's lesson for Schürmann would be a sobering one, resisting all consolation and consolidation of an ultimate yet fantasmic referent that would guide and orient our actions. The (presencing of the) world has become a contingent and goalless process.

Schürmann will see the event of presencing as that which liberates us from the anthropocentrism that still accompanied modern philosophy, according to which nothing can be said to come to pass if it does not appear to the transcendental subject. To temporalize the ontological difference between being and beings, Schürmann will distinguish between (originary) being as the event of presencing *and* the different, "original" and epochal economies of presence (the epoch of the cogito and of "God" is that which presences thus). If the phenomenologist wants "to address presencing and its manifold ways of differing from the economies of presence,"[24] the three terms of the ontological difference will have to be temporalized accordingly: whereas, in the unfolding of the ontological difference beings (*Seiendes*) lie present in their being (*Seiendheit*) from out of their difference with destinal being (*Sein*), the temporalized version of this difference states that the presence (*Anwesenheit*) of that which is present (*Anwesendes*) unfolds from out of the event of presencing (*Anwesen*)—the sheer coming of being.[25]

This "event" is sobering because it unfolds without why, without any other goal than its simple presencing of beings. *Ereignis* grants us its unfolding as, in the later Heideggerian terminology, world and thing (in its difference from objects). These terms try to suggest

> that the world, or contextuality, announces itself in the "as"—the thing "as" thing. This deals a blow to transcendence, since the world is not elsewhere than the thing [. . .] A phenomenon is taken as what it is only when we understand it as gathering its context, as "worlding." And the context is taken as such only when we understand it as gathering the phenomenon, as "thinging."[26]

The "worlding of the world," according to Schürmann, marginalizes human beings: they are only "one of the elements" of "the [. . .] autonomous play of the world."[27] Schürmann concludes that only this openness toward the presencing of the world allows the thing to appear, divorced from metaphysical overdeterminations that cover up radical finitude, thus "not in its unchangeable essence" but rather "in [its] singularity."[28] It is this contingent and historical process that is the issue of thought: bereft of any single origin (be it God, nature, or the cogito), presencing shows itself in its very contingency as the "ceaseless arrangements and rearrangements in phenomenal interconnectedness,"[29] as if thinking were thanking "the goalless showing-forth of phenomena."[30] *Ereignis*, then—and here is the sobering part—is "what establishes us in our precarious dwellings," not as "some thing," but rather as "nothing—a mere coming to pass."[31] The

(Heideggerian) worlding of the world, thus, and I will show that this is a major difference with Levinas's thought, conveys a "non-human facticity,"[32] as if being can do without beings or in any case without a subject to which it, since time immemorial, ought to appear.

All this might be unbearable for a modern mind. Nevertheless, it is close to what Heidegger's course on *Plato's Sophist* intimated already, namely that to philosophize is to make explicit the prereflexive and "pregiven [. . .] unitary being" from out of the "the whole, present, givenness":[33] the unity of the thing appears out of the givenness of the world *as* a world. It is to this unity of our contingent world that Schürmann still refers in his 1987 book when saying that "what is one is the process of *coming to* presence":[34] the world as it worlds, now, in our times, as *our* world, as qualitatively different from past worlds and modes of presencing. Common to all epochs is the presencing of the world, but the presencing of the world differs from epoch to epoch.[35]

A final point then is Schürmann's separation between the event of presencing, *Ereignis*, and the epochal "economies of presence." The first is deemed, rather surprisingly, ahistorical, albeit that our access to it is granted in and through its various, historical, and epochal expressions. The "ahistorical [. . .] showing-forth"[36] is however to be understood correctly: "the event itself has neither history nor destiny. [. . .] Not that the event is atemporal: its temporality is the coming about of any constellation of thing and world."[37] The presencing of the event is that which makes possible a gathering of things present, an "epoch." Such presencing pushes beyond modernity's one-sided emphasis on the human subject. An example will perhaps make this clear: whereas a modern mind would have a hard time affirming the "happening" of the world outside the solipsistic ego's lived experiences, Heidegger's thought of presencing would take into account how the world persists beyond and outside the subject. The world "worlds" outside the finite horizons set out by human beings and regardless of whether or not it appears *to* a finite subject. The event of presencing is not man-made: it "happens"—"worlds"—without any reference to the human being. The presencing of the event is irreducible to the given constellations of any epoch.

With this last point, Schürmann, not unlike Foucault, introduces the thought that there is a radical break between the different epochs: "past presencing is mute."[38] In each epoch newness arises, because the worlding of the world presences in ever new and manifold ways. That which was present in a past age, however, stamped and marked—Heidegger's *Prägung*—as it was by principles and ultimate referents that are no longer ours, lies beyond our understanding. Schürmann insists that the existential analytic turns into an "epochal analytic"[39] when Heidegger discovers that even everydayness has a history, that the being-in-the-world of the Ancients differs irreducibly from the presencing of the world that is the lot of our technological age. One is thrown not into a universal or ahistorical world, but into an epoch. The epochal analytic shows the different metaphysical options as ever so many illusory attempts at total reflection, to "grasp" the contingent world in eternal principles. The epochal analytic shows the return of what thus has been denied—because it could not be coped with: the simple presencing of world, of time and as time, of mere "happening"—as if being is a playful performance art without a performer. After the "turn," which for Schürmann is not an experience in Heidegger's life or writings but rather a "turn" we all could experience—the turn from metaphysics to that which will surpass it—"the reference to daily experience becomes inoperative [. . .] If presencing—"being"—is grasped only through its difference from epochal presence, then our everyday experience of being is *lost forever* as soon as a new fold unfurls presence in a new constellation."[40] This "epochal discordance"[41] should not be underestimated: it means that the *arche* of the Medieval age can tell us how medieval men and women lived; it does not tell *us* how to live. And die.

Technology, the Closure of Metaphysics, and Anarchic Praxis

Yet, according to Schürmann, our age, the technological one, stands out for a particular reason. With Heidegger, Schürmann agrees that technology inaugurates the closure of metaphysics, and that our age might be the one that witnesses the happening of such a turning. An "other beginning" (Heidegger) permeates the end of metaphysics. Technology exposes the illusory character of "past principles" in that it shows that all archic principles are maximizations of the regional "fabrication" and "representation." With the appearance of technology, the "metaphysical lineage comes to an end."[42] Schürmann's anarchy consists in rejecting all past principles, because technology shows the human, all too human character of all such principles: these epochal principles appear as every so many ontically originated, totalizing and hegemonic representations. Yet one might say that Schürmann is inspired by a sort of Heideggerian anarchy in that the (Heideggerian) phenomenology of presencing might indeed be taken to point to the difference between presencing—transcendental and a priori—and that which in each case, that is, in every given epoch, lies present to the subjects of that given age. It is in the latter sense that both Schürmann and Heidegger would agree that technology inaugurates the "annihilation" and "extinction" of metaphysical principles and positions and opens onto the anarchic origin of being as simple presencing—nothing more, nothing less.[43] An-archic, that is, without "a whence and a whither,"[44] existence without why, neither origin nor goal. Our technological metaphysics is, according to Schürmann, Janus headed: both the completion of metaphysics in espousing all its inherent possibilities *and* intimating in and through the crisis and absence of justification of past principles the anarchic presencing of the world and being.

The ontological and anarchic presencing of the event singles out being as a contingent process across the various ages, delivering to each its epoch and setting the standards of that which is epochally possible and that which is not. If technology is the inauguration of the withering away of every metaphysical principle because it exposes these as illusory, then what kind of praxis would be appropriate to correspond to this contingent event? According to Schürmann, this would be nothing less than an *anarchic praxis*, for "legitimate praxis can no longer mean to refer what is doable to a first ground or some supreme reason, to a final end or some ultimate goal."[45] If we must still learn to see "things" instead of objects, and if we still must learn to think instead of representing, then the Heideggerian candidate for accompanying action is releasement or *Gelassenheit* because "an acting other than 'being effective' and thinking other than strategical rationality is what Heidegger puts forward under the name of releasement."[46] Only then are we able to see the relation between liberation and releasement.[47] Releasement is freed from the hold that past principles exercised on thinking and is more properly attuned to the presencing of the network of "phenomenal interconnectedness": it corresponds to that which the event does—letting be. For Schürmann, releasement is to be taken both politically and philosophically. Philosophically, it is that responsiveness that makes possible the setting free of the "thing" out of the representational clutches of our epoch in which any phenomenon always already appears like a present-at-hand object.[48] It responds to the event of presencing without resorting to the objectivation of this presencing.[49] Politically, releasement is the act of a rebellious philosopher—Schürmann mentions Socrates—renouncing his or her age-old role as a "covert civil servant": once it is clear that a radical fluidity is introduced into social institutions as well as into practice in general, "the entry into the event [. . .] remains thinkable and doable only as the struggle against the injustice, the hubris, of enforced residence under principal surveillance."[50]

Rather than focusing on the concrete technological aspects of the metaphysical closure, the remainder of this chapter addresses Schürmann's relation to other continental philosophers precisely on this topic of a "possible" closure of metaphysics in order to confront the tragic thinker

Schürmann with a remainder of an unjustified "optimism" and "hope" when it comes to overcoming metaphysics.

Levinasian Anarchy

The relation between Schürmann and Levinas is an odd one. Schürmann's Heidegger book seemed to be sympathetic to Levinas's anti-metaphysical and anarchic attempt to think the approach of the Other. For Schürmann, Levinas seemed, unlike Deleuze (who turns to jubilation) and Derrida (who mourns its loss), sufficiently sober to cope with the loss of the One.[51] On the back of the book, Levinas in turn praises Schürmann's work for its "speculative and pedagogical value [which] make[s] it a highly welcome publication." In this respect, it is all the more striking that *Broken Hegemonies* does not even mention Levinas by name.

Identities: Totality and Hegemony

The similarities between Levinas and Schürmann may be obvious: just as Schürmann rejects at the end of metaphysics any hegemonic fantasm, so too Levinas is wary of the idea of a closed totality. Both Levinas and Schürmann then display an attentiveness toward that which cannot be represented and thus forced into a system. Moreover, both thinkers would in and through their rejection of the monism and the quest for unity characteristic of metaphysics endorse a fundamental plurality and multiplicity of being. Schürmann's "radical multiplicity"[52] thus might very well be, for Levinas as it is for Schürmann, accompanied by a certain anarchism—taken as the absence of any common or unifying principle or foundation of our world once all "*archai*" have shown themselves to have originated in an ontic "projective" manner—for "there is an anarchy essential to multiplicity."[53] Levinas and Schürmann furthermore share a similar attentiveness to the inner divide that haunts the human being once thrown upon its span between birth and death. A certain form of such "tragedy" might be discerned primarily in Levinas's early works and their effort to "break with Parmenides" through a pluralism that "appears [in] the very existing of the existent itself."[54] By that token, the existence of the human being is, according to Levinas, double: at once chained to itself and turned to the other. Chained to itself, that is, to the impersonal nature of the "*il y a*" contaminating the human being's person, which Levinas describes through the analysis of insomnia, in which it is not "I" that is awake but rather an impersonal "me" that is waking.[55]

Chained to itself, because in this rift between the "I" of consciousness and the "*il y a*" of impersonal existence threatening it from within, the human being inevitably has an awareness of its imminent death. Turned to the other, for existence's duality might take another direction and accomplish itself in fecundity.

This latter route is taken by Levinas's *Totality and Infinity*, which still affirms the necessary break with Parmenides to think transcendence's anarchic plurality. *Totality and Infinity*, moreover, conveys its philosophy of pluralism in the same formula as Levinas's earlier works. In this work—and even more so in his later works—Levinas will identify the rupture with the system of being with the very existence of the human subject: "the break-up of totality, the denunciation of the panoramic structure of being, concerns the very existing of being."[56] It is true that in Levinas's works this interruption or "distance" will be progressively connected with (divine or not) transcendence, because "the distance [transcendence] expresses [. . .] enters into the *way of existing* of the exterior being."[57] Concerning the debate between Levinas and Schürmann, it matters little whether Levinas associated the anarchic undertow accompanying all discourse on being with divine transcendence; it matters all the more that Levinas consigned his anarchism to a principle nevertheless: the "exterior being" is to be equated with the face of the other, and only the face in turn is to be equated with that which forever disrupts the system. Levinas's "essential anarchy" thus concerns only the intersubjective encounter. Therefore indeed "a principle breaks through" this essential anarchy "when the face presents itself, and demands justice."[58] The essential anarchy is undone by the principle of the face.

Differences: With/out principle

In this sense, the debate between Schürmann and Levinas might turn on the latter's humanism and anthropocentrism, for even if it is a "humanism of the other man," it is a humanism nonetheless. Let us turn to Schürmann again to consider what the difference between the presencing of being and the interruption of the exterior being or the face might be. Commenting on Heidegger's pathway to presencing, Schürmann writes: "in *Being and Time*, to be present still means to be present 'for man' [. . .] A new way of thinking is required to understand presencing independently of such a reference."[59] Now, if Schürmann is considering the presencing of being(s) "independently of every position we would have taken in its regard," then it is obvious that that which Levinas reserves for one region of phenomenality, namely the human being, must be extended to the whole of phenomenality.

It would thus be necessary to state that for Schürmann not only the human face but also the world and perhaps nature would be able to occur independently of any reference to "man."[60]

Not only Schürmann would deem this anthropocentrism in Levinas a residue of metaphysical thought, Derrida has also accused the ontotheological character of the excessive importance Levinas attributed to the face: this *"intra-ontic* movement of ethical transcendence" props "up thought by means of a transhistoricity."[61] This intra-ontic movement, which, just as traditional ontotheology does, thinks beings ("the face") rather than being, seems to be in need of some theological legitimation. Indeed, because "the Other resembles God"[62] it seems that it is ultimately God who, like a supreme being, bestows the face of the human other with the power to interrupt the subject's egoistic being. Hence Derrida's critique, for, in his words, "the question of Being is nothing less than a disputation of the metaphysical truth of this schema."[63]

Again, it is not because Levinas resorts to God to justify the interruption and the distance of the other that his endeavor is "ontotheological." It is rather that through this recourse to God the human face is attributed the rank of a "principle"—an ultimate referent—which attests to Levinas's metaphysics. In this way, Derrida's and Schürmann's critiques of Levinasian humanism would coincide: the critique of ontotheology does not point to one or the other "theological" residue in Levinas; it is rather that "the human face" still functions as an "ultimate signifier" that orients all other significations that accounts for Levinas's ontotheology. In Schürmann's words: the face turns out to be yet another hegemonic fantasm in that it inappropriately singles out one phenomenal region (intersubjectivity) at the expense of all other regions (e.g., nature).

In this respect, it might be good to turn to Levinas's later work, especially *Otherwise than Being* and *God, Death and Time*, in which Levinas proceeds to a separation of anarchy and principle.[64] Indeed, in these later works divine transcendence is utterly separated from any principle, even that of the human face: "this glory is without principle: there is in this infinity an *anarchical* element."[65] If the face at the time of *Totality and Infinity* was erected to the point of a principle—a being that would be singled out as the highest of beings—and if it therefore would be subject to that which *Broken Hegemonies* would deem a "maximization" of one phenomenal region over others, then it must be noted that the face in *Otherwise than Being* is de-phenomenalized to a great extent: it is not so much the concrete encounter with a human face that is at issue but rather our pre-original trauma or susceptiveness toward the other's otherness that is judged to be anarchic, that is, without principle.[66] This susceptibility, always and already turned toward otherness, is called by Levinas "a bottomless passivity"; it is without ground.[67] The primacy of otherness thus makes up a susceptibility of all for all, which Levinas interprets as fraternity. One might formulate the difference between the early and later Levinasian anarchy in this way: whereas *Totality and Infinity*, although it agreed on the essential anarchism of intersubjective pluralism, assumed and perhaps had to assume "the commonness of a father," which according to Levinas is the great contribution to thought of "monotheism,"[68] in *Otherwise than Being* fraternity is given a strictly philosophical explanation,[69] and the face is so to say replaced by the trace. The trace is not a unifying principle, it is an "outside" of thinking that somehow operates from within my being and orients (my) existence toward otherness. It is an "*à Dieu*," which implies a goodbye to a (certain) God as well. It might be such a trace, which is just as much "without why" and "without ground" as Schürmann's and Heidegger's presencing of being, with which Schürmann agreed when confirming, with Levinas, that "being is exteriority."[70] Considering the later Levinas's assertion concerning the "impossible indifference with regard to the human,"[71] one can safely conclude that on the topic of humanism the differences between Schürmann and Levinas would still stand.

If the difference between the early and the later Levinas thus implies a difference in the status of "anarchy," then it is worth noting the confusion this thinking "with/out principle" has caused among commentators: Abensour celebrates Levinas's distinction between anarchy and principle *because* it refuses a political conception of anarchy that would impose yet another principle on anarchy,[72] while Rolland suggests that the unprincipled anarchism *includes* such a political conception—I come back to this below.[73]

Schürmann might have experienced a similar confusion, considering that *Broken Hegemonies* makes little mention of "a principle of anarchy"—if at all. This confusion comes to the fore in both Rudolphe Gasché's article on Schürmann's work, which inspired the thesis of the last section, and the brief but harsh discussion between Derrida and Schürmann.

Derridean Anarchy

The thesis of this section is that the definition of "hegemony" of *Broken Hegemonies* might be applied to the thematic of Schürmann's book on

Heidegger as well. Schürmann's debate with Derrida will then help us to underscore the shifts in Schürmann's conception of the "closure of metaphysics" and in the conception of its humble everyday origins.

The whole debate centers on one citation of Derrida—to which Schürmann tirelessly returns—from Derrida's *Margins of Philosophy*: at the end of metaphysics it is for Derrida a matter "to decide to change terrain, in a discontinuous and irruptive fashion, by brutally placing oneself outside, and by affirming an absolute break and difference."[74] Schürmann has most forcefully responded to Derrida's "deconstructive naiveté" and its desire to switch terrains, to go to an anti-metaphysical site, when stating that the philosopher's task "[is] more modest, for from what lofty position would we be able to draw the geographic map of discontinuous planes? What field outside the terrain must one occupy in order to affirm rupture? I know of no other place than the one whereupon the waning twentieth century has planted us," commenting in a note: "Derrida seems to speak here as a chronicler of what was going on in France at the time he signed the text—'May 12, 1968,'"[75] implying, importantly, that Derrida mistakenly took an ontic event to have (anti)metaphysical significance. Schürmann's desire, then, was not to "change terrain" but to change to another thinking, "beyond deconstruction."[76] Janicaud confirms: "[Schürmann] neither accepted the idea of an end of metaphysics nor the possibility of 'placing oneself outside,' even if by a kind of play."[77] Yet the latter point stands in need of some proof, for it might be the case that at the time of his Heidegger book Schürmann was himself riveted to a naive deconstructive site. Indeed, several passages show that Schürmann envisaged an "outside of ontotheology," or at least that an other than metaphysical thinking was a "possibility."[78]

In this way, Derrida's *History of the Lie*, which appeared in a volume dedicated to the memory of Schürmann but which cites him merely two times, might be read as turning Schürmann's critique against himself. Derrida's text, though it deals mainly with Arendt, can indeed be read as a critique of the grand Heideggerian rhetoric, recounting *a* history of being and of metaphysics, for is not such a rhetoric compromised by "an indestructible optimism" in that it seems to presuppose *already* how the lie or the error of metaphysics might be overcome?[79] This optimism is concerned not with a personal attitude but with claiming to be "in the know," whether it concerns the end of metaphysics or truth in general.

But let us not agree with Derrida too easily and turn to Schürmann's critique of Derrida in the 1982 book to understand what the difference between this book and the later *Broken Hegemonies* might be. Schürmann criticizes Derrida for a large part in the notes of the first-mentioned book. Schürmann mentions the game Heidegger played with Nietzsche and poses that Derrida is playing a similar game with Heidegger: just as Heidegger could turn Nietzsche into the "last metaphysician," so too can Derrida, by ruse, turn Heidegger into the "last metaphysician."[80] Schürmann argues that Derrida can only turn Heidegger into the last metaphysician of presence by forgetting the temporalizing of the ontological difference, the difference between presencing and that which is present in each given epoch. Derrida can only claim that Heidegger's question of being remained an "intra-metaphysical effect" by obliterating presencing and reducing Heidegger's dwelling to a homecoming that interpreted being as "maintaining" and "belonging" and thus as presence. In this way, Derrida can play with Heidegger as Heidegger played with Nietzsche: just as Nietzsche remained "metaphysical" for Heidegger and therefore "attempted an exit and a deconstruction" from metaphysics "without changing terrains," so too, for Derrida, Heidegger is still metaphysical without switching terrains. Deconstruction then would be anti-metaphysical insofar it knows how to change terrains.[81] For Schürmann, the difference between presencing and presence means precisely that being cannot be understood in an optimistic sense as the place where we dwell and belong. Because of "epochal discordance," the presencing of our world radically differs from the presencing of any other epoch. For Schürmann, we indeed dwell in the world, but this world now worlds in ways it hasn't worlded before—if I may play with Heidegger's vocabulary—and resists therefore any sense of "belonging."[82]

Thus, just as Derrida criticizes Schürmann for being optimistic concerning the matter of overcoming metaphysics, so Schürmann criticizes Derrida for being too optimistic when depicting Heidegger as the *last* metaphysician. Might it be that the confusion comes from the fact that both adversaries are "playing a game," even more grave than that which prevails in Derrida's "step outside the destruction game" and which "watch[es] the destroyers destroy each other reciprocally"?[83] This game, then, would concern "the natural metaphysician in us," and I risk a bold hypothesis in favor of this natural metaphysics in the conclusion to this chapter.

Conclusion: In Praise of Everydayness

If, then, Derrida utters a similar objection to Schürmann as Schürmann toward Derrida, it might be the case that Schürmann's accusation of a "deconstructive naiveté" can be turned against himself. I turn to Rodolphe

Gasché's article and to the remarkable conclusion of *Broken Hegemonies* to make this point. In this conclusion, Schürmann seems to address this game, which throws the accusation of metaphysics around and around. This is a game, so it seems, of endless reversals in and of metaphysics in which in the end no one escapes the accusation of being the "last metaphysician"— Schürmann calls it "the inversion thesis." For instance,

> to report that sometime after 1830 values got inverted [. . .]— such storytelling is not exactly free of interest. It allows one to classify one's neighbor, if he locates his referents up high, as "still a metaphysician," for two centuries now, a professional insult.[84]

It is, however, such insults that accompanied the debate between Derrida and Schürmann and through which the destroyers of metaphysics are destroying themselves. It seems, therefore, that the concept of "counter-philosophers" that Gasché has drawn from *Broken Hegemonies* is applicable to both Schürmann and Derrida as well. Counter-philosophers are those who, in a given epoch, emphasize the negative, the pull to singularity and mortality, and thereby tend to "maximize" these negative experiences as if they merely reverse the "maximization" of metaphysics' ultimate referents.[85] The danger, then, is that both positions would miss the originary double bind and *différend* of natality and mortality, which posits that "metaphysics" is "natural," "ontic," or "existential" because it originates in the natural tendency to look away from that from which one cannot not look away from, namely death and finitude. Thus, while "metaphysicians" stress the aspect of natality, the "counter-philosophers" seem to stress the aspect of negativity and mortality. It is at this point, however, that the conclusion of *Broken Hegemonies* gets enigmatic, for if Gasché is right when saying that a hegemonic fantasm is accomplished when the phenomenality of the phenomenon is constituted by turning this phenomenality "into parts of an interconnected world,"[86] then this is, as I have shown, exactly what Schürmann's Heidegger book sought to do when insisting on the oneness and the unity of the presencing of a world.

It is thus a possible escape of metaphysics that is at stake in the conclusion to *Broken Hegemonies*. On the one hand, one still finds statements in line with the Heidegger book. Gasché, for instance, scrutinizes Schürmann's treatment of Eckhart, for whom it would have been a matter of "leaving [the principles] behind, of no longer having recourse to them," and then asks poignantly: "one may question this possibility by recalling everything that Schürmann has established in this work [*Broken Hegemonies*]."[87] One may question Gasché's statement in turn, though, because Schürmann's point was that the "natural metaphysician in us" *inevitably* has recourse to principles and ultimate referents. But, on the other hand, it is the latter thesis that the conclusion to *Broken Hegemonies* seeks to overturn in sticking to the ultimate double bind as much as possible by stating that the natality "impulse that unifies life" cannot be equated with the good just as the singularization to come of death cannot be equated with "evil pure and simple."[88] In this sense, Schürmann realizes that unifying principles and hegemonies are not in advance to be considered as "bad," "evil," and "insulting," as the Heidegger book would have it. In this way, it opens the terrain from which an escape might be possible, rather than leaping into an "other terrain."

The "escape" of metaphysics, then, it seems, has to do with the question of just how far we can heed Nietzsche's "extra-moral" view on metaphysics. For, if the unitary presencing and "the oneness of 'phenomenal interconnectedness' (Schürmann), or the one fraternal humanity for that matter (Levinas), shows itself to be yet another metaphysical convulsion, then the most sobering question to ask is to where the "epochal discordance" extends. The question of the relation between the one and the pluralistic manifold would then need to address a possible discordance not only between epochs (as in the grand Heideggerian rhetoric) but also between cultures and perhaps individuals. Another warning of Derrida to Schürmann might thus be incorporated into the debate over the end of metaphysics, namely that if one wants to philosophize in a manner free of interest, then the history of metaphysics must be recounted free of moral denunciation.[89]

To conclude: to understand the fact that the end of metaphysics might be related to the question of whether we can still attain to the level of transcendental, ontological, and therefore extra-moral thinking, it is useful to turn to the debate between Schürmann and Levinas. For if Schürmann at the end of *Broken Hegemonies* realized that the natural metaphysician in all of us cannot do without ultimate referents, that thus anarchy is from time immemorial indebted to a "principle," it is not sure whether Schürmann would have applauded the later Levinas's contention that anarchy is separated from any principle (be it a political one). It is furthermore worth noting that Rolland's appreciation of the political anarchism depends on an *ontic* argument. It can also be shown that Levinas's distinction between anarchism and politics is indeed dependent on the turmoil of 1968.[90] It is only then that we can understand Schürmann's ultimate reluctance toward any such ontic point of reference for the question of the end of metaphysics, for such a point would make the issue of metaphysics an issue for a report in a chronicle (whether it is 1830, 1933, or 1968). Schürmann indeed never considered May 1968 as one of the "rare moments of freedom" that Arendt noticed in history.[91] On the contrary, he seems to have recoiled before any such ontic point of reference, as is obvious from his recounting of the events of 1933 surrounding Heidegger.[92]

It is surprising indeed that a thinker who takes great pains to show the ontic origin of epochal presence, who singles out the exceptional nature of our age of technology, and moreover advances the public character of philosophy, ignores the ontic events of our current epoch. It is strange finally that a thinker concerned to such an extent with freedom and everydayness (to the point that an intellectual always and already is a "public intellectual") remained silent on the cultural and everyday implications of *our* metaphysics.

The reason for this? Perhaps even Schürmann had too much reverence for the hubris of the hegemonies he contested. Indeed, if the Heidegger book hesitates to criticize Heidegger for the "inability" of this thinking "to emerge effectively from the philosophical tradition,"[93] this might be the case precisely because, even in Schürmann and even though he has pointed to it, the relation between the ontic and the ontological realm, between everydayness and epochal presence, between the public realm and philosophy, is left hanging. Even more grave, precisely because it remains unclear how one can change terrain from everydayness to the terrain of ontology, Schürmann may repeat one of the most traditional hierarchies since the inception of metaphysics: the hierarchy (and the hubris) that separates "ontology" from all things ontic, philosophy from culture, authenticity from everydayness.

2
———

What Comes after Christianity?

Jean-Luc Nancy's Deconstruction of Christianity

Nancy's project of a deconstruction of Christianity was announced already in the 1992 book *Le sens du monde*. Nancy had written: "that which we need to think cannot but consist in the abandonment of the Christian sense," the sense of which "cannot but proceed by a deconstruction of Christianity."[1] This abandonment has to be understood in both an active and a passive manner: active because we have, in our culture, abandoned and are abandoning Christianity; passive because for Nancy something within Christianity's very constitution is such that the disappearance of Christianity seems unavoidable. This chapter tries to forge a distinction between Nancy's project, the questions it asks, and the ways in which Nancy's project unfolds. This chapter therefore describes, first, the links between Nancy's approach to the problem of sense and the deconstruction of Christianity that follows from it to show, second, some problems surrounding the very possibility of deconstructing the Christian tradition. The abandonment of Christianity seems to coincide here with the end or the "exhaustion," as Sloterdijk will put it, of metaphysics: the West has grown tired of itself.

The End of Metaphysics and the Deconstruction of Christianity

The end of metaphysics is not the end of the world. This sentence aptly summarizes, it seems, Jean-Luc Nancy's philosophy. Now that the grand narratives and the ultimate signifiers have withered away, we find ourselves in a world that is not bereft of any sense—as nihilists or their adversaries would have it—but, on the contrary, in a world where sense is always and already there.

The sense of the world, according to Nancy, is not to be sought in one or the other transcendental signifier that would, once and for all, decide on the meaning of our preoccupations in this world. Rather, Nancy's project tries to make sense of the fact that, now that all origins and foundations have fled, sense emerges and is present in any innerworldly encounter thinkable. This sense is not to be found in whatever grand narrative; it arises, rather, from out of our everyday encounters with one another. That is why, ultimately, Nancy proposes a "banal phenomenology" of our being-with-one-another.[2] Such a banal phenomenology directs itself mostly against Heidegger: over and against the latter's supposed "disdain for the ordinary," Nancy advances what one can call a praise of everydayness.[3]

Nancy's deconstruction of Christianity squares with his phenomenological ontology of "being-with" in the sense that Christianity has from time immemorial been exposed both to metaphysical structures and that which remained outside of them. In this way, Christianity, for Nancy, occupies an exceptional and paradigmatic place: although it is metaphysical to its very core, it simultaneously has sown the seeds of its (own) overcoming. Nancy is quite clear on this: for him, Christianity and "monotheism [oppose], as much as [they comfort] the reign of the principle."[4] The deconstruction of Christianity is, however, not to be taken as a provocation.[5] Nancy rather asks how Christianity can still make sense in a culture that is no longer Christian, that is, a culture that no longer shares all Christian presuppositions.[6] The deconstruction of Christianity is thus a comportment toward what one can call the relics and the remainder of the Christian culture. It is, according to Nancy, precisely from out of Christianity's vanishing that a thought of the world or of our being-with might appear, for "already in the most classical metaphysical representations of [. . .] God, nothing else was at stake, in the end, than the world itself."[7] The attempt to grasp the world within a single worldview or to comprehend the totality of beings from out of a highest being or principle will, when faded away, give way to the thought of the world without principle, without sufficient reason. If all historical highest beings—God, nature, reason, history—have functioned as a sort of filling in the gaps by, for instance, explaining that which could not and cannot be explained—the existence of the world for instance—then the deconstruction of Christianity aims to attend to the nothingness, the void, and the gap left after the flight of the Gods. Nancy's rather straightforward response to Marion is telling: "[Marion's] proposition does not emerge yet out of a 'self-giving' (and of 'self-showing' of the phenomenon, whereas I propose here, simply, that nothing gives *itself* and that *nothing* shows *itself*—and that is what is."[8] Nancy's thought, therefore, must be seen as an attempt to cope with a world *without givenness*, without any principle *being given*, and to stick to the world *as* it (now) worlds considered from the fact *that* it worlds (and that it is only the world that worlds). This "worlding of the world" is *ours:* its worlding is neither regulated by something or someone "out there" nor controlled by an ideal somewhere "in" the world. Hence what can be called Nancy's axiom: "we who are no more than us in a world, which is itself no more than the world."[9]

It is in *this* world that Christianity is auto-deconstructing. And it is important to note that for Nancy Christianity vanishes in a quasi-automatic way. Such an *auto-deconstruction* only ever occurs if the (metaphysical) system of Christianity "has contained its fatal agent within itself ever since its conception."[10] Such a "fatal agent," for Nancy, seems to be whatever givenness that has been posed, presupposed, or otherwise taken for granted: from the very moment the presupposition is made that God is the foundation and ultimate unification of the world (ontotheology) or that such a unification is left to the transcendental postulates (Kant and modernity), it must be stated that such a "presupposition also contains the principle of its own deposition."[11] Concretely, this means that Christianity will break under the pressure of the divides and the divisions that have constituted it in the first place. Nancy's project tries to expose and disassemble those "internal divisions" within Christianity that will eventually cause the disintegration of its assembly and be the death of it. Nancy mentions several examples of these divisions. One can, for instance, think of the Christian quarrel over the prohibition of images, on the one hand, and the right to represent the sacred, on the other. Derrida has noted another division: the portrayal of the Gospel of Jesus as touching and touched by human beings and Jesus's own prohibition of any such touch ("*Noli me tangere*"). Nancy added that it is precisely this paradox of Christianity—the paradox connecting "*hoc est corpus meum*" and "*noli me tangere*"—that is at issue.[12] Most important, however, is the division between a Christianity that lets itself be reduced to metaphysics and a Christianity that precisely resists such a reduction. Christianity, for Nancy, would be at the heart of both the closure of metaphysics and its overcoming.

The auto-deconstruction of Christianity therefore consists of the (progressive) disappearance of power, of presence, of the givenness of myths due to the contingent character of its composition and the internal divide on which it draws. One might exaggerate somewhat and say that, for Nancy, Christianity cannot not disappear because it is, and has to be, its own disappearance. Nancy indeed writes that "everything takes place as though Christianity had developed [. . .] *at once* [. . .] an affirmation of power, domination and exploitation *and* an [. . .] affirmation of the destitution and abandonment of self whose vanishing point is its auto-disappearance."[13]

Thinking the World: Between Heidegger and Levinas

Nancy's most audacious claim is to be found in one of his major works, *Being Singular Plural*, which can be read as a response to both Heidegger and Levinas. Let us have a look at Nancy's admittedly rather blunt response to Heidegger. According to Nancy, indeed one has "to refigure [Heidegger's] fundamental ontology"; that is, "it is necessary to rewrite *Being and Time*." Nancy, however, immediately nuances this bold claim by adding a few lines that will turn out to be indicative of his entire philosophy. For, according to Nancy, "this is not a ridiculous pretension, and it is not 'mine'; it is the necessity of all the major works insofar as they are *ours*."[14]

Nancy's philosophy indeed revolves around a philosophy of the "we," "of the 'with' of all things."[15] It is in this sense that Nancy's comment on Heidegger's fundamental ontology must be understood. The rewriting of *Being and Time* falls upon all of us, philosophers and theologians alike. For, in the aftermath of metaphysics and after Heidegger's obscuring of precisely this "with" through insisting on the election of one or the other people or *Volk*—be it the Greeks or the Germans—it is of urgent need to reflect on our being-together-in-a-world. In 1927, Heidegger had already written that "the world of Dasein is a with-world [*Mit-Welt*]."[16] It is all the more striking that Heidegger, if not having eradicated, at least has downplayed the importance of being-with already in *Being and Time*: either by insisting on authentic Dasein's "existential solipsism" or by letting this authenticity merge with the supreme "destiny" of this or that people that would come to the fore in the later Heidegger.[17] In this regard, Nancy's thought can be regarded as unsettling the difference between the philosopher and what Nancy labels the people or "gents," which he distinguishes from Heidegger's portrayal of "the They" ("*das Man*").[18] Whereas Heidegger could be interpreted as portraying some kind of heroic effort of "authentic" Dasein to free itself from the inauthentic clutches of "the They," Nancy insists that there is no such possible extrication: even authentic Dasein would be immersed in and forced to deal with the inauthenticity of "the They."[19]

One might expect Nancy to turn to Levinas to elucidate the "with" of all beings, for was not Levinas the one who had given the Other central stage?[20] The debate between Levinas and Nancy is, however, a complex one, and Nancy disagrees with Levinas on various points. First, Nancy would not agree with Levinas's indeed somewhat artificial separation between (Heideggerian) ontology and ethics by arguing that every ontology is already ethical and vice versa.[21] Second, and in perfect accordance with the *Miteinandersein* of all beings, Nancy diverges from both Levinas's exclusive focus on the human other and from Levinas's hesitations about the theological reference of this capitalized Other. Nancy writes that the alterity that he seeks has nothing to do with "an Other (the inevitably 'capitalized Other') *than* the world; it is a question of the alterity or alteration *of* the world."[22] One might object, of course, in Levinas's name and state that, for Levinas, the world is not another world or a *Hinterwelt* either, but that the world is precisely that which happens between the Other and I. For did not Levinas insist "that the relationship with the Other is not produced outside the world" or "outside economy"?[23] This is ultimately the reason why Levinas emphasizes the importance of not approaching the Other with empty hands. On the contrary, everything that makes up the world—foods, beverages, representations, and so forth—only makes sense *from within* the social relation with the Other, that is, if they attain to the level of some*thing* one can give to the Other.

Yet even then Nancy would beg to differ, for his (Lacanian) point of capitalizing the other would in the end also deconstruct these lines of demarcations between the Other and the (other) others as well as the Levinasian bifurcation between humanity and animality.[24] One might already surmise that at the root of Nancy's criticism of Levinas, one can hear the echo of Derrida's infamous phrase in which he confesses "[his] deafness to [. . .] the division of being between the same and the other"[25] in Levinas. In its stead, Nancy advances contra Levinas a "plurality *in* being,"[26] which passes well beyond both the pluralism of the two monolithic blocks constituted by the Same (or ontology) and the Other (or ethics) or the division between the inauthentic form of Dasein—everydayness—and the solitude of authentic Dasein, as Heidegger would have wanted it.

Nancy's own position, then, is what one could call a more "existential" version of Derrida's *différance*. Nancy is envisioning the event of being as the arrival of a surprise that surpasses our anticipations or representations. Being is what happens in however minute an occasion, but always according to the logic of the "with." The meaning of being, then, cannot occur "for one alone": this is Nancy's version of what I later, with Binswanger, call the "greeting" that is being.

Take, for instance, the Cartesian *cogito*: I can doubt the existence of others; I can even doubt the existence of a world out there; but I cannot doubt the very fact that it is I who doubts. Descartes's conclusion is that because

I think, I must also be: I am not sure that there are others at all, I am sure only of the fact that I exist. Nancy comments: for such a solipsistic phrase to be true, it must presuppose that others, namely "each one of Descartes' readers," must also be able to understand this solitude of the Cartesian cogito and so confirm this solipsism (all the while rendering it inoperative).[27]

In this way, being—existence—is for Nancy made up each time of different encounters, by our dwelling in different groups, by our attending to and tarrying with others each time anew. Nancy thus describes the ontology of being-with as a worldwide web of relationships in which all are dependent on all and supplement one another and in which no relation takes precedence over another to the point of eclipsing all essence (substance, *ousia*, etc.). Being, for Nancy, is that which is always and already shared: it is what takes place between us and on which no one can lay hold. In this sense, one might compare Nancy's envisioning of being with the way in which a deck of cards is distributed among its players: though all players share in the same deck of cards, the deck of cards itself is not appropriated once and for all by the players, and although the players share in the same set, the hands of all players are different each time. The set of cards "is" nowhere else than in its being shared among all of the players.

The Deconstruction of Christianity

What One Inherits from Christianity: Our Christian Provenance

Nancy's thought of the world emerges out of the progressive disappearance—the auto-deconstruction—of Christianity and its ontotheological variations. In a way, Nancy is trying to make sense of our Christian provenance, for the deconstruction of Christianity seems to follow from Nancy's own self-evident presupposition: if it takes two (or more) for there to be sense and signification at all, how then can Christianity still have meaning in a culture that no longer *shares* all Christian presuppositions?[28] The deconstruction of Christianity is thus a comportment toward what one can call the relics and the remainder of the Christian culture.

It is, according to Nancy, from out of Christianity's vanishing that a thought of the world might appear. This is, of course, not without consequences for the thinking of transcendence. The relation to transcendence is no longer a relation to one or the other term(inus) outside the world—God, for example. Instead of such a relation to the Transcendent, this relation now is rather a movement of transcend*ing* toward nothing in particular: it is a comportment of transcending without a Transcendent, without anywhere or anyone to transcend to except for the gap that is the world. This "immanent transcendence"[29] is thus nothing, nothing given—nothing in particular: it is the "with" of all beings-with-one-another, the "ad" of *esse ad*, a *coram* without *Deo*, if you like.

Nancy's rephrasing of what "transcending" means is the result of a long meditation on Heidegger's statement that modern humanism did not succeed in seeing the true "height" of the human being.[30] For Nancy, "transcending" does not mean the movement "towards a height, an altitude, or toward a summit (sovereign, *ens summum*)"; transcendence rather is always and already "*transcending*. It is passing-to-the-outside, and passing to-the-other."[31] This transcending of one being to another being, of all beings to one another, thus *takes place* within the world. From this follows "that the 'divine,' from now on, does neither have a place in the world nor outside the world because there is no other world. That which is 'not of this world' [i.e., transcendence, JS] is not elsewhere: it is the opening in the world."[32] Such transcending is, in its own way, Nancy's response to Schürmann's question "What is to be done at the end of metaphysics?" For to live in a world without any principles or guidelines given is for Nancy equal to the question of a certain praxis—a sort of savoir faire, a "know-how" to cope with the nothingness of the world.[33] That is why, for Nancy,

> Christianity designates nothing other, essentially [. . .] than the demand to open in this world an unconditional alterity or alienation [. . .] and can be summed up [. . .] in the precept of living in this world as outside of it—in the sense that this "outside" is not, or is not an entity. It does not exist, but it [. . .] defines and mobilizes ex-istence: the opening of the world to inaccessible alterity.[34]

Christianity's contribution is thus to have capitalized in the world on the very idea of a "beyond." It is only now, according to Nancy, that one is able to see that this "beyond" itself has not vanished. On the contrary, there is a "beyond" (to) this world, but this "transcendence" is not elsewhere than [in] the world, and it is not a supreme being. And yet it cannot be deconstructed.

At least this is what Nancy intends to convey in his discussion with Lyotard: if for Lyotard it is a matter of advancing toward a judgment without criteria—a judgment over a given, empirical, and particular case without a standard set of universal criteria—for Nancy it is a matter of raising the stakes of Kant's reflective judgment—a judgment that has to decide (and decides) on the empirical manifold in the absence *even* of any (empirical) intuition—to do justice to what Nancy calls the singular plurality as such (in which all beings receive and obtain their being in and through existing *next to* other beings and for which, consequently, no single form of intuition of an "essence" suffices).[35]

Whereas for Lyotard, one might say, it is a matter of constructing a concept with which to judge the plurality of diverse empirical cases and intuitions, for Nancy both the concepts and the intuitions are, so to say, ruled out: "the judgment without criteria [. . .] is placed before [. . .] something that cannot be constructed, which responds to an absence of intuition [and] which moreover *produces* an absence of concept." Furthermore, Nancy adds: "to encounter the *inconstructible* in the Kantian sense, this is also and at the very least is what 'to deconstruct' means [. . .] This word would [thus] have led us toward what is neither constructed nor constructible."[36] That which cannot be deconstructed is thus nothing less than the very happening of the world itself. One should not read Nancy here in nihilistic terms, for the gap or the nothingness that is left once metaphysics' foundational presence and absolute significations have reached their expiration date, an opening to the sense of all that is becomes possible. "Sense" for Nancy is neither the full presence of (metaphysical) signification construed by a subject nor the passive reception of the "meaning" that a supreme being would bestow on us; on the contrary, "sense" is always and already there and always only coming (and going): it is the awareness that, even though full presence cannot be achieved, this does not mean that all sense has abandoned us. Rather, it is that we are abandoned to sense when (and even though) this sense can never attain the level of a clear and distinct signification.[37] "Sense" is precisely the very *retreat* of signification—the retreating of full presence: it is this "retreat" that we will "have to be," and the fact that this sense only ever occurs among two (or more) is why we need to rewrite *Being and Time*.[38] It is a relationality that in no way whatsoever can be reified: it is precisely because it escapes all the characteristics of (a) being that Nancy terms it "nothing."

This alterity within the world, its opening onto sense, is the shared event of being and world that can never be at the disposal of one (highest) being (or disposed to a highest being); it cannot be elucidated without an inquiry into our Christianity provenance as well as its future fate. Nancy's concept of "provenance" is important to his deconstruction of Christianity. "Provenance," he writes, "is never simply a past; it informs the present, produces new effects therein without ceasing to have its own effects." In the case of the demise and the deconstruction of Christianity, this means that "our time is thus one in which it is urgent that the West—or what remains of it—analyze its own becoming, turn back to examine its provenance and its trajectory, and question itself concerning the process of decomposition of sense to which it has given rise."[39]

This provenance, then, should teach us not only under which pressure Christianity breaks but also how the exhaustion and possible extinction of Christianity might give way to a confrontation with that which "comes to the West and Christianity from beyond themselves, what comes toward us from the depths of our tradition as more archaic than Christianity."[40] It is this downfall of Christianity that according to Nancy instructs us about our present and our future:

> Christianity's fate is perhaps the fate of sense in general, that is, what has been called in the last few years the "end of ideologies." The "end of ideologies" is at least the end of promised sense or the end of the promise of sense as an intention, goal, and fulfilment. That is doubtless what it is: the end of the self-sur-passing of Christianity.[41]

This is indeed what Nancy thinks is the case: what we are witnessing today is the "paradoxical fulfilment of Christianity in its own exhaustion."[42]

This intertwining of Christianity's fulfilment and its exhaustion is, for Nancy, only possible because at the heart of Christianity there is an internal divide that causes it to disrupt from within. Christianity is at a crossroads, or, rather, it *is* this crossroads: "Christianity [. . .] dis-encloses in its essential gesture the closure that it had constructed and that it perfects, lending to the metaphysics of presence its strongest imaginary resource."[43] Christianity, as the metaphysics that is closest to us, gives, by way of its own closure and exhaustion, way to the opening of something new. It is thus because Christianity is, from the outset, a "divided integrality"[44] that its conflicting constituents will cause it to decompose and dissolve. It is exactly these divisions that Nancy seeks to deconstruct, for "to deconstruct means to take apart, to disassemble, to loosen the assembled structure in order to give some play to the possibility from which it emerged but which it, qua assembled structure, hides."[45] The deconstruction of Christianity will therefore penetrate the assembly or the composition of Christianity to trace that resource that makes it possible but no longer belongs to it. In the next section, I look at those particular divisions that Nancy has in mind.

The Auto-Deconstruction of Christianity

According to the most concise definition Nancy provides for the deconstruction of Christianity, it is "both an analysis of Christianity—from a position presumed to be capable of moving beyond it—as well as the displacement [. . .] proper to Christianity [. . .] inclining toward resources [. . .] that it both conceals and recuperates."⁴⁶ Whereas the first is, so to speak, an act of deconstruction that falls to us in the twenty-first century, the second is the passive observation of Christianity deconstructing itself from within, its auto-deconstruction. The latter, passive, component can be likened to observing Christianity's quasi-automatic disintegration, a disintegration that follows the death of God and that will eventually bring about the death of Christianity.

Probably the most important argument that Nancy advances is that Christianity lets itself be reduced to metaphysics all the while having the resources to remain outside of it: Nancy points to such divisions within Christianity in all of the crucial "moments" of salvation history.⁴⁷ The first one is the relation between the Creator and the creature that, because of its contingency—God did not need any reason to create—already differs from the relation between a cause and an effect. Nancy then points to the act of creating ex nihilo itself, which, for Nancy, already attests to a nothingness undoing the possibility of all "principles" and of all metaphysics. The second counter principle to metaphysics lies in the Incarnation, which for Nancy as such points to a metaphysics of presence (Christ being the permanent mediator between heaven and earth), but which now, "after" Christianity, receives a new assembly in what Nancy calls "spacing." "Spacing" points to the brute materiality of all beings, a mute materiality that knows that its meaning is solely dependent on death as the "end" of materiality. The third counterattack on metaphysical thinking is the possibility of a faith entirely bereft of any form of belief. Here there is, for Nancy, a salvation by faith alone, a salvation that resists the certainties and the dogmas of beliefs of all kinds. It is a salvation that knows nothing of "the whence and the whither" of this salvation.

These three revolts—of a Christianity both with and without metaphysics—are now caught in the middle of their classical Christian interpretation and an interpretation from out of a world that is no longer Christian: faith, in its "post-Christian" posture, is nothing more and nothing less than a sort of faithfulness to world,⁴⁸ to a world without manual or director. Creation ex nihilo comes to mean that the responsibility for the world and for the others, for the endless materiality of all that is, is entrusted to the human being alone.

The active part of Christianity's deconstruction then resides in attending to the void that is left by Christianity's fading away in understanding the need for a new concept of this collapse and especially why the West experiences this collapse "as deprived of sense" while it might, for Nancy at least, very well be one of the first opportunities to touch on something like "sense" in a proper manner.⁴⁹

Entheologisierung

The auto-deconstruction of Christianity in this way entails what Nancy calls the "detheologization" of the world. This concept shows Nancy at his most innovative. Detheologization aims to think the "sense" of Christianity's deconstruction. Sense might be interpreted here as "direction," as to where exactly this auto-deconstruction is heading. For this, it is important to understand contemporary culture not only as one that is "no longer" Christian but also as one that is not, for all that, "unchristian." This is what I intend to convey with a "not-quite non-Christian culture." It is such a situation that makes for the originality if not novelty of the contemporary era and to which a great many contemporary theologies fail to relate.

This situation forbids the classic thesis of Löwith, for instance, for whom the (post)modern era was but a secular version of what religion once had to offer. The deconstruction of Christianity aims at a "detheologization" and not a "secularization" of the theological, because this latter option would entail that all happenings within our culture, in one way or another, still be Christian. "Secularizing the theological" would mean not only that all events within the world could be answered for and recuperated by theology but also that there could be something like a permanent presence or identical core to Christianity that could in principle be transmitted from one culture to another without this core being altered or contaminated by such a transmission. There would then be nothing that would not be Christian. This is, as I will show, the critique that Derrida will level against Nancy. But, for Löwith too, modernity would still be a Christian phenomenon because, for instance, Christianity is precisely the religion that departs from religion (Marcel Gauchet) and in this way always and already incorporated the modern tendencies within itself.

Nancy does not deny that certain of these secularizing tendencies do take place, as is indicated already by his "translations" of salvation history; he denies that these translations will always lead to the greater benefit and glory of Christianity. On the contrary, these secular translations are able to run their own course and at times even *depart* from Christianity. In this way, these translations can create a cultural situation where questions arise that can no longer be answered by Christianity or theology and for which the old Christian answer would simply be unfit. One might think here of the contemporary indifference toward religion, which presence in popular culture, in the Catholic teachings at least, is simply denied and which, in Marion, as I will later show, is *immediately* interpreted as a hatred toward the divine.[50] Secular translations of religion can therefore create the space for a deconstruction of Christianity where contemporary culture is, if not non-Christian, than at least other-than-Christianity. With this, Nancy is close to Hans Blumenberg, who argued that the "legitimacy" or "novelty" of modernity was precisely that it moved beyond Christianity and introduced humanity to new questions and situations (e.g., through science and technology) for which the Christian tradition contained no answer, very much like Christianity itself, and its question of the "sense" and "direction" of history, outstripped the Greek thought of cyclic time.[51]

This is why Nancy poses, in our "post-metaphysical" situation, the question of the "sense of sense." The very fact that the collapse of Christianity today is "first and foremost" experienced as bereft of any sense would only show, according to Nancy, that the secularized West has not yet emancipated itself enough from Christianity's clutches and that the West has not yet been prepared for something "other" than Christianity that would be able to give meaning to and make sense of the contemporary situation. This is another reason why the deconstruction of Christianity incorporates a more active gesture to understand this world in an other than theological fashion.

Nancy thus distinguishes this "detheologization" carefully from "a secularization of the theological."[52] The latter would mean, indeed, that the world would again play a role in the theological drama according to which "in the beginning" there is creation and "in the end" there is the resurrection of the dead. A secularization of the theological does not attend sufficiently to the demise of Christianity. What Nancy has in mind, with the concept of a "detheologization," is rather a complete displacement of all things theological: no longer the valuation of a Transcendent, but rather the absolute value of all things immanent, of the world that is.

The difference between the "secularizing of the theological" and Nancy's account of "detheologization" lies precisely in the fact that the former would still reserve some sort of theological role to play for the world—as when one is tempted to read into the emphasis in *Being and Time* on guilt and authenticity a secular version of Christianity's narrative of the fall and redemption—while the latter tries to conceive of the fact that the fallen nature of the world has been assumed and taken up by this global world itself while no longer awaiting its satisfaction from whatever "outside" one can imagine. The world now has to "be" this lack, this fallenness without a place from which to have fallen in the first place; it merely has to transcend into nothing without expecting a redemption that will alleviate this lack somehow. Nancy adds: "it is from this feature of 'creation' that an inscription is thus transmitted to the global world"—this is how creation, for Nancy, becomes "de-onto-theologized."[53] The inhabitant of the contemporary world must "erase sin," at least in Nancy's mind, through resigning both from regarding its own existence as a fault and from conceiving every salvation as an abandonment of this very world (for another world, for instance).[54] Redemption, for Nancy, is nothing other than no longer perceiving existence as faulty or guilty. On the contrary: existence consists of experiencing in the world that which is not of the world but which is not of another world either. But this transcendence within the immanence of world, this nothingness is nothing less than the nongeometrical space *between* all beings, the "with" of all things.

Nancy's concept of detheologization thus tries to convey the fact that, although some phenomena in the contemporary world no doubt derive from the Christian tradition, their signification is completely devoid of any Christian resonance. Next to the pair sin/redemption, Nancy quite explicitly mentions capitalism as one of the legacies of (Christian) monotheism. In fact, Nancy argues, capitalism might be summed up as the monotonous "mono-" of monotheism. It is indeed important to know that, for Nancy, both capitalism and nihilism are the inevitable outcome of Christianity, for the one God supposedly gives way to both nihil-ism[55]—nothing has any value—and capitalism—everything has the same value, quantifiable through money.[56]

Such a "detheologization" also accounts for today's "difficult atheism," which all too often is simply parasitic of theism or, as Milbank once put it, turns into a parody of theism. Nancy, however, notes that not only capitalism and nihilism but also atheism enjoy a Christian provenance (something Milbank would not easily concede).[57] A certain reappraisal of atheism is indeed one of the possibilities for Christianity to regain some "credibility." One could point to diverse contemporary, strictly cultural meanings given to the *word* God (in Levinas and Derrida, for instance) or to an odd dismissal of atheism in the question of God. For the latter, one can think of Marion's portrayal of atheism, which, for him, would only ever be a-theistic toward a certain conception of God, and all indifference toward God is immediately interpreted in a theological and privative fashion, namely as a "hatred" of the divine: for Marion, all absence of love is immediately interpreted normatively. Detheologization therefore allows one to see the indifference to religion in a more positive, neutral, and decidedly nontheological manner, for theology can only interpret this indifference negatively and privatively, namely as the absence of that which, properly speaking, ought to be there, faith for instance. This is why we will later see Marion confusing such indifference with hate. For Nancy, then, the problem rather is that today we are not yet atheistic enough. In a culture that is not yet non-Christian, we would not even know how to be pagans!

Nancy's merit is that he seeks an atheism that is willing to deal with the "sense" and the "truth" of a world that no longer feels the need even to relate God to this very world. Nancy is therefore to be distinguished for what one could call the contemporary postsecular rage, where the limits of secular reason are immediately seen as a possibility for a renewed theology: because, in reason, there can be detected a sort of faith, all at once everything turns into a faith. The real relativism today is the dogma according to which everything is interpretation and "a way of seeing." For Nancy, it is not the case that, because of these limits of reason, one can immediately jump to a (theological) faith underlying the presuppositions of secular reason; it is rather to remain within the limits of reason and rationality as something one "has to be" without presupposing that this "lack" will ever be remedied and redeemed by a plenitude "to come." In this way, Nancy's thinking is able to open onto an atheism and indifference toward religion *without fault*. This is atheism today. Yet it is not to be excluded either that from such a nontheological account a genuine theology might once follow. But, in more ways than one, for Nancy it is simply too soon to start doing theology: first comes world.

In this sense, it is for Nancy a matter of understanding both how and why our contemporary world, despite its Christian provenance, now interprets itself as bereft of and lacking all meaning and just which "secret [. . .] resource"[58] might have assured the linkage between monotheism and the monotony of money today. Nancy's question is whether there can be any sort of *tertium datur* between the modern and premodern verticality ("God") and the postmodern horizontality of monetary ontology (where everything can be turned into a commodity), between either a supreme value or a general equivalency. Earlier Nancy had already written that nothing is to be expected from a "theologization" of the alterity of the world:

> there is no theology that does not turn out [. . .] to be either ontological or anthropological—saying nothing about the god that cannot immediately be said about "event," about "love," about "poetry" and so on and so forth. Why not recognize, on the contrary, that thought, in this age of ours, is in the process of wresting from so-called theology the prerogative of talking about the Other, the Infinitely-other, the Other-infinite. It is taking away from theology the privilege of expressing the *absconditum* of experience and discourse.[59]

It is precisely this *absconditum* of experience, the emptiness and nonidentity at the heart of every experience, that is essential to Nancy's deconstruction of Christianity, for which Christianity empties itself of itself precisely in the consummation of its metaphysics. This *absconditum* is Nancy's existential addendum to Derrida's *différance*, for we "have to be" this difference between metaphysical Signification and worldly sense; we cannot fill the gap between sense in the world and the full-fletched metaphysics of presence that was once, supposedly, feasible.

Even the most respectable systems of the old metaphysics, for Nancy, already show the cracks through which being-in-the-world makes its presence felt. It is thus that Nancy's resistance to Marion and Levinas can be explained: for both, according to Nancy, explain the spacing between sense and signification away by opting for one or the other signification or a given. Consider for instance Nancy's rather straightforward portrayal response to Marion and Levinas: "Marion [proposes] the 'distance' between beings, as opposed to the fullness of metaphysical being. In fact this was tantamount to proving the opposite: far from being rediscovered, God disappears even more surely and definitively through bearing all the names of a generalized and multiplied difference," and then adding, concerning Levinas this time, "Levinas may well say [. . .] that God is 'Infinite,' in the sense of 'unthematizable': the very term 'Infinite' thematizes him."[60]

It is here, with an *absconditum* at the heart of experience, that Nancy claims to have discovered some common ground between Heidegger and Levinas: "I should like here [. . .] to force together Levinas and Heidegger momentarily and say: the lack of sacred names is the *à-Dieu* of the sacred." It is precisely this kinship between Heidegger's flight of the gods and the *à-Dieu* of the Levinasian God that Nancy will elaborate in his deconstruction of Christianity, for it is through such a departure that the *absconditum* of experience can be named. For Nancy, it matters to attend to this lack at the heart of experience properly, not by reverting and relating it to a plenitude to come (filling the gap through one or another metaphysical signification), but rather by attending to the emptiness and void raging through every experience and so resisting an ultimate signifier and even resisting to be signified at all. It matters to attend to this gap otherwise than as an absence of signification, but to see the "sense" of this as an alterity within experience, within the experience of world disrupting our cravings for identity and signification from within.

Absentheism, or Why God Cannot Not Flee

Nancy's ruminations on God and the Gods can be summed up in what he coins as *absentheism*. Absentheism, for Nancy, means that the Gods cannot not be their own disappearance, and even that it is necessary that they flee (Heidegger), for us to be able to attain to the world without any principle or postulate being given.

> At the end of monotheism, there is world without God, that is to say, without another world, but we still need to reflect on what this means, for we know nothing of it, no truth, neither "theistic" nor "atheistic"—let us say [. . .] that it is *absentheistic* [:] an absent God and an absence in place of God.⁶¹

All that the deconstruction of Christianity will need to do is to make sense of this fleeing and retreating of the God(s), because "for us, up to now, such an orientation of thinking—thinking without end, finitude without end—remains privative [. . .] and, in sum, defective,"⁶² that is, we cannot yet understand this retreat of the divine otherwise than as deprived of any sense.

In this way, Nancy's deconstruction of Christianity is one of the first philosophies that tries to forge an opening onto a new thinking appropriate for this thoroughly "detheologized" world, that is, Nancy will try, in and out of the demise of Christianity, to make sense of that which is experienced only as lacking all meaning through "a new understanding [. . .] of this collapse and of the void that has resulted from it."⁶³

For this, one needs to expound once again on Nancy's account of sense and its difference from metaphysical signification, which was one of the central themes of Nancy's œuvre well before the topic of a deconstruction of Christianity came into view. Already in the short essay *The Gravity of Thought* (1991), one is able to note several themes that also run through the later deconstruction of Christianity. Nancy writes:

> [T]he demand for meaning has to go through the exhaustion of significations. This exhaustion does not imply that all significations will have been null and void. They had their meaning, they cleared the way for this destination that leads beyond them without itself [. . .] Christianity [has] led us to ourselves. [In] the end, the system and end history of signification have come to signify their own annulment, turning upon themselves only to reveal the infinite withdrawal of signified meaning.⁶⁴

Meaning (or sense), then, is mobile and floating: it can never be appropriated. Signification, then, is sterile and immobile and always and already suffers from the somewhat cumbersome unification of a concept and its respective intuition, of the one-way traffic between the noesis and the noema if you like. But, Nancy argues, signification always is also (at) a dead end: it cannot take notice of that which escapes and retreats from its drive to represent, and its claim on whatever sort of full-presence. And it is precisely this retreat and this withdrawal, this gap within whatever full-presence, that Nancy calls "sense":

> the meaning offered at the limit of signification takes us into the movement of a presentation *to* . . . which is a rupture of presence itself: not only a rupture of evidences, certainties, and assurances [. . .] but, more deeply, a rupture of signification itself and its order.[65]

Nancy's distinction between sense (or meaning) and signification and full-presence bears some similarities, it seems, with Heidegger's distinction between present-at-hand and ready-to-hand beings: whereas the first stands for, say, a scientific approach to beings to the point of "[prescribing] for the world its 'real' being," the second conveys the fact that we are thrown into a world that is made up of always and already meaningful referential contexts.[66] Whereas, the first, to use Nancy's words, is the sometimes somewhat artificial construction of the link between a concept and an intuition, or of the constitution of the unity of a noesis and its noema, in the second such constitution and construction always come too late, for we "bathe in sense."[67] The *absconditum* at the heart of experience is such that experience always and already deals with the lack of Signification, whose concepts always come too late and which is always marked and stamped by an otherness that disrupts the drive toward the Same and the Concept. Experience itself *dis-encloses*: the compulsion toward closure and unification that is Signification is being deconstructed and opened by the passing of time, the coming and going of world(s).

It is this retreating of sense from signification that will prove to be a distinctive mark of Nancy's deconstruction of Christianity, for what "sense" exactly is one only comes across when something (e.g., Christianity) stops making sense, when the larger bulk of its significations stop "signifying," when within Christianity there is found something older—historically: the paganism within Christianity—and more original—transcendentally: the condition of possibility of Christianity—than Christianity. It is clear already that the concept that stands out to understand all of this is that of the Incarnation, where matter is inspirited, enflamed, set on fire with sense but also with Signification.

The Space of an Incarnation: Deifying/Reifying the Deviance

Because a clear and distinct signification can no longer be attained, one will nevertheless need to cope with some degree of obscurity when it comes to our dealings with "sense." It is here that the theme of incarnation shows itself to be one of the central themes of Nancy's deconstruction of Christianity. If the Incarnation suggests a certain intertwining of the divine and the human, then one might argue that it is precisely this problem of intertwining, of mingling, and of mixture that is the main question of Nancy's philosophy. Nancy thus advances toward a thorough *philosophical* understanding of incarnation. Such a conception seeks to understand just how the intelligible *dwells in* the sensible. It is the awareness that at times the transcendental is not the condition of possibility of the empirical at all, but rather the other way around: how the empirical serves as the condition of possibility of the transcendental in such a way that it is the transcendental itself that *takes on body,* or *becomes flesh*.[68]

For Nancy, this means that philosophy "can only be materialistic," albeit that a sort of "transcendental materiality" is at issue.[69] The "obscurity" of sense stems from the fact that it is dependent, in a certain way, on the muteness of matter. That is why Nancy corrects Heidegger's analysis of the stone, which, according to Heidegger, would be "world-less."[70] Nancy asks whether it is not exactly the impenetrability of this concrete stone here that makes up the sense of the world. Instead of juxtaposing Dasein and material things such as stones, as Heidegger does, Nancy sees the sense of the world arising from out of their touching one another. Indeed: our world would not be "our" world (as we know it) without the very materiality of the stone, without the impenetrability of this very stone over which we trip, for instance, without the door's hardness against which we bump, and so forth. In a certain sense, one can say that were it not for this materiality of the stone (or any other material thing), we would not even know what "to trip" would mean. That is why Nancy states that "impenetrability [is necessary] for there to be access, penetration": it is only through this materiality and this hardness that one can know what one's "access," ecstasy, and openness toward beings might mean.[71]

Nancy says this in(de)constructible happening of the world in many ways, the most important of which is: "*espacement.*" This "spacing" already indicates the material component of Nancy's thought of being—beings take place in space. The transcendental component of this "espacement," however, resides in a meditation on the taking place of the very taking place of (all) beings, the condition of possibility for anything to take place at all—which Nancy also calls "the Being of Being."[72] This "spacing" then, the creation of "the *with* of all things,"[73] borders on being a-historical: it is that which escapes history, the symbolic order, and all narratives but makes them nevertheless possible; it is, to use Schürmann's words again, the a-historical event that has neither history nor destiny but makes possible the coming about of all the historical epochs within history. Nancy's account of this event of the happening of the world is seemingly dependent on a major distinction that Heidegger drew between that which is man-made and that which is not. Though the fact of, for instance, meeting you there is within the power of both of us, the very fact of us being able to meet anywhere at all is something that exceeds our powers.[74]

One should note, however, that on the question of the relation between this philosophical understanding of incarnation and the theology of the Incarnation, Nancy adopts a rather peculiar stance: whereas, for theologians, it is more often than not the latter that justifies the former, for Nancy the former in fact exceeds the latter to the point that the latter becomes but an illustration (albeit a paradigmatic one) of the former. One might ask, indeed, whether such theological shortcuts are not begging the question, if only because they miss the "rather troubling [. . .] duality" of "the spacing *within* the Incarnation," of the mute matter that crosses (theological) intelligibility.[75]

To paraphrase Nancy, then: it is not the Christ with whom I am concerned; it is not the Cross; it is only the question of the crossing, of the intersection. It is the retreat in the middle of the world that is at issue here.[76] For Nancy, it matters to understand just how this excess of the already incarnational spacing toward Christianity's understanding of the Incarnation can be assessed *in* and *from within* a Christian culture. The Incarnation, which understands Christ as the mediator between the divine and the human, is thus superseded by this spacing, which is a mediation both without mediator and without mediating anything—no (clear and) distinct entities.[77] It mediates, if anything, the nothingness of all beings for beings to be able to come into being out of that very nothingness and to differ from one another. It is in this sense that this infinitely finite spacing of singulars accounts for the event of being. But the event of being happens only in and to beings: it takes on body, materiality, place, and space. It is of this, according to Nancy, that the Christian idea of Incarnation was a foreshadowing.

The deconstruction of Christianity, for Nancy, evolves around the question of just what "secret [. . .] resource"[78] or fatal agent has accompanied it since its inception and now delivers the Incarnation of which theology speaks to a spacing of incarnation(s). The "secret" resource Nancy is looking for is something more archaic than Christianity itself: it is that which reveals the possibility from which Christianity proceeds. It is this possibility that Derrida has aptly called "the paganism within Christianity."[79] One can already surmise that the result of such a deconstruction of Christianity would, according to Nancy, deliver the sense of deconstruction, a sense that no longer belongs to this deconstruction. In this way, the deconstruction of Christianity would give rise to the indeconstructible.[80]

And it is here that Derrida and Nancy part ways: Derrida's "transcendental historicity" is concerned precisely with the matter of history or with the history of matter—the fact that there are essence and ideality arising out of mute matter at all—whereas for Nancy the retreating of signification leads to an eclipse of all essence amounting, paradoxically, to a materiality entirely without any meaning—matter would be so contaminated by the passing of time that no ideality or essence can ever arise.[81] In philosophical terms, the difference is this: for Derrida, signifiers signify always and already *insufficiently*, but they do *signify*, and it is so that materiality and historicity are impregnated with meaning (although only for a while and never permanently) and why their *Verflechtung* is a philosophical problem; for Nancy, ultimately signifiers fail to signify: "sense" is such that it will forever elude Signification. But, and this will be Derrida's point, if such "sense" is "what there is," then, by the same token, Nancy again prescribes for the world its being and is close to some sort of empiricism: it is the case that there is sense.

I return to this in the conclusion to this chapter, but for now it is to be noted that Derrida's assessment of Nancy's deconstruction is rather complex. More than once, Derrida deems Nancy's project both necessary and impossible.[82] By stating that the deconstruction of Christianity might be impossible, Derrida is, with Bataille, pointing to the fact that every deconstruction of Christianity might only bring us ever more Christianity, albeit in one or the other hyperbolic form. Nancy, however, has responded to this quite forcefully: if Christianity is nothing other than that which opens the world onto an unconditional alterity or alienation, then, Nancy notes, "'unconditional' means: not undeconstructible. It must also denote the range, by right infinite, of the very movement of deconstruction."[83] It is, for Nancy, the infinitely finite movement of deconstructions that delivers the sense of deconstruction. Nancy proceeds in a note: "the indeconstructible [. . .] can have no other form than that of the active infinite: thus, the act, the actual and active presence of the *nothing* qua thing (*res*) of the opening itself."[84] The indeconstructible, for Nancy, is the very happening and passing of world, lest, of course, we "prescribe for the world its real being." For Nancy, being-in-the-world opens through my being-there (empirically) to the transcendental happening of the world as to a "permanence without substance" of the worlding of the world.[85]

For this, Nancy turns to an ontology of kenosis, to an elaboration of the emptiness of something like sense in and over against the full-presence of metaphysical and Christian signification, in short: of the rupture within presence that makes that all presence is, from the outset and according to the logic of the "with," dependent on and related to other presences. There is no substance or essence that is so absolute that it would absolve from all relationality.

This ontology of kenosis, however, shows one of the most remarkable features of Nancy's deconstruction of Christianity, namely that it retains something of the divine names, for what is at stake is not so much a "*Deus absconditus*" but rather "the divinity of the *absconditus*," not so much of that which retreats, but rather the divinity of the retreat of itself.[86] It is this retreat, that is, that which flees from full-presence, that preoccupies Nancy and that provides an opportunity to develop the ontology of the "with." This retreat, or the "ungraspability of being," denotes first and foremost—as Nancy quotes Gerhard Granel: "the withdrawal of the 'how' that occurs in every phenomenal field—at once its finesse, its total novelty, and its unproducibility."[87] The surging-forth of the world, our world, for Nancy cannot be reduced to causation or to creation as a product of some sort of a divine producer. If it were to be reduced to causation, there would not be a fundamental difference between one moment and the next, and the temporal sequence of events would be explained on the basis of some prior causation or cause, leaving no space at all for novelty. Similarly, if the world were to be reduced to the end result of divine act of creation, all of its beings and all of its events would be contained and predestined by the divine mind, and the sense of the world as something that cannot be produced and constructed (whether by God or the human being) would be lost. Such would be the Nancyean understanding of the world as appearing to me "without there being a movement of appropriation of the real but also no movement of reference to me, on the part of the real."[88] This world, then, is neither an outcome of a divine act or process of thought nor a correlate of the subject's intentionality: it is that which precisely defies any production and constitution.

To develop this "deification of the deviance," Nancy then turns to the thought of Maurice Blanchot, for it is his (non-)concept of "writing" that instructs about "the movement of exposure to the flight of sense that withdraws signification from "sense" to give it the very sense of that flight"; to Derrida, for it is différ*a*nce that puts one on the track of an "absenting of presence at the heart of its present and its presentation"[89]; and to Heidegger's thinking of a divine *Wink*, for in such a wink, the wink of an eye, Nancy finds a space and a place for the passing and the passage of the divine.

Such an absence or an absenting at the heart of every presence or the passing of every presence into an absence, then, points to a "prae(s)ens that exceeds beings [. . .] the passing designates [. . .] not something situated beyond being. [It] is [. . .] an always other sense that begins freely [. . .] This inaugural [. . .] freedom accedes to [the] excess of sense, which is [. . .] the sense of being."[90] This passing presence, "the ever-renewed distancing of the other in being, and of the absent in the present," according to Nancy, "delivers the divine from itself in both senses of the expression: it frees it from the theological and disengages it in its own gesture."[91]

The most remarkable effect of Nancy's deconstruction is therefore that it configures the divine in a new way rather than, as one would expect, abandoning it. Indeed, Nancy's philosophy does not attempt "to theologize *différance* [or] the 'last god' [. . .] but to discern what is divine in the *Wink* as different, radically different from the *theos*."[92] This divinity Nancy perceives in the, shall I say, ordinary passing of night and day—playing here with the kinship between *deus* and *dies*: the

> divine is always a way of naming, in regard to the world, the constitutive alterity of its opening. Divine is the division that creates a world [. . .] this division according to which it is possible to have the order of things and (distinguishing itself from them in order to distinguish them) of the "non-thing of the sky."[93]

This "non-thing of the sky," which Nancy now denotes as divine and which in his earlier writings was also called nothingness, will be progressively linked to creation *ex nihilo*. Consider, for instance, *Being Singular Plural*:

> [I]f creation is *ex nihilo*, this does not signify that a creator operates "starting from nothing." [This fact] instead signifies two things: on the one hand, it signifies that the "creator" itself is the *nihil*; on the other, it signifies that the *nihil* is not something "from which" what is created would come [*provenir*], but the very origin [*provenance*], and destination, of some thing in general and of everything. The *nihil* [is] nothing prior [;] it is the act of appearing. [If] the nothing is not anything prior, then only the *ex* remains. [The origin] is a distancing that immediately has the magnitude of all space-time and is also nothing other than the interstice of the intimacy of the world: the being-between all beings. The being-between is itself is not a being, and has not other consistency, movement [. . .] than that of the being-a-being of all beings.[94]

All of this, finally, is implicated in that which *Dis-Enclosure* announces programmatically as the end of nihilism: "'Nihil*ism*' means, in effect: making a principle of nothing. But *ex nihilo* means: undoing all principle, included that of nothing. That means: to empty nothing of any quality as principle. That is creation."[95]

Nancy's Exegesis of the Resurrection Story: *Noli me Tangere* and the Faith in Sense

Theologians, obviously, might wonder whether Nancy is not simply retrieving here a pagan notion of the eternity of the world. Indeed, for Nancy, the world is nothing but a "permanence without substance." Similarly, the theologian might ask whether Nancy is sufficiently informed about the different accounts of creation in the Judeo-Christian tradition: it is not sure whether his account of a *creatio ex nihilo* could not be countered with Augustine's analysis of *creatio de nihilo*, in which, it seems, God exercises power over the nothingness of the world without turning it into a principle or metaphysical signifier.[96]

Be that as it may, Nancy has recently provided an intriguing exegesis of the Resurrection narratives in the Gospel in which both the main themes that this chapter has highlighted recur and, moreover, the theme of an absence amid all presence is, so to say, "existentialized" through a particular notion of faith. It is time, then, to turn to one of Nancy's more constructive proposals.

Noli me tangere dwells with another important division in Christianity, the paradox between "*hoc est corpus meum*" and the words of Christ after the Resurrection, "*noli me tangere*." Nancy recognizes that, although Christianity for the most part is "the invention of the religion of touch, of the sensible, of presence that is immediate to the body and to the heart,"[97] it also incorporates a strange kind of prohibition of a point of contact with the Resurrected One. After having noted that the verb *haptein* also means "to hold back, to stop," Nancy writes:

> Christ does not want to be held back, for he is leaving. He says it immediately: he has not yet returned to the Father [. . .]. To touch him or to hold him back would be to adhere to immediate presence, and just as this would be to believe in touching (to believe in the presence of the present), it would be to miss the departing according to which the touch and the presence come

to us. Only thus does the "resurrection" find its *non-religious meaning*. What for religion is the renewal of a presence that bears the phantasmatic assurance of immortality is revealed here to be nothing other than the departing into which presence actually withdraws, bearing its sense in accordance with this parting. Just as it comes, so it goes: [. . .] it is not [. . .] fixed within presence, immobile, identical to itself [. . .]. "Resurrection" is the uprising, the sudden appearance of the unavailable, of the other and of the one disappearing in the body and as the body itself.[98]

Nancy's jargon should now be (more or less) clear. What interests us here, however, is how Nancy depicts Mary Magdalene's response to the appearance of the Christ, through which Nancy delineates his own version of a (postmodern) faith. Commenting on Christ's appearance to Mary and her impression that she was speaking to the gardener, Nancy adds about this difficult course of recognition:

[O]n the one hand, it is as if [Christ's] resemblance to himself is, for a moment, suspended and floating. He is the same without being the same, changed into himself. Is it not thus that the dead appear? [. . .] The same is no longer the same [. . .] the visage is made absent right in the face; the body is sinking into the body [and] the departing is inscribed onto presence, presence is presenting its vacating.[99]

In this sense, Mary sees a dead man and has lost all previous tools to identify and recognize the figure speaking to her. This is, however, the reason why, Nancy argues, "the difficult and uncertain recognition bears the stakes of faith. It does not consist in recognizing the known but in entrusting oneself to the unknown."[100] This is also why Mary Magdalene's answer in faith mimes the movement of the one she encounters, because, upon hearing her name, "she, in turn, is to leave and announce the departure"[101]: faith is the proper comportment to the fleeing and floating of sense.

This nonreligious meaning of the resurrection leads Nancy again to praise what one could call the divine eternity of the world, for just as much this revelation and resurrection only reveal that there is nothing here to be revealed—except perhaps the revelation of the retreat—so too this story of the Resurrection, according to Nancy, merely reveals the endless coming and going of the living and the dying, for it is only "death [that] opens the relation, that is, the sharing of the departure"[102] And it is this opening of the departure, this revelation of the withdrawal within the world that is again called divine: "the "divine" henceforth no longer has a place either in the world or outside it, for there is no other world. What is "not of this world" is not elsewhere: it is the opening of the world, the separation [and] the parting."[103]

All of these somewhat morbid metaphors already suggest that Nancy's message, if any, is not one of hope. In a discussion with Roland Barthes, Nancy argues that the disorientation of the "Occidental way of signifying" need not be turned into a reorientation, but rather that "an "exempting from sense" is at issue, namely a complete liberation from the injunction coming from God knows where that the history and destiny of the West "has to make sense."[104] Such a liberation, of course, would also free us from experiencing the current crisis of Christianity as bereft of all sense.

On the contrary, and to use the terminology that has been advanced throughout this text, our contemporary situation entails the recognition that the lack of signification is not equal to a lack of sense. On the contrary: at issue for Nancy is precisely the fact that, because of the end of all final goals and signification (which, for him, is both the erection of an absolute value—God *et les autres*—and the absolute generalization of value as it occurs in the general equivalency of capitalism), one is abandoned to sense and needs only to consent to the present/absent sense in the absence of all metaphysical significations. It is this consent that Nancy will label as faith. This faith, then, is the rather banal recognition (but the banal can be important) that this sense is all there is. It is faith in the fact that sense is what happens between us, in "the back and forth from one to the other," like in making love: "the truth of sense is properly nothing but its being shared, that is, at once its passage between us [. . .] and its internal and sovereign dehiscence."[105]

For Nancy, it is, however, only when all holy places and persons that could serve as a guarantee and assurance for such faith have disappeared that a faith in such sense could arise. Such a faith, Nancy explains, "is the non-knowledge [. . .] of the necessity of the other in every act," a "faith in the other" that precisely is not able to, and does not want to, recuperate this otherness into a conceptuality and so turn it into a knowledge.[106] This faith would, finally, be one without belief(s): it is a praxis precisely because it does not resort to dogmas, theses, explanations or reasons. Hence Nancy's preference for James (rather than Paul), for it is in James that Nancy finds "not [a] theological thinness, but [a] retreat of theology [. . .] that is, a withdrawal of any representation of contents in favor of an active affirmation of faith."[107]

This affirmation would then be the always renewed consenting with sense as the consent with the absence at the heart of all presence, for the absent sense is not an ontic property or quality of beings that, once for all, could be established or reified. The only reality that corresponds to this sense is, according to Nancy, the endless finitude of all that is. That is why this consent, ultimately, is "a correspondence with the very real of dying,"[108] with the fact that there is a skeleton in every man and woman.

L'adoration extends this line of thinking: it is important to see that lived existence entails neither the verticality of a Signification nor the mere horizontality of death and the corpse. For death too has something of a verticality: this is the nonreligious meaning of the resurrection that we already encountered in the "announcement of the departing" in Nancy's reading of the Gospels. One needs to understand such a resurrection no longer from out of a knowing about something beyond life, but rather from out of the relation that death always and already entertains with life. The "place of the dead," for instance (of which Sloterdijk will also speak), is such that their place is indeed one within the lives of us all: the grave, for instance, is a place where we can still "encounter" and speak to the departed one. This encounter and this speech, furthermore, instruct that the dead still have a place within the world: "Relations do not die."[109] The place of the deceased friend and lover is the place reserved for him and her in my memory of him and her, precisely. For Nancy, however, it is not the "dead within life" that are worthy of thought but also *our* "living with death." For this, Nancy turns to the remarkable fact that death's ever-present possibility does not entail for us that life would not be worth living; to the fact that, despite death, all of us find life (more or less) interesting and are, despite everything, still standing. This "living with death," then, is to be related to desire: the joy of relating to others and to the world is greater than the end of the relation that death entails. This desire, which makes that "life can pass by death,"[110] is the faith in the sense of our relations despite death.

Deconstructing Nancy with Derrida

It may be clear that, in its current state, Nancy's deconstruction of Christianity will not unsettle a great many of Christianity's theologians, which, in a certain way, is a pity, for if one cannot avoid the impression that certain philosophers are more than happy to dance on Christianity's grave (and Nancy might be one of them), one equally cannot avoid the impression that certain theologians somewhat resemble the band that kept on playing on the Titanic, not realizing that their audience had already left and that the relic that was their stage would afterward be used only in museums and movie theaters. It may be Nancy's merit to have put theology in its proper place and to return theology to the place from where it should start: the very happening of world. Theology can only do this, it seems, if it refrains from judging what happens there from out of a tradition that would itself be unmoved from what precisely is happening.

On an Apocalyptical Tone in Nancy's Philosophy

Derrida complains that Nancy still has hope, close to the hope he once detected in Heidegger, the hope for a First Word, for a Beginning that would not be contaminated by how it ends. The problem for Derrida, however, is not that there (still) is hope, but rather how such a hope in Nancy is configured. For this hope needs a zero point of sorts: between the "old" metaphysics and the creation of the world that is a'coming, a gap and a cleft need to be installed. This gap, then, would reveal the promise according to which we can *never again* think metaphysically and ontotheologically, and that now the time has come to think nonmetaphysically. Such a hope, for Derrida, would be in vain, for it presupposes that we would have an adequate and transparent vantage point on all the wrongs of the ontotheological tradition, on the entirety of the *Seinsgeschick*. And even though such a judgment might turn out to be inevitable, modesty might command that we know *just as little* as the thinkers of the so-called ontotheological eras and that we, just as well, have a compulsion toward ultimate signifiers.

"Nancy's hope," then, can be understood from out of the "destructive effects,"[111] namely the strange mixture of hope and apocalypticism, of *our* beginning that would be entirely new, that Derrida signals in Nancy's works. In this section, I ask of what precisely these gestures are "destructive." First, however, some examples of this hope and of its accompanying apocalypticism are provided.

A first example needs to focus on Nancy's somewhat desperate call for a new era. Consider, for instance, Nancy's statement that doing justice to the event of being is "one of the concerns left to us by that time which, as "post," could well be a first time, a time suspended in the preexistence of another time, another beginning and another end."[112] A second example, then, needs to show that such a new era has already been inaugurated. The Kingdom, so to say, "is near." Consider, for instance, this somewhat utopian hope in *Being Singular Plural*, where Nancy states that *from the moment and henceforth* the global space of the world is understood as spacing, our history comes upon [. . .] its greatest danger and its greatest opportunity. It is here in the still poorly perceived imperative of a world that is in the process of creating its global conditions, in order to render untenable and catastrophic the sharing of riches and poverty, of integration and exclusion, of every North and every South.[113]

Such an inauguration needs, third, to be accompanied by a sort of repentance—the invocation to change one's wicked ways. Hence Nancy's apocalyptic tone in, for instance, *Dis-Enclosure*. Here Nancy infuses the planetary and cosmic dimensions of the globalized world with a peculiar kind of Heideggerian nostalgia for a time prior to our technological age. It is said, for instance, that "for the first time" the expansion of the world is not only the end result of the technological means human beings employ and control, but also that these means and instruments take control themselves: they are "at once tools but also agents [. . .] of expansion" to the point even that "space is not conquered without space conquering its conquerors as well."[114] Now is the time, according to Nancy that is, that the spacing of space, so to say, rears its ugly head; it is "a new departure for creation: *nothing*, which moves over to make a place or give occasion to *something*," for now that "the space-time is becoming that of the transmission of satellite signals," "locations are delocalized and put to flight by a spacing that precedes them and only later will give rise to new places."[115] But for now, it seems, all this has "a character that is close to an explosion."[116]

If Derrida directs us to this apocalyptical tone in Nancy's thinking, then this is the case because these somewhat morbid metaphors are by no means innocent. Raffoul and Pettigrew, for instance, pointed out that the title of the book, *The Creation of the World* or *Globalization*, has to be read in disjunctive fashion, for these terms "reveal two distinct, if not opposite, meanings": whereas globalization stands for the global uniformity and its sometimes indeed disastrous effects, the creation of the world "is the possibility of an authentic *world-forming*, that is, of a making of the world and of a making sense."[117] It is in this way that Nancy's statement in *Being Singular Plural* that today "our history comes upon its greatest dangers and its greatest opportunity" has to be understood: *either* the dawn of a new and just era *or* the apocalypse.

According to Derrida, then, it is precisely such a disjunction that is destructive of Nancy's thought, for it implies an absolute rupture between our era and earlier metaphysical times. This already indicates that Nancy might be not so much forging a way out of the (Christian) tradition from within the tradition, but rather trying to operate from outside the tradition as if an absolute break with it is nevertheless possible, thus forgetting that "it is *not* enough to 'believe' or believe oneself and declare oneself *non*-Christian in order to utter a discourse, speak a language [. . .] safely sheltered from Christianity."[118]

One should thus ask, with regard to this "still poorly perceived imperative," not only whether Nancy does not make the same mistake for which he reproached Heidegger—after all, is there any difference between those able to "hear" the voice of Being and those able to perceive the imperative to create the world?—but also whether the institution of an absolute cleft between our age and the previous ones is philosophically valid at all. Ultimately, Nancy is not the first philosopher to proclaim the end and fulfillment of history. The point, however, is that if such a cleft would be valid—as the indications of temporality in the quotes seem to indicate—then, by the same token, *all* previous eras are—to play Nancy against himself[119]—taken *en bloc*, that is, grasped as a totality. From this follows that one can oversee all of its history, the entirety of its assembly; in short: all of it is (fully) present. Over and against this totality, one can then have "all sorts of opinions." The conclusion thus seems to be that the ontological language Nancy is using here for his account of the creation and "worlding of the world" suddenly turns very ontic and is on the verge of becoming a form of a metaphysical ideology. In short, the mixture of hope and apocalypticism indicates that Nancy himself has not yet been emancipated "from a certain thinking of emancipation"[120] and flies the same flight as once did Hegel's owl, viewing from above all of its chances as well as its perils. This, finally, seems to be the reason why Derrida keeps pointing to a nostalgia and to a hope even in Nancy's work. For if there remains any hope for salvation and resurrection in Nancy's work, then Derrida's closing address in *On Touching*[121] indeed has to be read as a warning about the destructive gestures of Nancy's work, for even the one without hope can make the error of "getting the others' hopes up" through postulating a salvation that is always deferred as "yet to come."

Otherwise Than Metaphysics, or the Eclipse of Essence

The question therefore is whether metaphysics makes a return even in Nancy's philosophy, for the hope of an entirely new beginning might simply repeat the gesture with which Heidegger, for instance, wanted to be "in touch" with the origins (of being). Metaphysics here means simply the possibility of the pure gaze, perceiving what it perceives in a clear and distinct manner, touching whatever it touches on in manners unmediated and untainted by history, interpretative maneuvers or (con)texts.

Derrida's argument in this regard is quite complex, but it runs, if one turns to the language of phenomenology, something like this: even though one wants to escape the logic of immediacy or of intuitive fulfilment of intentionality by pointing to whatever resists such fulfilment—what remains absent or does not give itself—this resistance itself will, in turn, give way to effects and illusions of immediacy. It is as if Husserl's break with the natural attitude in order to attain the phenomenological attitude will inevitably pass into some sort of natural and realist attitude. Let us listen to Derrida: "[The] dehiscence of the outside and the other comes to inscribe an irreparable disorganization, a spacing that dislocates, a non-coincidence (which *also* yields the chance effects of full intuition, the fortune of immediacy effects) wherever Husserl speaks of 'coincidence.'"[122] In other words: even if one believes in the interruption (or mediation) by the other or by otherness, chances are, still, that this will "produce an *illusory* belief in immediacy of contact."[123] According to Derrida, it would thus be to such a metaphysics that we all fall prey, and Nancy is no exception: "for it can also happen, it can moreover *always* happen—we have to insist on it—that the intuitionistic [. . .] logic of immediacy shows itself to be irrepressible [. . .] not only here and there in Nancy's text, but massively elsewhere."[124] Such an "intuitive" metaphysics, then, would give rise to a realist naiveté—as if one can touch without remainder or residue on that which obstructs, hinders, and resists the immediate grasping of all touching. Derrida again: "Nancy has written moreover: there is that there is: creation of the world."[125] In other words: it is as if, in the end, Nancy sees himself able to answer the age-old metaphysical question—*tode ti*? What is?—in a rather straightforward way: the world is what there is.[126]

To be sure, for Derrida, it is not a matter of denying this dehiscence; it is rather to respect the fact both that this dehiscence *will* be denied—turn into realism, declaring and prescribing what is real—and that one will have to reckon with this dehiscence and interruption that is an "archi-facticity" precisely as "contingency"—and, in this sense, "real."[127] To put it in phenomenological terms again: it is not only a matter "to reintroduce a priori what is constituted into what is constituting"[128] or "the antecedence of what I constitute to this very constitution,"[129] but it is also, and above all, a matter of knowing *just how* this contingent archi-facticity crosses the very act of constitution.[130] And it is here, I contend, that Nancy's thought shows itself to be phenomenologically inadequate. Two examples illustrate this.

Faith and/in Belief

The first example is Nancy's utter separation between faith and belief. Nancy asks rhetorically: "whether faith has ever, in truth, been confused with belief"?[131] To be sure, Nancy is well aware that belief without faith is empty, for one needs the personal stance of faith to put into practice one's beliefs.[132] What Nancy does not take into account, however, is that, phenomenologically speaking, reciprocally faith without belief is—to stick to Kantian terms—blind: for just as "it takes two to explain a thought,"[133] so too it takes (at least) two things, statements or propositions, for faith to be able to discern and discriminate between contents at all. The return to such a self-evidence is by no means a coincidence: for one to be able to have faith, one has to be acquainted with the contents of a tradition from within, that is, one has to be aware of the existing set of propositions to discriminate between those propositions that are outdated, in need of recontextualization, and those that, perhaps, are not. At the same time, however, the act of faith actualizes such propositions if and only if this or that proposition can be taken as true, but the fact remains that such an act is only possible if it is preceded, and thus *constituted*, by some sort of acquaintance with the culture and propositions available.

An example might elucidate this. One can think, for instance, of the debate between the anticorrelational theology of Karl Barth and the correlational theology of Emil Brunner on the topic of the virgin birth—a proposition one might deem "unbelievable" in all senses of the word. This debate can be summarized as follows: whereas Barth stressed the primacy of God's revelation over and against human beings' capacity to receive God's revelation, Brunner insisted on the necessity of some point of contact between God's revelation and the human condition in order for revelation to be received at all. Whereas Barth, then, stresses the virgin birth as illustrative of the discontinuity between God's grace and the *capax Dei* of the human being, James Smith, argues the other way around: "while the central truth here is certainly God's gracious initiative, [. . .] it does not occur without reference to the "conditions of the receiver." For if God really wanted to demonstrate the utter incapacity of humanity and assert his free (re)creative powers, should God not have impregnated a man?"[134] The point is that for a believer to have faith, discernments of this kind are a prerequisite: only if one balances, and has balanced, between the doctrine of virgin birth taken as a somewhat mythical proposition and an understanding showing the—albeit theological—logic of it, a faith can arise that *actualizes* its content: there is no faith if faith does not have anything to activate in the first place. Such a mediation and entanglement of faith and belief preclude both any primacy of faith over belief (Nancy) as well as any primacy of belief over faith (as Nancy interprets "religion").

Derrida and Nancy's Shorthands

Another example: for, even if this was put in theological terms, it surely is not a matter of theology alone. One finds, in Derrida's *On Touching*, quite a revealing comment on the two shorthands the two thinkers use to designate the gesture of deconstruction.[135] Whereas Derrida's "if there is any" [*s'il y en a*] may be known, Nancy's "there is no 'the'" [*il n'y a pas le/la . . .*] perhaps is not. And yet the difference here, however minute, is of utmost importance. As we all can recognize, as Derrida does, the necessity of Nancy's phrase, it is necessary as well to recognize, just as Derrida does, the limits of it. Imagine a conversation in which someone says, "all politicians are bad." The response, obviously, is that not all politicians are the same and that, thus, there is no such thing as "the" politician. And yet, for speech, communication, interactions to occur at all between us, it is necessary just the same that both of us, and all of us, *do* have a concept, an essence, of that which is understood as "the" politician; otherwise a response to such a statement would not even be possible. In other words: one cannot do without representations, essences, concepts, and so forth. *Il faut généraliser*—one must generalize. In Derrida's words: "Nancy knows that one has to use cunning, make deals, and negotiate with it [since] the definite or defining article is already engaged or required by the discourse that disputes it."[136]

This imperative is precisely what is left open in Derrida's "if there is any" and what Nancy's shorthand forecloses. Derrida's "if there is any" leaves room for more interpretations: because we sometimes must generalize, however violent toward this other here and that being there, however impossible in the face of this singular existence and the plurality out there, one will have to recognize a sort of soothing of such general concepts to reality, a sort of aspiring of the concept toward the purity of that which it designates, an existence of ideality and signification. If Derrida mentions time and again, for example, that a pure hospitality is forever presupposed, his "if there is any" such hospitality not only, and simply, indicates that one cannot speak of this general and absolute hospitality without taking all the concrete and empirical forms of hospitalities into account, it *simultaneously* admits that one will need to speak of a general form of hospitality whenever and if—*s'il en y a*—such a concrete hospitality has occurred or *once* an act of hospitality has happened. This is why Derrida explains his shorthand: "each time, it was necessary to point to the possible (the condition of possibility) *as* to the impossible itself. 'If there is any' does not say there is none." The point is that Nancy, and his tendency to dismantle and dislocate the possibility of concepts and essences of all sorts, seems to reduce philosophical discourse to the singularities of all sorts of empirical events to the point of *eclipsing* essence. It would be such an abandonment of signification and essences that Derrida has in mind when commenting on Nancy's line of reasoning: for Nancy indeed, "it is because there is *some* technical [. . .] that there isn't this or that ["there is no 'the' technical"] and that one can infinitely repeat [. . .] gestures that deconstruct the very unity or the properness *itself* of all essences."[137] In other words: it is because there are these very different forms of hospitalities that one cannot conclude to the one and single essence of hospitality—there is no such thing as (the) one hospitality.

We know that Derrida would not agree. On the contrary, Derrida would write: it is necessary to say "the" hospitality in the singular again to say it in the plural. Derrida, then, notes the difference between his "if there is any" and Nancy's "there is not 'the'": if the former turns *to a conditional*—hence it can also be read: once, whenever and if there is such a thing as an act of hospitality—the latter turns to a negative modality—there is no such thing as Hospitality. Consider the difference, then, between "a good politician, if there is any" (Derrida) and "there is no 'the' good politician" (Nancy): the former speaks in a provisional manner—while it is highly unlikely that any such thing will occur, one cannot exclude the fact that it might occur either—the latter speaks in a negative and almost dogmatic matter: even if there would be such a thing, one cannot and may not conclude that this would be a general thing, a group of people that could be comprehended through an essence. Nancy is thus already in denial of any factuality: there cannot be, and there never will be, "the" . . .

Conclusion: What Comes after Christianity?

The abandonment of all essences, their eclipse, that Nancy is looking for in this way comes close to that haunting picture Levinas once painted, namely that in a world without the Other, "absolute silence [. . .] would reign"—one would not know whom to speak *to*. It is to forget, moreover, that "to the ineffable ideality [. . .] there responds an echo of the world in which significations are said"—in the world, one always and already speaks *of* something *to* someone.[138] For Levinas, then, and because the social relation is "not produced outside the world,"[139] it is in discourse that things acquire "fixity," a "name" and an "identity," in short: an essence. It is only through this naming and this fixity that we can speak of the same things in (more or less) the same way: for instance, that "the same train is the train that leaves at the same hour."[140] What seems to be lacking in Nancy's account of the world thus seems to be a phenomenology of language, that is, a phenomenological account of the echo between the (ideal) signification of the word and the world in which these significations and essences are *already* used, of the fact that language is, at any rate, always the speaking of some*thing* to someone.[141]

The consequences that need to be drawn from this discussion are severe. Should one conclude for instance that, contrary to appearances Nancy's ontology occurs, unlike Levinas's, "outside the world"? In a certain sense, yes. For if one follows Derrida's contention that the eclipse of essence in a way obscures the "archifacticity of contingency" because it is always and already on the verge of *reifying* this very eclipse by bordering on realism, and if one follows Levinas's conclusion that the Saying or the address of the Other occurs always and already in, and from out of the said or that which is being addressed, then one cannot *not* conclude that Nancy's thought of "the creation of the world" *forgets* that even this speaking of the world happens from out of a *determinate*, definite world, culture, or being-with-one-another.[142]

Thus, the irrepressibility of essence we are advancing here, because of the noted return of metaphysics and some sort of "essence" and ideality, implies that Nancy's thought of the world in some sort of way *posits* a point outside the world, which, even in his case, functions as the postulation of a sort of givenness, a concept(ion), albeit the givenness of the nothingness of sense. It is such an "outside" that accounts for the fact that Nancy's thought of the world nevertheless seems to merge with a (subjective) "worldview" in the Heideggerian sense. Because Nancy's proposed eclipse of essence shows itself impossible, it becomes thus legitimate to ask whether Nancy's project on Christianity really takes place from within this determinate and definite Christian culture that is ours—however "post-" we are—that is, whether it can take into account the peculiarities, the differences, and the contexts that determine, precisely, this culture. For just as the distinction between faith and belief does not hold, so too Nancy's attempt to deconstruct Christianity, speaking of it as if already outside it, to have surpassed or overcome it, to dwell beyond its essence, seems to lack the means to confront the relics of this culture, that is, the propositions and the discourse that constitute it, to discriminate between, or even to deconstruct, its ruling distinctions, demarcations, and so on. One thus might wonder whether Nancy's distinction between the "creation" of the world and its alternative, which he calls the "unworld" of globalization, has not, because in his account of this creation there already is the "unworldly" lure of absolute silence and muteness, already deconstructed itself.

What, then, comes after Christianity? The question deserves to be posed, even though Derrida has deemed it impossible. This chapter only ever wanted to utter a warning about the terms of this debate. "The test of a de-christianizing of the world," for Derrida, is destined to fail because "only Christianity can do this work, that is, undoing it while doing it. Heidegger, too [. . .] has only succeeded in failing at this. Dechristianization will be a Christian victory."[143] The de-christianization or detheologization, then, would be destined to come up with ever-more Christianities and crypto-theologies. Likewise, the theologians decry the loss of bits and pieces of the Christian tradition. Nancy's "wrestling match of thinking,"[144] however, and this is what is indicated here, might be fighting an invisible opponent, for it should not matter who wins and who loses here, and even less what is lost and what is won; it matters what is to be done: "after" Christianity, "after" metaphysics, "after" the spectating subject indeed.

Nancy's mis-take on essence and on metaphysics—not its eclipse, but its haunting, like a ghost—should shed light on just how to proceed here. Consider, for instance, Nancy's approach to Levinas's beyond of essence: "many pages and accentuations in Levinas can lead one to belief that there is a 'God' or some form of capitalized 'Other'—and hence [that Levinas is] at the risk of essence [*au risque d'essence*] with the foundation of this un-ground."[145] One should thus wonder whether this risk of essence is really to be avoided and even whether it can be avoided at all. The suggestion is therefore that the demarcation line should not run between *either* a thought of the world *or* the lure of essence; the question is how this given set of essences merges with the facticity of "already" being-thrown-in-a-world and so contributes to any thinking of world.

Thus, even when it comes to the deconstruction of Christianity, then, being-in-the-world is communication if and only if we know *what* we are saying. Speaking of the world is possible *à condition de s'entendre*.[146] This also means that there indeed *is* a *condition* (of possibility) for us to understand one another, and it is because of this "echo" of, this "link" with and "attachment" to the world in which essences are used, that one can criticize Nancy for *not enough* having thought *with* Merleau-Ponty, that is, for not having recognized that "without the necessities by essence [. . .] there would be neither a world, nor something in general, nor Being."[147]

For Merleau-Ponty, then, these essences, these constitutions of ideality, are rooted in our encounter with the world, and therefore their (albeit unstable) authority is always and already conditioned, (co-)constituted, and "borne by the tree of my duration and other durations."[148]

In short, the newness and the novelty of our contemporary situation—the "creating" of the world—that Nancy wants to convey cannot be attained at the expense of everything that has occurred before. The rigorous cleft that Nancy enforces between our age and everything that preceded it seems phenomenologically untenable: just as one cannot have a "faith" entirely bereft of belief,[149] so too the novelty about which Nancy wants to inform us cannot do without a rigorous taking into account of what showed itself, so to say, previously on the happening of the world. This is exactly the point where Merleau-Ponty's thought would touch, to my mind, Nancy's philosophy: all new constellations of thought only ever happen through a novel figuration arising out of the already instituted and constituted configurations. There is no new formation of thought and world if there is no transformation of (all) the earlier sedimentations and configurations of sense and signification—the new happens only through the transformation of the old.[150] It is on this intertwining between the contemporary constitution or creation of the world and its older configurations that Nancy remains silent, perhaps all too silent. It seems, then, that, even "after" Nancy's deconstruction of Christianity, one is not done with the i/Incarnation. That is why one might salute Nancy, as Derrida seems to have done somewhat, with the advice Ignatius of Loyola once gave to his pupils, that is, not "to turn or incline to one side or the other," but "to find [oneself] as in the middle of a balance."[15]

3

Exercises in Religion I

Peter Sloterdijk and the Matrix of Monotheism

"A spectre is haunting the Western world—the spectre of religion." So goes the telling opening line of Sloterdijk's recent meditation on the ghostly return of religion in contemporary societies, a meditation not unlike Nancy's project but more attentive to recent developments in postmodern culture.[1] Just when we thought we were safely sheltered from the redemptions of all sorts of theology and thier parade of capitals, these capitals and capitalist accounts of redemption make an ominous return. Yet Sloterdijk's phrase sets the stage for a virulent critique, a critique of what he calls "verticality," where "religion" (if such a thing exists; Sloterdijk says it does not) is, if not outdated, then at least recuperated by the world of sports and the capitalist market. Religions cannot do anything today, according to Sloterdijk, other than evaporate in and extend into "the domain of struggle" (Houellebecq). What remains, then, is a terrestrial globe for the ones exercising and training, the ones attempting to be, to exist or deal in any other way with the highs and the lows of "being-in-a-globe"—Sloterdijk's interpretation of Heidegger's being-in-the-world. One must note that the theme of religion has figured quite some times already in Sloterdijk's work. In his first main work, for instance, *Critique of Cynical Reason*, the theme pops up regularly and, more recently, the works *God's Zeal* and *Rage and Time* are both almost book-length studies of religion and what remains of it today.

In this chapter, I browse these diverse works to gain an overview of Sloterdijk's works, a philosophy that may serve as one of the most exciting of our era, if only because Sloterdijk approaches topics and themes that no philosopher other than he has tried to confront. I do so in a few, distinct steps. First, I take up our "exercises" in the deconstruction of religion again by elaborating on Sloterdijk's theory of the "desuprematicization" of the supreme being. In a second step, then, I turn to Sloterdijk's proposal of a secular translation of religion, if not its utter illegitimacy and inadequacy when it comes to understanding the contemporary world.

How to Change Your Life: An Ontological Self-Help Group

When Sloterdijk speaks of a "theological blockade of the superlative" and of the maximum, then his version of the deconstruction of Christianity, as portrayed in *God's Zeal*, has to be read as an attempt to remove the blockage, that "age-old attempt to secure it through *nec-plus-ultra* fences."[2] *Rien ne va plus*: *God's Zeal* presents itself as a book meditating on the violence and the conflicts (all too) proper to religion. Sloterdijk proposes a "blasphemy clause" and a "safety procedure" in which one may easily recognize a sad sign of the times. What is required before reading the book is:

> an arrangement as to which aspects of religion and religious faith can and must be discussed [. . .] According to this arrangement, a number of phenomena traditionally assigned to the realm of the transcendent or holy would be released for non-religious reinterpretation (of potential blasphemous appearance, though not intended as such).[3]

Such a clause obviously is no stranger to what I call here the question of presuppositions and the concomitant "soft" pluralism, where everything can be discussed and debated on the condition that no one is offended (through which, in turn, nothing can really be discussed or debated). The ruling ideology, religious or not, acts like a sovereign: it determines both what can be said and, even more, what cannot be said. Once all clauses are signed and agreed on, Sloterdijk proceeds (or better yet, once Sloterdijk has *phenomenologically reduced* these contemporary ideologies) discusses the inherent violence of monotheism. This meditation will "from the perspective of faith [. . .] no doubt seem grossly unjust in many places—in so far as most things said about faith without allowing it a chance to revise it are unjust."[4] Our religious rulers, too, love to make an exception for themselves. They too, if I'm allowed to refer to one of the most famous examples of "the question of presuppositions," think themselves "more popular than Jesus."

> Today's children of the banalized Enlightenment are [. . .] meant to burn what they worshipped and worship what they burned

[and] the novices of post-secular society [see the European Enlightenment as an] anomaly [and a] metaphysical diet when the rest of the world continues to dine unperturbed at the richly decked tables of illusion.[5]

The reader may notice that, with Nancy and Sloterdijk, we arrive at another terrain than that of Caputo, who, as we will see, can still speak of the "great indeconstructible secret" and who can see nothing but analogies between faithful premodernity and irreligious postmodernity. However, with Sloterdijk, the phenomenon of religion is finally seen with a nonreligious gaze. One of his main accomplishments lies in confronting the phenomenon of religion and the concomitant question of the presuppositions separate from all question of emotion. Sloterdijk ventures on a sort of ultimate deconstruction, in which there is no illusion that would not be shattered and no dream that would not be broken. This already marks an important difference between *God's Zeal*, *Rage and Time* on the one hand and the more recent *Life* on the other: whereas the first-mentioned works do presuppose the possibility of "secular translations of religious transcendence" (Karl Löwith), they also indicate domains in which such a translation would not be possible because of the irreducibility of the religious phenomenon. It is the latter that is completely abandoned in Sloterdijk's recent work. Sloterdijk now proceeds toward a complete reduction of religion to one of those "systems of an exercising and training humanity" in a world filled with struggle where all are wolves to all. *God's Zeal* distinguishes three features of religion "for which there are no functionalist or naturalist substitute descriptions of a binding nature" that can be given, namely: the power to think (of) something that transcends thought ("that than which no greater can be thought": Anselm, Descartes); the transcendent topology implied in the locus of the dead (a "beyond," a "hereafter" of sorts); and, finally, the idea of a revelation in which there is the possibility of God descending toward the world and one or the other prophet.[6] All things considered, it seems that several, some would say even crucial, features of the phenomenon of religion can still be maintained. The question as to the translation of religious features in secular terms still encounters something "irreducible," or at least something that would be impossible to translate in which religious persons could then still recognize what is most proper to it.

Things differ considerably in Sloterdijk's more recent work. Here, even that which remained irreducible to naturalistic and functionalistic descriptions is inserted in making explicit just that which remains implicit in every religious and spiritual system. Sloterdijk attempts some sort of "internal translation" in which religion is understood in terms other than itself, such as "market," "struggle," and "sport." Yet Sloterdijk insists that his attempt in no way amounts to a reductionist account of religion. On the contrary, his quasi-phenomenological reduction of religion claims to lay bare that which religion, in a sense, has always been. Furthermore, such a reduction is called for in the interest of the "acquisition of better knowledge" of this particular phenomenon, an improvement forcing us to a revision of the phenomenon of religion.[7]

Sloterdijk aligns his thought to the tradition of the Enlightenment and more particularly with Hume's handling of religion. David Hume, as is well known, interpreted religion as stemming from our natural desires, our hopes, and fears for the future, for instance. Sloterdijk adds to this position the results of contemporary biology and the sciences of culture, from which one, according to Sloterdijk, needs to learn that the cultural superstructure functions exactly like an immune system. Religion helps us deal with and handle the disturbance that death always is, just as our immune system is in advance of those bacteria that attack and disturb our biological system. This is what Sloterdijk names *thymotology* (from the Greek *thymos*, drive and desire): whoever wants to understand the human being first has to understand his or her desires, wishes, and drives.

And yet although these desires and drives can coexist with cultural and natural phenomena, these phenomena cannot be thoroughly understood or accounted for by these drives and desires alone. This, then, is where philosophy and phenomenology come in. Ontology is the science well aware that the human being is always different and always other than what reductionist accounts presuppose ("I am nothing but the pool of genes handed down to me"; "I am nothing other than the context from which I sprang," etc.), the science of "man infinitely exceeding man" (Pascal). In Sloterdijk's terms, this means that the human being is, naturally and culturally, "raised upward" (Levinas), open to what is above and possibly higher or at least other than him or her. The human being exists in a vertical tension. The immune system, then, turns this human being into a self-organizing and auto-therapeutic being. This capacity has to be understood in both biological and cultural terms. Although the biological understanding of the immune system is largely self-evident, its cultural understanding requires some additional explanation. Cultural systems, for Sloterdijk, operate just like an immune system. So the constant alteration that these systems undergo in and through contact with otherness is at the origin of a capability and aptitude possessed by these cultural systems which allows for them to undergo such changes.

These cultural systems, then, are marked with and stamped by vertical tensions and tend to organize themselves precisely in view of such tensions. Sloterdijk calls the handling of these tensions "the passion of being-in-the-world."[8] Once more, Sloterdijk attempts to make explicit what was implicit (in cultural systems) until now, namely that "things or facts [. . .] are by their nature subject to a tendency to unfold themselves and become more comprehensible" and that only then one can speak of a "true increase in knowledge."[9] Self-organization, according to Sloterdijk, belongs both to the order of things (realism) and to the order of what is culturally manageable. Sloterdijk again aligns himself to the tradition of the Enlightenment, because a certain idea of progress is present in his work, especially when it concerns the possibility of an acquisition and concomitant accumulation of knowledge. "Progress" here is motivated and caused by a continued "tendency into the open"[10]—a transcendence beyond ourselves, once the theological blockade has been released and one learns to distinguish, for instance, between being and God. This "fall upward," toward the open, is held in vertical tension (although "the vertical" nowadays has many names: better, faster, stronger; where it once was only called that which is "higher"). These vertical tensions, also called "normative differences," are, according to Sloterdijk, numerous: perfect and imperfect; holy and profane; courageous and cowardly; powerful and powerless, and so forth. All cultures are both organized and organize themselves around these differences. Yet, Sloterdijk argues, contaminations arise in the course of history, and these confused differences and hybrids "still fascinate us as the higher and highest possibilities of human beings."[11]

It is here that Sloterdijk's version of the deconstruction of Christianity (recall the subject and the object genitive) comes into view. Religion obviously has had, and continues to have, a role to play in the deconstruction of these normative differences. In the chapter on Caputo and Marion, I point, for instance, to the Christian inversion of all values as the exodus out of what the world deems powerful, efficient, and useful. But such a deconstruction can obviously be applied to Christianity as well. More often than not, Christianity too has sided with the primary term of these normative differences and tends to the rich and the powerful rather than to the inversion of these values, which Christianity itself nevertheless had proposed. This is what *God's Zeal* aims to demonstrate: the perpetual bond between monotheistic metaphysics and violence. Sloterdijk's deconstruction of Christianity then delineates the following possibilities as describing the highest tension, both of and for humanity today: "a non-economic definition of wealth, a non-aristocratic definition of the noble, a non-athletic definition of high achievement."[12]

This perpetual "migration toward what is outside" attempts to think the perpetual alteration through our *passio*: our being affected by that which is other, thereby affecting and infecting ourselves and our immune systems. And even though this transformation (which ultimately is the flux of life and which I name here "the event of world") can be said to be both innate and acquired, both nature and nurture, it is never a choice. On the contrary: this passion is a being affected prior to any choice of mine and any accord on my part. This is what explains the title of Sloterdijk's recent work, "Whoever notes that it reads 'You Must Change *Your* Life' rather than 'You Must Change *Life*' has immediately understood what is important here."[13] The imperative thus belongs to the sheer fact of my life, as such. If I could, as Heidegger argued, will no longer to will—the definition of *Gelassenheit* or releasement—I cannot desire not to desire or crave not to crave, for a man (or woman) without desire or without cravings can perhaps no longer be called a man (or woman).

One can elucidate this phenomenologically by pointing, once more, to finitude and death. Could one not say that death, as "the possibility of impossibility" (Heidegger), is precisely what escapes any choice of ours and is prior to any accord one could think of? And if this is indeed the case, must one not state that even in the case of euthanasia, death happens without our consent, because no one has freely decided to be so sick that death would now be the only viable option? And could one, in this regard, not suspect suicide not to be a choice, because no one can voluntarily be so unhappy that he or she would freely choose to end his or her life? "Freedom or the grave," as the oldest bills of human rights have it, because, and simply, no one has chosen one's own freedom.

Once Again: Violence and Metaphysics

Sloterdijk's sober analysis of the various monotheisms starts, on the one hand, from what one could call a market-oriented approach in which the historical successions of these religions are seen as "enemy takeovers."[14] On the other hand, the perpetual causes of conflicts between these religions arise from their respective "zealous universalism," which forces them to develop a "world strategy" in which frictions and collisions between them simply become inevitable.[15] In what follows, I portray Sloterdijk's "deconstruction of monotheism" through his version of the "deconstruction of Christianity"

In a phrase reminiscent of Nancy's project, where Christianity suffers and ultimately suffocates from its own internal divisions, Sloterdijk points to an internal inconsistency of Christianity: "[it] saw itself *in principle* as a religion of love, freedom and warm-hearted inclusion, [but] *in fact* also practiced ruthlessness, rigorism and terror on a large scale."[16] Christianity, therefore, on the one hand, is aware of that which "morally speaking [is] one of the best things humanity had ever heard"—the dream of free beings under God and the "dissolution of [. . .] the enmities"—but also of its own Fall, so to speak, at the moment when it "began to cohabit with worldly power" and in this way puts perpetual enmities in play both between religion and the state and between religions themselves.[17]

The latter happens in such a way that Derrida's thought of sovereignty comes to mind. Christianity proclaims the "gospel of love" to everyone without exception, yet it does make an exception of itself when it turns the gospel of love into "the gospel of fear." The latter, then, *criminalizes* all forms of unfaith and unbelief: we will force you to love using all means necessary. "The zealots took revenge by branding those who did not share their faith 'infidels' [,] declared a spiritual crime [.] This is why, from its earliest days, the message of salvation has been accompanied by an escort of threats predicting the worst for unbelievers."[18] The faith of the other (insofar it entails a faith different from the Christian faith) is criminalized through being "privatized," that is, understood in a privative manner. Unbelief is then no longer the mere *absence* of belief (which could still understand in a neutral sense, the absence of faith of those people who had not yet heard of Christ, for instance), but is now turned into a *lack* of faith, understood obviously in a non-neutral way, as the lack of that which, properly speaking, ought to be there, namely faith. This difference between this simple absence of faith and the apparent lack of faith should allow us to understand not only the "theological blockade of the maximum" and its concomitant "suprematicization" but also how we, in our times, could venture to deal more *positively* with the sheer indifference against all things religious. Other than, for instance, Marion, where such indifference is immediately criminalized as a "hatred over and against God," one could at least try to deal with this phenomenon of indifference, say, less violently and thus, possibly, in a more Christian manner.

It might be no coincidence that Sloterdijk focuses on Augustine to elaborate the theological halting of the maximum. Augustine, for Sloterdijk at least, intensified the resistance against the cruelty of the world, exemplified through the Roman gladiator's games "[. . .] by striving for a moderation of human behavior through the threat of maximum cruelty in the life beyond [so risking to overshoot] the mark: with his [. . .] theological absolutism, [he] inflated the diabolical aspect of God to the point of sacred terrorism." In this way, Augustine served as the basis for a Christianity that "often furthered the evil from which it subsequently offered deliverance."[19] Yet another time Christianity shows its sovereign guise: it knows both what is lacking (unbelief as the lack of faith) and that which cures and relieves the lack (redemption has, classically, been understood as the *privatio peccatum*, as "the lacking of sin").[20] In Augustine, one can in effect find the roots of a "merciless" God who, as a sinister sovereign, rules over both what is hidden and what is manifest.

Sloterdijk does not answer the question of whether this contradiction is inherent to Christianity and has plagued it from the very beginning, or whether it would concern a contingent matter through which a religion first and foremost good has been corrupted. He does show himself to be particularly mild when it comes to the history of Christianity as the history of violence: "[its] intentional universalism was inevitably foiled [. . .] by pragmatic necessities arising from coexistence. [The] Christian confessions [. . .] became predictable factors in the world ecumenical movement."[21]

In the contemporary world, the struggle and the battle between religions has begun its "post-imperial period," which, according to Sloterdijk, is "irreversible."[22] All claims to imperialism will from now on be accompanied by a claim to "de-imperialization" or "de-suprematicization."

The De-suprematicization of the World: The Matrix of Monotheism

This de-suprematicization can be seen as the predecessor of Sloterdijk's recent "critique of the vertical." It tries to decipher in the totalitarian character of the various monotheisms a "logical problem [that] follows, prior to the concomitant psychological tension, a *strictly internally conditioned grammar*."[23] Sloterdijk, for instance, detects a religious as well as an ontological "supremacism." The first climbs toward what is "most-high," as toward a person, whereas the second, inspired by the deisms of the Enlightenment, attains an impersonal One through ever higher generalizations and abstractions ("one," "simple," maximum"). Yet both share a sort of aspiration to what is "high," "up there," and both, Sloterdijk claims, will inevitably tend toward their own unblocking and de-suprematicization.

Here is where one might see Sloterdijk's version of the end of metaphysics and deconstruction of metaphysics. Monotheism and its metaphysics rest on a matrix that, while obeying an internal grammar and a logical program—you will aspire the most-high—will at a given point in time be "exhausted"[24] and all its possibilities overused and overseen.

This "exhaustion of the monotheist matrix" corresponds with the end of metaphysics: something of the sort has occurred, for instance, to Nietzsche when realizing that the answers given to the question "Why is there something at all?" could be countered by yet another "Why?" and thus rendered inoperative. For, one might argue, it is at this very instance that the awareness has arisen that the Ground and Foundation of all beings—God, Man, and so forth—never really has been a ground and/or a foundation and was, at best, something that held the floodwaters of finitude and of contingency at bay for a while. In other words, the awareness is that the function that metaphysics once performed no longer works and, quite possibly, has never really worked at all (because there is no such Ground to being, for instance). This is why Nancy sought for that factor within Christianity that in a sense came from without and that is, thus, "older" than Christianity and might have served a condition of possibility for a while but will now outrun it and deem it outdated.[25]

How does Sloterdijk then describe the suggestion of a ground and foundation as proper to metaphysics? Sloterdijk points to the way, analogous to the way in which unbelief becomes a criminal offense, in which "the extremisms" of monotheisms combine a "rigid [. . .] monovalent ontology" with "a bivalent logic."[26] Such a monovalent ontology reduces the multiformity of appearances to one single principle, of which a participationist ontology serves as a prime example. All appearances or phenomena are reduced as "instantiations" or "effects" of the one sole ground of Being (which obviously is to be named "God"). "Monovalence of speech about that which is means this: the thing of which it is said that they are actually are, and are not not; nor are they anything other than what they are. Hence they share in being, both in the fact *that* and the fact of *what* and how."[27] For Heidegger as well, metaphysics speaks without blushing of the existence (the "that" and "how" X is) as well as of the essence of a being ("what" X is). Metaphysics can do this because of its desire and its craving for a ground and a foundation to all being(s), which almost in advance determined "that," "how," and as "what" a being "in general" could appear, namely as "produced," "caused," and "mutable" beings held fast in their being and kept in check by a Being that is "unproduced," "uncaused," and obviously "immutable."

Metaphysics, in effect, installed a cleft in being, of which the most notable was the one between the "real" being "up there" and the barely real, finite beings "down here" or, in Sloterdijk's phrasings, between monovalent supremacism of the highest being and the bivalent logic to which beings fall prey down here. Monovalence ("a being is what it is") means that which is said of the highest cannot be untrue (because it is the whole truth and nothing but the truth); bivalence ("a being is always already other than it is") stands for the possibility that that which is said of these beings might be untrue as well. Bivalence first and foremost concerns language. "The introduction of the second value made the human capacity for true statements unstable, as these—being a reflection in the other of that which is—were now accompanied by the fatal possibility of being false."[28] Language, then, is not a mirror of nature, but rather that which, through the use of words, might possibly substitute itself for the thing itself or, even worse, that which might insinuate that there is no being outside the texts of language. There is no necessary link between signifiers and their signified. It goes without saying, so to say, that with Sloterdijk, one is, once again, in Derrida's companionship.[29]

Yet metaphysics will hold fast, and if necessary violently, to monovalence. The possibility of utter true speech is grounded in the one being that, because of its supremacy, provides and supplies the possibility of truth. The possibility of uttering true, univocal, and adequate propositions is thus grounded in ultimate Being, which, through distributing itself in all other beings, again "supplies" in and "delivers" to these beings their "truth," "presence," and ultimately their univocity. But such a "distribution" of truth from Being to all beings, this availability of a certain immediacy through linking these beings to their source in Being, can only happen in a sovereign manner, namely through monopolizing the happening of untruth as well: univocity (either/or) will also mark the event of plurivocity (and/and).

> the zealotic monotheism and their universalist mission [. . .] rest on the intention of eliminating the risk of failure introduced by the second value at all costs—even if that implies removing the errant along with the error. In fact, the errant himself, viewed in terms of the ideal of monovalent being and its reflection in the true sentence, is merely a form of real nothingness.[30]

The cleft installed by metaphysics is therefore essentially hierarchical. While certainly it will not deny that true speech can happen, it will firmly state who can utter such speech and, with no less zeal, affirm who cannot do so. In metaphysics, sovereignty entails the monopolization of both truth and untruth through criminalizing or at least culpabilizing the latter.

It is Sloterdijk's merit to have shown just how this process occurs. According to Sloterdijk, the "true proposition" best relies on the immediacy of a revelation ("Here I am, I tell you the truth"), which, in turn, depends on an authority that shuns all dealings with uncertain and finite beings. And, furthermore, if it cannot avoid this interference, it remains immune from contamination with finitude through proclaiming itself to be the exception to the (finite) rule (of the finite). In this way, the end of metaphysics coincided with the awareness that there *are* sovereign commands without any legitimacy. In other words, this means that for Sloterdijk too there might always occur a discrepancy between justice and the force of law. Or, more positively, that there might be an authority other than the sovereignty of the law: if such sovereignty is to be construed as a power without authority, it remains to be seen how we might construe today an authority without power. For Sloterdijk too would probably subscribe to Derrida's search for a nonsovereign account of authority and would consider this too as one of those instances in which the best of humanity shows itself.

Such is the tenor of Sloterdijk's remarkable interpretation of the prohibition of images, which, for him, "stems from the observation that they never serve purely to reproduce that which is represented, but always assert their own significance in addition."[31] The image thus always risks taking the place of the imagined. Thus considered, the prohibition of images implies that those claiming to have an immediate link to "what is up there" must be reduced to the utmost minimum—recall that "icons of Christ" are claimed not to be "man-made"—and thus function as a sort limiting of the untruth in order that what is imagined in these images not be forgotten or in any other way go out of use through what is so imagined. One is reminded here of what Lacoste calls the danger pertaining to the distinction between the *res* and the *sacramentum* within Catholic theology, tending more to such images than the other suprematicisms. Here as well, the danger consists of the fact that the incognito of the *res* can be such that it hides completely behind the *sacramentum*, through which the latter gains momentum to such an extent that the *res*, in fact, can be forgotten and no divine presence other than the Eucharist (as *sacramentum*) can be imagined.[32]

Just how such worldly signs gain an unworldly authority and how worldly authorities grant themselves a supernatural aura and substitute the provisional laws of this world for a necessity is of no less than ontological importance, Sloterdijk notes in terms that once again recall Heidegger's thinking:

> Depending on the type of supremacization they tend towards, their agents choose typical procedures for returning from ambigu-

ity to certainty, from the fallibility of idle talk to the infallibility of the original text. [The aim] is to block out human language as it was spoken after the Fall. Its replacement is a code still untarnished by the negations, contradictions, and capacity for error inherent in bivalent speech.[33]

Heidegger had indeed interpreted the metaphysical code as an assurance of that which in no way can be assured, as an ascertaining of that which in every way remains an uncertainty, namely (my) being-in-the-world and the "fundamental uncertainty with regard to being," which extends to every being in its very finitude and contingency. Traditionally, this occurred symptomatically and systematically with regard to the problem of evil, in which evil is explained away as a lesser good but in no way as totally deprived of the Good. In modern times, something similar can be noted in Descartes's treatment of uncertainty, where all uncertainty is explained away as deprived (although not totally) of certainty and where the guarantee of certainty ultimately lies in God. In both cases, thinking and imagining that there really is such a thing as evil or uncertainty cannot accord with the nature of things but rather pertains, necessarily, to an improper use of reason, which improperly ascribes "being" to something that, properly speaking, is nothing. The question now is obvious: what happens exactly when the metaphysical code is broken? And what is to be done once the "logical program" is revealed and, through such a revelation, no longer functions? This is what Sloterdijk labels as "desuprematicization" or "the exhaustion of the monotheistic matrix."

An Exhausted Matrix?

A first answer comes to us through Derrida, who stated that one must learn to think without nostalgia and without too much hope. Being, for Derrida, has no monovalent mother tongue in which things can be signified clearly and distinctly once for all. Yet our studies have shown that one best not dream of the total eradication of such a nostalgia. One cannot abandon all nostalgia in a whim. In both Caputo's and Nancy's work, one can in effect detect a longing for a pure faith, untroubled and uncontaminated by the doctrines of established and institutionalized religions. For this reason alone, one needs to reckon with the fact that the most nonmetaphysical account can suddenly turn very metaphysical. Every "Anti-" "is held fast in the essence of that over against which it moves."[34] Hence some reluctance is appropriate when querying for the exhausted matrix. One should simultaneously ask, for instance, whether the ontotheological code has in effect been broken and even if such a thing is possible at all.

Sloterdijk's proposal of the "de-supremacization of the supremacisms" does, in the long run, aim at "dissolving [. . .] the matrix."[35] Sloterdijk can once again be aligned here to Derrida, when opting for lesser violence, for the battle of monotheisms is concerned "with how to ensure control of the extremist potentials within each of the zealotically disposed religions. [Such] tensions cannot be made to disappear, only diverted into less harmful expressions."[36] This means concretely that one has to collaborate on "dampen[ing] the extremism of service" to the personal as well as the impersonal Highest Being through a "decoupling of affect and religious code" and the eradication of all zeal from the latter.[37]

In this regard, the "exhaustion" of the matrix does not entail the total elimination of this code but rather to free the matrix, as much as possible, from its zealots and their fanaticism in a world "full of minorities that claim to constitute humanity."[38] Sloterdijk's "politics of being" once again adheres to the Enlightenment tradition by attempting to trace "the general quality present in all concepts of God that conformed to the personal-supremacist type" through breaking through the "symbolic shells" of "the historical style of zealous universalisms."[39] What remains of the matrix is nothing but its exhausted code: "On the one hand 'exhausted' means fully developed and realized, while on the other it means entirely used up and seen though in its fundamentally limited and erroneous nature."[40]

Let us consider the first sense of "exhaustion": the historical religions have deployed themselves completely and are fully realized. This means that they have actualized all of their possibilities and that, once these possibilities are exhausted, they can be left to their own demise. Sloterdijk's analysis of this first trait of "the exhaustion of the monotheistic matrix" consists of showing just how the three monotheistic religions introduce a "de-radicalization of alternatives,"[41] through a concession of sorts to polyvalent meaning (and/and) as a response to an ongoing demise of monovalence (either/or). Yet another time Sloterdijk turns against Augustine and the adjustments to the Christian thought of sin and redemption stemming from the bishop of Hippo that are made by the theory of purgatory. For purgatory offers a *tertium datur* between eternal damnation and eternal bliss. The eternal damnation emanating from Augustine is, according to Sloterdijk, based on an account of sinful human nature that is constituted so poorly and so weakly that its free will constantly stands between God and the human being to such an extent that its freedom is an obstacle to the reception of grace. It is likely that a free being will not choose for God. Yet this unredeemedness is to be conceived here in a privative manner. It is a condition of the human being for which this being is solely and fully responsible itself. The lack of will and of faith is an absence of which, properly speaking, ought to be present if only we would sufficiently will and desire this faith and the good.

In a cosmology in which all beings are immediately attuned to the good, that which seems to be lacking in goodness and so disrupt this order—*in* and *of* being—can only be conceived as a privation. It is not within the order of creation itself that something is missing or lacking in order to be able to receive redemption. It is rather due to the free human being, which lacks in obedience or servitude to freely subject itself to God. The *ordo* is such that "the human being [. . .] can only use its freedom without fault if he decides not to use this freedom."[42] According to Sloterdijk, Augustine is the founding father of the overburdening, the culpabilization, and even criminalization of the human being, which can still be attested to, if we follow Sloterdijk, in modern times as well as in postmodernity—in Marion too, as I will show, there is no such thing as an indifference toward God without fault.

The conception of purgatory can thus be seen as a first concession to the changed circumstances since Augustine preached eternal damnation (almost) for all and eternal bliss for the happy few. For purgatory offers a *tertium datur* between sin and redemption:

> In order to establish the otherworldly place of purgatory as a third eschatological place, the introduction of a processual moment into the heretofore timeless and statically conceived divine world became necessary. [. . .] If it is the case that in the beyond we still find catharsis (or progress), transformation, and "development," then the place of purification becomes latently historical.[43]

The discovery of something like purgatory therefore opens new possibilities for Christian monotheism. It is from such a moment onward that "things can be arranged" and that the issue of salvation merges with the symbolic actions of transaction and of commerce. Thus purgatory, Sloterdijk somewhat exaggeratingly states, is a sort of general "revenge bank" in which one can invest and from which one can borrow what one needs in advance. Just, as in Nancy, one can once again associate the complicity of capitalism to the "mono" of monotheism—this "mono" being transcribed in our society as the monotony of money. One is a long way off from those contemporary theologians claiming that the good features of modernity are obviously

Christian, whereas all that cannot be traced to such a Christian origin are merely instances of nihilism. Perhaps, then, it would be possible to take theology seriously when it learns to admit that capitalism, too, might have been inherited from our Christian tradition.[44]

For Sloterdijk, though, it goes without saying that this currency of salvation ends up being devalued. If Christianity opens itself to the world through turning the place of salvation into something dynamic and historical, a decisive step is taken, it seems, to conceive of a salvation and purging that end up being merely historical and on worldly terms. The decay is initiated when purgatory "assumed characteristics of both places: the grisly décor and gruesome punishment of hell, but also the confidence and the certainty of a favourable conclusion found in heaven."[45] What remains, in effect, is the obscuring of both orders while now conceiving of redemption as an outdated superstructure and sin as a somewhat faulty word for the condition of being-in-the-world.

Conclusion: Sloterdijk and "The Legitimacy of Postmodernity"

It is, however, important to note that these practices of de-supremacization are, according to Sloterdijk, inherent to all monotheisms. Sloterdijk therefore confirms what Nancy had called "the auto-deconstruction of Christianity," the limits of which have yet to be determined. In Sloterdijk's *Life*, one will observe that the zeal and the concomitant wrath—frustrated zeal equals wrath—are in effect undermined from within through those exercises that seemingly belonged to monotheism from the outset. Sloterdijk argues that monotheism "has always included [. . .] a series of spiritual exercises that contributed implicitly to overcoming the dangerous rigidity of the founding matrix."[46] The practice of negative theology would be one of those methods to disrupt and deconstruct the strictness and rigidity of the monotheistic matrix handed down to us in the concepts of the sub- and superlunary. Such "exercises in religion," one might say, always have consequences. That which is supposed to be "up above" turns out to be "down below," or, more positively, they somewhat take down what is "up above" to uplift what is "down below." Such a displacement can indeed be detected in negative theology, which states that one cannot even say of God that he does not exist. In such a way, the negative theologian him- or herself occupies the *tertium datur* between total distance from God and the complete lack of distance (as exemplified in theories of deification, for instance). The negative theologian thus is midway between the exclusion of God—nothing in and of being resembles God—and God's complete inclusion—nothing in and of being is not God. It is no coincidence then that Sloterdijk describes negative theology as "God's last intellectual chance," as the enterprise able to show that even today there is some space for "what is above," "what is outside," or as the gently falling upward that, according to Sloterdijk, is the human being.[47]

Here I have arrived at the second signification of the supposed "exhaustion of the monotheistic matrix." For, according to Sloterdijk, even these attempts to adjust the matrix from within, internally, can, once its possibilities are actualized, no longer make the matrix function within societies, cultures, or even individuals—recall the secularization of salvation through purgatory—simply because this opening to the modern world serves as the condition of possibility for Christianity to succumb to this context and evaporate as sugar does in coffee.

Such a "secularization of religious metaphors" (Löwith) or the "transcription of theological concepts in the thought of world" (Nancy) is therefore not the whole story when it comes to today's deconstruction of Christianity. In today's context, questions might in fact arise that old theories and old theologies, secularized or not, cannot answer. This is where Löwith's theory of a secularization of transcendence yields to Blumenberg's account of the legitimacy of modernity, which is "legitimate" and "new" only because questions have arisen that Christianity can no longer answer and for which it does not answer at all (because it no longer understands the question). This is exhausting the monotheistic metaphysics to such an extent that, in Sloterdijk and Nancy, *even* Christianity's effort to adapt to or to recontextualize in the modern context—through a "return of religion," for instance—does not suffice to revive the Christian tradition and ultimately turns out to be unable to respond to the modern context at all.

This is the second signification of the exhaustion Sloterdijk has in mind. Despite its urge for adaptation and adjustments, the matrix is itself no longer adjusted to the new distribution of roles making up the (post) modern context and to the opening of a world "coming to terms with itself" (Nancy). Sloterdijk would say that no religion, or return to religion, can save us now. What comes "from above" and "weighs" upon the human being is no longer something "outside" this world—as certain science-fiction films, secularized versions of religion as they are, have shown. Nor is it the highest being, directing and steering the world from without. Rather, it is the "nothing in particular," the "nothing" of being-always already-in-the-world to which the human being, held aloft only by gravity, can comport only from within, that is, from out of his or her own worldliness without this "world" being able to occupy this verticality totally.

This, then, for Sloterdijk, is the moment one ought to change one's life.

4

Exercises in Religion II

Living With Exhaustion

Before elaborating on Sloterdijk's recent somewhat estranging work, *You Must Change Your Life*, one ought to recall his functionalist and naturalist approach to religion. Sloterdijk starts from a biological account of what it is to be human. Just as all biological systems succeed, through trial and error, that is, through exercise, to immunize themselves from outward threats, so cultural systems too are attempts to undo the threat of what comes from without. Religion, then, is one of those units of meaning that have accompanied the human being in its effort to reduce the "vertical tension"—the weight of the outside. This weight, of course, takes on different postures in the course of history. In this sense, one can read Sloterdijk's *Life* as an inversion of Kierkegaard's stages on a life path, the result of which is that Sloterdijk seems closer to the likes of Auguste Comte than one first might have expected. For in Sloterdijk too there is, first, a religious phase of humanity, in which the weight of the outside and what is "out there" could only be named God. Next to this first phase, there is a second, ethical stage in which the trend "upward" is soothed with and relieved by the horizontal idea of progress. Finally, there is our postmodern, esthetical position, where it is the artist and the athlete who accompany one's climbing and counting up to the highest. The first by proclaiming "art for art's sake," whereby the sublime (dis)figures as what is above and beyond us. The latter shows us the void and complete exhaustion of the maximum of records that still need to be better, faster, and stronger. In this regard, Sloterdijk's stages almost correspond to the classical transcendentalia. In the first stage, the human being is measured against his or her holiness or truth; in the second stage, over and against his or her goodness; and in the final phase, over and against his or her beauty.

Sloterdijk here opts for an ontological approach. The a priori of the opening is older than the diverse ontic forms it has taken in the course of history. This a priori openness consists ultimately of the immunological commerce and dealings with the outside, which always and already impose some kind of alienation on the human being. The human being is therefore ontologically speaking an *outsider*. This means two things here. On the one hand, the human being has no natural place in the world and is thrown into this world without a goal or an origin. On the other hand, the human being cannot *not* open onto this world and stands—at least through the opening that is one's body and one's consciousness—always and already on the outside of its world.

This ontological approach allows Sloterdijk to interpret religion as but one attempt to immunize this threat coming from the outside. (Note that it took a very long time before this "outside" was just called "world"). To explore this history, one needs to turn to Sloterdijk's magnificent *Spheres*, in which he shows how the peculiarity of the postmodern situation is to be portrayed. In this regard, one might note that the idea of the outside today has been exposed to a *loss of face*. No one looks back to us when we gaze toward the heavens. And when we look straight ahead, we cannot see any light at the end of the tunnel. This makes for the fact that, for Sloterdijk, "the question of 'where?' " posed by the human being needs to be addressed anew, given, of course, that, after the "globalization wars and technological departures" that marked the past century, we finally realize "that the question should rather be: where are we when we are in the monstrous?"[1]

Sloterdijk's topology or "ontobiology" tries to deliver a dynamized version of Heidegger's being-in-the-world, no longer the static world of the 1927 interbellum dominated by angst but a being conditioned by world each time again, reminiscent of Nancy's retrieval of being-with-one-another: "What recent philosophers refer to as being-in-the-world first of all, and in most cases, means being-in-spheres. If humans are *there*, it is initially in spaces that have opened for them, because, by inhabiting them, humans have given them form, content [and] relative duration."[2]

Insofar as Heidegger's conception of being-in-the-world can in effect be interpreted as somewhat static—everyone is always and everywhere in the world—Sloterdijk tries to take hold of the alterations that make up one's being-in-the-world, attempting to show just how the atmo*sphere* of being-in-the-world can change from one moment to the next. Just as for Nancy, then, being-with is not the immobile limitation of one's being-in-the-world to *"einen bestimmten Umkreis"*—"a determinate circle" of others and things,[3] so too Sloterdijk takes into account how a different *Umkreis* or circle of friends or of random people might alter one's being-in-the-world. Being-with-the-others, our being *in* the world, according to Sloterdijk, is not always and already the "same" for everyone at every time—with anxiety quietly hovering over everyone's being-in-the-world—but is *lived* each time differently. The fact, moreover, that it is lived differently will come to mean, for Sloterdijk, that it *is* differently as well. To put it in Heideggerian terms: the altered mode of the being of being-with transforms the being of being-with. So, for instance, when I attend a lecture in an academic setting, the world "worlds" differently than when I spend an evening with my friends. And although this change of setting might be considered, in a Heideggerian manner, as being only of "ontic" and empirical relevance, the change *itself*, the *fact(icity)* of such changing, is not without ontological importance. "Being-in-spheres" then denotes both a psychological ontic component with an ontological component ("the mood changed") and a biological, spatial component ("I am in another sphere").[4] It is this dynamical interpretation of being-in-the-world that Sloterdijk, as we later point out, appreciates in Binswanger's work.

Modernity and the Emergence into History

Spheres, in effect, points to the ontobiology of the immune system as one of the main causes of the course of history. Unlike *Life*, this ontobiology is not yet the only the cause of the course. The "spherological drama of development" resulting in the "emergence into history" undergoes something like a tipping point with the downfall of the medieval theory of participation and the corresponding metaphysics.[5] This crisis has caused not only what one can call the modern *shrinking* of the world—to what is experimentable, provable, visible, and so forth—but also a growing *muteness* of being. This muteness, then, serves as the "entry in history": "this is where the birth of the outside takes place: upon emerging into the open, humans discover what they initially think can never become part of their own, inner, co-animated realm."[6] Recall that, for Blumenberg, the entrance of Christianity on the stage of the world consisted of bringing the very question of "the meaning of history" to the old circular systems of ancient culture. It was, moreover, this question that Greek and Roman culture could not answer (again: because they did not understand the question—the question of the course and direction of history simply does not arise in cultures which maintain that time is circular). What Sloterdijk shares with Nancy therefore is precisely that our era, whether we call it postmodern or not, asks us to no longer elucidate the meaning of being-with and of history from out of the exhausted possibilities of the Christian epoch, which easily turns this "mundane" meaning into a full-fledged metaphysical Signification. Sloterdijk adds, though, that this entry or "emergence into history" realizes and actualizes itself today and is on the verge of becoming conscious of itself. This means that this entrance, once the *Hinterwelterei* is left behind, is itself "nothing but historical." The awareness can then arise that the human being has *always* been an outsider and takes its stance, so to say, precisely as a vertical animal, with urges for and impulses to what is outside and what is above.

> The moderns hardly have any access to the forgotten worlds of metaphysical bubbleglory [. . .] It was never the goal of the classic thinkers [. . .] to attain to what one calls in an (anti) cartesian vein, the ultimate ground, but it was rather to enclose ultimately everything [and to reach for] total immunity.

The message of this immunization or of the attempt "to enclose everything in one stroke" in this way is that:

> every point in the world space, even if it is far removed from the center [. . .] is potentially and actually made possible through a ray from out of this center and reached through it. And because everything which is, springs from an all-effectuating, good center (*omne ens est bonum*: all goodness has an immunological power) my own life and light is secured of its own place in an [. . .] animated and totally immunizing whole.[7]

This is why the end of metaphysics is portrayed by Sloterdijk as a "crisis of the heavens" and a "loss of the middle."[8] This "end" displaces the human being: no place or space can ever be secured for him or her. From the "bubble" that is the cosmos, in which every being speaks of God to a universe (or better: to impersonal space, sphere, or globe). In such a universe, being is silent, not because it would not want to speak—privative negation: being or God ought to speak, but chooses not to—but because it is mute and bereft of all ensoulment. This is why modernity can be seen as a "return of gnosis" (Blumenberg), and the evil and unjust Being can be placed over and against the goodness of the face of the other, which, of course, speaks (Levinas).

One has yet to understand how it can happen that the matrix of monotheism exhausts itself or, to use Nancy's words, auto-deconstructs.

Sloterdijk contends that the issue with this metaphysics gone weary is precisely that it suffers from its own supremacy and cannot uphold the pressure of its own maximum. Despite all adaptations and desuprematicizations, it does not succeed to once again animate what is now bereft of any spirit. On the contrary, the "inanimate"—without *animus*—will strike back with a sort of *vengeance* and haunt the attempts to reanimate and immunize the "inanimate," somewhat like a ghost. If metaphysics is auto-deconstructive, this means: it cannot immunize against itself and is consumed by its own phantasm of supremacy. The "inanimate"—a term used here for that which is not "inspirited" and knows not of any in-spiration from God knows where—is of course evil, which in the reign of metaphysics only appeared to be "inanimate" but was quickly "inspirited," albeit as a lesser *good*—and perhaps the problem of sin and incompleteness. Thus, history and historicity emerge in the awareness that there is no direction and orientation to history other than mere historicity: absolute spirits of all sorts are fading away, if they have not burned out already.

How does this happen, and, more specifically, how does incomplete immunization happen? Sloterdijk, in this regard, points in different directions. On the one hand, there is a tendency to totalize, starting from a highest being that would not want to exclude any of the (ordinary) beings. This is what Sloterdijk calls the "the immune reaction of the bubble"[9] against everything that would want to posit itself outside the sphere of the bubble and the totality it contains and reaches for, as for instance atheism would do. The result of this is that the One God of monotheism or the one absolute being knows of no outside. One might say, in a Derridean vein, that there is nothing outside the God of monotheism. God is immune against everything that could posit itself outside of God or that could otherwise contaminate God. This is one more reason why indeed evil had to be interpreted as a lesser *good* and is, in this way, included in the order of creation, which is to be deemed "good," "very good even."

On the other hand, it is precisely experiences of evil that have convinced the moderns of the exact opposite of the goodness of creation and, in this sense too, orient modernity toward a new kind of gnosis. The world, indeed, for most of the moderns, had come to be a mechanistic system that is fairly easy, if we are to follow Descartes, to imagine as an *automaton*. In modernity, then, for Sloterdijk, the ontotheological "ritual" ends (and no longer works) by means of the (secularized) "devastating attribute that is the infinite,"[10] one of the concepts that had issued from this very ritual in the first place. This infinite, in effect, is no longer personal, but an impersonal, mathematical structure that extends to the whole "that is extended"

(Descartes again). There is nothing outside that which can be mathematicized or mechanized. But the dream of such a universal *mathesis* of course is such that there no longer can be conceived "the middle" or "the center" to which the human being was always and already related, whether this center was named God, Being, or Christ as the mediator par excellence. The Infinite One, one could say, becomes *an* infinite. This no longer left a space for a center that could orient the human being which, in turn, has lost its central place in the cosmos. In this regard, it might be no coincidence that Descartes stated that the characteristics of the *automaton* could pertain not only to animals but *also* to the human being "walking outside his house." The loss of the center is of course one of those fundamental experiences that Pascal underwent when writing about "the eternal silence of these infinite spaces." This silence is frightening indeed, and its numinosity makes, for Pascal but no less for us, the question that is the human being all the more urgent.

This is why one can regard Pascal's "man exceeds man infinitely" as a more accurate, although more pessimistic, rendition of the experience making up the modern mind than Kant's famous admiration for the "starry heaven above" and the "moral law" within him, which of course has secretly summoned Being to speak again. Pascal, then, voices the experience of the outside brilliantly: the outside, the ecstasy of the human being toward the world now no longer concerns a world that bathes in and is sheltered by God's presence. Rather, the ecstasy now experiences itself as a historical openness through and in which nothing in particular appears necessary (except perhaps what I call here the appearing of appearing or the event of world). Such ecstasy merely observes, so to say, the "coming to pass" of all appearances to which Schürmann already hinted. Being-in-a-bubble turns out to be being-in-the-void, or as Sloterdijk had aptly put it: "Spheres stop being round when they burst."[11] Such a destruction, obviously, is accompanied by "the abandonment of God's immunity."[12] The infinite is no longer defined as that which includes and encloses, but rather as that which cannot be enclosed and included totally. An infinite is like a black hole, a tear in the fabric of what once was a uni-verse: a "a non-container" and "a non-ground."[13] It is the fact of history and the fundamental historicity of all beings that now estranges and causes awe, although the "entry into the open" now becomes "the entry in the uncanny" too.

Still this experience of modernity will first be disputed with entirely medieval means. The "exhaustion of the matrix" and the "abandonment of immunization" encounter resistance from the matrix itself, and the latter delivers one more possibility to save it from exhaustion. Sloterdijk already recounts the mode of procedure in the opening pages of *Bubbles*:

it would not be [viable] if they would not bring a dowry of memories of the symbiotic field and its enclosing power with them into the strange new land. It is this power to transfer the integral space to new circumstances that ultimately also overcomes the intruder trauma [through integrating] the disrupter like a new sibling—as if, in fact, it were a necessary element of its own system.[14]

This makes for the continuity as well as the discontinuity of the event. Continuity, in that the past is taken up and informs the present. Discontinuity, because the uncanny or unusual can be such that it is no longer integrated in what is considered to be usual and familiar (for instance, the family, the homeland, etc.), thus causing the bubble to burst. This is also the reason why Sloterdijk suspect a fundamental continuity between the "dark" medieval ages and the later Enlightenment. This continuity, according to Sloterdijk, shows in the culpabilization of the human being. Yet even this remainder of guilt will prove to be, at least according to our author, but one more possibility the matrix comes up with to save it from de(con)struction. Christianity's auto-deconstruction means that it will wither away in and through its endless adaptation to newly arisen contexts and circumstances. It will reorient and redirect its message to the changed context just so long as this context needs and understands the answer Christianity would bring to its questions. These questions are ultimately "identical" through different epochs: the meaning of being, of love, and of death. The outdated and worn-out system of participation (in being, *in Christo*, or *in Deo*) and the concomitant overburdening of sinful, all too sinful freedom, is transposed to and *translated* in the modern context as follows: "if the consensus of all is that the praxis of freedom has now come to power, how come then that this praxis has *not yet* resulted in a permanent good world?"[15] The "old" answer to the newly arisen question of freedom is first sustained and *continued* (this freedom, too, is insufficiently able to establish the new, brave world once and for all) but will ultimately be falsified, *done away with*, and proclaimed to be maladjusted to answer the new question that freedom entails. For the idea of freedom, according to Sloterdijk, will finally abandon the thought of a universal world *as well*. It will be considered a mere remainder of the matrix and will settle for a purely individualistic era.[16] It is this latter process that we, according to Sloterdijk, are witnessing today.

The "culpabilizing matrix"[17] will remain in function and in power for just a little while, although new candidates for the "origin of evil" quickly arrive: the right to property, class society, capital, the univocal logic of identity, and so forth. One might be reminded just as well of Levinas's "subject," subjected to the other to such an extent that it can never attend to this or that other *sufficiently* and can never experience its indifference to the other without guilt. Just as, for Marion, hate is but a lack of love, so too, for Levinas, every not attending to the other is but a lack of attending the other and will be interpreted as egoism. One can also think of the version of the decentered subject such as provided in psychoanalytical circles, where, obviously, the intention of the analytic can never be to heal or deem the patient healthy *enough*, but rather to perpetuate the sickness by convincing the patient of the permanence of an insufficient health. Because one here can only be declared healthy against all odds or through a fault in proceedings, one cannot conceive of any being unhealthy without guilt. On the contrary, lobbies and markets will be created to culpabilize the civilian's unhealthy lifestyle. I return to the phenomenon of the health hype below.

The fundamental continuity between the medieval and the modern politics of such a culpabilization points, for Sloterdijk, in the direction of an *ontological continuity*, valid for human beings at all times and all places, and which accordingly does not really change. Such a continuity makes Sloterdijk wonder about a "determinate function" that, then, would be neither young nor old, "neither a word nor a concept" (Derrida) and that can never be exhausted. This is the final reason why the "entrance in history" would not itself be historical and ultimately leaps "beyond" history and borders on being "ahistorical." The appearing of the appearance of "history" was not of our accord, but has becomes a reality nevertheless.

One can illustrate this well with a passage of *Life* in which Sloterdijk highlights the difference between Nietzsche's utterance "God is dead!" and the contemporary "the king is dead!" Whereas the first expression requires the addendum that this God now has to remain dead, the second's addendum, "Long live the king," indicates something else entirely. Sloterdijk intends the following: if the function of a king has, in effect, lost its function, then even the kings and queens of Europe have now indeed become nothing more than "symbolic" powers: "the royal function as such, understood as a pole of attraction to the pure Above, Over and Upwards, remains imaginarily intact in many individuals despite real circumstances and demands a new interpretation" and implementation.[18] It is for these "new implementations," fulfilled namely through postmodern aesthetics and athleticism, that the older religious answers can no longer fit the profile. These implementations therefore mark the transition to the "exhaustion of metaphysics" in its second, more definitive, meaning.

In a more concrete manner, and this is where *Life* sets off, one can state that religion is itself outdated, undone, or maladjusted once new knowledge has arrived coming to us through changed circumstances. And by this, Sloterdijk has in mind the current financial and ecological crises. This is the decision that seems to be made by Sloterdijk somewhere between writing *God's Zeal* and *Life*. Whereas the first still sees opportunities for religion in the contemporary context, the latter opts, it seems, for a nullification when it comes to the possibilities for religion to fulfill the "function of the king" in a contemporary context. One has nevertheless arrived at a crossroads. This crossroads converges between the exhaustion of possibilities that still can fulfill and satisfy certain needs and certain implementations of some functions in the contemporary context and the matrix, which, itself, will suffer from such an exhaustion and is bound to perish. This hesitation can easily be demonstrated in Sloterdijk's works. Even *God's Zeal*, which still reserves a role to be played by religion, ultimately doubts the possibility of such a role:

> the new interest in the great religions can be attributed primarily to the fact that, since the self-renunciation of Communist and Socialist humanity politics, *the traditional religious codes have been all that is available* when people look for more comprehensive forms of communal consciousness—at least, for as long as there are no transculturally convincing formulations of a general theory of culture on offer.[19]

What remains for a while is simply the matrix itself and the code in which it ultimately consists and which, if we are to seriously ponder its fate, we need to untie of all affective and emotional components. Religion therefore only has a provisional role to play in the universal and global response to the emerging crises facing humanity. It might, for instance, seek and establish even renewed forms of being-with or of "co-immunity" (to turn to the term used by *Life*)—causing our "globe" to turn into a "bubble" again—in which a universal, if not unified, humanity could *live*. One can suspect indeed that, for Sloterdijk, religion is a valid response to the question posed by what he deems a "demographic Enlightenment": the overpopulation of the planet, as "one of those crises that is 'already here' and 'still to come,'" which, in turn, points to the problem of a more just sharing of the natural riches of the earth.[20]

Yet even in *God's Zeal* Sloterdijk will ultimately deny a religious implementation of some functions or roles in contemporary societies and will do so, remarkably, on strictly epistemological grounds. In effect, one has to understand that Sloterdijk is not at all bothered with the fate, so to say, of the monotheistic matrix. This is the problem for those who have not yet eradicated all emotion and sentiment when it comes to the code onto which monotheism is grafted. Sloterdijk's problem with religion is strictly epistemological (and one that deserves to be posed—it is one of the reasons why this work here clings to the philosophical method from the beginning right to the end), for the revealed religions "deny [. . .] the possibility and inevitability of finding new truths, if these happen to produce results leading to revisions in the text of the holy scriptures."[21] If it is easy to imagine the response of the zealot to Sloterdijk's proposal—even today people take God's supposed Word all too literally—it needs to be considered too whether these religions, structurally, are unable to adjust properly to new and expanding knowledge. For it would, of course, not be the first time that religion stands in the way of genuine human development (of which Galileo is only the paradigmatic case). Consider, for instance, the fact that Christ's coming, in the Christian religion, has to be regarded as the absolute null point: it is "unique," "unrepeatable" to such an extent that the Christian no longer has to expect anything from (ordinary) human history. These religions, Sloterdijk argues, prefer the past rather than the future, and it is this that makes them in the end unapt for the present. This is why they are bound to *disappear*, because they become useless for the fulfillment of certain functions in society and, secondly, because they are structurally unable to deal with the changing circumstances and the concomitant renewal.

Postmodern Life: Ascetic, Aesthetic, and Athletic Religion

This inaptitude of religion to fulfill certain functions in contemporary society is the reason why Sloterdijk writes that it was only at first sight that the exhaustion of the matrix appeared to be "a new religious question," because this exhaustion confronts us with a new situation that comes to threaten this matrix as such:

> whoever acknowledges the possibility of fundamentally new insights is admitting something that older historical metaphysics would not have accepted at any price: that truth is subject to evolution, and that in the historical succession of knowledge something else is to be seen as a random sequence [. . .] The fact that the acquisition of knowledge lasts indeterminately forms the ontological foundation of history.[22]

Here is the entrance into history: human beings step outside only to find there the world "revealed"! The new knowledge stemming from changed circumstances forces the establishment of new answers and the abandonment of older ones. This is why *Life* opens precisely by arguing that the status of this knowledge will cause the matrix to fade away, and by leaving aside all natural and functionalist explanations of religion.[23] Sloterdijk's recent work, in effect, proposes what one can call an "ontobiological reduction," which, starting from the strategies for immunization that envelop both biological and cultural life, takes up the matrix constituting religion in exposing or at least making explicit what is only implicitly present in these religious exercises: their trafficking with verticality, the exposure to the outside in and as being-in-the-world. The aim of this reduction is therefore not only to propose a compete translation of religion in terms of the "outside" of world but also an elucidation—"explicitation"—of what the end of religion itself had always and already been.

In the remaining sections of this chapter, we first briefly delve into the position Sloterdijk's recent work takes in order to see, second, just why the religious matrix would evaporate in the domain of market and other struggles, such as the battle of athletes against each other and against themselves. I already indicated that Sloterdijk's book on life can be read as a reversal of Kierkegaard's "stages on a life path." These stages here will lead from the religious path, over the ethical-metaphysical one, and finally to the catastrophic existence of the aesthete. However, in Sloterdijk, too, whenever there is a catastrophe and a desert, so too is there hope and a saving power of sorts.[24] This is why in a third step I show how the minimal universalism—one of the aims of this work—in Sloterdijk takes the form of a "co-immunity" in which religion no longer seems to have any function at all.

The core thesis of the book on life is indeed that religions are *nothing but* (old) attempts to deal and interact with "the open" and "the outside," as particular instantiations of what it is to be in the outside or in the world. Religion, for Sloterdijk, has been nothing but the attempt to immunize against "the above" and "the open" through installing a kind of "trafficking" with this outside. This functionalization of "the higher" has in our era been taken over by other domains. The religious and ascetic exercise has become mainly an athletic one. What once was the "highest" has become the "fastest," "strongest," and so forth."

Such rupture will find an aesthetic replacement as well. In *Life*, Sloterdijk appeals to Kafka and Cioran to illustrate this. In Kafka's *A Hunger Artist* (1923), in which a trapeze artist decides not to descend after his shows, Sloterdijk detects the prime example of what he sees as an existentialism for dandies through which the aesthetic rupture with world becomes "an earnest parody of [. . .] the religiously motivated renunciation of the profane world."[25] The rupture with world, in effect, is performed as a sort of semi-rupture. Whereas the end of the religious rupture was an end other-than-itself, namely to please God, this end now has become internal to the dynamics of aestheticism itself: *l'art pour l'art*. The artist lives for his or her art only, and this means that he or she wants to experience the break with world *for the sake of* breaking with world. "The urge to go further is as inherent in art as the will to transcend reality in religious asceticism: perfection is not enough,"[26] as when the artist decides to stay longer, much longer on the trapeze for instance. A decisive step in this "despiritualization of asceticism" has been taken in Kafka's portrayal of the hunger artist. Whereas the trapeze artist no longer wanted to "please God," he at least had an audience to please, entertain, and excite; the weal and the woe of the hunger artist is such that he knows no tendency to please or any other goal. For Sloterdijk, it is here that Kafka most definitely describes the end of metaphysics and the death of God. The hunger artist not only no longer knows of any goal of his exercise, but he in no way rejoices in or enjoys his shortage (of food, of an audience, of a goal) as some sort of romantic hero or other Werthers would have done. On the contrary, the hunger artist simply admits that he would have gormandized if only he had found something to his liking. If, in effect, the trapeze artist wants to be admired for his abilities, the hunger artist wants nothing of the sort. This artist says: "but you shouldn't have admired this." Sloterdijk calls this "the most spiritual European pronouncement" of the twentieth century because it shows "what remains of metaphysical desire when its transcendent goal is eliminated. What transpires is a form of beheaded asceticism in which the supposed tensile strain from above proves to be an aversive tension from within."[27]

What remains of the metaphysical shortages and the hunger for God is the art of hunger, in addition to a certain delight derived from a lack. Unaware of any goal, this kind of delight for Sloterdijk evolves into the "lack of hunger" that currently characterizes our welfare economics. In the latter, Sloterdijk argues, people become like wolves to one another and resemble the panther that devoured the hunger artist, of which it was said that "he had more than enough." Here the human being becomes like the animal that knows no other lack than a biological one.

The abandonment of higher goals and of admiration, through giving but banal reasons for his odd, impossible art, is an anticipation of our capitalist age in the sense that the logic of welfare economics does indeed indicate that it wants the maximum of wealth for a maximum amount of people while at the same time remaining blind to what it might lack itself or even to the fact that there is such a lack—those who experience shortages of food, for instance. It will no longer show the least bit of understanding for those who do in effect lack anything.

Cioran adds a second observation to the ongoing despiritualization and decapitation of asceticism, which in Kafka was already bereft of its goal and ultimately of its audience. The latter is important for Sloterdijk's interpretation of Cioran, in whose writings Sloterdijk discovers "a new type of practising person whose originality consists in that [. . .] he practises rejecting every goal-directed way of practising."[28] Someone who does not seek to please God or attempt to become a "great artist" by making art for art's sake or want to be an illuminating example for his audience. "Methodical exercises [. . .] are only possible if there is a fixed practice goal in sight. It is precisely the authority of this goal that Cioran contests. Accepting a practice goal would mean believing—and 'believing' refers here to the mental act whereby the beginner anticipates its goal":[29] I believe it to be possible to reach my goal.

This religious and faithful '"anticipation of a goal" is the most important behavioral attitude that Sloterdijk's "ontobiological reduction"—the reduction of what is only implicit in this kind of attitude in order to make it explicit—wants to expose. Once religion, too, falls prey to a lack of goal, it becomes hollowed out from within. It no longer has a place to transcend to once all otherworldly goals have been eradicated. The exhaustion of the monotheist matrix, in its second meaning, signifies that all teleology, all "playing for the coach," so to speak, has come to an end. There is no one left to please, not even oneself. Other than the hunger and the trapeze artist, Cioran had "discovered the healthiest way of being incurable."[30]

What remains of metaphysical hunger once no one hungers for God anymore is but an ascetic flight from the world, an "exercise" or "practice" in which one can still see the structure or foundation of a rupture with world but no longer the place to which such a rupture would take the ascetic. No safe havens and afterworlds are admitted. This is what is manifested of the religious attitude once the phenomenological reduction is performed and completed and once the traditions in and through which this exercise received its meaning have faded away. Just as, in the case of the hunger artist, the interest of the audience in his performance only lasted for forty days (not because of any religious indication but because the attention, after this period, for his performance was gone) and then rendered this exercise superfluous as to the sense of the flight as well as to its goal, just so "the conditions of possibility of their survival [i.e., of religious traditions and exercises] will themselves become conspicuous"³¹ in Cioran's ascetic "redemption without redemption," that is, once the tradition is sufficiently uprooted.

This is Sloterdijk's version of a phenomenological reduction of religion: once its experiences and its exercises disappear, the conditions of possibility of this experience and exercise will appear. These conditions can now be made explicit and will expose the fact that the religious exercise simply grafted itself onto that which Sloterdijk calls "anthropotechnics." The climbing out of one's world, the vertical tensions that the human being "has to be" (just as long as he or she has "to be its Dasein"), is a climb and a tension that now no longer can be filled in with a religious meaning.

Next to the ascetic-aesthetic transgression of the artist, suffering from (his or her) world, the transgression will receive an athletic signification. The world of sports will come to dominate the world of aesthetics, just as the latter had already conquered the religious world. The "loss of interest" in religious traditions shows the exhaustion of the monotheist matrix to itself in "a zeitgeist that wants to speak the final word on the world of hunger: over and finished."³² What remains, to return to Blumenberg's terms, are not questions that can be answered religiously. What remains, it seems, is but "bread and circuses"—and, perhaps, the flag.³³ It are these three things that, according to Sloterdijk, fulfill all quasi (onto)biological needs of postmodernity.

It is not difficult to imagine just how the transformation of religion into athletics occurs. Just as religion is for Sloterdijk originally a "commotion around ecstasy,"³⁴ so too the sporting event functions as a temporary sedation or opium for the people attending. Just as religion once claimed the capacity to substitute the usual for the unusual, so sports has since become the domain par excellence in which one "extraordinary" performance succeeds the other and the athlete is adored by the audience. The difference, however, once the religious blockade of the maximum has been banned, is that no such maximum or limit is allowed any longer. While in sports, there is, literally, no limit to what can be accomplished and records only stand in order to be broken. This is what Sloterdijk calls the "mount impropable." Here, the maximum is not defined by a summit that is already there, but rather is invented or imagined while climbing and ascending.³⁵

In what follows, I would like to point to the somewhat ambivalent attitude toward religion that Sloterdijk demonstrates in his recent work. For, next to the postmodern—aesthetic and athletic—and the rather ancient and medieval—ascetic—rupture with world, there is also an ethical interruption with world. It is, however, in this ethical rupture, which Sloterdijk situates in the Greek world, that Christianity nevertheless seems to play a central role. A role moreover that seems to resist the reduction of religion to but one more player in the global (far from) free-market economy in which Sloterdijk sees the definitive Gestalt of the exhaustion of the monotheist matrix.

Life, and Nothing but Life: The Liberation from the Matrix?

Sloterdijk's solution to the crisis of the postmodern world will ultimately consist of the erection of a new kind of ethical rupture, now interpreted as a distinguished distinction, with world, in which an enlightened elite will lead the masses to a new phase in the community of human beings worldwide. For this, Sloterdijk returns to the "non-aristocratic definition of the noble"—one of the highest possibilities for humanity. Sloterdijk does not seem able to eradicate all aristocratic and elitist connotations entirely. On some other points, too, Sloterdijk seems to contradict himself, for instance, in his quest for an ecological and economic answer to the contemporary crisis. I will, for instance, show that the "culpabilizing" potential of the monotheistic matrix is not as exhausted as Sloterdijk wants us to believe. In his plea for a universal co–immunity, aiming at an ethics fit for the globalized world, it is exactly this sort of culpabilization, albeit in a *secular translation*, that returns.

Of what does the ethical transgression consist exactly, and what is Christianity's relation, if any, to such a transgression? To obtain a new ethical orientation, Sloterdijk meditates on Heraclitus's mysterious saying *"ethos anthropoi daimon."* For our purposes here it is best to stick to Heidegger's translation: "the human being dwells, insofar he is a human being, in the uncanny."[36] The uncanny is perhaps the better translation of *"das Ungeheure,"* which in our text has also been referred to as the unusual, the extraordinary, or the monstrous. Being ethically oriented is, for Sloterdijk, the human being who has a taste for the uncanny or the extraordinary within the ordinary and the usual being-in-a-world or at least a sense for that which "weighs" on the human animal from the outside and the above.

And yet Sloterdijk attempts to correct Heidegger here. Whereas Heidegger seems to presuppose a quasi-automatic connection—one might risk thinking of an "ontotheology of the uncanny"—between human dwelling "down here" and the higher abode of the "daimon" up there, Sloterdijk does not think that such a necessary link is given in and through Heraclitus's thought. For Heraclitus, Sloterdijk argues, the human being can choose to be nothing but human (and most of us, according to Heraclitus, will do so) and so decide not to establish a link with the higher place of the "gods" up there. Yet the human being can also decide to transcend his or her dwelling in the world and so be uplifted toward what most properly belongs to the gods. What Sloterdijk takes from this (his forgetfulness of Heidegger's "*Das Man*," which would disrupt the link between the ordinary and the extraordinary, excepted) is that, for him, it is in Heraclitus that an ethical transgression of the world has become possible: it is good, better even, to think than not to think, for those who think are at least "awake," whereas the others simply sleep and slumber. It is through an attentiveness to *logos* (to thought, that is) that thinkers (and the thinkers only: here originates something like aristocracy and elitism) are able to break with everydayness and all that is ordinary, all too ordinary. This rupture, as is well known, is expressed in Heraclitus's utter contempt for all those *hoi polloi* who cannot think. "The difference within each human manifests itself as a difference between humans,"[37] between those, the philosophers, attentive to the appeal of the *logos*, the *Anspruch* of being or the cry of the absolute imperative "you must change your life," and those who evidently are not.

It is Plato who, for Sloterdijk, takes the next and decisive step in the ethical transgression. The contempt is now no longer directed and projected on the others, the *alogon*, but rather onto oneself. This is Sloterdijk's version of Derrida's primacy of the bad conscience, which I will point to later: "whoever is able to feel self-contempt has already mastered the decisive step."[38] This step, then, is what makes this transgression from the onset, that is, before it is codified and mummified in the matrix of monotheism, culpabilizing: the human being's score, qua logos, is always and already unsatisfactory—one is *never* thoughtful *enough*; one cannot attain to the level of the *idea tou agathou* properly. The one who shows no contempt for him- or herself would not even be "logical" or wise enough to even judge that one is insufficiently aware of and attentive to the uncanny creeping into one's dwelling places.

This, however, for Sloterdijk, is not Plato's only addition to the ethical transgression. The transgression toward or exercise in the uncanny—what Heidegger would deem a sort of *readiness* for the uncanny and the open—is here turned into a pedagogy. Recall, for instance, the famous allegory of the cave, where the one "enlightened" returns to the others to enlighten them as well. From that moment onward, it seems, the break with the ordinary is no longer a "free exercise" but some kind of drill disciplining the ones exercising. The "idea of restraint comes from an internalization"[39] of the transgression, which is now converted in a hierarchical tension as the difference between the (enlightened) teacher and the (sleepy) student, between the one who is advanced and the one who is still an absolute beginner. This inward transgression therefore will almost automatically appeal to the presence of a teacher or a king: here one might think of Plato's infamous philosopher-king as the one "who knows the drill" (simply, perhaps, because he or she knows *how* to drill). In any case, this "king" would be able to master the transgression from the ordinary to the extraordinary and could, in principle, lay down the codes of the rupture to show the masses just how to follow one's leader.

One could indeed exaggerate somewhat and state that Sloterdijk here shows "the birth of the matrix from the spirit of hierarchy." What originally seemed a quasi-anarchic transgression now becomes an exercise that lets "the difference between dominance and practice" evaporate.[40] For one who takes the primacy of bad conscience seriously, it is evident that all of us are only "exercising" and that all of us can be both teacher and student at once, master and servant alike; civilian in some respects but king in another; free and slave at the same time. The aim and the instruction of the anarchistic transgression could in effect be that one best exercises in such a way that one is neither master nor servant.

In Heideggerian terms, one could state that the discipline of pedagogy makes the transgression itself present-at-hand and therefore turns it into some sort of permanent presence. Techniques and drills will be constructed to obtain from the ones exercising more efficient results. This is how the difference between power and authority, between dominance and practice, or even between "power and virtue" will be forgotten.[41] The exercise, in this way, becomes an (anthropo)technics: a means to optimize the pupil with a view to total mastery over the pupil. This teleology occurs in several phases, Sloterdijk argues, but each phase aims for a mechanistic integration of the unguided projectile (one's) life can be.

In this respect, Sloterdijk speaks of "codings of the highest and the last," which can differ from culture to culture, and although one cannot find a culture without such codifications or hierarchy, such codifications have to be:

> realized in actually lived time. The things lying on top of one another in the illustration are projected onto the time axis, after which the beginner's position can be identified with the Now, the advanced position with the Later and the position of perfection with the Finally. From now on, onwards and upwards mean the same thing.[42]

The hierarchization of exercising becomes, through the insertion of *techne*, rigid and binary according to the strict logic of monovalence. There is no pupil who can be a teacher and no teacher who at times can be pupil too. Through this technological insertion of teleology in the exercise that is life, the universal and absolute imperative of life, "You must change your life," undergoes a change. It will concern very concrete and particular guidelines as to how exactly life (in general) needs to be lived. Just as there is only exercising and not "the" exercise, so there are only living beings and not "life" in general. The "ascetic or perfectionist imperative"[43] functions as some sort of sovereignty. It will tell others how life should be led without this imperative necessarily pertaining to the sovereign him- or herself. In this regard, Sloterdijk mentions "two misconstruable factors"[44] when it comes to the absolute imperative of life. In its purest form, this imperative would concern in effect only *my* life in the very act of living it as an exercise for which, in this world without a manual, one can hardly find general rules at all. The misunderstanding of "pedagogy," of the attempt of mastery over the exercise, begins already in Plato's work. For here, the philosopher is the one who is "in the know" about both the rupture with the habitual world and about the "correct" comportment toward the "fall in everydayness" (Heidegger). Such is the case because he or she

> has discovered the cave's exit. He understands what it means to have turned himself around and ventured outside. What he has achieved should not, he feels, be impossible for his fellow humans. Never is [Plato] more generous and more of a stranger to the world than when, as here, he projected his own character onto others.[45]

What is forgotten here by Plato, Sloterdijk suggests, is that that which pertains to his individual being does not necessarily pertain to the lives of others as well. The "falling upward" or "the pull toward the open," and the feel for the openness of our finite world, is now confused with a present-at-hand technique transposable from one individual to the other. Such "relinquishment of the particular in favour of the general"[46] changes the absolute imperative "You must change your life" in a double manner. First, the "change" itself is now interpreted as some sort of originary *mimesis*, where everyone does the same thing as everyone else, and over which pedagogy exerts mastery as a form of "applied mechanics"—I will teach you to be like me.[47] Secondly, the possessive pronoun is erased. The one exercising is, in and through such a sovereign pedagogy, bereft of the possibility to lead *his* or *her* life and should now lead *the* life everyone else (or "they") is leading. Hence, the "general cause" prescribes for the absolute imperative its being. The peculiarity and particularity of *my* life, then, its existential seriousness—the fact that no one can be my being in my place—is overtaken by general rules, the *mores* and the *ethos* of prevailing culture. Just *what* is forgotten in this overtaking of the singular by the general, Sloterdijk contends, is that "life,"[48] and thus the exercise concerning us all, is self-organizing and autoimmune and itself anticipates more or less resolutely the theories and pedagogies that the politics of the day imagine about this life. Namely, the "simple" fact that life is "led" before it becomes an "object of thought." This is also the reason why certain moralisms and theories can become maladjusted to and sometimes simply inappropriate for contemporary life and are threatened with "exhaustion," if not extinction, for instance when certain new forms of cohabitation in fact *already* set new standards well before theory accepts or rejects them. Theory, in fact, comes after the fact of life. Sloterdijk might align himself here once again to the phenomenological project, as the theory that is wary of all theory.

This is finally why heeding to the absolute imperative of life can count as a *liberation* and an appeal to a *fundamental modesty*. "You must change your life," on the one hand, forces one to recognize that in fact *my* life has no manual that accompanies it and that the codifications of life that have been handed down to us are not *automatically* meaningful today because, for instance, "it is tradition," "it is customary," and so forth. On the other hand, it is also the case that this lack of guidelines should prevent me from prescribing this "end-less" exercise to others (and perhaps sometimes even incite one to listen and learn from traditional practices).

Changing Codes

It is uncertain whether or not the Christian religion has a role to play in this liberation from the code or the exhaustion of the monotheist matrix. Sloterdijk indeed suggests that it does not. Sloterdijk's portrayal of postmodern times seems to assume that religion *evaporates* in the domain of markets and struggle. On the other hand, Sloterdijk still holds onto the culpabilizing tendencies of this very matrix. Sloterdijk therefore does not think the exhaustion of the matrix through to the very end. This is why I now point to the fact that Sloterdijk ignores the role Christianity played and has to play in quite a crucial case of his thought of the exercising life, namely in distinguishing between power and authority. Modernity, as the era of belief in progress, is characterized by Sloterdijk as a "deverticalization of existence."[49] Such a leveling of hierarchical distinction eases, in a certain sense, the being-in-the-outside-of-the-world. The transgression of, or the transcendence to, the openness of world now becomes a craving for the far off instead of climbing toward the highest being. In this regard, Sloterdijk is eager to point to exotic escapism of mass tourism and the, through the internet incited, "renewal for renewal's sake"—a new world is only a mouse click away. In any case, what seems to follow the theological blockade, the being-in-the-being-of-God, is simply the being "everywhere and nowhere" of modern man (and woman).

It is obvious that this causes considerable problems. Sloterdijk's criticism of Heidegger's static account of "being-in-the-world" has to be understood as a critique and portrayal of contemporary culture as well. "Falling" into the world of everydayness can indeed be such that a simple repetition of the "being-in-God" occurs, and an "outside" of this world would become impossible (just as, in the earlier days, there was no outside of God, now there might be nothing but everydayness). The Heideggerian being-in-the-world is understood by Sloterdijk as a return, an immersion or handing over of the human to its very world, causing the loss of distance with this very world and so abandoning the very possibility of transgression.[50] The catchphrase of Heidegger's "the they," in which one usually is not one's own self but more often than not unfaithful to the *eigentliche* Selbst,[51] is rephrased in mass tourism as follows: the tourist, in effect, is not only unfaithful to his or hers "ownmost" self but also serves to symbolize the "wanting-to-be-always-and-already-elsewhere." The fear of, say, treading water once no transgression from on high is to be found is simply replaced through the continual changing of places.[52]

Hence Sloterdijk's shivering for the massification of man in what he calls the "United States of Ordinariness" where "what was [once] reserved for the king, nowadays is wanted by the democracy of all and sundry."[53] It is such a leveling that plagues late capitalist culture. Capitalism, then, in effect shows itself as the *last sovereign*, by turning that which was once held in "high" esteem into but one more "product" to be sold as a mere commodity while granting no exception to the rule of the market. The bankruptcy of religion, for Sloterdijk, is due to religion's total evaporation in the spirit of capitalism (if a spirit would indeed belong to it), for religion is just as well forced into and onto the markets and their concomitant logic of supply and demand. This issues a religion tied to the straightjacket of competition, in which it has to offer its services and obtain customers better (or rather *more*)[54] than other religions do. It is important indeed to note that capitalism clothes itself in the robes of the sovereign: it monopolizes all competitiveness by allowing no competition for itself. Thus capitalism makes an exception for itself.[55]

For Sloterdijk, all of this seems to point to some sort of rupture or new axial period (Karl Jaspers). Just like Nancy, Sloterdijk is not wary of some apocalypticism. And just as in Nancy, it is, of course, *our* time that proclaims itself to be a time of rupture and the inauguration of something totally other and new. This is why, for Sloterdijk, in the time of metaphysical and theological blockades of the maximum, a conversion was strictly speaking impossible. The famous conversions of Augustine and of Paul, for instance, are nothing more than a changing of codes and drills within the matrix that left the matrix itself untouched.[56] In modern times, Sloterdijk argues, one witnesses a complete metamorphosis of what is deemed "above" and "outside" human beings. The absolute imperative of the extraordinary now appears as the global crisis, which is to be identified as a *crisis of the world*. Sloterdijk, for instance, not only mentions the financial crisis but also global warming, which, as an "overheated evolution," seems to function for him as a sort of *veritas redarguens*: a truth that forces one to act and see things in a different perspective.[57] Hence Sloterdijk's closing plea for "another cycle of secessions [. . .] in order to lead humans out once again—if not out the world, then at least out of dullness, dejection and [. . .] above all out of banality"[58] for which nothing can and must change. No exuberant and extravagant transgression is needed: you must not change your life but simply act as everyone else acts. Act, as it were, as if your maxims were to be universalized instantly. As far as the ecological crisis is concerned, we have yet to awaken from our dogmatic slumber.

Whether or not religions could play a role in the reversal of the crisis is not entirely clear. Sloterdijk writes that it is uncertain whether "monotheism is able to serve as the matrix for contemporary ethics" because of its privileging of guilt and such a culpabilization is not an appropriate affect to turn the global apocalypse around.[59] The co-immunity that *Leven* prescribes, which entails a renewed universalism in which the future of humanity and the world seems to take precedence over the fate of individuals within this world, is for Sloterdijk the only "legitimate successor" of the various monotheisms. Once again, then, it seems confirmed and certain that for Sloterdijk "the post-Christianity of our world situation is an historical fact."[60]

Conclusion: Deconstructing Christianity?

Yet one can wonder whether Sloterdijk is able to eradicate the culpabilizing character of the matrix from his appeal to a new ecological ethics. One might indeed not only be reminded of the role humanity has played in global warming and the guilt or blame it has to take for this crisis, but also understand just how Sloterdijk's plea for a new ethical transgression is accompanied by a new form of "bad conscience." Sloterdijk, as I have shown, indeed highlights self-contempt as the basic mode or mood of this transgression. Something of the sort lingers, it seems, in the exposure of the exercise of life. Does not the imperative to "keep" practicing imply that one has yet not practiced *enough*?

One could, furthermore, suspect that the very sovereignty of the crisis, as a sovereignty without a determinate sovereign, and the concomitant appeal to a "recentering" and a new "orientation"[61] of the happening of the world might have been inspired by Christianity just as well. Sloterdijk in effect seems to subscribe to what I will call the Christian "reversal of all values" in and through which the powerful appear without power and the poor turn out to be the rich. This indeed is what transpires from his critique of Nietzsche's contention that Christianity would be nothing more than "a revolt of slaves" and thus a praise of submission and servitude. Christianity, for Sloterdijk, has contributed considerably to the ethical transgression of the world, and it is unclear why this could no longer be the case. If one can grant Sloterdijk that a theology without cosmology or ecology agrees to its own disappearance and, through this "half-atheism,"[62] already seems to evaporate into the world within which being is mute, it should not be granted that Christianity has no means at all to counter the monotony of the market and the corresponding leveling of all that is. One might wonder just the same whether Christianity has not been an instigator and has not played a role *continuously* in developing those possibilities that Sloterdijk esteemed to be "the highest ever produced by humanity," namely an authority that is not solely based on raw power. Does not Sloterdijk himself state that, for instance, Matthew 19:30 "the first will be last" was involved in the renewal that the ethical transgression brought to humanity. For this passage (and others) "could be saying that the hierarchy resulting from the conditions of power and ownership should not remain the only permissible view—in fact, not even the central one—of intellectual rankings."[63] This would mean that Christianity has quite some means available when it comes to countering the crises facing the contemporary world.

A second reason why Sloterdijk's deconstruction of Christianity remains indebted to Christianity is that the transition from the "individual" fate to the fate of humanity in general, which rules over the individual exercise, seems to be Christian as well. This is a point of which Sloterdijk seems to be unaware in this nevertheless crucial stage of his enquiries. For when Sloterdijk wants to underscore the universal extension of the ethics of co-immunity, it is precisely to Matthew 10.37 that he turns: "those who love their father or mother more than me are not fit to be my disciples."[64] This means that at least a part of Christian universalism is repeated, not only by Derrida's unconditional universalism of hospitality (which overcomes both love of self and the *moral division of labor*), but also by Sloterdijk's desire for a universal humanity that overrides and can at times overrule the fate of the individual. All of this, obviously, brings the overburdening of the individual back into play, simply because the "bad conscience" has not been overcome. One might wonder, quite rightly, whether this in effect would be necessary or even desirable.

One might conclude that Sloterdijk's deconstruction of Christianity, like Nancy's, does not overcome Christianity. Just as is the case when it comes to metaphysics, we seem to have not yet recovered from our Christian past. One might wonder here whether such a recovery is in effect desirable.

Conclusion to Part 1

One may in effect not forget that these respective "deconstructions of Christianity" are a criticism of the end of metaphysics as well. This part will hopefully have shown that the "exhaustion of metaphysics" has entered a critical phase. With regards to metaphysics too, the exhaustion has reached the first signification Sloterdijk mentioned: all possibilities for metaphysics seem exhausted.

One can call out for a complete inversion of all values (Nietzsche). One might counteract and state that such an inversion remains stuck in what it wants to invert (Heidegger). One might just as well say that the critic of metaphysics still clings to this very metaphysics and thus figures as "the last metaphysician," unable to think without nostalgia (Derrida's Heidegger). One might enter into this auction by an even higher offer and attempt to speak of the end of metaphysics from out of an "entirely different terrain" (Derrida).[1] One might even remain indifferent to this auction itself and state that this struggle is of no concern because one claims to have found an even "better" metaphysics (Milbank) or a total "anti-metaphysics" (Caputo). Or one might even let metaphysics be, in a curious case of *Gelassenheit*, and leave it to its auto-deconstruction (Nancy) and aim for what is to come (Sloterdijk and Caputo).

With these positions in effect, all the possibilities of (the end of) metaphysics are overseen and in a certain sense already actualized, unless one yields, again, to the second signification of the intended (or not) exhaustion. Here the limitations and uselessness of metaphysics come in sight, and the metaphysical attempt as such is deemed unusable in its effort to comprehend, found, or otherwise understand this world of ours. This means that the novelty—better, if we are to avoid apocalypses: peculiarity—of our context and situation is to be taken seriously. And, if we are to avoid illusions of overcomings at all, the deconstruction of Christianity and metaphysics "to come" has to take into account both the eternal return of a certain metaphysics and that which, *amid* a culture that is marked and stamped by metaphysics and Christianity, might forge positions and postures "beyond" outworn metaphysics. If the adjustments to metaphysics (for example, the positive evaluation of embodiment) do not suffice to remedy the problem that metaphysics poses (for instance, its aversion for all things bodily) to such an extent that metaphysics seems maladapted to and even *unzeitgemässig* for contemporary times, then the time has come to comport oneself properly to the remains of metaphysics and of a certain strand of Christianity as well. This is what Heidegger had in mind when stating, decades ago, that metaphysics "will not remain a choice."[2] It is acknowledged, or can be acknowledged, that still we cannot think non-metaphysically, nor do we already live in a non-Christian culture.

In this part, I have shown that metaphysics and ontotheology return in various ways. Nancy's "eclipse of essence," pretending to do away with metaphysics and ontotheology in one stroke, has as a remarkable presupposition that it can take the entire (metaphysical) tradition in view, condemn it, and then put it aside. All of a sudden this apocalypticism, which also surfaced in Sloterdijk's thought of the contemporary world, seems able to oversee the entirety of the tradition, which is a very metaphysical move indeed. In Schürmann's thinking, something similar occurred when he insisted that past presencing (of being and beings) is mute and in his willingness to dismiss all things ontic when it comes to considering the event of world: as if the world and everydayness are not thoughtworthy in themselves or, at least, do not add to philosophical thinking. It is as if Derrida's warning that all deconstructions of Christianity are condemned to repeat Christianity is true for metaphysics and ontotheology as well: all supposed "overcoming" of ontotheology is destined to repeat it.

Yet on this question of metaphysics some results need to be taken into account as well. Schürmann's concept of the "natural metaphysician" allowed us to see the question concerning ontotheology as an ontological problem rather than as something that happens to this or that thinker in the tradition. This concept will therefore play a role in the second part as well, especially when I play out Derrida against Caputo and imagine the former as a "natural metaphysician." I have also considered ontotheology's inevitability as political problem: there is not one ideology, for instance, that has no highest being. The problem of ontotheology is, again, not that it uses the word and concept "God"; it is that it thinks so highly of reason that it allows reason and logos to completely determine what is real and what is not. This is where Heidegger's critique of science and technology starts. Anything, in fact, can be a highest being. Derrida's and Sloterdijk's quest for a sovereignty without sovereign or an authority without power stems in fact from the realization that the medieval and modern monarch echoed theology's highest being: the "theological" heritage of this idea of sovereignty lies precisely in the fact that the sovereign *can* make an exception of him- or herself, like the Uncaused cause of medieval metaphysics is not caused by itself or Aristotle's Unmoved Mover moves everything all the while remaining unmoved by what it so moves. Yet it is not to be excluded that this political strand of the problem of metaphysics might be to theology's benefit: this is why in the second part I consider, with Caputo, the Christian idea of a reversal of values and Jesus of Nazareth as a sacred anarchist who knew of and embodied even an authority without power.

On the philosophical import of ontotheology, its extension, and its limits, one might argue that our findings confirm Heidegger. Heidegger seems to have foreseen that metaphysics is not only not a choice of ours—it happens "unbeknownst to oneself"—but also that it happens always and everywhere. Here is the passage of Heidegger that has given us to think a bit more than others and in which one receives a phenomenological "Wink" as to the "how" of ontotheology:

> if God [. . .] has disappeared from his authoritative position in the suprasensory world, then *this authoritative place itself is still always preserved*, even though as that which has become empty [. . .]. What is more, the empty place *demands to be occupied anew*."[3]

It is here too that one can surmise why ontotheology, for us natural metaphysicians, is not to be avoided: thinking "without" ontotheology is impossible because the position of a highest being is always occupied by one or the other instance, whether it is God (in a certain theology), money (in contemporary capitalism), or the very idea of certainty (which occupied modern philosophy and later science). On this very point, it seems in effect quite reasonable to follow Heidegger and try not to dream too prematurely about a postmetaphysical era, if at all. For Heidegger indeed, the foundation was indeed an "illusion" but, on the other hand, a "perhaps necessary" one at that.[4]

Apart from such politics, this interpretation of ontotheology also hints at a more existential version of ontotheology: the very "want of a hold" on being and beings (Schürmann), the "tranquillization" that is everydayness (Heidegger) cannot and will not be eradicated. Perhaps these ontotheological strategies and compulsions have made it into the philosophical and theological tradition because it is first an ontic and existential issue.

On the other hand, for those who want to avoid metaphysical stifling and coagulations (of one aspect of being, one region of the tradition rather than others) as much as possible, this part might have brought about some indications as well. If we are to avoid such fanaticism, then one pathway might be not to dismiss the philosophical and theological tradition entirely, as Nancy, Schürmann, and Sloterdijk are wont to do, but rather to aim for the long detour *through* the tradition where, here and there, some less metaphysical thinking might be encountered: even if ontotheology and the concomitant "natural metaphysics" happen always and everywhere, it is perhaps still not sure whether it happens all the time. At least we need to realize that our "postmetaphysical" period can only benefit from thorough and patient readings of the "metaphysical" tradition.

If the postmetaphyiscal era, then, is in need of an evolution rather than a revolution, then this has consequences for deconstructing Christianity and, more broadly, for the secular phenomenology of religious life as well. Just as one cannot rid oneself of metaphysics, so too one does not abandon Christianity that easily. I have shown that Sloterdijk too, as if unbeknownst to himself, repeats essential traits of the Christian tradition. Another problem with Nancy's and Sloterdijk's "reduction" of religion is not that it rejects religion—after all, one can hardly object to someone claiming to do away with religion that he does away with religion—but consists rather of the procedure with which religion is rejected here.

Just like Nancy's auto-deconstruction, Sloterdijk's deconstruction of religion and metaphysics quickly become reduction*ist* and totalitarian even. There is nothing outside the unifying principle of auto-deconstruction—*everything* auto-deconstructs—and the explicitation of the exercise that is life—*all* we do is but exercise. Like Nancy's attempt to create the world ex nihilo, so too does Sloterdijk seem to be in need of a rupture between the old matrix of monotheism and the completely "new" exercises in religion. A rupture that, of course, takes the contours of an apocalypse and crisis that we now can only "see through a glass, darkly." The problem with this is that this "new ontological knowledge" would exclude all previous knowledge as worn-out, outdated, and exhausted and so absolutely hail the advent of this "new" knowledge at the expense of all other bases of knowledge (whether this would be the tradition or other branches of science matters little). This, however, is exactly what Sloterdijk reproaches religion for. In other words, the ontobiological reduction is as reductionist as the revealed religion Sloterdijk is claiming to replace because it, too, would leave no room for new and other knowledge!

Rather than insisting on such ruptures and on the utter "legitimacy" of modernity or postmodernity, it seems more reasonable to mediate between the "old" monotheism and the new religions of consumption and athletics. Even if this era of ours is "legitimate" to such an extent that its questions can find no direct answers in the past traditions, it is not to be excluded that, at least for a little while, the answers we come up with to face the current crises (the indifference to the other, the world, and to the transcendent to name but the most important) will, at least in the West, be stamped and marked by the Christian philosophical and theological tradition.

Part 2

Between

5

In Defense of Deconstruction

John D. Caputo and his Critics

John D. Caputo, too, has been involved in deconstructing Christianity. Unlike Nancy, however, Caputo's attempt is not to retrieve from Christianity something more ancient than Christianity—its fatal agent (as Schürmann would have it) or its auto-immune heart (as Nancy would have it—but rather to "repeat Christianity" in order "to expose it to its future."[1] Such a *Wiederholung*, then, would be the attempt "to expose what is going on in Christianity to the event by which it is nourished" in order that "a Christianity to come" might be "released."[2] What Caputo shares with Nancy through Derrida, then, is that the truth of Christianity does not lie within Christianity. Christianity, for Caputo, is but a name for a historical set of beliefs that is always but a historical construction (and therefore subject to change and to deconstruction). Christianity is immersed in the deconstructive play of the traces, where what we are trying to name can only ever be named inappropriately. Yet the very act of naming or, in this case, being a Christian, is from the outset "exposed" and "nourished" by an event that keeps the very act of naming going. What lies outside the "system of Christianity," for Caputo, is not, as it is in Nancy, the mute matter of spacing that lies at the origin of sense but rather a vitalistic force that rages through or haunts being and beings from beyond being. It is this "weak force," for Caputo, that directs us and our systems toward the future or what is "to come."

One can hardly accuse Caputo of the same grand apocalyptical tone that I have found in Nancy, although for Caputo, too, it is no less urgent to think nonmetaphysically. Yet some of the criticisms I have advanced against Nancy can be directed toward Caputo as well, namely the deconstruction of the distinction of faith and belief to such a point even that a faith "without" belief (and a fortiori a "religion without religion") is simply, phenomenologically, impossible. The question of the "with" therefore resurfaces in this chapter more poignantly than ever.

This chapter also addresses the question of the scope of a concept like auto-deconstruction—which is a problem for Nancy too. The problem is as simple as it is disturbing: if this method of auto-deconstruction is to be both valid for the entirety of the Western history and applicable even to one's own personal life,[3] then the question needs to be posed of just how far this auto-deconstruction extends. The problem is well known: if the method is universal—applicable to all beings—then it borders on becoming a totalizing one, for such a unified method risks, by making no exception between beings (or texts), both to extend its auto-deconstructive move to that which cannot be deconstructed and to interpret that which is not (yet) deconstructed as auto-deconstructive. In both cases, the method of auto-deconstruction turns out to be "destructive": in the first case it would be overly revolutionary: it would relentlessly deconstruct no matter what—and in the latter case it would be overly conservative—it would stop deconstructing simply because "things are autodeconstructing"[4] anyway.

Auto-immunity, aporias, and auto-deconstruction are all around. This is apparent from Caputo's (a bit frivolous) notion of a "Christianity to come." First, it seems to turn Christianity into one of the unconditionals Derrida had already mentioned, such as hospitality and justice. Derrida has never, to my mind, granted as much, although we owe him the question and exclamation marks around the very theme itself: "Christianity's indeconstructible? What a scene!"[5] Let us, secondly, imagine this scene then and expose its aporetic structure. An unconditional Christianity to come would be nowhere else than in the diverse empirical Christianities that one comes across here and there. Yet these diverse empirical forms of Christianity never incarnate (?) or instantiate the idea of Christianity properly, that is, essentially or once and for all. If Christianity is as aporetic as, say, hospitality, then one can never have (the idea of) Christianity without the (empirical) Christianities as little as one ever grasp the idea of Christianity from out of just one empirical Christianity.

Caputo does not configure the idea of a Christianity to come in just this way. However, the totalizing, if not paralyzing, aspects of this aporetic structure flow quite naturally from his account of "the how of deconstruction." Deconstruction, Caputo argues, is a *modus* irrealis:[6] it merely turns "nouns" into an "infinitive"[7] and so exposes the named thing to the event that is going on in these things. This is how it is exposed to its future and how a promise of sorts inhabits deconstruction. Let us take "democracy" as an example. The idea of democracy is unconditional. Yet democracy only ever happens in very conditional and institutional democracies. But these democracies breathe somehow a promise of a democracy to come, a democracy that would be, say, less unequal to the point that existent democracies are always and already haunted by a democracy to come that would force them to turn their institutions "more" democratic or at least less undemocratic. It is, if you like, a force forcing us gently (perhaps all too gently) to a "never finished production of an idea to come."[8]

Is this all that deconstruction can do? And would it not risk, ultimately, not producing anything at all, precisely in the name of what is to come? Would it not risk, because of the totalizing nature of such a conceptuality, both legitimizing the revolutionaries eager to overthrow the system in the name of an even better democracy that is on its way and supporting the tyrant who effaces the 'to come' by explaining that his (or her) democracy here is not all that bad, perhaps even the least bad given this and that situation? The point, however, is not only a political one but rather philosophical: if everything is auto-deconstructive, then, well, nothing is auto-deconstructive, and one can erect aporias pretty much everywhere—what noun is there that could not be put in an infinitive form and could resist such a (Levinasian) *infinition*?[9]

Yet if Christianity is a witness to its own deconstruction, then Caputo might have found a means to respond to some of his critics. One recalls from Chapter 2 that Derrida's "*s'il y en a*" employs a conditional: because, whenever and if there is such a thing as hospitality, that is, because there are *different* empirical hospitalities, it is always possible to come to an idea of a hospitality to come (even though there is no such thing as "hospitality": Derrida is integrating Nancy's thought here). Now imagine that something similar happened to Christianity in Caputo's thought: because, whenever and if there are these very *different* Christianities, it is always possible to arrive at a Christianity to come (even though there is no "essence of Christianity"). The point is that *here* a passageway could be found *from out of* the different Christianities *toward* something like a "Christianity without Christianity" or "religion without religion" even. Such a passageway, however, requires one to make sense, pass through, "reduce" even the different traditions to arrive at a Christianity to come (or one that still can be meaningful): it is, in short, to take "religion *with* religion" seriously if one is to come to a religion to come.

The idea is surely not absent from Caputo's work. My suggestion, however, is that for the most part Caputo wants to do away with "the with" and that this is phenomenologically, philosophically, and perhaps even theologically impossible: the "with" haunts the "without" more than does the "without" the "with." The question of the "with" is then insufficiently taken into account. One should recall, in effect, that this question of "the with," the question of the effectivity of the "hegemonic fantasm" (Schürmann), could be addressed to both Hägglund and Caputo—*bien étonnés de se trouver ensemble.*

How (Not) to Do Away With "The With"?

Faith versus Belief Revisited

The first of these remarks concerning "the with" pertains again to the relation between faith and belief, which is no less present in Caputo's work than it is in Nancy's, although the former gives it a more theological spin. Religion without religion would be a faith that can do (almost) without belief or at least one that assents to beliefs minimally, that is, only insofar as they occasion or allow for a passageway to faith. These empirical and local beliefs, for instance that Jesus is the Son of God, would then serve as an empirical prolegomenon to the ontological faith in the event, as a faith in that which "is going on in" these beliefs or that which these beliefs are, all illusions aside, "really about." It is, however, with this distinction especially that one senses that Caputo's is not the long road of a deconstructive reopening and repetition of Christianity, but rather a sort of shortcut through the tradition of Christianity: a passing through Christianity only to pass over certain strands of Christianity and to hark back to a rather pure "origin" of this faith not yet tainted by anything Greek.

Caputo will in effect argue that there is an analogy between the precritical thought of the Middle Ages and postcritical postmodernity: it is not that we all of a sudden have relapsed in an age of obscurity (although some might like to see postmodernity in this way) in which faith is accorded a more primordial role than reason; it is rather that the postsecular account of deconstruction now notes that faith is not entirely bereft of reason just as reason does not seem to be entirely exempt of belief. In this way, deconstruction is held between premodern and modern thought: it opts for neither blind faith without reason nor for a pure reason without faith but rather for a faith in and of rationality. The era of the end of metaphysics, which is ours, echoes in Caputo's mind the biblical and apologetical times in which the faithful search for the divine was not yet corrupted and contaminated with the *logos* of Greek metaphysics.[10] "Uncontaminated"? I will question whether Caputo is able to avoid what one can call one of the peculiarities of modern thought, the mysophobia showing itself in the search for pure reason and pure consciousness, when calling for a "pure" messianism.

Be that as it may, a certain analogy between postmodernity, which no longer believes in an ultimate signifier or grand story accompanying life from the cradle to the grave, and the ancient world, which did not yet have such a systematized story at its disposal, may in fact be present. The quest for certainty, permanence, and immutability perhaps had not yet begun. One may, on the other hand, very well wonder what precisely is gained by such an analogy: it might simply be the case that such an interpretation of the end of metaphysics only succeeds in starting the metaphysical game all over again: nothing is more certain, in fact, than a human being trying to do away with, or at least sedating, uncertainty.

The analogy gains force, however, when Caputo proceeds to clarify his notion of "desecularization" by turning to Nietzsche. Something strange has happened, Caputo writes, on the way to God's funeral: "Enlightenment secularism *also* got crucified on the same Cross, and that spelled the death of the death of God."[11] The appeal to neutrality and rationality is itself turned into fiction. This, for Caputo, does not have to mean that we have arrived at the dictatorship of relativism or of conservatism even. On the contrary, this enlightenment of the Enlightenment should lead to a "a heightened sense of the contingency and revisability of our constructions, not the jettisoning of reason but a redescription of reason, one that is a lot more reasonable than [the] overarching, transhistorical Rationality that the Enlightenment tried to sell us."[12]

Caputo argues that, once the idea of a neutral and "objective" rationality is abandoned, one has arrived at a new form of reasonableness that cannot except itself from a sort of fundamental modesty. On the contrary, once the metaphysical dream of a complete grasp of reality, of an adequate and transparent knowledge of the things surrounding us, has been expelled, another facet of reasonableness still remains and now shows itself in and as the "historically contingent 'take' we have on things—which makes it look a lot more like 'faith'": a sort of belief or basic trust that the take on reality we have at the moment really has a grip on or a firm footing in that very reality.[13] All of a sudden then, for Caputo at least, "the still small voice of religion could once again be heard."[14] The criticism of religion's despisers initiated in this way a new conception of religion, of reason, and of religion's reasonableness.

This analogy between premodernity and postmodernity—the fact, if you will, that one cannot exist without (some form of) faith—of course does not mean that the accomplishments of the Enlightenment—"freedom! or the grave" can be read on the first engravings of human rights—should now be abandoned as well. The Enlightenment, for Caputo, rather has to be seen as a necessary correction to the competing claims of "blind" faith and "pure" reason, for just as in postmodernity there seems to be no such thing as reason without faith, the other way around works just as well: there might be no faith without (some form of) reason. This, then, is the Enlightenment: a necessary injection of reason and understanding in the body of faith, an extension, if you will, from Kant's "*sapere aude*" to "*sapere aude fidum.*"[15]

But how? For this, Caputo turns to Heidegger, one of the first thinkers to point to the historical character of the supposedly "pure" reason. Being-in-the-world, for Heidegger, is a complex interweaving of always and already comprehending the beings-within-the-world—are there others?—and of the moods (or *Befindlichkeit*) that accompany this pre-comprehension and pre-understanding of these beings. Such affectivity shows the revelatory and "reflective" role of moods. It is my mood that tells me what the world looks like: if I am bored, the world will indeed appear as boring; to heartfelt joy, the world will appear as the source of all things joyful and a "good, indeed very good" place, and so forth. The point, for Heidegger as well as Caputo, is that being-in-the-world already testifies to a certain reasonableness (well before the scientific understanding even arises), for such a being-attuned-to beings never occurs ex nihilo but is established through an understanding (of being and beings) that grants these entities (and ourselves) a certain kind of stability and permanence—this is why fallenness to the world, for Heidegger, is never far away.

This "understanding of being/s" thus can count on a certain pre-understanding: it conveys the fact, so to say, that one is not surprised each time one sees a table (even if this table here is seen for the first time). This has also been called "the hermeneutical 'as,' the 'interpretative' fore-structure" by which we take this table *as* a table. It is these structures that shape how I perceive my world; it familiarizes my perceptions and my understandings every time I encounter a new but relatable object or environment. It turns the "face of the earth" into a familiar *milieu*. Perception, then, does not start from scratch: I am not frightened when I see a table even if for the first time, but am *used to* and rather *familiar* with seeing tables as tables. With all this, Heidegger wanted to point out a certain familiarity with the world, for each "seeing" is always and already a "seeing (this) as (that)," an anticipation of these beings-within-the-world that are, precisely through this anticipation, always and already familiar when one comes upon them.

For Caputo, then, this "hermeneutical seeing as" blurs the traditional distinction between faith and reason: whereas the latter was to be defined as a "clear and distinct" way of seeing and of knowing, or even as a "*lumen naturale*" that, with a little help from God, succeeded in the correspondence between thought ("*intellectus*") and being ("*res*"), the first was dismissed as a blind belief in that which "the eyes cannot see." Caputo writes: " 'Seeing as' weakens the idea of 'pure seeing' defended in the camp of reason and strengthens the idea of 'seeing in part' defended in the camp of faith."[16] For "seeing as," as such, is a precarious and sometimes perilous endeavor: my pre-understanding indeed can be mistaken, and what I thought was a table ended up being a designer table that forces me to revise my entire idea (and pre-understanding) of what a table actually is!

Suddenly the idea of a pure reason, bereft of any faith, somewhat seems like an illusion. The pre-understanding conditioning the scientific endeavor, for instance, for which water can be reduced to H_2O is valid *as long as* the scientific attitude can be maintained, namely *just* as long as the scientist is in his or her laboratory but no more once he or she notices that the water he or she is drinking never is H_2O. Furthermore, one must consider that the very objects that the scientific attitude can take into account as valid for scientific description change over time: science evolves in a somewhat "epochal" manner in which one paradigm can hardly communicate with the other, and its pre-understanding (prescribing and determining what counts as a "scientific" object) cannot extricate itself from the finite and limited conditions of knowledge entirely. Caputo therefore concludes: "we are ready to recall [such a rational, scientific understanding] as soon as it outlives its usefulness and our faith in it [in one or the other paradigm, for instance, JS] is shaken. So *seeing* is starting to look something like believing."[17]

This deconstruction of the distinction between faith and reason alters the conception of faith as well. For, if reason is not entirely bereft of a certain faith, then faith too is not to be seen as exempt of all reason, as lacking all rationality and reasonableness. Quite to the contrary: it is reasonable to believe something like faith is always and already in play. Faith, for Caputo at least, can no longer be conceived in the classical sense, namely as a blindness of sorts and a trust into things the eye cannot see. It is quite reasonable to state that without faith, nothing would be seen at all. It takes faith, then, to see the scientific object as an object, just as it requires some kind of trust that being-in-the-world will display a sort of stability and permanence (even only of "everydayness") from one day to the next: one must, to hint at Husserl, have faith that the earth will not move tomorrow. This is why Caputo writes: "To believe is to take something 'as' [like the scientist trusts that, given the right circumstances in the laboratory, he or she will be able to 'see' water 'as' pure H$_2$O, JS] and to proceed with some confidence in our perspective, in order that we may see and understand. So believing is starting to look a lot like seeing."[18]

This is what constitutes the complexity of postmodernity: all of a sudden rationality itself is not exempt from hopes, beliefs, trusts (whether or not misplaced). All of a sudden reason relies on presuppositions that are not, for that matter, always "conscious" and self-evident, and it becomes important to approach beings, objects, words, and things with the "right" presuppositions and pre-understanding if we are to learn to see and to understand them, to see and understand, for instance, that the world is boring *only* when bored, a source of joy when joyful, and so forth.

All of this allows Caputo to conclude that a revision is needed when it comes to the border zones between philosophy and theology and between faith and reason. This relation is now to be regarded as a relation between "two kinds of faith [. . .] two kinds of seeing-as"[19] where philosophy delineates the basic structures of a reasonable pre-understanding of what it is to be in-the-world and theological faith grafts itself onto this very same structure and, although "seeing" it in more a confessional manner, nothing human is alien to this type of faith: it is not *per se* an alienating belief in something illusory.

From "Is" to "Ought" (and Back Again)

With this, one is of course returned to the question of presuppositions—of the philosophical import (or not) of something like postsecularism or the "apathetic pluralism" where nothing is left but *faith-based* rationalities. For, however tempting Caputo's description and deconstruction of the relation between faith and reason may be, it is not without its problems. Caputo, for instance, does mention that his position would in effect need to concern itself with the question of the "right" presuppositions but never seems to supply any criteria—rational ones, I would add—with which one would be able to differentiate and distinguish between the different forms these presuppositions and these faiths can take. In this regard, Caputo is closer to the "resigned pluralism" one can detect in the defenders of a postsecularist stance, which is hard to distinguish from the nihilism and the relativism plaguing our times, in which "you believe what you want" and every person has presuppositions that are, a priori, as valuable as the opinion of everyone else and valid notwithstanding the knowledge this or that person has (or has not) from the thing or being at issue. (Think of Twitter here.) This pluralism resigns from rational debate simply because it does not amount to much more than saying that it is good that there are many presuppositions and many faiths. It does not offer any help when one of these faiths shows itself to be *worse* than another. Again: one must be willing to consider that Christianity, too, can cause or at least cooperate in the dictatorship of relativism of which it accuses other parties so easily.

This leads to a second, even more grave problem. Not only does Caputo not tell us how to distinguish between valid, less valid, and invalid presuppositions—creationism might just as well be a "way of seeing" things: this follows from the fact that this faith is *just as good* as any other—but this thought "from out of one's presuppositions" never really addresses how it comes about (and, more importantly, how we could avoid) that the "equivalidity" of these faiths always and already seems to lead to the tendency to regard one set of presuppositions as *better* than any other set. It goes without saying that the presuppositions so proclaimed to be better (better in the sense of preferred) are often, all too often, one's own presuppositions rather than the faith or the presuppositions of the other. Phenomenologically speaking, it would therefore be better (better in the sense of more rational) to stick to the "thing" at hand and, instead of hoping and dreaming of a world of "universal justice and hospitality," to realize that what remains once this question of presuppositions has run its course are nothing but stories, interpretations, and faiths *each of which* displays the tendency to prefer its own presuppositions rather than those of the other. "Rational" means here: always, everywhere, and by everyone. If one were to reduce phenomenologically this conflict of presuppositions, one would in effect not see any justice but, in each case, the never-ending nature of the conflict that *has no reason* to jump to the conclusion of a universal justice and hospitality. This signifies, just as well, that the end of metaphysics (in which one's own narrative is exemplary for all other narratives—even when seen *as* narratives of the Other) might not yet be attained by the weak religion that Caputo proposes and, I would venture, presupposes. It might be things like this that incite "the younger generation to [. . .] become impatient with Derrida and all the *soixante-huitaires*" and invite Hägglund to strip all these conditionals and beliefs of whatever there is "to come."[20]

Yet even on philosophical and phenomenological grounds this mixture of faith and reason seems somewhat untenable. Let us have a look at the example of water again: for someone to be able to really attest that this thing here, in the laboratory, under the right conditions, is in effect H_2O, he or she would need to compare the constitution of such an ideality with other instances of H_2O, for instance, with plain, not so purely constituted, water. The "invention" of H_2O, then, would be *dependent* on the possibility of comparison—repetition and iteration Derrida would say—with "impure water," somewhat like the omnitemporality of geometry is dependent on the empirical condition of possibility of someone, in some empirical space and time, Galileo for instance, stumbling upon the idealities of geometry.[21] In a quasi-transcendental phenomenology, even the act of constitution is constituted. Yet, and this is the "quasi-transcendental dizziness"[22] I will show Derrida advances, it will never become clear, nor distinct for that matter, just how (much) this empiricism penetrates the very idea of ideality. Another aporia if you like: one cannot decide whether "plain water" is prior to H_2O or whether H_2O lies prior to water. So much for Derrida.

What Caputo wants us to believe, however, is that in one way or another one can do away with the "quasi." At his most empirical, Caputo would say that this mixture between faith and reason, between water and H_2O, between conditional presuppositions and the unconditional "to come" is *really* all there is, one will have to work with all these "withs" simply because this *is* all there is to work with. Yet, as with every empiricism, there seems to be a naturalistic fallacy here: it is not because something is the case that it ought to be the case. Hence the need for comparison, negotiating, mediating, etc. between the different beliefs. Yet, at this point, Caputo is at his most transcendental: for such a comparison, one would need a vantage-point of sorts, a truth of the system not contained by the system: one would need to hark back "beyond" the tradition, "beyond" all these different beliefs to an originary faith not yet tainted by these particular beliefs, to a Christianity, for instance, that would not be wounded by Philo Judaeus's Greek. In short: one would need to bracket and reduce the *entire* tradition and its beliefs in order to come to this pure faith and so forget about the need to mediate and negotiate between beliefs. But my question of the "with," of a quasi-transcendental *Verflechtung*[23] of this faith and the different beliefs, would argue that one cannot have it both ways. From such slumber and such dizziness, there might be no awakening.

Religion without Religion versus Religion with Religion

Contra Apologia

"Nobody trusts theology," and rightly so. This is one of the catchphrases of Caputo's proposal of a religion without religion.[24] Nobody trusts theology, first of all, because theology all too easily shifts towards ontotheology and places God (or a similar referent) up on high, "up there," and then congratulates itself with this complacent ability to place God in the exact space where it wanted![25] Such a theology is, in effect, a sovereign in all the political meanings that can be attached to the word: sovereign is he or she who is able to distribute the monopoly on power and violence in such a way that he or she is able to control both the public realm (where nonviolence is the rule) and that which can legitimately, and if necessary violently, disturb the peaceful public order (the nation-state, the king, or anyone else with the power vested in him or her to speak "in the name of God"). Sovereign, therefore, is he or she who can make an exception to the state of nonviolence characteristic of the public order and who can enforce this nonviolence with violent means if he or she should so choose.

This is the infamous "*state of exception*" of political theology so popular even in mainstream continental philosophy today: the state is sovereign because it can monopolize both the rule—the nonviolence of the public order—and the exception to the rule—"waging war" is a legitimate exception to nonviolence because its goal would ultimately be to maintain nonviolence. In theology, this would run somewhat like this: the God looking upon us from "above" holds a monopoly both over that which is "uncaused" (Aquinas already said: only God knows God) and over that which is "caused," created and thus contingent. This is why one can think that in a traditional metaphysical worldview the human being would be like a puppet on a divine string: God as "the director of the world" could for instance declare a state of exception over the finite world and decide, negatively, to leave the finite to the finite and so return it to nothing but "dust and ashes" or, positively, to intervene temporarily in the finite, contingent course of things to change its course precisely—the infamous "contradiction" (of experience, of the laws of nature) of the miracle might be elucidated along these lines. In both cases, however, the unchangeable and transcendent God makes an exception of Godself: this God remains, in effect, unrelated to the sublunary world which, in turn, cannot *but* relate to all that is outside of itself and thus change and alter permanently and constantly.

Why does no one trust theology? Because theology—at least in a culture that is still sufficiently Christian for theology to be able to have a hold over what can be proclaimed to be the "highest being" (and what not)—holds a monopoly, violently if necessary, over both that which can be considered as the truth as well as what can be considered the untruth. This is why such a theology is sovereign: it is able to discern and to dictate "What is truth?" and, in the very same movement, able to delineate what *cannot* be true. It is against such a theology, a theology concerned only about beings that are the highest that Caputo protests. "Nowadays," Caputo writes, such "strong theologies" are to be found in the works of Milbank and Marion.[26] Of particular note, is Caputo's growing mischief with Marion's thinking whose configuring of the idea of God as the "impossibility of impossibility"—from *The Erotic Phenomenon* onward—for Caputo seems to border on the classical doctrine of omnipotence.[27] Marion's "God without Being," then, would be an attempt to do away with the historical play of differences, an erecting a strong God as the "infinite center independent of the play of traces."[28] I will later come back to this claim (Marion, for instance, never uses the word omnipotence), but for now it is important to note Caputo's rather harsh remarks when it comes to this "new apologetical phenomenology": all these apologetics would be a "strictly local discourse driven by the same local confessional interests," "a fodder [. . .] purely for local consumption; it is strictly a phenomenology for Catholic campfires."[29] Apologetics, then, is a strategic abridging of deconstruction: On this

> Kantian model, postmodernism is an epistemology that limits knowledge to make possible a faith in metaphysical realities [. . .] Everyone crowds under the umbrella of "overcoming ontotheology." But for them that is a highly circumscribed expression limited to getting past "objectifying thinking," say a rationalist proof for the existence of God, so that it remains safe to retain faith without proof in the classical metaphysical theology.[30]

It is true that the strong theologians Milbank and Marion (and Westphal to whom Caputo is referring here) have a way of delimiting metaphysics and ontotheology to a strictly modern phenomenon in order to safeguard, precisely, the theologies of Augustine and Neo-Platonism. "After" ontotheology, then, these theologians can go on with their business as if nothing has happened. They reason that if no one is really able to disprove the existence of some sort of highest being, nothing prevents them from believing in it anyway. Caputo brilliantly exposes the flawed *argumentum ad ignorantium* at work here turning "thought" and "deconstruction" into a "deconstruction *light*" as it were: since you cannot prove that there is no highest being up there, I am free just the same to believe in such a being.

Caputo attempts to configure a weak theology in line with the event (of the world, of being or of being-in-the-world), an event that transpires in and is testified to in the different historical forms all these strong theologies have taken. This theology, for Caputo, remains indifferent toward the question whether or not there were would be a highest being somewhere outside space and time, and whether this being would be "accessible" through faith or through reason, but does attempt to show that whatever theory that is constructed about such a highest being is a construction in space and time and therefore *as contingent as* anything else in this world, so that no discourse, neither "Christian faith" nor, perhaps, religion without religion is safely sheltered from "the postmodern critique of metaphysics."[31]

One might want to call such an event, with Heidegger, *Ereignis* (as the event of world and being) and point to the fact that, despite all efforts to turn this world itself in a manageable "product," the event of the world, itself, eludes all attempts at manageability and production. I might well be able to decide autonomously that I will show up for this meeting at that particular time and that particular place, the very fact itself of my being able to move about in this world is not one of my own making nor one, for that matter, of my accord. All "immanent" autonomy, then, takes place within the "transcendent"—transcendental, rather—heteronomy of the world. The event of world, then, eludes the last of the utopian projects, namely the one of a global and total *Machenschaft* and can be defined as "that which cannot be made and is not of our own making," that is: being, time and world. For this event, it seems fitting (at times) to introduce the concept of the "ahistorical" again, for if all beings and events happen within time it might very well be that the event itself, while granting time, is extratemporal. One might, according to Caputo, liken the event just as well to Levinas' vision of an "otherwise than being," for this otherwise than being is that which disrupts and disturbs "being" (and its tendency to systematize, thematize, and totalize) and continually opens being towards its other. "Otherwise than being," then, arises out of being—borders on being being itself[32]—to displace the egocentric orientation of all beings but cannot itself be reduced to (a) being. Otherwise than being is that which flees from concepts and that which, in this flight, remains foreign to the will to power dominating being and beings. One might also wonder whether this event of world is not close, very close to what Derrida would call "the indeconstructible," for if all beings, events, and texts can be deconstructed, it might very well be that the event of world borders on being precisely that which eludes deconstruction. The event of this world, in this way, names a transcendental instance amidst all immanent, historical and finite constructions (contingent theologies, systems of Absolute Knowing that turned out to be not so absolute, etc.) that, itself, cannot be reduced to just such a finite construction. This appeal is transcendent to the extent that it exceeds (by conditioning) all finite experiences and historical constructions. It does appeal to us to deconstruct or otherwise critique all that is and especially that which thinks itself to be a "necessary" construction, tradition or invention, but this appeal itself cannot be deconstructed. The appeal therefore is closer to the modern idea of the "transcendental" than to the idea of the Transcendent, if only because it opens empirical, finite experience to that which conditions it as to its very possibility: the appeal to deconstruct all constructions is possible because these constructions only arise out a finite passing of time and of experiences and thus out of the finite character of all experience. Yet the "indeconstructible" appeal only ever is a "quasi-transcendental": it is not the transcendentality that is separated neatly from all empiricism; it is not "elsewhere" than or separated from the world, like Kant's noumena.[33] The indeconstructible appeal can only be read *in*(to) empirical constructions although it cannot be reduced to just such a construction.

Martin Hägglund's Radical Atheism: "infinite finitude" versus "finite infinity"

It is here that Hägglund and Caputo disagree and what separates Hägglund's (and also Nancy's) "infinite finitude" of being is the fact both that, for the latter, deconstruction itself is endless and limitless and can be applied to all beings and that finitude taints and constitutes all of these beings, from the highest to the lowest, without the possibility of ever leaping from these endless deconstructions of deconstructions of. . . to an instance that would unconditionally elude such deconstruction, whereas Caputo's "finite infinity" leaps precisely to such an instance or at least tries to inhabit the not-yet of the to-come. In short, for Hägglund, the spirit (if I may call it that) of deconstruction is such that its one and only aspiration is to show that every empirical and historical construction *can* be deconstructed and that the "overarching aim" of deconstruction *is* to show that all constructions *can* be reduced to just that, a contingent construction. To this, Caputo opposes, quite convincingly I must add[34], another "spirit" of deconstruction and another "overarching aspiration": the intention of deconstruction is in effect to show that *in and through* the finite constructions (beliefs, cultures, art, etc.) there transpires an in-finity that allows one to at least imagine that there might be more to these finite constructions than just finitude. This is what Caputo calls "finite infinity": finite conceptual constructions, democracies, hospitalities and "Christianities," perhaps, "contain what they cannot contain (the to-come)," an in-finity, *infinition* that *is* "what is possibly going on" in "what is actually happening."[35]

The appeal therefore only shows itself *in* the finite, endless range of possible deconstructions (of ideologies and of, who knows, Christianity) but is, according to Caputo at least, itself kept safe from deconstruction. Deconstruction is justice, Derrida tells us in *Force of Law*: it would convey an "increase of responsibility"[36] more than anything else. This means, among other things, that one must not and should not await the day when the Idea of Justice comes falling from the sky and "will be done" but rather that, in this world, one must construct patiently and in a just manner the least unjust world possible. The command "thou shalt deconstruct" is not itself deconstructible. For Caputo, then, there is no "religious turn" in Derrida. Rather, Caputo argues that "while "Derrida's topics of choice have changed over the years, he has not altered the basic structure of his thought, which is the passage through the universal to the singular."[37] For this basic structure, Caputo points to Derrida's "Linguistics and Grammatology" in *Of Grammatology* where Derrida in effect argues for a transcendental thinking arising out of the "double passage," from empiricism to transcendentality and then from transcendentality to empiricism. This is what later would become the "quasi-transcendental" in the later works and is here called "ultra-transcendental."[38]

The "finite infinity" of deconstruction is truly infinite, since it seeks what lies "beyond" the different hospitalities and Christianities *in* these different hospitalities and Christianities. It seeks, then, what Derrida—*with* Levinas—has called a "transcendence in immanence."[39] The transcendence of this infinity lies in the fact that it can never be reduced to just such an immanence. The infinity of this transcendence lies in the fact that this transcendence will never be attained as such, it is not an ideal that can or cannot be reached, and it only shows itself in the ongoing quest for a less inhospitable world.

Yet it is a finite infinity just as well. For this infinity is nowhere else than in the world, where its meaning incarnates[40] in ever so finite forms: "The to-come is infinite not with the infinity of Christian Neo-Platonism but with the infinity of grammatology, the infinity of an in-finitive, open-ended while endlessly contracted and determined in the finitude of the moment."[41] This finite infinity, then, is not the positive or actual infinite that would be somewhere "outside" the play of traces and of endless differences but neither is it the bad infinite or "infinite finitude" of Hägglund and Nancy, for whom all beings and empirical constructions are endlessly deconstructible. It is furthermore this "contraction" and "determination" of this infinite *in* the finite and immanent plane where Derrida differs from Levinas. This debate is not between a finite deconstruction and an all too infinite Other, as Hägglund has it, but rather between two ways of configuring and "inventing" the infinite. The disagreement between Levinas and

Derrida is not that the former adheres to an instance that would be wholly other and the latter does not, but rather between two ways of inventing the "wholly other." This "infinite other" of Levinas would be for Derrida not only human all too human (at the expense of animals for instance) but also too wholly, too holy an other to be true. Here is Caputo's earlier account of this contraction and determination of the wholly Other: "Derrida shows [. . .] that the *tout autre* comes but it comes relative to a horizon which it shocks."[42] *Contra* Levinas, then, Derrida shows that there indeed is exteriority, that there is nothing worthy of the name of thought if it does not reach for the wholly other, but that this Levinasian attempt—essay—at exteriority has to be conceived otherwise than Levinas, not so much "without context" and without "mediation" but rather in and through writing, in signs differing endlessly, not definitely but indefinitely and infinitely. Hägglund, as I will show, wants to repeat *Violence of Metaphysics* here (although he does a slightly lesser job than Derrida once did) and disregards Levinas' own developments in *Otherwise than Being*.[43]

What Caputo wants to do with the impulse coming to us from Heidegger, Levinas, and Derrida, and with the different names they have given to the event (*Ereignis, autrement qu'être*, etc.), is to show that these names are *but* names and, in this way, already do injustice to the event they are trying to name. None of the names for this event could be insulated from the deconstructibility of all names, which is why this radical hermeneutics and radical theology of Caputo's starts and ends with an appraisal of a radical historicity—close to the "fundamental uncertainty" Heidegger had already noted—if it is not to veer into an ontotheology, always on the verge of escaping the conditions of space and time put on thinking. Of such an event, then, Caputo wants to be the theologian and his deconstruction of Christianity shows him again as faithfully following Derrida:

> my idea [. . .] would be to expose what I take to be the events that circulate through the "religions" [. . .] to their non-Abrahamic other, to what is "impossible" from the Abrahamic horizon. The result would be not a fusion of horizons but the shock of alterity, of worlds with very different sense of time, death, and individuality, where *the shock of that difference would be the event*.[44]

With such a conditioning by space and time, then, we are where Hägglund starts and ends, to the point where he would strip from these conditions such an event entirely. Hägglund argues for a "non-ethical opening" toward the coming and spacing of time.[45] This spacing of time, then would be the only infinitely finite event, to which we are always and already exposed: it is to be opened toward "death, discrimination, and obliteration."[46] A life that is worth living, the only life actually extant, according to Hägglund, is a life that is continually exposed to its own corruption, to its own death. It is such an "infinite finitude" that would eradicate the immunity of the ideal of an eternal life which knows not of death, which Hägglund regards as the "foundation of religion."[47] For this spacing of time conveys the idea that it is time that distends and is dispended to all empirical beings. In this way, it is time itself that "takes on body" in the space between beings. Obviously, there is no outside of time. Nothing could be exempt from this spacing of time: nothing that could abandon this temporal realm "unscathed" or "indemnified" in any way. The spacing of time tries to intimate that life and finitude are co-extensive: for a being to be and to live, it is dependent and related upon other beings and otherness *tout court*. But this relationality is not the romantic idea of relationality to which the theologians today too often seem to resort, it is rather that such an exposure to otherness is what makes finite life all the more precious, because always and already open to that which will, eventually, obliterate it: the fact of dying. "The thinking of infinite finitude refutes the very Idea of positive infinity: [it] is self-refuting as such since everything is subjected to a temporal alteration that prevents it from ever being in itself. Alterity is thus irreducible because of the negative infinity of finitude, which undermines any possible totality from the outset."[48]

As I will show, there is nothing here with which Caputo would disagree: all such ideals of an immunity toward otherness, whether it would be the autonomous transcendental subject eradicating all traces of heteronomy or the God of ontotheology "unmoved" and "uncaused" by the conditions of space and time have, for Caputo just as well as Hägglund, proved to be untenable. Yet this is what Hägglund interprets as "Derrida's message," an originary finitude, "which from the very beginning exposes life to death, memory to forgetting, identity to alterity"[49] to such a point that the immune ideal of "pure" life, for instance, can only appear as an undesirable fiction or phantasm: the pure life of the Absolute then, unrelated to all things of the world in such a way that nothing can really happen to this Absolute, would in fact have nothing to do with "finite life" (as we know it) but all the more with death, as the state where we no longer relate to anything else and nothing really happens.[50] Only the dead, then, would be identical to themselves and completely at peace. The living, on the other hand, are for Hägglund, thrown into an auto-immune human condition, that is, the "illogical logic" through which a living being can autonomously destroy that which is supposed to protect it from the intrusion of heteronomy.[51] This being, then, would not be able to protect itself from otherness, as the autonomous subject would do, but rather see its autonomy destructed in face of otherness precisely—not a retreat in autonomy but an advance of heteronomy to the point of death. This is in any case, Derrida's version of the "fatal agent" present in the metaphysical hegemonies we saw Schürmann describing earlier. The best example of such auto-immune entities today is perhaps the "planned obsolescence" with which manufacturers endow their products so as to make sure that these products will soon after their creation break down and consumers need to buy another one: nothing, then, is built to last.

Hägglund disagrees with Caputo (and Levinas), in that he sees both thinkers erecting an ideal of immunity, exempt from time and worldly existence. Hägglund argues that the ideal of infinite alterity (in Levinas) or the Kingdom of God (in Caputo) is *posited* and *projected* over and against finitude, which then is turned into a "finite totality."[52] This is where Hägglund repeats Derrida's *Violence and Metaphysics* and its "deafness" toward Levinas' bifurcation between being and finitude—totality—and the other—infinity. Hägglund similarly rejects Caputo's "utterly deconstructible" bifurcation between the world and the Kingdom.

Such an ideal of immunity, then, would abandon the aim of deconstruction which for Hägglund is descriptive rather than prescriptive[53]: it describes the non-ethical finite exposure to otherness and substitutes the ethics stemming from Levinas and that would still be present in Caputo for a politics where the only undecidability and unconditionality is that one cannot do without decisions and conditions. Here lies the "ethico-political significance of deconstruction" for Hägglund: it is not only to "[expose] the internal contradictions of the doctrines that hold it to be desirable to eliminate exclusion once and for all," such as Caputo's Kingdom and Levinas' messianism, but, since, for Hägglund, violent discrimination (between others, between beliefs) is all there is, it is also "urgent to reflect on ethicopolitical questions, to work out strategies for a 'lesser violence.' "[54] For Hägglund, any attempt to overthrow the finite conditions of space and time, whether it be in the past where all was supposed to be "good, very good even" or in the future where, through one or the other teleological regulative ideal, all will be good, very good, is to forget that, for Hägglund's Derrida, all that exists is the unconditional coming of time which threatens all that would be promised in such a (metaphysical) way.[55]

Hägglund is certainly right in trying to establish the frontiers of finitude through his reading of Derrida. His argument against Caputo, however, is not that the latter would hold a "two-world Augustinianism,"[56] as Caputo has it, but rather that Caputo *stretches* the difference and the distance between what is conditional and what is unconditional in an inappropriate way. For Hägglund, "there is [. . .] no opposition between undecidability and decisions in Derrida" and "even the most conditional hospitality is unconditionally hospitable to that which may ruin it."[57] For Hägglund, then, there is no gap between what is unconditional (the coming of time) and what is conditional (the discrimination between others *in* time): there is nothing in particular, nothing special "going on" in what is actually happening. For Hägglund, Caputo stretches the distance between the unconditional(s) and the conditional *as far as* possible and, possibly, a bit too far, so that the distance between "religion with religion" and "religion without religion" possible becomes untenable and, who knows, "utterly deconstructible."

Mind the Gap! Of Unconditionals and Their Condition

Mary-Jane Rubenstein and Martin Hägglund

Before delving into this a bit further, it must be noted that one need not be a radical atheist to agree with Hägglund here. In her intriguing reading of Derrida's preference for aporias, Mary-Jane Rubenstein argues for a similar closing down of the gap between on the one hand unconditional hospitality and undecidability and conditional hospitality on the other. Rubenstein analyzes Derrida's notion of the impossible in regard to the decision. The decision, for Rubenstein, occurs in the happy medium between undecidability as the leap into the unknown and the instant of decision which, she argues, is to be calculated and prepared—through the gathering of knowledge—as much as possible. The decision, then, is made (or not made) at the very moment that, having gathered all possible knowledge (about how to arrange hospitality and accommodate the other for instance), one realizes that all this knowledge does not suffice for a completely just decision, for a wholly unconditional hospitality for instance.[58] Thus, for Derrida, one has to assume responsibility to welcome otherness and, more importantly, one must do so *responsibly*, that is, by gathering as much information and knowledge of the different forms of hospitality as possible. Yet this does not suffice, for this knowledge will never be able to dispel the fundamental uncertainty, indecision and division surrounding the just or less unjust decision (otherwise nothing would need to be decided). For Rubenstein, then, one has to remain undecided at the very moment of the decision through which this decision, for her, seems to take the form of a "faith in the absurd": no matter how much one knows, one will never know whether the decision taken is and will be, in fact, a just one. This is the outcome of her analysis: "the crucial passage with respect to decision, then, is not the so-called gap between undecidability and decision [. . .] for *there is no such gap* but rather the passage [. . .] from decidability out to undecidability. Which is to say out to decision."[59] Undecidability would be everywhere: that is why everything remains "to be decided." If I turn to Hägglund again, then this shows that, obviously, there is *more than one* reading of Derrida, but also that one can understand Hägglund's reading of Derrida a bit better, for here the unconditional coming of time would surround us to such an extent that all we want, desire and know is to have more time, to "live on" and "survive." This would be, for Hägglund, the ultimate (without ultimacy) of our lives and times.

What Hägglund and Rubenstein share, then, is the presupposition that the conditionality (of hospitalities) *is* what is unconditional. This is what one could call, with Caputo, the "hidden" empiricism or metaphysics—a metaphysics of becoming[60]—of these thinkers, trying to point to "what there is" in rather straightforward a manner. Rubenstein here relies (a bit too much) on Heidegger who states that the true aim of awe is to see that it is the ordinary that is extraordinary.[61]

Before showing how this is too empirical a reading of Heidegger and Derrida, let us note Hägglund's manner of collapsing the gap between unconditional and conditional hospitality, which ought to bring us closer to Derrida:

> Derrida says that unconditional hospitality is at once indissociable from and heterogeneous to conditional hospitality. On the one hand, unconditional hospitality is *indissociable* from conditional hospitality, since it is the exposure to the visitation of others that makes it necessary to establish conditions of hospitality [. . .]. On the other hand, unconditional hospitality is *heterogeneous* to conditional hospitality, since no regulation finally can master the exposure to the visitation of others.[62]

Hägglund seems to make a similar move as Rubenstein here: whereas the latter mentions the heterogeneous moment of the "leap into the unknown" only in order to see the indissociability of the conditional and the unconditional better—there is nothing else than (un-decision)—the former stresses the heterogeneous moment of unconditional hospitality only in order to better see the indissociability of this unconditional hospitality from all these, never-ending concrete and conditioned forms of hospitalities—there is nothing outside the violent discrimination between different forms of hospitality.

Be that as it may, this is not what Derrida says. For this, I will have to return (finally) to Derrida's debate with Levinas, and more in particular to his discussion of Levinas' silence when it comes to the difference between ethics and politics, a difference moreover to which Derrida fully seems to subscribe, although again this difference perhaps has to be considered otherwise than Levinas. Derrida even calls this difference a *Faktum*, as if Levinas could not have done otherwise than remain silent about how this "ethics" would pass into a "politics": it is indeed too little noticed that this supposedly "ethical" thinker Levinas does *not* give any ethical guidelines or rules to live by whatsoever. Hägglund would be hard pressed to find any prescriptions here. (In an odd sense, there is less hubris, "prescribing for the world its being," in Levinas here than there is in Hägglund, prescribing for us "survivors" just how to survive: it is not bad at all to establish borders and protect "what is your own").

An Essay at Exteriority: Otherwise than Survival

Let us read Derrida:

> This fact [this silence on the relation between ethics and politics, JS] is a fact that remains, and this fact is not some empirical contingency. But it must also remain between the messianic promise and the determination of a rule, norm, or political rights. It marks a *heterogeneity*, a *discontinuity* between two orders, even if this be on the *inside* of the earthly Jerusalem [. . .]. This discontinuity, moreover, allows us to subscribe to everything Levinas says about peace or messianic hospitality, about the beyond [*au-delà*] of the political in [*dans*] in the political.[63]

It would be by not giving any rules about just how to attend to the other that Levinas actually has preserved the fact that the other (and the others) must be attended to and welcomed. But the point lies elsewhere: it is again a question of a transcendence in immanence, of an immanence that "contains what it cannot contain," and therefore an immanence, whether it be radical atheist or full of awe, which is *more than* just an immanent plane. For it is a question here of the "beyond" of immanence (of politics, of drawing borders, of decisions) from within politics, of a peace "beyond" politics established/incarnated/presencing within politics: the "purely immanent" and the purely political would then, for Derrida *also*, contain (in an autoimmune manner) that which it cannot contain, namely a transcendence that disrupts the very possibility of this cocoon that would be immanence.[64] So we find Derrida argue contra (a certain) Levinas that there is neither a transcendence that would be wholly other than immanence nor an immanence that would be bereft of and immune to all transcendence whatsoever (contra Hägglund and Rubenstein). The transcendence of ethics (without "ethics") is therefore to be distinguished from the violence of immanent politics, although this transcendence occurs nowhere else than within the order of politics. Caputo is right in saying that the heterogeneous moment is "contracted" and "determined" by finitude, by conditional hospitalities, "relative to a horizon."

One might say that Hägglund and Rubenstein place the transcendent moment of the unconditionals without sovereignty too low, focusing on the "within," so missing that they indeed constitute two different orders. Yet, one might argue, as I will do, that Caputo locates these unconditionals a tiny bit too high, focusing on the "beyond," playing with the discontinuous moment at the expense of the continuity between the two orders.

For let us listen to just how the later Levinas has configured this interruption and contraction of the infinite, so that this contraction leaves room for the other of the other, for the third party that is. It is this contraction that Hägglund misses: at least in *Otherwise than Being*, there is no such thing as a finite totality, which is why indeed the third party does not wait patiently for the "end" of the ethical moment between you and me. Yet Caputo misses it as well: although he stresses the very moment of such contraction and determination of the infinite in and through finitude, he seems unaware just how this contraction for Levinas occurs.[65] For this interruption in Levinas occurs in a very particular way, pointing both to a silence of phenomenology—which is an interruption of a certain *voyeuristic* phenomenology that merely wants to see and describe—and to what I call the inevitability of ontotheology, that is, of the "with," of a religion *with* religion that is—so bordering upon Schürmann's concept of the "natural metaphysician" that I will advance against Caputo in the next chapters.

In *Otherwise than Being*, Levinas in effect seems to endorse the view that a "God without ontotheology"—the beyond—can only appear if the ontotheological God, the "permanent danger of turning [God] into a protector of all the egoisms,"[66] is forever presupposed—the *within*. One will have to query just how Levinas incorporates the problem of ontotheology. To develop this thesis, one needs to be aware of Levinas' distinction between the beyond of being ("*être autrement*") and (the) otherwise than being ("*autrement qu'être*").[67] The former, for Levinas, seems to play the role of a Hegelian bad infinite, in that it invokes a regress *ad infinitum* of the mathematical infinite of n+1 possibilities obtained by the negation (and somewhat Platonic depreciation) of all things finite. The latter is supposed to convey the "good" infinite, in that it communicates about the transcendence of human beings—you, me, us—which is irreducible to any operation of thought, and which is, indeed, "intolerable for thought."[68]

And yet: we think. Levinas states that the infinite is "intolerable for thought. Thus there is an exigency to stop."[69] At the end of the chain of negations of beings, at the end of the common horizon that unites beings and holds them together, the ontotheological "God of the gaps" makes an appearance. However: this God only ever appears there where thinking, first, thinks it, and, second, however and whenever it thinks it. The God of ontotheology is indeed an idol, but it is one that shan't die. This at least is what Levinas has in mind when stating that the negation of the imperfections of this world, thus of finitude, does not suffice for a genuine otherness: since the negation of something takes refuge in that which it negates and thus forms a system, the otherness or the divinity of the Highest Being, so obtained through negation, "is still within the same."[70] The ontotheological God, then, is the Infinite reduced to the negation of the imperfect beings of this world and in this sense remains indebted to the logic of finitude: the Highest Being, the halt of the literally endless negation of beings, turns out to be as finite as the instance that thinks it. Derrida rightly points out that this discontinuous moment of "exteriority," although it is indissociable from immanence, therefore requires a passage "beyond the totality of beings"[71] and that on this point Heidegger and Levinas (and, as I will show, Marion's account of God's indifference to being) converge.

One must nevertheless note that Levinas gives a very peculiar ring to this exigency to stop, to the halting of the infinite regress proper to dialectics and negation. This stop, I will show, is always and already produced by the third party: it is, for Levinas, the entry of politics in the intrigue of the Infinite. For this, one must first recall how Levinas reinterprets the relation between being and otherwise than being or between the same and the other. The subject—as "otherwise than being"—is a rupture with being and being's pretension to the absolute by, as a bad infinite, "cover[ing] over all ex-ception" and "filling every interval."[72] This break with being, however, at the same time binds the subject to the other. The subject is therefore at the same time "breaking-point and binding place," "a node and a denouement—of essence *and* essence's other."⁷³ This connection between the same and the other is not a dialectical relationship in which the one provokes, as if automatically, the other. For Levinas, it is nothing less than an enigma, for the signification of the one-for-the-other touches at and is befriended with being as if it was its neighbour "to the point that the one-for-the-other can be expressed as though it were a moment of being,"⁷⁴ to the point even "that the diachronic ambiguity of transcendence lends itself [. . .] to this option for the ultimacy of being.⁷⁵

It is only in the concluding pages of *Otherwise than Being* that Levinas explains *just why* the intrigue of "the" otherwise than being must appear to and show itself in—must be related to, contracted and determined by—being: "thematization is then inevitable, so that signification show itself [. . .] in the betrayal which philosophy is called upon to reduce."⁷⁶ The otherwise than being therefore shows itself necessarily in the logos of being and in "the said."

However, in this appearance in being the trace of the infinite shows itself *in a particular way*: the enigma of an alternating of meaning, which "is the very pivot of revelation," is, when appearing to thought and consciousness, brought back to a dilemma, as if it shows itself to be up for choice after all.⁷⁷ But this choice or dilemma shows itself only to "reflection on the condition of the statement that states this signification" beyond being.⁷⁸ And Levinas adds: it is only "in this reflection, that is, only after the event, *contradiction* appears: it does not break out between two simultaneous statements, but between a statement and its conditions, as though they were at the same time."⁷⁹ Thus, it is between the statement of "otherwise than being" and its condition, that is, being and language, that a contradiction appears: it is impossible that (the) otherwise than being be said from out of being. Levinas' point is that this contradiction only appears when thinking starts to reflect upon the (finite) conditions from out of which the infinite gives itself to thought. Note that Levinas mentions the same line of reasoning while trying to understand how the other can animate and dwell *in* the same:

> this signification in its very signifyingness is an accord or peace between planes which, *as soon as they are thematized*, make an irreparable cleavage. They then mark two Cartesian orders [. . .] which have no common space where they can touch [. . .]. Yet they are accord prior to thematization, in an accord, a chord, which is possible only as an arpeggio. [T]his kind of accord is the very rationality of signification in which the tautological

identity, the ego, receives the other, and takes on the meaning of an irreplaceable identity by giving to the other.[80]

Thematization and reflection therefore *oppose* being and otherwise than being, and become "a contestation of the infinite."[81] It is, thus, in and through thinking, that is, in representation and in reflection, that the infinite is "belied without any ambiguity," is taken as "the invisible behind the visible," and appears, perhaps, as "a great Other," a being par excellence.[82]

Levinas's argument is thus twofold: on the one hand, he argues that the same and the other properly belong together as in an arpeggio: the other dwells in the same *before* the same even knows it—this is why the *conatus essendi* or the perseverance in being that is mere survival is for Levinas, to use Marion's words, "at best, an illusion and at worst, if it's stubborn, a lie."[83] At the same time, however, when thinking starts to thematize or reflect on this relation between being and that which possibly escapes it, namely (the) otherwise than being, a contradiction appears between the statement of "otherwise than being" and the condition of this statement, that is, its being uttered by a being from out of being.

The ambiguity and ambivalence of the infinite signaling itself to thought is only then turned into a dilemma and logical opposition. Levinas argues that only when thinking starts to think and reflect on the "immemorial past" of the otherwise than being, it is brought back to the order of representation and ontology, which subsequently declares itself to be the ultimate: "the immemorial past is intolerable for thought. *Thus there is an exigency to stop*."[84] This is to say that thinking thinks the immemorial past or its "illeity" inevitably *as* an infinite regress, and that thinking *itself* configures the "exigency to stop" or the halting of the regress in the manner it thinks appropriate. Thought converts the otherwise than being into an "*être autrement*" or into a (mathematical) series of beings explaining being(s), into "an extrapolation of the finite,"[85] of which thinking *itself* will grasp the halt or stop.

It is important to note that, for Levinas, this "stop"—this ever-present invocation of the "God of the gaps"—is concretely produced by the advent of the third party. This is Levinas's reduction of ontotheology to politics. With this advent—the fact that there are other*s* besides the Other—Levinas tries to incorporate the phenomenon of ontotheology into his own discourse, precisely as an inevitable function of thought itself. Indeed, for Levinas, the infinite must appear (in being) and leave its ambiguous trace by betraying itself in and through its very appearing in being, that is, by appearing on being's terms. It is here that Levinas advances toward the mysteriousness of that which appears as twofold, and at the same time: "a face makes itself an apparition *and* an epiphany," an enigma and a phenomenon.[86] It is this doubling that thought reflects upon, then reduces to the form of a dilemma or choice, and what makes thought subsequently veer into the ontotheological direction.

All this is thus produced with the advent of the third party. For Levinas, "the relationship with the third party is an incessant correction of the asymmetry of proximity [. . .]. There is weighing, thought, objectification, and thus a stop in which my anarchic relationship with illeity is betrayed."[87] The Other becomes a phenomenon to be dealt with as if it were any other object. It is here as well that, according to Levinas, the Infinite is *necessarily* interrupted, halted, and fixed "in structures [and] totality," and it is this interruption that will give way to the "permanent danger of turning [God] into a protector of all the egoisms" to the politics and ontotheology of a *Gott mit uns*. All of this would seem far-fetched if Levinas had not explicitly linked this political "God of the gaps" with the theme of ontotheology. For it is only in an exacted stop that "the movement beyond being [. . .] become[s] ontology and theology."[88] This appearance of the two tentacles of the problem of ontotheology, moreover, "thereby [marks] a halt [*un arrêt*] in the halt-less quality [*non-arrêt*] of the relationship in which the infinite is traced [. . .]. Here, the gaze substitutes itself for God. With theology, which is linked to ontology, God is fixed in a concept."[89] This stop, then, is always and already there: there are others besides the Others; being is in the neighborhood of (the) otherwise than being; ontotheology haunts philosophy forever; and conditional hospitalities might always obscure the unconditional hospitality of being turned to otherness. Yet one must distinguish and discern.

One Never Knows: Il faut essayer

Let us, after this excursus into Levinas's account of the beyond of the infinite within finitude, return to Derrida and his interpreters. The unconditional and heterogeneous moment of a hospitality of all for all requires a stop. This stop happens with the advent of the third party. It is therefore with the third party that the heterogeneous moment is contracted in and determined by the different forms of finite hospitalities to the point that it is inevitable that this moment is swallowed, so to say, by these finite hospitalities, and the thought that there is nothing outside these finite hospitalities becomes legitimate. In Levinas's terms: it becomes inevitable that one thinks that being and finitude is indeed the ultimate or that there would be nothing outside politics. Second, and perhaps even more unavoidable, is the tendency that one's own politics, the conditional hospitality into which one happens to be thrown, will take precedence over all the other forms of hospitalities—that is what the appearance of the tentacles of ontotheology indicates and why, for Levinas too, we are all "natural metaphysicians." Third, this "stop," this interruption and this halting, appears in being and for beings as a contradiction—being and beings cannot state that which would be outside of being. They are "heterogenous," "allergic" to one another even. Yet, and here is where Derrida sides with Levinas, the two orders belong, "prior" to the stop, indissociably together as an "arpeggio," which means that even if it comes naturally to us to let the unconditional moment be swallowed by all the conditional moments, this moment would not be able to be "digested" to such an extent that it would completely evaporate or be evacuated: just as it is natural that the "beyond" is reduced to and betrayed by the "within," and the "within" will do its utmost best to contain and quarantine the moment of the beyond—declare all "instance[s] beyond temporality"[90] and beyond phenomenological viewing to be nonexistent, for instance—so this "beyond" will haunt all the existent hospitalities within being. It is to such a haunting that Derrida will subscribe (and that, for him, will even haunt Levinas's anthropocentrism). Caputo is right therefore to point Hägglund to Derrida's statement in *Questioning God* "that there is in forgiveness [one of Derrida's *unconditionals*, JS] a force, a desire, and impetus, a movement, an appeal (call it what you will) that demands that forgiveness be granted."[91] For Derrida, too, then, there is more between heaven and earth than the human being can fathom, more to finitude than just the finite, more to hope for than simply a marveling at the totality of beings (Rubenstein) or deplore the endless comings and goings of finite beings (Hägglund).

It is here that the halt or the interruption of a certain all too empirical and all too voyeuristic phenomenology is important and why Derrida indeed takes a transcendental vantage point that at other times he would be happy to criticize.[92]

For this, Derrida again sides with Levinas. Derrida turns to Levinas's argument that, with regard to the Other, phenomenology "finds itself abruptly thrown into a paradox" here, adding significantly that this interruption occurs from *within* phenomenology.[93] For all its reductions and all of its descriptions, the description of the other man and woman, of otherness in general perhaps, stumbles on a nonappearing in the very element of all appearances, a non-presence or invisibility at the heart of all presence and visibility. Such an interruption Derrida had already noted in Husserl's account of the alter ego, which obeys Levinas's demand of the otherness of the other more than Levinas was willing to admit at the time of *Totality and Infinity*. The alter ego, then, is surely available for description. I can see that your body is similar to mine. I can infer from the fact that when I see you crying, for instance, you must be sad, because, *similarly*, when I am sad I cry. The other, for Derrida, must be a phenomenon for me and thus appear according to the horizon and modes of my perceptions. Yet, for Husserl already, this description respects the other's otherness because it is only an "analogical appresentation" and an "originary nonpresence" that does appear to me: I can see that your body is similar, I cannot see what you think and feel. The other appears (to me) by, precisely, not appearing fully, as a full presence that is. In *Violence and Metaphysics*, Derrida thus already argues for the other as "a phenomenon of a certain non-phenomenality."[94]

Phenomenology would be, for Derrida, the description of the limits of description or, in more technical terms, a sort of reduction toward what is irreducible, an operation that realizes, while describing, that these descriptions are *prescribed* by and turned *to* the other. Yet what is important to us here, contra Hägglund's wish that deconstruction be all description and no prescription, is how Derrida, again *with* Levinas, has stressed the ethical interruption of phenomenology, no longer simply describing the other and otherness but rather responsibly, infinitely attending to the (beyond of) the non-presence (within) the empirical presence of the other. Here is Derrida: "this ethical language of phenomenology *describes prescription* at the point where prescription lets itself be described only by already prescribing, by still prescribing."[95] Every autonomous constitution, then, is already constitut*ed* by (and so directed *to*) the heterogeneity of otherness. This is also why Hägglund's omitting of the second source of religion—the greeting or the "to you" in everything that is said—is more grave than one would initially suspect: it is to omit the most daring aspect of deconstruction, of its being *infinitely and yet responsibly* being-turned-to-otherness.

It is to omit that the stakes of deconstruction as well as those of phenomenology lie not in the endless description of things visible but rather in the invisible meaning and sense that are addressed *within* these visible things and in what so addresses itself to us there. Derrida would surely agree with Hägglund (and even with Levinas) that it is quite likely that when addressing this address, this address will be thematized and turned into an ontotheology: chances indeed are that it will quickly be indemnified improperly.

But this does need not mean that the address itself would not escape these attempts to address it. Hägglund's stress on deconstructive description, on the description of the fact that in effect all things must pass, forgets that, for Derrida, there cannot be a "phenomenology of phenomenology" but only an "ethics of phenomenology"; Hägglund forgets that, in more contemporary terms, the appearing of appearing does not itself appear and that herein lies a being "responsible"[96] despite one's finitude: to attend responsibly to the appearing of appearing from within whatever appears. The event of world, *properly* indeconstructible, escapes all making, fabrication, and historical constructions although it is not foreign to these finite constructions either. In this happening of world, then, there is no escaping the fact that meaning is always and already incarnated. But the fact that one cannot escape these incarnations does not mean that, for Derrida (or for Levinas and Caputo), there would be a (theological) escape to *Incarnation*.

Conclusion: Begging to Differ

One cannot but conclude that what one finds in Hägglund's staccato of deconstructions is indeed an "abridged" edition of what Derrida presented in the name of deconstruction. This is not to say that there is nothing to learn from Hägglund's account of Caputo's religion without religion. This conclusion, and the next chapter, come back to this. Now one needs to keep in mind that some of Caputo's contemporary critics, such as Hägglund and Rubenstein, find that Caputo stretches the difference between what is unconditional and what is conditional, whereas they would want to close the gap between the two orders, so that the conditional *is* the unconditional and no leap could be made from, say, finitude to that which, possibly, escapes finitude.

One might in fact argue that Caputo's "religion without religion" is a bit of a stretch, insisting on both a *very* empirical stance when it comes to the mixture of faith and belief, for instance, and a *very* transcendental vantage point when leaping to the "without" religion that would be outside the system of beliefs. Caputo, then, seems to bet on multiple horses, insisting that the distinction between what is conditional and what is unconditional can be drawn quite neatly and the gap between the two stably maintained. For Caputo, then, even though one cannot "do without 'without,'" it is perhaps better to settle for "both with *and* without."[97] But this, obviously, does not answer the question of the "without" (or our question of "the with"), it merely restates it.

I have just shown that Levinas seemed to agree with Derrida in that the very movement of *infinition* is contracted and determined by finitude. More importantly, I have shown that this contraction and determination of the wholly other through the same occurs almost inevitably in an ontotheological way, which would mean that "the with" as such, claiming a God *pro nobis* (but not for the Other), would be ineradicable. It is hard to imagine where exactly Derrida would stand on this problem. One can only suggest that Derrida would at least recognize the difficulty, considering that his response to Nancy suggested that even the most anti-metaphysical of thoughts is susceptible to "destructive effects" that would make it more metaphysical and ontotheological than such thought would be willing to admit or even realize. This is why the next chapter imagines Derrida *as* a natural metaphysician, not willing to share his secret because we already know this secret, "we would indeed know everything."

When I state that Caputo's stress on the movement of the event, of the how of *infinition*, is a bit of a stretch, I mean that this movement of the "beyond" in Caputo sometimes seems to occur at the expense of finite historical constructions in which it nevertheless takes place. This is not to say that there is a disdain for the empirical in Caputo, but surely there is somewhat of a neglect of factual being-in-the-world. To be sure, this neglect is understandable, because, as a follower of Derrida, Caputo is well aware of the danger of a certain empiricism (which Derrida has noted not only in Levinas but also in Nancy). Empiricism is, for Derrida, the end of philosophy: philosophers would be out of a job. It would provide an "immediate access" to the things out there and forget that, at least for Derrida, there is no such thing as the thing as such (which, of course, is a problem for transcendental philosophy as well, claiming to attain the pure ego "as such" present to itself). This is why Caputo begins his response to Hägglund's materialism and a purely descriptive deconstruction with an account of his "hypermaterialism," in which "matter" would *matter* because there is more than mere matter.[98] To be sure, Caputo does recognize that there is description in deconstruction and that "things are autodeconstructive" and "deconstructors are at best good detectives," observing what is actually happening in this finite world of ours.[99] Yet this "hyper-realism" insists "that over and beyond the movement of the auto-deconstructive [. . .] *in which we are unavoidably lodged without having asked for it*, there is also the rest of the deconstructive story, the work of our deconstructive 'responsibility' which we may or may not avoid," obeying (or not) what is possibly going on in what is actually happening—every detective needs an intrigue.[100]

So I find Caputo stressing the *Entwurf* rather than our *Geworfenheit*.[101] But, with this, we are back where we started, at a certain *impossibility* of deconstructing Christianity, at an impossible passage from the different Christianities to a Christianity to come, with a certain Munchhausen drowning in the different beliefs and not able to reach out to an originary faith. And if this postmodern Munchhausen were able to do so and *project* a faith without belief, it is still not excluded that such a faith would be attained according to the very particular passage that Levinas stressed—one more ontotheology (Levinas), one more Christianity (Derrida).

Caputo insists with Derrida in effect on such a passage—the passage through the transcendental—but is unclear about just how such a passage would be effected. Caputo at times even omits that such a transition for Derrida is always and already double, that is, *back* to the empirical auto-deconstructive nature of things. Consider, for instance, the different, if not incompatible, accounts Caputo gives of such a passage: to be able to come to the hyperbolic vantage point of a "religion without religion," one would need to pass not only through the transcendental (exempt of empiricism) but also "through ordinary rule-governed experience (of the possible)" (which would *only* be universally and transcendentally true), through "the given category of prayer" (here one suddenly seems to pass through the "empiricism" of the different historical beliefs), "through negative theology" to learn to pray to "God knows what," and finally also through "the normative and ethical features [of the *tout autre*]" to "intensify [its injunction] and attain the somewhat supererogatory responsibility toward the singular."[102] The deconstructive detectives seem to have a lot on their plate! But one might wonder whether with such a list, even Caputo has fallen prey to a quasi-transcendental dizziness: in short, we would need to know *from where* we pass through the transcendental and *to where* this will in effect lead. It is here that Caputo, although not often at a loss for words it seems, remains silent.

How (not) to do away with the with, then? Here one might turn to one of Hägglund's objections to Caputo, where the former insists that in Caputo the Kingdom of God is circumscribed as an "absolute immunity, where the good would be immune to evil," thus erecting an "utterly deconstructible distinction" between our unfortunate human condition (where justice, gifts, are, alas, impossible) and God's Kingdom (where everything is possible)—a distinction, by the way, that recurs in *exactly* the same way in Marion's thought.[103] Here, then, this auto-deconstructive finitude is construed as a *finite totality* against which afterward is projected a God who would release these conditions from their debt to injustices and evil. Hägglund is right when pointing to Derrida's statement in *Violence and Metaphysics* that there is no such totality, nothing of "the Same" that Levinas projects in *Totality and Infinity*.

It is time that we dwell on Caputo's "religion without religion" more closely, but for now we know where passing through the transcendental might lead us, back to an auto-deconstructive and auto-immune human condition, to a not-so-planned obsolescence of the human being and its beliefs. Here the coming of the impossible needs not so much to "contain what it cannot contain," endlessly reaching for whatever is forever out of reach, but here finitude needs to *conserve* whatever is infinitely beyond its reach: the gap between the transcendental and empirical, as we will later see in Binswanger, contains and conserves an infinite through passing through a very ontic you, where it is the transcendental itself, so to say, that "takes on flesh."

6

Between Faith and Belief

Derrida versus Caputo

If the previous chapter showed that some of Derrida's (and Caputo's) critics are wrong when saying that there is no gap between what is unconditional and what is conditional in Derrida, this does not mean that one can, without critique, subscribe to Caputo's "religion without religion." Even though Derrida seemed to maintain a distinction between faith and belief, which roughly (but only roughly) would correspond to the distinction between a "religion without religion" and the beliefs of "religions with religion," Derrida, as this chapter aims to show, was much more attentive to the back and forth between these tenets of religion than Caputo is. In short, where Caputo aims for a "purer," "perfectible" faith—think of the Beatles tune "It's getting better all the time"—I argue that Derrida insists on an always impure and even "pervertible" faith—think of The Rolling Stones song "(I can't get no) Satisfaction." With this, then, Derrida comes close to the "natural metaphysician" that Schürmann and Levinas are describing.

The Event of Religion

For Caputo, however, religion is but one of the places where something happens that matters, makes a difference simply because it happens and doesn't stop happening; although it can neither contain nor domesticate the event itself and in its entirety. The event, then, for Caputo is greater than which nothing can be conceived. At best, religion is a trace of what could be called "the event of the event," bordering on the ahistorical "event of world" we have seen Schürmann describing, which initiates a "sense" of that which is more, different, and other than the contingency of all worldly constructs and a taste for the fact that even though there might be nothing but world, this world itself might best be understood as the ultimate event or at least as an event harboring some ultimacy.

Religion for Caputo remains one of the great inspirations narrating and recounting the event of the event that happens nowhere else than in the world, but cannot and may not be identified with that very world. Yet religion, for Caputo, is only one pathway toward this absolute and certainly not the only narrating and witnessing to an instance greater than world and finitude, for art might *just as well* be conceived of as an opening to that which cannot and must not be deconstructed. It is intriguing to see, however, that when it comes to examples of such an event—if there are any—his take on art is most clear about "the shock of the event relative to a horizon," to the point that one wonders whether there is for Caputo today anything worthy of the name event in religion and theology:

> [The shock of the event] would produce something new, quite in the way Picasso revolutionized art a hundred years ago by contemplating African masks, which were for him the visual impossible. That was exactly the terms in which Cubism was denounced by the critics of the day, who still played by the old rules of representational art and complained that it was "impossible" to make out the figures![1]

For Caputo, "truth" does not lie in what is represented but rather in how the event blurs preexistent conditions of possibility. The event has the "capacity to nourish our imagination [and this is] its truth, its vitality. This vitality is its truth."[2]

On the other hand, religions are, as is everything else, historical constructs themselves, and therefore they more often than not tend to contain the event of the world in the confines and closure of its own "circle." This is, according to Caputo, religion at its worst. What matters for him is to attend in each case to the openness to the event, even when this "openness" cannot be "maintained" or turned into something "present-at-hand"—no one is open to the other once and for all: the openness and transcendence toward the event is always and already disturbed and rendered inoperative from within. This means, to turn to a certain Augustinianism, that this openness toward the event of the world will always be insufficient. The dream of an opening to the other or of the pure address and adoration of otherness (Nancy) in effect quickly turns into its opposite, complacently congratulating itself with one's openness, and so reflect more one's closure than an actual openness: "Come and see how open-minded we are!" I return to this issue below, and the concomitant primacy of the bad conscience, when I rally Derrida against Caputo.

Such a readiness for the event is what Caputo prescribes after "the end of metaphysics." Once all grand stories are rendered incredulous, and with this all grand Goals and dreams of a divine Origin, what remains is nothing but a witness to a fundamental, metaphysical ignorance. All we have to do and know, according to Caputo, is confess that we do not know where to go and even less who we are—*das Woher und Wohin bleibt dunkel* (Heidegger).

Yet Caputo's is not a "theology of despair": it concerns a theology rather that, once the belief in a world behind the scenes is abandoned, concentrates on and concerns itself with this world here rather than other worlds over there, for this world here is the only world that one has at one's disposal (precisely because this world is *not* at our disposal): "to have a religious vocation [means] to make ourselves answerable to the world, to the voices that call us in and from the world, from within the world. [This] is very important, because it is very important that the world is not all in all, lest we are suffocated [. . .] by the world."[3] The very least that this religion without religion knows—and one will have to wonder later *just how much* this religion pretends to know—is that this world is not the be-all and end-all of being-in-the-world and that a proper religious stance begins with a *distance* or exodus from the world in order to see that not everything of this world can be called "good, very good even." In this distance, religion shows itself as one of the few instances left that is able to protest against and resist the current state of affairs or "course of things."

The first, although not final, word of such a religion is a "No" to the ways of the world: it confesses that there is much to be said for an unconditional and non-deconstructible event, which gives to the old critique of idolatry a new impulse. It admits just as well that not one name for this event harbors it exclusively and entirely. The nihilism of the present age could in effect be interpreted as stating something like "It is what it is" or "This is how things tend to go":[4] it not only denies the possibility of a final word (Lacoste) but also can no longer take into account that just because everything is contingent and finite, everything can change and is, in this sense, prone to difference. For Caputo, a religious act can be termed religious if and only if this act is one of resistance. It resists the modern "shrinking" of the world, where Descartes and Kant jointly prescribed for the world what could (and what could not) be experienced and known. In this regard, Caputo—rhetorically but elegantly—states that the act of resistance is a prayer for the impossible to be possible again, for a riot against the safety and security of the transcendental horizon in ways similar to Heidegger's anxiety, which turns the world toward nothingness only to finally face one's finite being-in-the-world. This prayer seeks to dismantle these "small" happenings of the modern age and its primacy of foreseeability, calculability, and efficiency and prays for a taste and a *sense* of the "greatness" of the event of world, which cannot be foreseen.

It goes without saying that Caputo's "religion without religion" is quite critical of established and institutionalized religion and other powers, not least because this "establishment" easily forgets the contingency of its very establishment. "Religion *with* Religion" is an attempt to secure the Infinite firmly in its place, to assign it its place and make the Infinite at the disposal—one might risk "disposable" here, as such an Infinite all too easily auto-deconstructs—of one community. Religion *with* religion asks the credentials both of its highest being ("you belong to us") and of the "lower" beings ("you are with us") by means of a signature to quite determinate propositions.

Yet Caputo argues that his "religion without religion" is not foreign to the institutionalized version: it belongs to it as much as the hornet belongs to the horse. "Any wider sense of religion, of a religiousness without the confessional religions [. . .] will always be *parasitic* upon the confessional forms, will always feed off them [and will] all the while be depending on [them]." Caputo desires nothing more of such confessional religion than that it is "disturbed from within by a radical non-knowing, [by] a sense of the secret"[5] through an appeal to those of us claiming to be "in the know" about God in order for them to confess their ignorance and unknowing just as well.

The calling accompanying this religion without religion is the call to negotiate and mediate between the unconditional appeal of the event and the worldly conditions in which and through which this event necessarily incarnates, takes form, and is, for better or for worse, conditioned. Caputo wants to turn the aporia into an axiom: if you think you know about hospitality and you do not receive every other—the good, the bad, and the ugly others alike—then you do not know about hospitality at all! The absolute idea of hospitality exceeds the empirical and concrete forms of hospitality—Levinas would say that we must still learn to desire the non-desirable Other—but, in and through this mediation between the conditional ("what is possible": I'll see what I can do) and the unconditional (the impossible turned possible), this idea and its very absoluteness and universality deliver us to the "finite promise of the world."[6] This makes for the fact that religion is always and already doing injustice to the event and is only ever but a contingent, all too contingent name for the event constantly exceeding that which it makes happen (and for which "God," too, is but a name, an example, perhaps only a manner of speaking). Yet, for Caputo at least, religion remains one of the best possible means—pun intended—to do the least possible injustice to the event without limits and conditions: the Unconditional is written straight in crooked and conditional lines.

In line with our earlier exposition of Caputo's idea of a "Christianity to come" as an appeal of Christianity harbored in the event of the different Christianities, it is perhaps fitting to comment briefly on Caputo's "turn to theology." I have noted already that Caputo's best examples of the shock of the event come from art rather than religion or theology. In this regard, it is remarkable that, as for now, no such "unconditional appeal of Christianity" is to be found in Caputo. Rather, one finds Caputo's "weakness for theology" circumscribed as a prayer "for the coming of the theological event," as if nothing in the actual state of theology and Christianities were sufficient to perceive therein already an event or at least the promise of a "Christianity to come."[7]

Prayers, Tears, and Gnashing of Teeth: On Attempting to be an Atheist

The Prayers and Tears of Jacques Derrida (1997) is perhaps Caputo's most famous book and in any case his most sustained effort to spell out the implications of Derrida's deconstruction for religious matters. Derrida's weeping song, if there is any, has never left Caputo, and the theology that comes afterward draws heavily on the results that this book delivered. Before delving into Caputo's magnum opus, I first follow the account he has given of his itinerary with Derrida in the booklet *Philosophy and Theology*. A single question is guiding our efforts here: if one could not dance and sing before the *causa sui*, why would one bow and kneel for "the impossible"? And if "the impossible" is one of those holy names that were and are lacking, will it *continue* to arouse our desire to dance and sing or to pray and weep?

Caputo meditates on one of Derrida's expressions that had caused quite some disturbance and controversy in the world of philosophy and theology. Derrida said: "I quite rightly pass for an atheist." But why, Caputo asks, would Derrida not simply say that he *is* an atheist? Because uncertainty—close to Heidegger's *Seinsunsicherheit*—and ignorance concern all, the atheist as well as the believer: both will need to recognize that an uncertainty and inoperativeness contaminate the dogmatic anti-theism as well as institutionalized theism. Derrida is close here to a certain view of Kant: whereas the latter condemned the *selbst verschuldeten Unmundigkeit*, the "self-incurred immaturity," in the name of the transcendentality of freedom, his argument is radical to such an extent that even this "immaturity" comes from the *freedom* to choose not to be free. Derrida, in turn, takes his infamous "destinerrancy"—we are destined not to reach one or the other destination, but rather to err—to a transcendental level, for when he criticizes institutional religion as being onto-theo-logical, prone to determining its (own) destiny, that is, he does so not by saying that it did not recognize the truth of destinerrancy, but rather by stating that this institutionalized form of the proper destiny is but a form, although not entirely illegitimate, of destinerrancy: even the one pretending be the "in the know" about his or her fate cannot cover over one's transcendental faithless and fate-less existence.[8]

But why does Derrida not simply state that "he is an atheist"? Because, again, the "fundamental uncertainty with regard to being" concerns us all: both the theist and the atheist will need to admit that this ignorance interrupts the dogmatics of faith as much as the rationality turned to rational*ism* of the atheist. After metaphysics, then, no one can rely on the permanence and the assurance that reason sought to postulate in the modern age. The "ego" is not only *not* the master of its own house; it is dispelled and looking for asylum elsewhere. Even when I piously would exclaim that "I believe in God," the atheist voice within will whisper that no one really knows what or who God is (and will, in this way, and as if unbeknownst to itself, repeat the most classical of theologies); but, similarly, even when I confidently claim that "I certainly do not believe in God," soon thereafter a similar haunting will take place, for it then becomes urgent to know to which "God" exactly such a claim pertains, as if an "atheist" claiming that "God" is inexistent would be something of a contradiction in terms—after all, what could the word "God" mean to an atheist?

Derrida argues for something similar when stating that even when you are a "radical atheist, and you just mention the word *God*, that means that you are supposed to understand what that word means, that you inherit the word in a culture [. . .] in which the word *God* means something."[9] The atheist therefore can and cannot deny the existence of God: if he or she denies the existence of God, what is so denied is the meaning and the mentions this word has in a certain not yet non-Christian culture. But this means that the atheist does not deny the existence of God at all, because, radical or not, he or she must first have presupposed and affirmed the meaning that this word has in this particular culture. It is not certain whether all this is but a play on words, and if it is, this might be exactly what constitutes the problem of our not quite non-Christian culture.

For what must be noted here is that Derrida, with his "passing for an atheist," is consonant with the aporia of the unconditional hospitality that *is* and *exists* only ever as conditioned. Let us listen to Caputo's account in his obituary for Derrida: "When asked why he does not say 'I am' an atheist, [he] said it was because he did not *know* if he were, that there are many voices within him that give one another no rest, and he lacks the absolute authority of an authorial 'I' to still this inner conflict. So *the best* he can do is to rightly pass for this or that, and he is very sorry that he cannot do better."[10] So if Derrida "passes for" an atheist, he does so because absolute atheism is as unreachable as an absolute hospitality is and therefore incarnates, again just as hospitality, in very conditional, perhaps even inappropriate forms of atheism. Just as we desire absolute hospitality only to incarnate the least inhospitable form of absolute Hospitality, just so an atheism worthy of the name can only take a stance while assuming the least possible faith/s. As little faith as possible: that is the best atheism can do today. But note that for Caputo's stance, who would like to "pass for a believer," the same holds true because unconditional belief is as impossible as absolute Justice would be and therefore incarnates, again just as Justice does, in very conditional, perhaps even inappropriate forms of belief. Just as we desire absolute justice only to incarnate the least unjust form of absolute justice, so a belief that "could pass the audition" can only take a stance while assuming the least possible atheism. As little atheism as possible: that is the best faith can do today.

In this way, "God" for Caputo becomes the name of a secret, the secret of being from time immemorial severed from Truth,[11] which concerns all, the ones erring as well as the ones fulfilling their supposed destiny. For this secret, then, it matters not whether you believe or not, for this secret is not asking you for credentials and a firm belief. So, for Caputo, it matters little if one would say that "one quite rightly would pass for a believer": I confess not to know what it is I ought to believe and even less how I should do so, but I cannot deny that a certain form of desire causes me to believe. Such a fundamental uncertainty takes, in Caputo as in Derrida, the form of a prayer, praying for "God knows what." "If you knew [. . .] my experience of prayers," Derrida confesses, "you would know everything, [you] would tell me whom to address them to."[12] You would then understand everything, Derrida fears, except that this life itself has been one of prayers and tears. You would tell me whom to pray to, whom to hope for and you will subsequently forget about all of my tears. You would above all forget that these tears were real and that this is why they forced me to pray. You will suspend, sublate, and even sublimate my prayer at the very moment I tell you that I pray. You will grasp this prayer in your concepts and will orient this religion of mine toward what you believe is "the religion of all religions," whereas "nobody understands anything" of this religious Derrida, not the least himself.[13]

Derrida (and Caputo, too, a bit too anxiously, as I will show) wants to pray without knowledge in order that life and prayer may be synonymous. Caputo asks: "to whom is he praying? And for what reason does he weep? If he knew that, if someone could tell him all that, *he would not need to pray*. He prays because he does not know whom to pray to or indeed if there is someone there to receive his prayers."[14] Moreover, Caputo likes to add, is this not the universal experience of prayer, the prayer of all and perhaps, who knows, for all, this prayer that confirms and confesses to its ignorance by confirming and confessing that it prays to be able to pray (as once, inversely, Eckhart prayed to God to rid him of God).

The border zone between those who pray and those who do not is thus rendered uncertain in order for those who pass for prayerful people, and quite rightly so, to get somewhat insecure as to their prayer, and in order for those who attempt or pretend not to pray nevertheless to pray their prayers as if unbeknownst to themselves, and perhaps just as rightly so, and in this way preserve and somewhat protect the secret that accompanies prayer and which we do injustice to if we name it, for example, God. If I would tell you that I pray, to whom I pray, and why I pray, you would know everything and you would suspend the secret, and I would no longer hide that I try to hide something (or that there is nothing to hide).

Caputo and Derrida are close to Augustine, that master of suspicion as well as of trust. Just like Augustine, Derrida recognizes a restlessness of the heart that perhaps is all too easily soothed and softened by the quietude of reason's contemplation. Unlike Augustine, though, Derrida is quick to suspend the teleology of this heart that "finds rest only in you, *deum meum*." Just like Augustine, however, Derrida is aware that a conversion is, most often, incomplete, in the sense that "Augustine's conversion lay in a transformation of what he loved [no longer just the world or only creation, but now only 'God,' JS], which involved a self-transformation of Augustine himself into a question unto himself, and a transformation of his love into a question about what he loved."[15] Unlike Augustine, Derrida confesses to an ignorance even when it comes to the incompleteness of conversion and certainly disregards the possibility of God coming to the rescue of this prayer: if Augustine determined the finite promise in and of the world concretely and empirically as it were from out of a religion "with" religion, which was dominant in his culture, then Derrida remains with a "faith without belief" and refuses to determine the promise of justice and hospitality with a certain name, word, or concept—one may not underestimate that this faith and this prayer is, just as *différance*, "neither a word nor a concept." Caputo concludes: "Derrida's *Circumfession* is even *more* prayerful than Augustine's *Confessions*, because the words are more wounded [Chrétien's '*wounded words*' or '*paroles blessées*,' JS] [. . .] for he lacks the community and the assurances of Augustine."¹⁶

The difference between Derrida and Augustine therefore is not that the former "passes for an atheist" and the latter "for a theist" (if that wouldn't be an anachronism), nor that the former despairs and the latter has faith. Rather, it concerns here "two different kinds of faith."¹⁷ The "postmodern" Derrida knows neither the faith without reason (for which one could still reproach a certain Augustine) nor a pure reason exempt of faith (in which the moderns believed) but realizes, recognizes, and confesses that these deconstructions of his are not without a certain faith either. The postmodern Derrida certainly refuses a faith that blindly trusts in the teachings of one particular community but equally mistrusts a reason that does not accept its blind spots or its faith. On the contrary: his faith is an "undeterminate one, a little more lost and astray, but for all that no less deeply set and resolved, perhaps even [. . .] *a purer faith*, a faith in faith itself."¹⁸

It is at this point that one will need to wonder whether or not Caputo still allows that "Derrida" speaks and whether he does not jump in for Derrida and take the latter's prayers and tears away, as in a moment of *uneigentliche Fürsorge*, to make them speak no longer of themselves but for-the-sake-of Caputo's own prayers and tears. Recall, then, the "essential corruptibility," of which Derrida spoke when circumscribing the Absolute idea of hospitality, meaning the very fact that the absoluteness of this idea does not exist otherwise than in the endless translations and betrayals of this idea in a manifold of empirical laws (of hospitalities, as very determinate ways of welcoming this rather than that other): the one Law does not exist outside the plurality of laws. Derrida writes:

> *the* unconditional law of hospitality needs the laws, it *requires* them. This demand is constitutive. It wouldn't be effectively unconditional, the law, if it didn't *have to become* effective, concrete, determined [. . .]. It would risk being abstract, utopian, illusory and so turning into its opposite. In order to be what it is, *the* law thus needs the laws which, however, deny it, or at

any rate threaten it, sometimes corrupt or pervert it [. . .]. *This pervertibility is essential, irreducible and necessary.*[19]

It is, then, quite obvious that something similar pertains to Caputo's postmodern "faith without belief" or "religion without religion" that we were here describing, up until now, with Caputo. For, if such a pervertibility expands to all the unconditionals Derrida has given us, not only can one imagine it to be detrimental to Caputo's idea of a "theology to come," as if the different Christianities cannot but ruin the law of a "Christianity" or "theology" to come (if there is such a thing), but it also would be closer to Derrida's thought of a quasi-transcendental *Verflechtung* to state that just as those enjoying a "stabilized relation to destiny" are not exempt from "destinerrancy," so those clinging to the law of "destinerrancy," as Caputo does, are not safely sheltered from the logic and the laws of "destiny" either. This is why, in the introduction, I wrote that "religion without religion" might be haunted by "religion with religion" more than the other way around.

Derrida as Natural Metaphysician: The Pervertibility of Pure Faith

All this, in any case, makes Caputo's very modern mysophobia, and his quest for a *purer* faith, highly suspect. For this, one could, for instance, elaborate on the logic of the secret at work in Derrida. The secret, Derrida argues, is in a sense always and already unfaithful to itself, for it takes two (at least) to have and share a secret. It is impossible that I keep something secret for myself. But if it takes two for the secret to be a secret at all, then at this very instant the secret is no longer a secret: it has been, in a way, delivered into the public realm already because "told to the Other." This "public" nature of even the most private of privacies means, for Derrida, that the secret has always and already been handed over to realm of "the They" in which the secret *is* only as already revealed, as *immer schon* passed on as the "latest news." Suddenly the secret is a lot less secretive! In technical terms: the conditions of possibility of the secret are at the same time the conditions of its impossibility: I can only keep something secret as soon as I decide to share this secret with at least one person. The secret presupposes the ever-present possibility of "going public."[20]

What could this secret be, about which we, according to Derrida at least, best avoid speaking? Why does Derrida state that "if you would know how I pray and what I pray for, you would know everything"? Because we would then have a transparent gaze upon his prayer and tears? Because we would then know what we in a certain sense know already, namely that this secretive faith is not as pure and not as secretive as it portends to be? Because the secret would then be no longer as grand, vital, and mysterious as Caputo, for instance, would like us to believe? Might it be the case, for example, that Derrida's faith then turns out not to be as pure as the modern and postmodern mysophobics have it?

Let us, then, imagine Derrida as a "natural metaphysician" for a moment. This would mean, first, that Derrida took in Levinas's argument of the ontotheological "halting" of the movement of "*infinition*" by the third party and would therefore be able to recognize that the distinction between the ethics of the Other and what Levinas called "*la foi du charbonnier*"[21] cannot be drawn easily: some instrumentalization of the divine does not let itself be eradicated, and philosophy and theology would forever be haunted by ontotheology. In this regard, it is worth pointing to Arto Paasilinna's character Pirjeri as one of the finest imaginings of the "natural ontotheologian." Pirjeri, an ordinary and not particularly pious Finnish peasant, is chosen to stand in for the tired, old God, who is in desperate need of a holiday. Here is what Paasilinna writes:

> Even now Pirjeri was in a certain sense a man of faith, albeit in a typical Finnish, unfaithful way. He did not practice his faith through attending Church, but was content with a personal relation to God. Pirjeri made a habit of sending juicy informal prayers to heaven whenever he thought necessary. If the prayer was answered and the problem solved, then, fine, and Pirjeri's faith in the Almighty was strengthened. If his wish would remain unanswered, he would shrug his shoulders and said: oh well, nothing ventured, nothing gained; apparently, God does not exist after all. During barren, cold winters [. . .] he asked, to pass time, for better weather and prayed to God that his joints would not be affected by rheumatism. On a sunny summer day, he would pray less often.[22]

Is it not here that one can see that our human, all too human prayers and tears know of no secret or cannot keep secret that a certain instrumentality of faith and of God cannot be avoided if we are to describe these prayers and these tears phenomenologically? And if these prayers and tears cannot avoid invoking God as a *Gott mit uns* rather than the "wholly other" God of the Other, would this not be *closer* to "everybody's autobiography,"[23] which

Derrida has in mind in *Circumfession*, rather than the solemn and lofty prayer Caputo wants us to pray? Lest, of course, Derrida's confession needs to be the autobiography not of everyone, but of "everyone and nobody," *für allen und keinen*, rather than the misery of a nobody like Pirjeri.

In short, I suspect that Derrida, unlike Caputo, would cling to the essential contamination or "pervertibility" of faith. In this way, the secret that incites and ignites faith would be that there is no secret to this faith and that it at least never is as pure as Caputo surmises: it is not without belief/s. Rather, one could contend that there is no such thing as a pure faith and that faith, if there is any such thing, elides the hierarchies of pur*er* and pur*est* faiths, for there to be in effect the possibility of something like "everybody's autobiography." This is why I insisted above on the "double passage" of the quasi-transcendental: it cuts both ways. Caputo forgets the tragic feel of deconstruction. The cut that is deconstruction therefore is directed not only against "strong" theology, against metaphysics and a stabilized destiny, but also against those who claim (hubristically?) to be forever outside of ontotheology and metaphysics and would so attain the purity of destinerrancy. Both the "impure" beliefs of ontotheology and the "pure" faith of Caputo would be cut off before even reaching their prime. This would mean that Caputo's anti-metaphysics suddenly turns very metaphysical and erects hierarchies as metaphysical and deconstructible as the ones he is trying to avoid. For Caputo, in effect, Derrida's prayer is "more aporetic, more uncertain [and] more desert-like" than the prayers prayed in any strong theology: in fact, it would be "*superior* to traditional orthodox views."[24] The fact that what once was "top-down" (strong theology) is now "bottom-up" (weak theology) therefore does not alter the fact that there is a mutually exclusive hierarchical distinction at work here. It is still a question, for Caputo, of *either* strong theology *or* weak theology: "the movement by which one determines the destination of prayer as [God] is an attempt to *still* or *arrest* [. . .] indeterminacy and destinerrancy," whereas, for Derrida, it might be a matter of realizing that it is precisely the thought of a stable destiny that can never be stilled or arrested.[25]

For what indeed would be the difference between Derrida's earliest memory of the word God, his mother thanking God for his temperature going down, and the horrible invocation of the name of God justifying the violence of the tsunami that Caputo evokes at the opening of his *The Weakness of God*?[26] Both instrumentalizations of the divine show that nothing is more common or natural than the human being trying to alleviate or otherwise explain away his or her being "cut off from the truth."[27] Nothing in effect would come more easily to the "natural ontotheologian" than to close the gap between him- or herself and the truth through relating this truth to his or her particular *Geworfenheit* and beliefs, just as Heidegger insisted that the "empty place" of the divine would, after metaphysics, soon be "occupied" anew because the "authoritative place" always remains. In short, whereas Caputo interprets Derrida as the beginning of prayer, as the way toward a more originary faith, nothing in Derrida prevents us from focusing on, exactly, "the end of prayer," where a certain ontotheological instrumentalization of the divine come naturally to us. Derrida would then not be describing the origin of faith, but rather the experience of the one who is always and already losing his faith, who suffers from always and already having lost his faith or only has faith "in a very unfaithful way." It is, then, in an ontotheological condition that the human being might be lodged, and it is, similarly, this condition that Caputo seems to dodge.

It is thus not that Caputo desires the permanence and assurance of premodern faith; it is rather that he seeks to reify somewhat "postmodern" restlessness and uncertainty so that this restlessness itself is stabilized and present permanently, so that the passion for the impossible itself "is the only permanence."[28] It is the latter, then, that phenomenology tries to expel from our desires and strip from referents up high, for nothing is permanent, not even uncertainty. In fact, what a phenomenology of religious life would show is that all of our prayers are rather impure, that what we share, as "natural ontotheologians," is an instrumentalization of the divine that cannot be avoided all the way. But this faith, by insisting on the impurities of these prayers, has the advantage of no longer differentiating between "pure" and "impure" prayers simply by taking into account the instrumental impurity of everyone's prayer—not the least that of myself, but if I'd tell you that you in effect would know everything. It is this that the idea of an unredeemedness within the human being intends to convey and to which I come back in the conclusion: the "Christian" has more in common with the sinner than with the saint.

If we are to follow Derrida, then it would be more appropriate to think through the dynamics if not dialectic between certainty and uncertainty, between Augustine the bishop and Augustine the seeker, to gain sight of the flux of faith, of a faith "which comes and which goes" and which fluctuates between atheism and theism. An *impure faith*, then, would be a faith that would *fail* when it comes to both the credentials asked for by a strong theology as well as the restlessness demanded by a weak theology. This is why I will turn to Derrida and describe the primacy of bad conscience for our portrayal of a phenomenology of a religious life. First, however, I inquire into Caputo's account of the "non-sovereign" God issuing from the later Derrida's works.

The Aporia, and the Great Unknown: God

One already knows that, for Caputo, conversion is a onetime, quasi-permanent endeavor, or that it at least should be as somewhat of a regulative ideal: "What do I love, when I love my God?" Caputo asks in the wake of Augustine. This question, for Caputo, changes everything—it therefore acquires a sort of permanence in the sense that things can *never* get back to the way they were: one can only ask this very question Caputo argues from within the horizon of love, that is, once the vain attempt to self-love has been abandoned and when one therefore has also abandoned the fate of the self to the possibility of love once and for all. It is then and only then, according to Caputo, that the human being becomes a question to him- or herself; thus revealing that love itself instigates the quest for knowledge. Caputo writes:

> Augustine's story shows us that religion kicks in, not necessarily when we sign on the dotted line of some *confessional* faith or other, but when we confess our love for something besides ourselves, when we [. . .] "bind ourselves over" (*re-ligare*) to something *other*, which means something other than ourselves or [. . .] when we gather ourselves together (*re-legere*) and center ourselves on a transforming focus of our love.[29]

Such transformation and conversion are radical. Caputo notes that when Augustine still attempted to love himself, for the sake of the self, he knew exactly what he wanted, who he was or was expected to be—a rhetorical master, for instance—but once the question of God is raised as precisely a question to God concerning himself/ourselves, everything is rendered uncertain, and "an abyss of endless questionability" is opened.[30] This transformation is a self-transformation in and through a center outside of ourselves. This is what constitutes the religious condition for Caputo: a never-ending response to a question without Answer ("Here I am"), to an unconditional event and appeal, through the permanent *service* to something other than myself, to that which is greater than all that which I can answer and of which I know the answer.[31] This service has to be interpreted as a passion, a passion for the impossible: a constant restlessness accompanying the fight for (universal) justice. In this search for justice, the ethical strand of deconstruction transpires, although the turn itself is inspired by Levinasian thought, for the latter already noted that "*la justice précède la vérité*," justice precedes truth. With this, Levinas underscores the fact that the truth of epistemology (of ontology, of being, etc.)—the truth that with a great sense of certainty can state that "snow is white if and only if snow is white"—is relative to the truth that gestures between the other and me. The truth, *even* ontological truth, is that truth only occurs in this bend toward the other, in this "intersubjective curvature" that is the most primordial opening to truth thinkable.

This Levinasian strand is Caputo's point of departure, although he will, more than Levinas did, emphasize the religious underpinnings of such an ethics of and for the Other. This religious inspiration takes the form of an unconditional primacy of love. Caputo confesses to a pluralist stance when it comes to the "question of the religions," for all concrete, empirical religions and their dogmas and doctrines can at any time be deconstructed—these are merely historical constructs that should not be confused with ontological or other necessities—but these deconstructions themselves are possible only "in the light of the love of God which is not deconstructible."[32]

The content of the "concrete" religions is thus open to deconstruction, and rightly so, while the "love for God," the name of God (or of justice or of love), will always—even when criticized and perhaps especially then—rise from the ashes and the ruins of its deconstructions. Caputo thus takes a stance against both an exclusivism with regard to revelation (We have the Truth and all the Answers and you don't) and an inclusivism (We have the Truth and all the Answers; it's only that you don't know it yet) and proposes to place the truth of religion where it is confessed that one knows neither of truth nor of any answers. Religion, Caputo argues, can never deny its contingent and finite origins, even though it originates

> in *response* to something that has swept us away, something impossible, something other or wholly other to which we are responding, which has driven us to the limit. But human beings are responsible for all the particulars of the response, for the vocabularies, for the theologies, and all the institutional structures which formulate in definite and determinate ways *just what* has swept them away.[33]

The difference between what can be deconstructed and what cannot be therefore does not pass through the human being: it is not up to us to criticize what cannot be criticized, for example, the event of world (escaping "our own making") or even the passion for the impossible (eliding all calculations and quantifications of the shrunken, modern world, where only what is rational is what is real). Therefore, it seems certain for Caputo—and perhaps *too* certain—that such an impulse found within "thou shalt not deconstruct what cannot be deconstructed" has to be interpreted religiously and ethically—if we can still tell the difference, that is—even though the impulse itself bears many names and is "said in many ways." What matters, for Caputo, is that this impulse resembles a revelation of sorts; minimally meaning that the truth of this impulse escapes all human grasping and is thus is a *given* (whereas, for Nancy and Schürmann, it is a matter of thinking without any such givens). What matters, after this recognition, is the realization that any name we would give to this impulse is first and foremost the name *we* give to this pulse and that these names therefore are as contingent, finite, and subject to change as we ourselves are; ever so many names for the unnameable.

This is the critique of idols: even the God *pro nobis*, who in the Christian teachings turns toward us, is first of all a name we have given to this God "for the sake of ourselves." The latter sense of "for us" can in effect have multiple meanings: it might be an alienating illusion (Marx), a projection (Feuerbach), an instrumental will to power proceeding from thought toward God even (ontotheology), but, even then, it cannot be excluded that the impulse and the drive toward the unnameable and the unconditional are given (religio-ethical deconstruction).

> When we put our head down and love God with all our strength, we do not know whether love is an exemplification of God or God is an exemplification of love. Or whether justice is one of the names we use to speak about God or whether the name of God is a way we have of speaking about justice. Or the impossible (the list goes on). We confess that we remain confused about this point.[34]

The confusion of names here is aporetic or inconclusive: we will never have the Knowledge at our disposal with which to decide whether God is love or rather that it is love that resembles something divine. One might compare this aporia with the manner in which Levinas understands the question of responsibility: this responsibility, in effect, wavers between that which philosophy calls the "bad infinite"—the mathematical series: n+1—and the "good infinite" that Levinas sees happening in the encounter with the Other. The "bad infinite" signifies the fact that my responsibility toward the other is in effect endless or limitless; the "good infinite," on the other hand, wagers on the fact that such a responsibility stems from the Infinite, as the movement of "infiniting," *l'infinition*. For this Infinite deflects the "natural" tendencies of the human being (which Levinas at times considers "evil") to interest itself in its self to, precisely, the nondesirable misery of the other. There is an aporia here as well: when confronted with the destitution of the other, we do not *know* whether it is some or other evil genius that cannot "leave us alone" or whether it is a good infinite stirring restlessness in us and so gently forcing us to serve the Other. The point, for Levinas as it would be for Caputo, is that the distinction between such a good and a bad infinite in the end does not really matter: what matters is that the other is served, whether it be through a "good" or "bad" inspiration.[35] In this respect, responsibility and servitude to the other come first, and the maintaining of a difference between the good and the bad infinite could be just another way to approach this transcendent impulse in too *abstract* a manner so as to turn it into a theory again and avoid all responsibility.

Conclusion: Between Faith and Belief

It is, with regard to the aporia, to be noted that Caputo lately has made some adjustments to what first appeared as a properly Derridean "double bind." Whereas first the aporetic relation without relation was to be configured as a relation between the diverse historical messianisms and their condition of possibility, messianicity in general, to such an extent that it would not be possible to say which comes first. It would, in other words, not be possible to see whether one comes from the extant religious tradition to the messianic impulse that inhabits them or the other way around, that is, from the messianic to the concrete messianisms. In terms of our debate here, it would not be detectable whether one comes from "religion with religion" to the impulse that "religion without religion" gives to the former or the other way around.

However, Caputo now insists that, instead of sticking to a Kantian interpretation of the messianic as a condition of possibility for the concrete messianisms, it is better to see the messianisms—all of them—as ever so many Heideggerian formal indications where "the singular is thought not as a particular under a universal but as an unrepeatable, irreplaceable individual" testifying, in effect, to that which possibly "is going on" *in* these actual and extant messianisms. It is here that Caputo moves beyond a certain Derrida, "help[ing him] out" as it were, to move beyond the clutches of Kantian formalism, where the concrete "religions with religion" would be but inferior instantiations of a condition of possibility prescribing for them how they ought to happen and toward an "indication" of what is (im)possible *within* the given traditions through unleashing "a potency that is actualized in the concrete performance."[36] The improvement is considerable, but it remains a sort of one-way traffic that disregards Derrida's "double passage" or attempt at "[doing] justice to the two possibilities" of going back and forth from the concrete revealed religions to the impulse inhabiting them *and* from such a quasi-transcendental impulse to the very concrete messianisms in which it, well, incarnates.[37]

The improvement is that Caputo now, especially after giving up his initial resistance toward "theology," seems more firmly footed in the history and the traditions of the concrete religions. *Il faut essayer* after all. Yet one might wonder whether Caputo is not simply substituting one aporia for another. Let us consider his response to Kevin Hart on this very problem, where Caputo seems to insist on a "proper way" to enter into aporetic problems, somewhat like Heidegger proposed to come into the hermeneutical circle in the right way.[38] Caputo then returns to a distinction between faith (*foi*) and belief (*croyance*), which, supposedly, both take place within the horizon of *khôra* or the secret—this is why the "unknowing" of destinerrancy is, for Derrida, not denied to those "believers" in a stable destiny: they would, perhaps, *only* flee for such unknowing, like *Das Man* flees into everydayness. The distinction between faith and belief then becomes a distinction "between the *indeterminate but indefinitely determinable structure of* foi, as a kind of archi-faith which goes to the heart of the human heart, and the variously determinate and historically concrete *croyances*."[39] Yet, even if one would concede the distinction (which, itself, is utterly deconstructible, as Chapter 2 has shown), it would still be indebted to some sort of Kantianism in the very precise sense that one or the other "a priori" horizon of human existence would again be presupposed (whether it is called *khôra* or not). And although one could easily concede that some givens pertain to the human condition, it need not be conceded just yet that this condition would be one of "love," "faith," or "religion" for that matter: for this, a phenomenological ontology of love with an eye to empirical beliefs would be needed and not an a priori judgment that it is religion or love that is present for everyone always and everywhere.[40]

The advantage of reconfiguring the aporia along Heidegger's notion of "formal indication" is surely that it allows one to rephrase the question of Christianity's deconstruction, for what if indeed there is only "the different empirical Christianities" to grasp what a "Christianity to come" might be? What if all the detectives have to work with and to investigate are these faiths that are always and already filled with beliefs? Then there would be no such thing as a *foi* that is "more pure" than any other of mixture of faith and belief.

At best, one would arrive at a less impure faith, and even Derrida's faith, if there is any, would be similar to the faith of a nobody like Pirjeri, mixed with beliefs that one believes are all too improper. In short, one would be hard-pressed to still distinguish between weak and strong theologies, because these latter theologies would be the only valid starting point if these beliefs are to function as formal indications of whatever "is going on" in these theologies. The deconstruction of Christianity, in a Derridean vein, would insist that there is in effect nothing outside the tradition, nothing outside the texts of these traditions; and even the ones who believe and hope that "the name of God cannot be contained by the historical contingency of the names [one has] inherited in [one's] tradition"[41] are destined to be more like Munchausen than Prometheus or, if you like, likely to be deconstruct*ed* more than they would deconstruct.

Instead of assuming that a "horizon" for human existence is always and already in place—was the whole point of the event not to shatter horizons?—it is therefore necessary that Caputo too turn to a phenomenology of religious life that knows of this mixture between faith and beliefs. This is why in the next chapter I align Caputo's thought to Marion's strong theology, if only to show that the distinction between weak and strong theology does not overlap with the distinction between faith and belief, as Caputo wants us to, well, believe, but also to take into account that a contemporary deconstruction of Christianity will need to take into account the sheer indifference to religion, the indifference of those for whom such a religious horizon is not always and already firmly in place. This is what the chapters on Sloterdijk already set out to do.

7

Between Weak and Strong Theology

Of a Sacred Anarchy in Caputo and Marion

A Christian Reversal of Values

Even though the distinction between "religion without religion" and "religion with religion" is not "airtight" and the demarcation line is drawn only to keep "the lines of communication open between them," this distinction might still be too sharp and too stark.[1] This chapter therefore seeks to expose some of the weaker points of Caputo's weak theology, for instance, that the "law of reversals"[2] is just as well made by the "strong theologian" Jean-Luc Marion, which would mean that Caputo's distinction between weak and strong theology does not always seem to hold. At the very least, this distinction can and needs some deconstruction. This chapter furthermore contends that on some parts of Derrida and Levinas's account of the "natural ontotheologian," Caputo remains all too silent. It concludes by presenting Marion's thought on nihilism and saturation and showing that Caputo's and Marion's proposals, on the indifference of our contemporaries toward the religious life, is, to say the least, less sensitive than Nancy, Derrida and, in later chapters, Binswanger.

Let us first dwell on the distinction between strong and weak theology. Caputo gives two reasons why he is attached to the Christian religion. The first is rather banal, the second, though, of utmost importance. The banal reason is that Caputo arguably "has a weakness for theology"[3] and is educated in a still quasi-Christian culture: one, quite automatically, uses the name and the names that belong to this culture. The second reason is considerably more important: the non-sovereign "God," which Derrida mentioned quite favorably in *Rogues*, is for Caputo Christianity's most radical contribution to the ethico-religious critique of idolatry. It is to this that I now turn.

The non-sovereign God is for Caputo a weak God, but a name used for the event that is being-in-the-world and for a God who does not make an exception of himself. God, for instance, does not *pretend* to be weak: it is not the case that God decides to give up, for the time being, all of his powerful properties. Rather, God disposes of no other power than precisely this weakness. With this, Caputo distinguishes himself from the entire tradition of *kenosis*, which one can still see (though in an ethical fashion) in Levinas's *Totality and Infinity*: it does not concern a subject, divine or not, that *first* can peacefully build and dwell in the world *only then* to be confronted with the other and "more or less" decide to do away with all of its possessions and its powers and deflect them to serve the other. In the very same way, Caputo is not aiming for a God who, at first, is all-powerful, omniscient, and so forth, who would only afterward decide to abandon such absolute properties.

This is ultimately what the narratives surrounding Jesus seem to indicate. Jesus, the anarchist, unleashed in the world something like a "divine disturbance"[4] of all worldly values. Jesus, then (Caputo does not speak easily of "Christ"), is "unique"[5] because he, contrary to the victorious and virile divinities of the Roman and Hellenistic worlds, did apparently not succeed in his mission but rather seemed powerless from the beginning and was ultimately tortured to death and publicly crucified.[6] Caputo meditates on the "foolishness of the Cross" to make room for the understanding that it was not all that foolish at all. On the contrary, the reasonableness of this foolishness consists in what I will call here, despite what Nietzsche thinks, the *Christian inversion of values*, of a "sacred anarchy."[7] This inversion issues from Caputo's penetrating reading of Mt. 22, 1–14, a wedding where none of the invited actually shows up and where the host decides to admit the passersby, though strangers to both the groom (Christ) and the bride (Church), to the feast. "The Kingdom is like this": "In the Kingdom, the insiders are out, have missed out, while the outsiders are in!"[8]

One of the core texts for this inversion certainly stems from Paul's letters, of which Caputo says that it is one of the charters of his weak theology:

> But God chose the foolish things of the world to shame the wise; God chose the weak things of the world to shame the strong. God chose the lowly things of this world and the despised things—and the things that are not (*ta me onta*)—to nullify the things that are, so that no one may boast before him. (1 Cor. 1, 27–29)

Caputo rightly reminds us of the fact that Jesus himself was one of those "things" that the world did not hold in high esteem (*ta me onta*) and, secondly, that "the religious relationship to the world arises in the face of this facelessness and hopelessness."[9] God's solidarity with the suffering of Jesus, who, in the world, was "less than nothing," accords a certain theological legitimacy to Caputo's ethics of resistance: for God, then, there might not be such a thing as the *ta me onta*. One might say that anyone who can still realize that the powerful are in essence powerless, that the rich have but a poor idea of what it is to be human or that the rulers are slaves to their power, and that that which for the world seems of no worth at all—the uselessness of love and faith, for instance—is what really counts, *then* he or she realizes something essential to Christianity, whether or not he or she has paid the entrance fee to the Kingdom.

Yet it is remarkable just how close Caputo's account here is to that of the "strong theology" of Marion and even seems to run into the same problems. Marion, for instance, mentions the exact same Bible pericopes when portraying God's descent—*condescendance*—toward the world as a continuous incarnation of sorts. In both Marion and Caputo, moreover, this descent "outwits" the play of being and beings, although in Caputo this would need to be interpreted as God's coming to and within the world without the world, as the "beyond" of world "within" the world. For Marion, God's incarnational movement is indifferent to all that "is" and that boasts upon being a high, if not the highest, being. What use is it, one could think, of the human intellect to ascend to an abstract Absolute—one that is all-powerful and overflowing of goodness—and of what use is it to have the capacity to think an essence of all essences if such a thing is immutable and unchanging? And finally, what use are "*the powers that be*" if these powers are rendered powerless in the face of the "great leveler" that is death?

But God, for Marion, is not indifferent to the individual being or the being of an individual as such. On the contrary, God's call consists precisely in calling the individual being (human or not) as such. God, "*[aborde] l'etant comme tel*," approaches a particular being as such, without taking into account the role this being plays in the world or in being as an individual being, but rather as an individual "You": "Where are you, Adam?" (Gen. 3: 8–9) in relation to the Father.[10] Such roles, turning the individual being into an anonymous anyone or into everyman (Philip Roth) or through which the individual inversely could boast on being "something" in this world, are obviously just as much roles "in a drama of which it is not the author" (Levinas). For such roles force this being here to *participate* in the rat race of today, forced to be "efficient," "productive," and "useful," brought outside of itself through the powers of the world over which it has no control whatsoever. It is this role, then, which is, through God's appeal, annulled, downplayed, and outwitted: "if you want to boast, boast on the Lord" (cf. 1 Cor. 1, 31).

For Marion, this indifference of God toward the ontic/ontological difference between being and beings has important consequences for ethics. This God, "coming from the outside," from without being, does not care for that for which the world cares—it is not inappropriate to think of *Sorge* here. God is indifferent, for instance, to ontic differences. This means that God is indifferent to both "absolute genesis" and "absolute corruption." The "absolute genesis" is the indifference toward anything that would think itself a highest being (and even toward the ontotheology that holds itself in high esteem through thinking the highest being), indifference toward the illusion of autonomy, of "not owing anything to anyone," as Marion repeatedly writes in *Being Given*.[11] Absolute genesis would be autonomous to such an extent that it cannot entertain relations with any otherness whatsoever and so turns, in the words of Martin Buber, "existence itself into a refuge."[12]

Over and against this "absolute genesis"—in which the nullity of existents pretends to be something—stands the absolute corruption of death, in which this "something" is turned to nothing. God is indifferent to this ontic difference just as well: God calls that which is "less than nothing" the *ta me onta*, as if it *is* something after all and turns it into a real being to such an extent that, for God, no such thing as the *ta me onta* exists. God, in Marion's thinking, is the one who perfectly controls the Christian inversion of values (and perhaps a bit too perfectly). Furthermore, this victory over "absolute corruption" is not only a triumph over death but also, for Marion at least, shows God as sovereign ruler over nothingness, over the *tohu vabohu* of which the book of Genesis speaks. In this way, the Lord "of heaven and earth" creates not only out of nothing—*ex nihilo*—but even nothingness itself—*de nihilo*. Hence Marion's statement that "the appeal of God" counters the absolute corruption of death as well.[13]

God, for Marion, surpasses not only the ontic differences between beings—that which is and is not—but also the ontological difference—the fact that beings are always and already lodged in being. One might interpret this "overcoming" therefore as follows: because the folding of individual beings into Being is annulled here, this very being is set free from its subjection to Being, where again "it would play a role in a drama of which it is not the author" because the beings that you and I are *are* beings that *have* to be their being without our prior accord. The individual being, then, appears for God without its lodging in (universal) Being.[14]

What exactly does this mean? Being, for Marion as for Levinas, is some sort neuter and, to follow Kant's saying, "not a real predicate," which means: being can be said *in the same way* about human beings and roses, for the rose *is* just as much as the human being *is*. Therefore Being (or even the being of this being) can never be what turns this being into a unique being or singular individual, for it is being precisely that this individual being would share with all other beings—this is the infamous *ens commune*. God, on the other hand, approaches, if God does so, that is, "the being as such," you just as well as me in "our" very singularity.

So, on this topic at least, Caputo and Marion are rather close. Caputo even applauds Marion's attempt at a God untied to and uncontaminated by being at times, which makes the harsh remarks against Marion even more awkward (see Chapter 5).[15] I have shown, moreover, that both God's turn to singularity as well as something of the sacred anarchy and the Christian reversal of values that Caputo proposes are present in Marion as well. Caputo is very much aware of these similarities and even anticipates a "formidable objection" to such a divinely instituted anarchy, namely that if "with God all things are possible, even the impossible [, one does not] enter into the very warp and woof of strong theology and the metaphysics of omnipotence, of miracles and divine intervention" and whether all this would not make "the name of God [. . .] the name of the strongest force of all"?[16] The question is in effect if God would be perfectly in control of this law of reversals and so would be, yet again, the authority of authorities.

A Sacred Anarchy, or the Authority of Authorities

It is on this issue of God that Caputo's distinction between the metaphysics of omnipotence and his poetics of the impossible seems to founder and becomes untenable, as we have seen Hägglund also observe. For here the demarcation line between what is possible for us and what is impossible becomes highly questionable, and Caputo omits the weal and the woe of us natural ontotheologians. Let us first consider the "strong theologian" Marion on the question of what exactly is possible for the human being with regard to the question of the divine. Rather late in *God without Being*, Marion asks the following question: "if the crossing of being and the distraction of ontological difference could be conceived only from the point of view of

God as agape, the analytic of man as Dasein would remain, *for us*, impassable, ontological difference, *for us*, unavoidable."[17] For Marion, just as for Caputo, faith necessarily turns to a certain ethics, because if "the being that it in each case is and has to be" and even that which this being could boast upon in being is of little concern to God, then this individual being rather has to *imitate* this divine indifference toward being and beings—by remaining indifferent for the play of being/s precisely and offering resistance whenever such indifference would no longer be the case. For Marion, this is accomplished, at the time of *God without Being* at least, foremost in boredom for which the play between being and beings obviously offers no solace. Boredom in Marion is in effect a precursor of the erotic reduction: when the play between being and beings disappears, it is the love of God that will appear. In more existential terms: if for the bored gaze, the meaning of being itself appears as something impossible—being does not make sense—then, at this very moment, the gaze is (still) envisaged by the gaze of God for whom nothing is impossible and so makes a true meaning possible. The possible "for us" and the impossible "for God" turn into logical and dialectical opposites: "the frontier between the possible and the impossible *for us* opens exactly this impossibility itself as the possible *for God*."[18] Even from this brief survey of Marion's thinking of the (im)possible, it might be clear that this "God without being" borders on an omnipotent being, if only because it ridicules both what is possible and what is impossible for us natural ontotheologians.

Yet the point is that things are not considerably different in Caputo's poetics of the impossible. Caputo's poetics suddenly veer into a very transcendental direction again, "bracketing" all thoughts of a superbeing existing somewhere "out there," bracketing in short everything we would know and be acquainted with from out of the text of the tradition to arrive at the "phenomenal field"[19] of the kingdom, which ought to inspire our imagination concerning the possibility of the impossible. For this, Caputo proposes a reduction of the word and the name of God:

> this is a reduction *from* any present determination or determinate form of the name of God, *from* what is happening or being named in the name of God at present, which contracts God to the order of being, *to* whatever event the name of God is promising."[20]

All of a sudden, then, Caputo shows himself again at his most transcendental, bracketing all actuality that could make for a formal indicator toward an event ridding itself of all proper names. Yet again one sees Caputo stretching the gap between the empirical and the transcendental by assuming, very much like Nancy, that the *entirety* of the empirical traditions falls neatly under the hatch of the reducing ego in order to jump to "the without" tradition as one would jump to a conclusion, forgetting in this regard that in the "originary" dizziness of a quasi-transcendental phenomenology, even that which the ego so transcendentally constitutes relies upon and is contaminated by its being, prior to the reduction, constitut*ed* by its thrownness in these very traditions.

But, as ever, the empirical strikes back with a vengeance, for, in Caputo as in Marion, these petty possibilities of finitude and the impossibility that is God are not matched that easily as any dialectics would want. So one sees Caputo erecting hierarchical distinctions very close to the ones Marion employs: on the one hand, there is the world, the biblical *cosmos* of which Saint Paul speaks, which "prevents the event,"[21], preventing the impossible by strictly staying within the limits of the possible alone; on the other hand, there is "God," for whom nothing of the sort is impossible and who certainly "is not conditioned by any conditions that would constrict God's giving under this or that finite measure or constraint."[22] All of a sudden, then, as Hägglund remarked, an utterly deconstructible distinction is erected between the finite totality of a world, constrained by its empirical conditions for which nothing is possible, and a "God," unconstrained and unconditioned, for whom nothing is impossible—outside of being, but not outside of ontotheology: *conditio sui*![23] All of a sudden, there appears an infinite in Caputo that never will be "contracted" or "determined," and that is anything but "relative to a horizon."[24]

The similarity between Marion and Caputo here shows itself in their respective responses to the question of just how one needs to attend to the experience of impossibility. Marion's answer is, as I will show later, inherited from the strongest of strong theologies: first and foremost, the human being lacks the will to love God's gaze upon him or her and ends up hating love: boredom will come to hate the gaze it feels weighing upon itself. There are no gradations here: either one loves God or one hates love. The "deformity of the sinner"[25] is such that one only ever loves insufficiently. In Marion, therefore, the human being lacks structurally (for theological reasons) the means to attend to the coming of the divine (as opposed to Christ, whose abandon to God will function as the norm and the criterion and the "perfection" of the human response to the divine).

Something similar happens in Caputo (although not theologically), for what would be the difference between accusing people of not attending to impossibility properly (through sin) or not loving love in the appropriate manner through sticking to the safety of a transcendental horizon of ethics (through just following the rules and not jumping to the supererogatory hyperbolic ethics). The latter is indeed what Caputo seems to suggest by increasingly likening Derrida's hyperbolic ethics to Heidegger's account of "the they," where the ones who stick to "what is possible" remain with an everyday "following the rules" and do not have the heroic courage to attend to the impossible by, for instance, turning the other cheek, greeting violence with kindness, and what not.[26] What for Marion amounts to a lack of will, for Caputo amounts to a lack of courage. Hägglund's analysis is acutely correct here:

> Caputo turns the passion for the impossible into a matter of heroism. [This] indicates how far he is willing to go to save the idea that there is an opposition between the possible and the impossible[:] Caputo has to assume that there is a "security" of the possible where things are safe, calculable, and free of risk, in order then to oppose it to the "insecurity" of "the impossible" [. . .] where only saints or monsters dare to go.[27]

One might indeed argue that here Caputo succumbs to a dialectics of the possible and the impossible, which Derrida was particularly keen to avoid, and turns, to use Levinas's words, the enigma into a simple dilemma (where "the same" is safely sheltered from "the other"), so forgetting the co-implication of the impossible *within* the possible, as two orders that accord as an arpeggio prior to hierarchical and heroic thematization: *either* one sticks to the safety of what can be done *or* one attends to the other in an impossible, supererogatory way. In Derrida's terms, the gap between the conditional and the unconditional here becomes one of "exteriority," where the one has nothing to do with the other, or one of "simple opposition and contradiction," where the possibility would simply yield to impossibility.

In the first case—of exteriority—the "sacred anarchy" again seems to be upheld by some sort of miraculous intervention of God, through which the impossible becomes possible after all; in the second case—of simple opposition—the passageway from what is possible to what is impossible is possible only once the realm of the possible is clearly and distinctly seen only then to revert (dialectically) to its reverse side, where the possible would yield the impossible (but, as such, is still "within the same").

These similarities between Caputo's weak theology and the strong theology of Marion seem to indicate that the distinction between these theologies cannot always be made as neatly as Caputo wants. Instead of opposing strong theology (to the point of fighting an invisible enemy), what is needed, it seems, is again an account of the degrees and the gradations between strong and weak theology. For, as it now stands, likening "strong theology" to the works of Marion and Milbank *and* to fundamentalism has the odd effect of producing both strong theologies *without* fundamentalism (Milbank and Marion) and fundamentalism *without* strong theology, without theology seeking to understand itself, that is. One would need an account of the *tertium datur* between strong and weak theology or, more modest, between "religion with religion" and "religion without religion." Let us listen to Caputo one more time:

> Fundamentalism [. . .] is an embarrassment to the orthodox. It shows what happens when people take what orthodoxy believes in the simplest way and carry it [. . .] to its more extreme conclusions. [But] fundamentalism and orthodoxy share a lot of core beliefs up to and including a common understanding of religious truth as representational.[28]

But, on this score, where would the dividing line lie between "religion with religion," "strong theology," and fundamentalism if all three of them err in sticking to representational truths: how does one differentiate exactly between less and more extreme; between, say, simple apologetics and warriors of faith? It seems more appropriate, then, instead of opposing the representational truths that are part and parcel of "religions with religion," to not rid ourselves of representational truths as easily as Caputo suggests and remain with a certain unavoidability of representation, thematization, and, as I will show in Marion, conceptual idolatry. This, at least, would bring the "reduction" back to its starting point within the *tertium datur* that are the beliefs, the representations, and the traditions of the extant religious traditions and within the ontotheological condition that is ours and is unable to do away with "the with."

From Caputo to Marion: Abandoned to Love?

For Marion, just as for Caputo, faith necessarily turns to an active stance or to some form of existential engagement close to Schürmann's "practical apriori": an attending to that which ties us the other and to what therefore functions as a given or as givenness (and in which Caputo too quickly sees a metaphysical superstructure of sorts). The gift of all beings, of all that is, means that the beings-within-the-world (and the beings that we ourselves are) can never be interpreted as a "possession" or as something "at our disposal," but rather as something like a "borrowed item" that turns "my being" into something that never is "mine" or my "own," but always and already is given by (and thus received from) the other.[29] To see the givenness of beings—what the believer would call "creation"—signifies that we can appropriate neither beings nor "the being that I in each case am and have to be" to such a point that being (or the being of these beings) can never turn into our complete, total possession and is, simply, never at our disposal. On the contrary, the believer, for Marion as for Caputo, will here subscribe completely to a philosophy of finitude and speak of the "things that pass" and of a world where all that seems necessary is as contingent as the next thing. This obviously does not mean that there is nothing to do or that there is nothing to act on in this finite world of ours. It does mean, however, that all actions and all deeds have to be relativized and nuanced from within—one would be tempted to use the term "autodeconstructive acts" here. Surely the believer can dwell, enjoy, and work within the world, to use Levinas's phrasings, but both the believer and the philosopher of finitude will confirm that, just as in the parable of the prodigal Son, the complaining son, for Marion, is wrong simply because he sees the gift of his father as a possession and no longer sees that even the possibility to possess first needs to be given: both the believer and the atheist will have to deal with the "transitory" character of all things.[30] But, before developing this philosophy of finitude a bit more, let us have a look at Marion's account of this sin, this lack of will to attend to givenness, which for him is a lack of openness to love.

Metaphysics and Nihilism

It has become customary to complain, especially in theological circles, about contemporary culture's lack of transcendence. In our days, so goes the complaint, "Appearances do not exceed themselves."[31] James Smith adds that because these appearances are "no longer appearances *of* a transcendent original or prototype, they are no longer 'appearances' at all."[32] The immanence of our finite being-in-the-world has stripped itself of its transcendent origin, leaving only a realm of mere appearance seemingly marked by superficiality. We have, supposedly, lost the depth in and of all appearances, and banality would govern over our era.

The phenomenological theology of Marion tries to retrieve just such a depth in phenomena, first in a theological fashion and only later through the means of the phenomenological method. In fact, the transcendence and the depth envisaged by Marion is, in his oeuvre, said in many names, most notably, "distance," "saturation," "excess," and "gift." The following sections provide an alternative reading of Marion's work by arguing that the transcendence of distance of the so-called early works is entirely maintained in Marion's later phenomenological work and that, in fact, one single theological figure governs both the thinking of distance and the later thought of givenness: revelation as God's full, definitive, unique, and universal abandonment to the world through love.

Before, however, looking at the details of Marion's proposal to remedy the contemporary lack and loss of transcendence, it is perhaps fitting to see just what the diagnosis of our contemporary culture actually is. For even if one can disagree with the proposed remedy of the contemporary situation by the theologians, it is hard not to agree with their diagnosis: our era is marked and stamped by the end of metaphysics and the nihilism issuing forth from it. All of these, nowadays, have to be "overcome": "in the times that nihilism makes epoch, our times," it is no less than urgent to surpass the denegation of all values, the death of everything that formerly was considered as what was most important.[33]

What is, according to Marion, nihilism exactly, and why is it the accomplice of metaphysics? If the metaphysical God for a time succeeded in guaranteeing and ascertaining the value of the highest and even the lowest values, then it is with the death of this God that nihilism, as the movement in which everyone can value and evaluate in the manner he or she wishes, comes to the fore: "it falls to man to establish the value of every being without exception."[34]

Marion's *God without Being* explains: "Nihilism begins with the devaluation of the highest values; this devaluation itself follows from the discovery that every value [. . .] loses its dignity simply because it receives such a dignity from a foreign evaluation, that of the will to power."[35] Every being is then put under the guard of the subject and is submitted to the subject's power to know and represent in the manner it thinks appropriate. In the words of Marion: "nihilism [. . .] assigns to every being a new way of Being—evaluation by the *Wille zur Macht*. [Only] this nihilistic foundation of the beingness of beings allows one to understand how *nihilism itself* [. . .] completes metaphysics."[36] Once "God" as the—perhaps illusory—highest value, or as at least an instance that prevented the subject from valuing everything at its whims, has faded away, being and beings now only ever come into view if and only if the subject can evaluate these beings at will and at command.

This is also why, for Marion, nihilism marks "the exasperation of idolatry": if the subject can value whatever it likes and whenever it feels so, it follows that there are as many idols as subjects.[37] The distinction between the idol and the icon in Marion's thought is well known: an "idol," obviously, does not mean that David Beckham (or whoever you like) is (a) God; it means rather that (post)modernity cannot imagine anything else, when it thinks of divinity, than the idolatry surrounding someone like Beckham: the paparazzi may follow Beckham as if they were apostles following (their) Christ, but the point is that the paparazzi, unlike the apostles, follow whomever (and wherever) they like. "The will to power," Marion adds, forges 'gods' at every instant: there is nothing, in the modern sense, more *banal* than a 'god.'"[38]

Idolatry, although a grave phenomenon, is therefore marked by banality and superficiality, as if what Marion calls the "platitude of *différance*," valid for every phenomenon and text without exception, has come to life.[39] Idolatry misses the depth that Marion wants to insert and assert, first, in iconic appearance and, later on, into the phenomenon's appearing. "[T]he "depth" of distance" allows for the overcoming of metaphysics and its nihilism and "holds back any threat of idolatry," which, consequently, is a "mask without depth" and only offers the "fallacious depth of a mirror," revealing ultimately the human being's ownmost evaluation of him- or herself.[40] The idol fills the gap between the visible and the invisible with a permanent, fixed, and available god, just like "*différance* fills any [of the trace's] depth."[41]

What, then, does the depth of the icon reveal, for surely it is an account of revelation that is given and offered here—a revelation outside, beyond, *hyper* the reach of the subject's evaluations and representations? Nothing, at least no thing, no being: nothing that can be reified, substantialized, or in any other way caught in the logic of essence. Revelation offers a face, but a "face without mask." No features of this face may be functionalized, and no properties appropriated. Instead of an essence of a substance, "the icon manifests [the] relation" between the Father and the Son in the face of Christ.[42] It thus reveals "the abyssal depth of the Father," but not in a visible figure or mask. Instead of congealing it in a visible form—a substance that could be fixed and identified and, ultimately, evaluated once for all—to view and receive the divinity's iconic appearance is no other than "traversing the depth that surfaces in the visibility of the face," and *relating* to the invisibility that orients the visibility of the world by showing the divine "intention [that] saturates with meaning" through, again, bringing the world into relation with the divine.[43]

Here one sees the theological version of the "eclipse of essence" I noted earlier in Nancy: a complete (and questionable) abandonment of concepts, essences—everything thinking should hold dear: just as religion ought to be "without religion" for Caputo, so for Marion the human being ought to be "without essence." Metaphysics and idolatry for Marion consist mainly of the precedence that a concept takes over a particular being or in the equivalence a concept claims with "God" (or anything else),[44] this is due less to the divinity of God than to the way in which conceptual representations operate, to the point even that conceptual idolatry signals a pleonasm. The logic of representation is such that it fills in the gap between the representation and the being itself: it fills the depth of a being with the represented essence of it, like a designer table could not be conceived as long as the essence of table is to be merely a plateau with four legs. It is for this very reason that Marion, from his early to his later work, attacks such a logic of essence: over and against the reduction to an essence, there needs to be something that cannot be reified: referral, relation, *renvoi*.

Marion's recent works confirm this strict dualism between essence (what is possible) and relation (what is impossible). These texts privilege "unknowing" over all will to know, for the will to know (which is also a will to power) only ever proceeds to improper and even unjust representations or conceptualizations of the human being. Marion mentions three such objectifications: when the human being, for instance, is reduced to a body in a medicalized situation, to a consumer in economic theory, to his or her sociability in and through belonging to a nation-state.[45] The conclusion, for Marion at least, imposes itself: "to claim to define what a man is [. . .] opens the possibility of leading to the elimination of that which does not correspond to this definition,"[46] like the essence of the table precludes certain designer tables to appear at all. It follows that it is only proper for the human being to be "without essence." And here Marion succumbs to what nowadays seems to rage through contemporary philosophy: the attempt, at all costs, to go beyond essence.[47] The "without essence"—the withdrawal from concepts, representations—can, for Marion, only consists of resisting definition and of an "absent essence" and thus of "a reference to an other than him":[48] in its reporting back and relating to the Creator. The likeness to God consists of not being like anything that has an essence: both the human being and God are incomprehensible.

In the icon, then, the invisible God not only "enters" visibility to the point that the visible and the invisible "become acquainted," but it also "inscrib[es]" itself in the visible "by the very reference it imposes": the *renvoi*, referral or the relation of the visible to the invisible.[49] Just as Smith was pleading for a renewed transcendent underpinning of immanence, so too (the early) Marion has recourse to divine revelation to overcome the *Unheimlichkeit* of nihilism.

It remains for us, in the course of this chapter, to better understand the theological figure of revelation offered here. One more quote will serve as a guide through Marion's later philosophy and phenomenology: "the icon [unbalances] human sight in order to engulf it in infinite depth [and] marks such *an advance of God* that even in times of worst distress indifference cannot ruin it. For, to give itself to be seen, the icon needs only itself. This is why it indeed can demand, patiently, that one receive *its abandon*."[50] It is such an advance that the phenomenology of givenness will mimic, albeit, if one is to believe Marion, on strict phenomenological grounds.[51]

Of Givenness and the Revelation of Transcendence

A profound continuity between Marion's early theological works and the later philosophical works is, however, to be noted. Marion's response to the question "What is to be done at the end of metaphysics?" is to counter, once again, this end of metaphysics with theology: only theology is able to surpass and overcome the nihilism that emerges from the end of metaphysics.

Just as the tradition has placed "God" as the totalizing instance of all thoughts and ideas, so Marion seems to portray love as the totalizing instance of our lives. It goes without saying that this experience par excellence, for Marion, merges with the erecting of a totalizing religious horizon of our lives. What Marion and Caputo share here is in effect that it would be love, as the "ultimate" passion for the impossible, which now functions as the paradigmatic experience of life. But as every paradigmatic and totalizing experience, it is somewhat exclusive if not violent even: for Marion, all absence of love is immediately configured as a hatred against God, whereas, for Caputo, a sort of heroism and passion for the impossible is constituted that seems to indicate that a life without such passion would not be worth living or at least would miss something of the truth of our being. It would be to remain, to use Heideggerian terms, in "the untruth." Because of all these similarities between Caputo and Marion, it remains for us in this chapter to see how strong such "strong theology" actually is.

For this, I now turn to Marion's account of revelation. Superficial and idolatrous phenomena—powered by the subject—are in Marion's later works countered by the depth and the distance that givenness introduces in a phenomenon's appearance. Givenness gives that which remains forever outside, other than, and irreducible to consciousness' conceptual representations. One might argue that Marion enlarges the Husserlian transcendence of the object—the fact, for instance, that the fourth leg of the table remains outside of my glance at a table—to the transcendence of the given by asking if that which appears always has to correspond to the contours of an object "or if it can be understood within the immense possibilities of what shows itself."[52] And the latter is, for Marion, "*the* givenness: that of transcendence in immanence."[53] It is this transcendence as well that will allow, now no longer only through theological means, to distinguish "between a film without depth and the figure of a reality [*la figure d'un réel*],"[54] between mere subjective lived experiences and givens to consciousness independent from consciousness as a reality always and already given from "elsewhere" than consciousness.

In a meticulous analysis of Husserl, Marion establishes precisely this: the broadening of Husserlian "evidence" (of something "real" and *other* than consciousness) to givenness:[55] if there is any evidence of such a reality at all, this is so because such evidence and reality are, first of all, given. Marion therefore comments on the Husserlian thought of "the "essential correlation" between appearing and that which appears."[56] In consequence of this correlation, Marion had in an earlier phenomenological work already noted that "appearing [. . .] no longer counts as a datum for the single conscious subject, but first as the givenness of what thus appears: the appearing [. . .] *gives* that which appears [l'apparaître *donne* l'apparaissant]."[57] It is here, Marion argues, that "phenomenology begins," because "thought sees that which appears appear in appearance [la pensée voit apparaître l'apparaisant dans l'apparition]; it manages to do this only by conceiving the appearing itself no longer as a 'given *of* consciousness,' but indeed as the givenness *to* consciousness [. . .] of the thing itself."[58] The essential correlation of appearing and that which appears opens unto the givenness of both the appearing and that which appears: both intention and intuition are being given. It is this correlation that intimates that the "appearing of appearing" is not dependent on any subject whatsoever. Rather, the fact that there "is" this appearing testifies to the fact that the subject is always and already instituted "after the fact," a posteriori: the constituting subject undergoes a delay over and against "the advance of givenness" that constitutes the subject in the first place.[59]

Whereas metaphysics maintained a cleft between the appearing of a thing and the thing as it is in itself, in that a thing "is" without even appearing to someone (realism), and modern philosophy distinguished between subjective impressions of a thing and the thing in itself (transcendentalism), phenomenology succeeds in bridging this cleft, in that the appearance of a thing in and through its various modes of appearing gives *the thing itself* to consciousness. Only in phenomenology "appearances no longer mask what appears," because givenness allows for the appearing and that which appears to arise at the very same moment: "givenness breaks out because the appearing of appearance becomes the apparition *of* what appears [l'apparaître de l'apparence se fait l'apparaître *de* l'apparaissant]."[60]

In this way, it is givenness that liberates phenomenology from being merely a narration of subjective lived experiences. Phenomenology needs "to give more than a state or lived experience of consciousness."[61] For this, it is necessary "that on its screen [of consciousness, JS] there be projected and come forward something other than it—the unevident, the phenomenon itself."[62] It is on the screen of consciousness that the phenomenon gives itself of itself and as its self, that is, as the other of consciousness such that consciousness and its intuition are finally "uproot[ed] from [their] idolatrous death" in which, indeed, appearances would not be appearances of anything at all and the subject would only ever see, mirror, and constitute itself.[63]

But, and this is Marion's point, what is other than and transcendent to consciousness is always and already given. In the case of the given phenomenon—the phenomenon reduced to its most pure status: as gift—then, the phenomenon gives itself to consciousness, "as such, and not as the appearance of something else more essential to it than itself [. . .] Appearing must thus remove itself [. . .] from the imperial rule of the a priori conditions of knowledge by requiring that what appears [*l'apparaissant*] force its entry onto the scene of the world without a [. . .] double, [. . .] abandoned to the world."[64]

It is here too that Marion immanentizes the earlier theological version of "distance." In a strictly phenomenological regime that analyzes only what gives itself to consciousness, no transcendent giver is, well, a given. Phenomenology only attests to the fact that something other than consciousness is indeed given but does not claim that a giver causes this givenness or lies at its origin. This (phenomenological) "distance" denotes the impact of the reception of the given phenomenon, which is given *to* consciousness *from* elsewhere than consciousness (such that consciousness can only describes its impact after the event of its appearing). Marion calls this anamorphosis: the process through which the subject moves from a vague awareness of a given *of* consciousness—an intuition of God knows what—to, by the effort of the phenomenological reduction, the recognition that indeed something is given *to* consciousness that cannot be reduced to consciousness itself and thus is best described as a gift or a given—my intuition is indeed an intuition of this phenomenon rather than that, as when one would measure the distance or the gap between a Photoshopped image and the figure of the reality belonging to it. This process is, for the phenomenon, a crossing of a distance: to "accede to visibility" and "to rise to its appearing [, the phenomenon] must cross a distance (an "elsewhere") that separates it from visibility and must (sur)render itself to the visible (in the double sense of abandoning itself and reaching out to the visible)."[65]

God, Abandonment, and Love

It is true that there are some shifts in Marion's thought. The later phenomenological thought is more nuanced in its account of deconstruction than the earlier theological ones, for instance (perhaps because, in the meanwhile, deconstruction has found something "indeconstructible" as well). It is not true, however, that the later phenomenological works would no longer speak of transcendence and of distance. Both terms are present in rather central places of Marion's phenomenology, even if they are rather infrequently used. This makes for profound continuity between Marion's phenomenology and theology. This continuity comes from his thought of revelation as an abandonment of God to the world that the world is not able to receive.

This thought of revelation as abandonment, and all of its Johannine undertones, is indeed barely noticed, although it runs through both Marion's phenomenology and theology and even explains Marion's more recent emphasis on love as "the transcendence par excellence."[66] God's Incarnation, in the early Marion, is conceived of as an advance of God such that God abandons Himself completely to this world even if this world does not receive it and "loves the darkness more than the light" (John 3, 19). Givenness, too, one recalls, advances and abandons toward visibility with a similar indifference to whether or not it is received there at all.

One will therefore need to interpret just how "distance"—both distances perhaps—"accomplish[es] a similar gesture of abandon and of gift" right up to the "abandon of love" that Nietzsche, according to Marion, already premeditates.[67] This abandon is, in the early theological works, inscribed in Trinitarian relations between the Father and the Son, and the Church where, through the Spirit's grace, this relation is, so to say, reenacted. The Son's "kenotic abandon of the Cross"[68] serves here as the norm and criterion for all other relations, for "the conjunction between abandon and the person" not only denotes the revelation in and as a face—an icon—but also becomes paradigmatic for all nonconceptual, nonidolatrous, nonontotheological relations between the visible and the invisible. It is only "this play of donation, abandon, and pardon" that opens from without being "an entirely other exchange than that of beings."[69]

The ultimate name of this abandonment and this "exchange" will be love, because obviously, "God so loved the world that he gave his one and only Son" (John 3:16). Love for Marion is, surprisingly, the only "thing" that can be said univocally from both God and being/beings. God and beings meet and cross precisely in the logic of love: it is in love, then, that Marion finds a relation that resists all reification and all metaphysical substance. If univocity between God and beings cannot be said through the concept—for God is not a concept—the essence—for God does not have an essence—nor even Being itself—for God is "without" being—then it is only love that can save us now, for "God loves *like* we love, with *the same love* as us."[70]

Love then is the answer to the question of just how we should abandon or give—*s'abandonner* or *s'adonner*—ourselves (over) to that which has always and already been given to us and has advanced toward us. The only appropriate response for the human being to God's gift is indeed to equally abandon ourselves to God with the very same love than Christ has shown to the world. It is here that another important symmetry, if not univocity, must be noted between God's crossing of being and the human being's possibility to cross being and thus reach out for that which is "without" being.

Recall that Marion envisions boredom as that particular gaze that undergoes an indifference toward being. Boredom, for Marion, proceeds toward an almost perfect inversion of God's agapeic and iconic crossing of being: just as God neither "destroys" nor "annihilates" being, so too the bored human being is not able to "annihilate" or even "destroy" being.[71] If God's call, then, remains indifferent to being and to beings, so too the bored human being puts his or her non-indifference toward being between brackets and will become indifferent to all ontic differences between beings.[72] Just as God exceeds being, the human being, too, exceeds Dasein: boredom "displaces man—at least in part—outside of his status as *Dasein*."[73] This inversion, then, is to serve as a figure of a mutual and univocal abandon of God toward the human being and of the human being toward God, for what indeed does "the gaze of boredom" do? It "neither denies nor affirms; it *abandons*, so far as *to abandon itself* [. . .] through pure indifference" to the vanity of the world and being.[74]

And it is just such a "pour[ing] out in an abandon that," like the gift, causes to human being to "be" truly and finally, for boredom is only the reverse of vanity, and this reverse will reveal, in a curious dialectics, the loving gaze of God because

> the world suffers vanity only by comparison with another sun [. . .] which lights it up and invades it from an absolutely extraworldly Orient [. . .] Vanity strikes the world as soon as the world finds itself taken in view [. . .] by another gaze than its own, under the gaze [. . .] of God.[75]

It is here then that the "privileged relation"[76] between vanity and agape appears: the abandonment of and indifference toward being and the ontological difference performed by the bored gaze are *already* taken up and inscribed by love's very same indifference toward being and *already* marked by love's advance toward each individual being as such: God's indifference to being and love for each being separately dislodges being and beings only to appeal and to "approach the being [*l'étant*] as such." For love repeats the indifference toward ontology's difference and inscribes it in the greater play of God's abandonment to the world: "that which is, if it does not receive love, is as if it were not, while that which is not, if love polarizes it, is as if it were."[77] The basics of the erotic reduction of *The Erotic Phenomenon* were given well before its appearance: as long as I am not with my lover, the world will remain vain and indifferent to me, and yet, my lover will orient everything in the world from out of her loving advance toward me; nothing happens when she is absent, and everything is oriented around her presence.[78]

It is only through this thought of God's revelation as abandonment as the one who gives himself to such an extent that my advance toward God always only discovers "God's advance towards me, from all eternity"[79] that certain statements, which at first sight seem overly metaphorical and lyrical, can be explained. Compare, for instance: "there is no worse deaf man than the one who does not want to hear" with the parallel, a little later, in the phenomenology of givenness: "there is no worse blind man than the one who does not want to see."[80] And, also in a book of phenomenology: "no mortal can ask, 'why have you abandoned me?' For us, all abandon like all abandoned [. . .] remains under the guard of givenness."[81]

One therefore might argue that from the early theological to the later phenomenological works it is one thought that obsessed Marion's thinking:

the thought of God's condescension toward the human being as if unbeknownst to him or her, that of a God incarnate who as it were cannot stop incarnating, to the point that even if one seeks this God, one can only discover that this God is already there and has found us.

Conclusion: Between Phenomenology and Theology

Thus one is at back at the "formidable objection" Caputo noted: just as it is truly impossible for us to avoid this God (of Marion), it seems impossible to abandon the "impulse" and the givenness of the "X to come" in Caputo's work. One or the other instance is always keeping the balance between what is possible and impossible firmly in check. It is not sure whether Caputo's sacred anarchy, and all its talk about the weak God, does not have a similar strong God in hiding there. And strong Gods make for strong theologies. Marion and Caputo cannot avoid the figure of God, as the authority of authorities, behind their respective theologies. Both make sure that religious questions always linger in the background of our thinking and even *impose* love as the transcendental horizon of our lives on theology and philosophy. Consider, for instance, Caputo's rendering of his passion, if not obsession, with Augustine's "what do I love?"

> What's really interesting to me about the sentence, of course, is that Augustine is *assuming* we love God. He's *assuming* there's a God, and he's *assuming* we love Him. So the vocabulary of God, the notion of God [. . .] *is in place* [. . .] What do I love when I love my God? That's a question for anyone, for everyone. We may or may not be using religious discourse: we may or may not find the name of God the vehicle for configuring our concern.[82]

One might very well "turn the aporia into an axiom,"[83] but along with axioms, apparently, come assumptions, and assumptions display a tendency not to tend to the things themselves. Yet what is needed is not so much theology's pessimism against the culture of today (through which all indifference toward God would be a hatred of God, as in Marion, or a lack of courage to love, as in Caputo), but a phenomenology that can admit to and deals with our culture's indifference to what matters utmost (the other, the world, and, who knows, God) and that shows a more viable way to speak phenomenologically of an ontology of love through our ontic encounters with our love and lovers.

If, then, in Marion givenness is always and already, well, given, and God's grace is offered for all to see, it remains to be seen just to what extent it is possible for the human being to receive such grace. "Reception," the early Marion argues, "imposes dispossession and abandon to the point of death."[84] It is, at this time, obviously Christ who lived such a reception "divinely, which means to say, in all abandon,"[85] just as it is obviously Christ only who could genuinely ask why God abandoned him. The distinctive mark of Christ, then, is that he imposed the measure, offering the paradigm for all of us willing to receive, if I may say so, the givenness of grace. For all of us mere mortals, the reception of the gift would imply, according to the logic of Marion's metaphors, seeing and hearing what there is to see and hear already and to give ourselves over to that which already has abandoned itself to the visibility of the world whether it be God or givenness.

It is precisely this that is confirmed in Marion's rather voluntaristic account of the decision to receive givenness. Let us have a look at another parallel between Marion's theology of the icon and the phenomenology of givenness: if it is indeed the case that God and givenness abandon themselves to the world in such a way that they appear there without withholding themselves, then the movement of this givenness can only be named a "love without reserve"—because love only gives itself completely and totally, and advances toward the beloved without expecting anything in return.[86]

But why then, if indeed "'giving itself' is equal here to 'letting appear without reserve and in person,' to the pure appearing of a phenomenon," that the receiver of such a givenness or grace so poorly and badly can recognize this givenness?[87] How does such thinking explain that one sees objects more often than not rather than the abandonment of (saturated) phenomena without reserve? Or, in theological terms: how to explain that even Christ's contemporaries did not receive and recognize the one appearing to them in the flesh?[88]

The answer to these questions in *Being Given* is strikingly similar to what Marion's theology tells us: the excess of saturation and its abandonment to the world throws the *adonné* into "a pre-phenomenological and pre-rational obscurity," wherein "the choice or the refusal of the 'great reason'" has to be made entirely guided by "the will to see."[89] The *adonné* here must choose between either a nonsaturated or a saturated phenomenon: the former will deliver to him or her "the enjoyment of a power adequate to constituting," whereas the latter will "expose [the *adonné*] to the humiliation of never constituting [. . .] in order to gain the enjoyment of a givenness of paradoxes."[90] This counter-experience therefore is "not equivalent to a non-experience," for the *adonné* is never abandoned and always and already is surrounded by givenness.⁹¹ The *adonné* knows not of any solitude.

Things differ only slightly in Marion's theology: if the phenomenology of givenness is reluctant to determine the decision of the will to "dodge" and "flee"⁹² from the evidence of givenness along theological lines and at times even grants the inevitability of this flight,⁹³ Marion's theology seems to add merely that *even* the decision to see is given—by God, this time—to the *adonné*: "what my will absolutely cannot will, God can permit it to will, provided that he *give* it to will it."⁹⁴

The theology of givenness therefore seems to haunt the phenomenology of givenness, as its double, which answers the questions left hanging by the phenomenology, just as in Caputo's case a strong theology and a God controlling the "law of reversals" is *already* there in his weak theology: the beliefs of "religion with religion" haunt "religion without religion" more than it is willing to acknowledge. Yet, as a theologian, Caputo might want to consider whether this God descending to singularities from without being and beings really is to be avoided. What might need to be avoided theologically, though, is the constant presence of such a God and the being-already-in-place of such a religious horizon: God's coming might be elucidated "relative to the horizon" that is our ontic and everyday world. In such a way, this concept of God might be closer to the idea of an "authority without power" I am hinting at here.

Marion's recent theology furthermore proceeds toward some straightforward identifications between givenness and creation, between the gift and grace, between the response of love that might, after all, "risk"⁹⁵ identifying the giver in and of givenness. As the *doublure* of the phenomenology of givenness, this theology risks identifying the lack of willingness to see the givenness of all beings along moral and theological lines as well: not to see the given would then be to appropriate God's creation as if it were my own; to appropriate it without admitting its reference to God, and therefore as *sinful*, just as in Caputo's weak theology every lack of a passion for the impossible is to be regarded as (morally) depreciatory, namely as a lack of courage to open onto what is impossible.⁹⁶

Accepting a phenomenology of givenness might mean *as well* that responding to the saturated phenomenon is *also already* responding to the one who lived the abandonment to the fullest and practiced such a love "in a mode nevertheless radically different than us,"⁹⁷ that is, perfectly and divinely, *without refusal* (Mt. 26:39), but who nonetheless offers the norm and the criterion for all other (even non-theological) responses to God's abandonment to the world, to the point of making Augustine's "too late I have loved you" sound like a tautology. For if the difference between the phenomenology and the theology of givenness lies in a will that is divinely given to the latter, and if this will is perfectly incarnated in Christ, then even those who amongst us who are non-willing to see would nonetheless need to be interpreted from out of this theological model: He came to the world, and the world did not receive him. The situation, for Marion, is no different for us as for Christ's contemporaries. "If we do not love, this is not all because we cannot love, but because we do not *want* to love. We therefore hate this love, of which we want nothing. Love is not loved. And God neither. Thus the refusal of God becomes intelligible insofar "God is love," insofar only love permits that one refuses it."[98]

It is clear that every non-response and all indifference to love is inscribed in a theological horizon. One should therefore ask whether the figure of reality offered by this phenomenology is not one that is tainted by theology to such an extent that it might be of little help for philosophy's (and our culture's) struggle with nihilism, simply because only those who believe in God's loving gaze would be "saved" from nihilism.[99]

One should ask, too, whether Marion does not abandon phenomenology altogether. Such a suspicion seems justified since Marion never tells us just why boredom would have "a privileged relation" with love and it seems that it is here that an extra-phenomenological argument overrides his phenomenology. The dialectics between love and boredom substitutes itself for the phenomenon of boredom and, in one way or another, prescribes for boredom its being. The precise point where such a substitution occurs is to be found in, again, a book of phenomenology, in *Reduction and Givenness*' extensive discussion of a boredom of the depths.[100] Here Marion writes, while distinguishing boredom from anxiety:

> Boredom [. . .] leaves beings in place, without affecting them, above all without being affected by them; it peaceably and serenely abandons beings to themselves [. . .] But that very abandonment defines it: [it] removes itself from [Being and beings], [it] covers itself, refuses to expose itself [. . .] Boredom *hates*.[101]

Suddenly boredom, dialectically, turns into something else: Marion is no longer strictly describing boredom but is already interpreting it as hate: a hate, obviously, of love itself. All of a sudden, too, the indifference proper to boredom—and despite Marion's protestations on the same page—turns into a non-indifference, for is not the difference between boredom and hate precisely that the latter presupposes one or the other relation to that which it hates (albeit a negative one) whereas the former does not? Does not the very fact of hating someone or something speak for some relation to the person or being at issue? And would a phenomenology of boredom not need to state that boredom abandons precisely such a relation?

If our phenomenology of religious life aims for the erection of a transcendence able to be welcomed by all, it is however precisely such a secular indifference (to values, to religion, to reality) that needs to be taken into account. Marion and Caputo's imposition of love as the ultimate horizon of our lives, a horizon that seems fueled by more than one theological assumption, might prove to be of little help for this. It is for such a transcendence that our third part aims, when giving some *ontic* relief to the salutation and the elementary faith Derrida has detected. For, if I opt for a phenomenological stance here, it is, first, because not all (postmodern) phenomena are experienced as being "without depth" (e.g., friendship, love, work) and, secondly, these phenomena are not lived and experienced exclusively, as Binswanger will show us, as religious or theological phenomena.

Conclusion to Part 2

The reader will have surmised that, in a way, I find that there is too little of phenomenology in Marion and Caputo. For all its talk of bedazzlement and excess, Marion's thought ends up being a phenomenology without phenomenon: one does not see or hear or really experience a saturated phenomenon. Marion's most dear example, love and the erotic phenomenon, comes with such a theological bias that it is hard to see how such a phenomenon could appeal to non-believers or those indifferent to matters transcending our mundane, all too mundane, affairs. Caputo's repeated insistence on a "vital," "elemental" impulse, raging through being and beyond, seems to impose more than one assumption of which one needs to be suspicious. Is this "energy" or this vitalism always and constantly present? Does it ever incarnate in a phenomenological intuition, which we can share and discuss? Is this "mysterious force" not just romanticism revisited? And, for the theological reader, why would one theologically insist on a nonsovereign God, and not rather on a God as the authority even of authorities, particularly when these seem very close on some points. Yet, on the other hand, all this need not turn us to the other extreme, portrayed by Hägglund's interpretation of Derrida, and insist on the idea of a finite survival of all against all. This might be but a poor idea of "what is going on" in (and perhaps with) being. For such a phenomenology, I will turn to Binswanger's account of love in Part 3. In the remainder of this conclusion, I focus on those traits that I deem essential for a secular phenomenology of religious life.

Facere Veritatem: The Primacy of Bad Conscience

What to do as a finite being after metaphysics? It is at this juncture that Caputo's "religion without religion" is most compelling. For the truth of this religion does not concern this or that statement or proposition (of which we could afterward ascertain that this is indeed the case) but rather a truth-seeking practice, a truth in the making as it were, which can only be truly verified in a life living out this truth, on the condition perhaps that it does more than ascertain the survival of self and of one's own.

"Religion without religion" only ever begins when the individual is being put into question by God knows what and is so forced to act, act on this questioning, that is. Such *veritas redarguens* is a truth that judges you and forces you to put this truth into action. Religion, according to Caputo, is a question directed toward the individual, a sort of summoning by it knows not what. Perhaps one need not think here only of the Augustinian *mihi magna quaestio sum* but also of the New Testament pericopes "and who do you say I am?" echoing a "who do you think you are?" of sorts.

This is the reason why Caputo distinguishes his religion without religion from both "religion with religion" and the "tragic sense of life." Whereas the former signifies a faith that is all too assured of its truth, complacently knows the answer to all of life's questions but does not act (perhaps only prays, dances, and kneels), the latter concerns the tragic feel of the one for whom "nothing really matters" and "anything goes" without actually going for anything at all. The "religion without religion" feels for the three passions toward the impossible, "faith, hope and love" but for the latter the most, because only love can save the faith that gets caught in the mazes of a doctrinal and institutional web—similar to how the "spirit" of the law saves the "letter"—but also because love is perhaps the only suitable answer to the tragedies, irony, and cynicism plaguing contemporary societies.

Tragedy knows the cruelties and atrocities happening within the world and aims to endure these—somewhat like Heidegger's *aushalten* of the *Hineingehaltenheit* in the nothing—as long and as proudly as possible. It knows that "being is evil," or at least "injust," to speak like Levinas, yet tries to counter it by proclaiming a sort of *amor fati* over being: a love for being that, itself, is blind, mute, and cruel and only knows "no." Tragedy feeds off a certain primacy of the negative. It is for this reason that Caputo distances himself from this tragic feel: in the end, the tragic condition no longer *does* anything at all. It merely quietly, and perhaps with somewhat of a grudge, contemplates the course of things.

The ethics of this religion aims for another "yes,"[1] a yes that does not deny the "no" of negativity, but says "no" to negativity as well: it cannot be that . . . The ethics of a religion without religion cannot be indifferent toward the course of things, it says "no" both against the status quo (which excludes) and to cruel fate (which hardly excludes), in the name of the impossible if necessary, with no more knowledge in support of this resistance than the knowledge that, for the love of God, things can be different and nothing seems to indicate that the current state of affairs is necessary. "Faith is faith that we can say certain things are wrong."[2] Religion can then play a role in the struggle with postmodern life remaining for the most part indifferent to and untouched by the current state of affairs and for which nothing makes a difference really.

This is close to what Ignace Verhack has called an "originary affirmation," for which being is *first of all* experienced as a "favor" given or granted and for this very reason cannot and may not be denied *to others*.[3] This, too, then, is the reason why Levinas's question "Do I have a right to be?" is *not* a Christian question and can at times even appear nonreligious. For indeed one may wonder whether this subject that is "de-nucleated" or "de-cored," if not raped, *by* the other is able and willing to do anything for the other at all. This, then, would be what the tragic and traumatized subject would have in common: both are paralyzed and can no longer act. The tragic subject because, for him or her, action would make no difference; the traumatized subject because he or she is robbed of the possibility to act, whether it is ethically or not.[4] Caputo's point is well taken.

Yet one needs to wonder whether this dichotomy between tragic and religious thought actually holds: after all, rather than boasting of one's love for God or one or the other passion for the impossible, Derrida seems to know that all we can do in this finite world of ours is (give it a) try: *Il faut essayer*, even when we do so badly. It might be that again one has to take one's distance from Caputo and balance Caputo's all too cheerful dealing with the "invention" of the impossible with the tragic feel issuing out of Derrida's works. I do so by highlighting what I call *the primacy of bad conscience* as the basic stance of a contemporary phenomenology of religious life. It is in effect not clear whether Derrida's experience with the aporia lends itself that easily to Caputo's experience of the impossible, for which everything, at any time, still is possible (and if not, it should be invented).

The experience of the aporia for Derrida has, as is well known, to be interpreted in relation to justice and law, or rather: the *justesse*, the correctness if you like, of justice, with the "justice" or "justness" of the laws beings enforced. I have already shown another aporia: it is impossible to consider oneself hospitable if one is not hospitable to every other. And every other is (the) *wholly* other. Considered from the fact that one always welcomes some others more than others, it follows that no one can consider himself, justly, hospitable. And yet: one must be hospitable: *il faut l'hospitalité*. It therefore follows that "I try my best" to be hospitable: *Je ne sais pas. Il faut essayer*—one must try. Yet this attempt can only be truly hospitable if it welcomes every other . . .

Something similar occurs in the aporia concerning justice. Consider, for instance, the case in which a judge deals with a specific violation from out of the general rule and so enforces the law. The application of the general rule—theft is illegal—to a specific case—imagine a young child stealing a pear to heal his sister suffering from diabetes and not just to "dump it out to the hogs"—prescribes for these specific circumstances a generality that loses sight of, precisely, the specific, individual and circumstantial coordinates of this case. "Enforcing the (general) law" can thus border on being unjust: the child may have stolen the pear to increase the sugar levels of his sick sister quickly. Justice itself demanded that the general rule "thou shalt not steal" be transgressed here: the child in effect has *good* and *just* reasons to steal this particular pear. "It is just that there be law, but justice is incalculable, it demands that one calculates with the incalculable; and aporetic experiences [are] moments in which the *decision* between just and unjust is never ensured by a rule."[5]

Yet it would be unjust just the same if there would be no law or rule at all. There is no (sacred) anarchy in Derrida's deconstruction here—not here at least. The aporia demands that there be rules *at the very moment* in which these rules are suspended. Imagine, once more, that each child would be judged differently in each case and that therefore rules would be established or invented at the particular moment of each crime. Justice then demands laws or in any case cannot do without laws, for this would make of justice and law a completely arbitrary event. Stealing would this time be just and, at another, completely wrong. The judge, according to Derrida, will have to decide—speak justly, and enforce a judgment—*at the very moment* when he or she is well aware that justice *both* "overrules" the law (a blind application of the law/s to all individual cases borders on injustice) *and* is in need of the law (the total suspension of all laws would be completely arbitrary and, again, unjust). For the judge to be just, then, it is necessary that a decision be made concerning that which cannot be decided once and for all: it is never certain whether or not the laws apply to this particular case, and neither is it certain whether this concrete case surpasses the laws in its generality.

And yet: it is demanded that "justice be done." "For a decision to be just and responsible, it must, in its proper moment, if there is one, be both regulated and without regulation, it must preserve the law and also destroy or suspend it enough to have to reinvent it in each case."[6] It is thus that compromises, the taking care of one's own, gets temporarily suspended, and it is just that all this is suspended. And yet it is, in turn, unjust too when laws as a whole are suspended and the judgment takes place without a rule entirely. The law, in this sense, is useless and without value but appears as a promise of value and meaning just as well.

Derrida concludes, and this is the primacy of bad conscience we have in mind here: "it follows from this paradox that at no time can one say *presently* that a decision is just, purely just (that is to say, free and responsible), or that someone *is* just, and even less, '*I am* just.'"[7] There is for Derrida no way out of the aporia and even less a right way to come into the aporia. For we do not *know* what justice is and even less how to be just, and even if we could boast on this decision being legal or at least legitimate, we cannot exclude that this decision here, however legitimate and legal, has been unjust toward the others of this other over there, toward those particular cases that cannot be subsumed under this general law here. Yet we cannot do *without* justice, without a certain lawfulness or law and order even. One has to decide, one cannot wait eternally, justice *demands* to be done: it is just that here and now the law is enforced, even though this law is unfair to some and unjust to every other (which is every other).

For:

> This excess of justice over law and calculation [. . .] cannot and should not serve as an alibi for staying out of juridico-political battles. [. . .] Abandoned to itself, the incalculable [. . .] idea of justice is always very close to the bad, even to the worst, for it can always be reappropriated by the most perverse calculation.[8]

One would, then, claim to speak *in the name* of justice, in its very name, incarnating justice once and for all. This, then, is the aporia: there is an element of indecision in every decision taken, an element of incalculability present *in* all kinds of calculation, making the decisive step more than a little insecure. Even if no one can take a decision in my place, I can never be certain that this indeed was a good decision and a good call. For, at the very moment I would boast of having made a good decision, one can be quite certain of the opposite, and I have decided in a sense for the worst, because one does not *know* what the good decision is at the moment of deciding; if one would know, in effect, nothing would have to be decided.

The primacy of bad conscience is such that it, at best, states that here or there a less bad decision can be taken and sometimes is taken too (justice is done, or *can be* done), while knowing all too well that an absolute

Good decision does not exist or, if it would, can hardly be called "good," because it would be used as an alibi (for instance, for not doing the good any longer) and also because it would be indifferent to the ways of the world where evil can have good consequences and where a good decision likewise can culminate in evil.

Let us give the final word to Derrida, when it concerns the difficult balance between an endless/infinite responsibility of all for all and the unique one—you, me—who always has to decide, and decides poorly, for everyone and everything. To a question posed to him by John Milbank, namely whether it would not be better to substitute this endless responsibility for a more concrete and mundane form of ethics, for a moral division of labor—where everyone takes care "of their own" and only afterward turns to others—Derrida replies:

> I, of course, have preferences. I am one of the common people who prefer their cat to their neighbor's cat and my family to others. But I do not have a good conscience about that. I know that if I transform this into a general rule it would be the ruin of ethics. If I put as a principle that I will feed first of all my cat, my family, my nation, that would be the end of any ethical politics. So when I give a preference to my cat, which I do, that will not prevent me from having some remorse for the cat dying or starving next door, or, to change the example, for all the people on earth who are starving and dying today. So you cannot prevent me from having a bad conscience, and that is the main motivation of my ethics and my politics . . . It is not because I am indifferent, but because I am not indifferent, that I try not to make a difference, not to make a difference ethically and politically, between my family and his family and your family. I confess that it is not easy.[9]

Ethics is abandoned or at least suspended at the very moment one thinks that "all things are well" when "well considered," calculated, or negotiated. This is why this deconstruction must be endless—I am almost inclined to say *"il faut l'infini"*: every position deconstruction assumes, every stance it takes, and all of the decisions it makes will constantly be challenged by all other positions, by the other others, by the other of this Other here, by the others excluded when I feed first of all my dog or when I seek shelter for my family first: " 'One must avoid good conscience at all costs.' I must *never* be able to say 'I have decided' much less 'I have decided well,' much less '*I am all square*, and my duty is done."¹⁰ All of a sudden, then, one is close to a certain Augustinianism or even to the Catholicism of guilt and sin we are so desperately seeking to shed, shaking the sand off our feet as it were. It matters little: religion starts here, and if God should not exist, we should invent him. There is no shelter for one alone. Caputo's cheerful insistence on the ever-present possibility of attending to the other seems to forget that, for Derrida, all such attending is only ever insufficient and borders on the tragic.

Not Yet Rid of God?
Of a Religion Not Quite without Religion

What, in effect, would this primacy of bad conscience mean for a contemporary phenomenology of religion? It could mean that the borderline between an ontotheological "rest" and deconstructive restlessness cannot be as neatly drawn as Caputo thinks. It might mean, in effect, that the primacy of restlessness that Caputo prescribes is an illusion and that all, ourselves most of all, "have faith in a very unfaithful way" (Pirjeri) and that no one is able to ban this God who would be "a protector of all the egoisms" from thought entirely.

This is, for instance, what Žižek also advances against Caputo. Caputo for Žižek (and Marion on certain points as well, I would add) misses the moment "by means of which the very excess of the Event over its embodiment in name(s) has to be remarked in a name,"¹¹ that is, the moment when and the reason why a religion without religion, a religion *sans*, constantly veers into a religion *avec* as well and names the event that it says it does not name. But this is the moment on which everything turns! Even when Caputo's deconstruction of Christianity tirelessly tries not to fill the gap between the event and the names for this event—a critique of idols it is—it omits to think that "very moment" in which this "between" and this space is occupied and instrumentalized. Remember what happened to the empty space Heidegger mentioned! This is the moment, then, in which *even* deconstruction turns into an idol, which is the moment of an incarnation, mere play, mirroring itself more than it would mirror "the" event. This is why Caputo's anti-metaphysics suddenly can seem very metaphysical.

No doubt that this is a problem for philosophy, but surely theology cannot quietly contemplate these debates as if it were still enthroned as the queen of the sciences, overseeing the battleground of its empire with a good amount of *ataraxia*. For if this "event" really may not bear a name and is perhaps "what has no name in any philosophy" (Merleau-Ponty), Caputo is bordering, venturing on an anti-Christian pathway. One should not underestimate the fact that it is the atheist Žižek who points this out to Caputo: "within this space, there is simply no place for the paradox of the Christian Incarnation: in Christ, this miserable individual, we see God himself. The properly Christian is the "leap of faith" by means of which we take the risk to fully engage in a singular instantiation as the Truth embodied,"[12] even if no embodiment is just enough, to embody the absolute appeal of love and justice (just) enough. Caputo configures, then, a deconstruction for dreamers, a religious bone *sans* flesh as it were, and forgets, omits, and neglects the role that concrete religions, religious positions, here, in the sublunary realm that is ours, play for the good and of course also for the worst.

Suddenly problems seem to multiply—this is why one needs philosophy. It in effect appears that Caputo, quite *unlike* Derrida, rejects the long detour around "the destruction of the history of ontology" (Heidegger) and opts for a shortcut right through or "after" the tradition as it were. Caputo *opts* out, then, *chooses* or *prefers* to leave the old metaphysics behind, whereas metaphysics might precisely be that which is not available for any choice of ours. *Der Metaphysik bleibt keinen Wahl,* Heidegger writes: it is not the case that one can decide no longer to invoke one or the other metaphysical function (that unites, gathers, connects, or unifies in any other way); it is the case rather that, more often than not, if one thinks that avoiding such a metaphysics is just a choice, a matter of taste and preference if you like, it is quite likely that such a metaphysics will be exactly what is repeated, copied, and transmitted: this is why the thought of the "without" is haunted more by the metaphysical "with" than the other way around.

This means concretely that Caputo's "religion without religion" underestimates the concrete religions, and their clinging to the *avec*. Caputo forgets that the parasite (religion without religion) feeds off that of which it is parasitical and so can never establish a definite, determinate distance between the parasite and its host. In short: Caputo emphasizes the absolute appeal that justice and love would be a bit too much and in doing so forgets the struggles, the sighs, and the wrestling with concrete, all too particular incarnations in finite and historical constellations and constructions. Caputo therefore forgets what I would call "the politics of being": the fact that there is, there must be, and there always will be mediation and negotiation between the different empirical versions of absolute ideas (even between the ideas of the Absolute) and that it is *within* being and being-in-the-world that things must change (or at least be improved) if one is to speak of a justice for all.

Conclusion to Part 2

This, then, is a problem that seems to rage through contemporary philosophy and can be found in a great many of political philosophies, such as Nancy's. Nancy's solution in effect to the question of such mediation and negotiation lies in what is called an "arbitration without arbitration."[13] Nancy's innovative thinking of community runs as follows: the sharing of sense without (metaphysical) signification is all that the others and I share. What we share is therefore not a stable and permanently present signification: no family ties, no national identity, no essence whatsoever is given here. We share only the sharing of sense: everyone experiences the world as (more or less) meaningful. It is the very fact of this sharing, the "community of those without community" that would transcend the incommensurable and conflicting significations within-the-world. This sharing of and in being is what is "beyond" and "above" the resigned pluralism where every other values other things than all the others: "What is shared therefore is [. . .] sharing itself, and consequently everyone's nonidentity, each one's nonidentity to himself and to others."[14] Watkin comments: "It is not meanings [Significations, JS] that are shared, but the absence of meaning itself that insists on being shared."[15] One can, of course, also think of Marion's configuring of the essence of the human being as an "absent essence" here: the essence of the human is to be without essence.

Here then one can again find a sort of overstepping or "*Übersprung*" out of contingency, and an instance is invoked that would raise itself above the mowing field, standing out in a quasi-permanent way as it were—and we already know that by no means such an instance still needs to be called "God." Such an "arbitration without arbitration" or "essence without essence" would in effect only be suitable if no one really clung to his or her tradition, identity, or religion and, secondly, if it would not be the case that because of such an attachment I value my own attachments a bit *more* than the attachments of others and if, finally, when everyone would agree that that my particular and empirical sense, my *Geworfenheit* in this culture here rather than in another really is of no particular importance in comparison to the sense that is shared absolutely. Arbitration without arbitration would therefore only be feasible if all would distinguish between "signification" and "sense" or between "religion *avec*" and "religion *sans*" *in the exact same way* and if all of us would subsequently agree that this particular attachment to this rather than that culture has to be "founded" in a "shared sense" that is *without* a metaphysical Signification entirely. *Quod non.*

Being-in-the-world shows a different state of affairs, namely one in which these different "incarnations" of sense *do* matter: the sense "without essence" of which Nancy and Marion speak or the "religion without religion" Caputo is claiming omits the sense that arises within being-in-the-world where certain practices always and already seem more meaningful than others.

If theology thinks the Incarnation, as "the word that became flesh," then philosophy hinges at an incarnation where sense or signification is born from out of our concrete dealings with the flesh of the world, so to say, for here too "signification" (even the metaphysical ones) cannot be dissociated from concrete words and wordings. This is why, for example, the raising of a German flag in Leuven is at one time experienced as appropriate and at another time as completely inappropriate even though the act of raising the flag shows the same state of affairs. It is appropriate when the world championship soccer match is being played and these Germans cheer for their team; it is inappropriate at other times because it was the Germans too who burned Leuven during the two world wars: the meaning changes through its use in different, concrete practices.[16] It is such a continuous contamination between ideality (logos, essence, Signification) and materiality that Caputo seems to underestimate and that accounts for the fact that even a religion without religion is not quite without religion (and especially not as much as it likes or chooses to be). This contamination, then, is a place of contingency where these contaminations continuously change and always can be altered. This is why one should not overestimate the concrete "religions with religion" (as the theologians tend to do). For, in this case, one would be returned to the resigned pluralism that states that all presuppositions, all faiths, and all beliefs are just as good as all the others. One might indeed ask whether the latter is not simply an instance of what philosophy would call a "*naturalistic fallacy*," arguing that "no ought"—no prescription—be inferred from an "is"—description. It is not because things are the way they are that one should accept that this is how things ought to be. On the contrary, perhaps: it is urgent to realize that we always and already *overestimate* our concrete attachments to this or that culture and religion and are always on the verge of confusing its historicity with a necessity.

It is to such an incarnation of meaning in embodied practices that we should attend, not by stretching the gap between the transcendental impulse and the empirical tradition in which it incarnates or by stressing a theological version of the Incarnation where one name would embody meaning and signification once and for all, but rather by speaking of multiple incarnations, as ever so many *Verflechtungen* of meaning in and through embodiments, which never would exhaust the mysteriousness of the mute matter (of being) into which all of us are thrown and through which we never jump to the complacency of the mere "with" or to the dream of the pure "without."[17]

Caputo misses, in effect, the moment of an incarnation, of an ontic figure filling in the gap between the conditional and the unconditional, of a very ontic you that would make for an empiricism and a transcendentalism at once and from which phenomenology and its reduction only ever begins.

This, as I will show, is what happens in the thought of Binswanger, whose phenomenology of love will in the remainder of this work be contrasted with Marion's idea of love and who will present us with a "real presence" of otherness (as opposed to the rage against essence I have detected in the previous chapters).

But to make things even worse, let me conclude with one more aporia: it is not certain whether it is because of this philosophical idea of incarnations that one, once, started to speak of a divine Incarnation, or, the other way around whether it is because of the divine Incarnation that one speaks of philosophical and contingent incarnations.

Part 3

Within

8

Ludwig Binswanger's Phenomenology of Love

"During the long work on this book, I was very surprised that the problem of love has been neglected by the philosophers, with only few exceptions [. . .]. For me, however, life without love is 'blind,' and love without life 'empty.'"[1] More than sixty years later, however, it has not become any easier to speak of the question of love. Certainly not if one keeps in mind that Binswanger's monumental *Grundformen und Erkenntnis menschlichen Daseins*—a work of more than 600 pages—was written in a time of war, which is not the last time one will encounter an odd coincidence between an ontic state of affairs and the ontology of love in this chapter.

Binswanger (1891–1966) was a Swiss psychiatrist who soon came under phenomenology's spell. After a first phase in which his work on psychiatric practices was dominated by Husserlian views, the second Heideggerian phase started as soon as *Being and Time* was published. His later works on melancholy, mania, and delirium show a tendency to return to Husserl's transcendental phenomenology. For our interests, it is important to note that the *Grundformen* belong to this second phase and present a forceful critique of Heidegger's existential analytic through precisely the problem of love. Binswanger's critique issues from two main disagreements with Heidegger, namely that my being, first, would be most proper or "authentic" when it faces its own finitude and upcoming death and, secondly, that it would precisely be this "encounter" with being-toward-death that would deliver and reveal being as most properly "my own." Against this stress on finite, *Jemeinig* Dasein, Binswanger introduces the thought of love as an existence that, though not distinct from (Heidegger's) being-in-the-world, does not coincide with the stakes of this being-in-the-world as outlined by Heidegger. The fullness of being, revealed through us in love, intimates a "being-beyond-the-world-in-the-world" ("*über die Welt hinaus sein*") that overpowers and empowers the existential structures of care and concern. It does so, moreover, by showing "being" as fundamentally relational or intersubjective, for even if one, in a way, always dies alone, one never loves alone as well: it takes two to love—at least.

Binswanger's, however, is not only a critique of Heidegger but is also a profound attempt to extend Heidegger's insights into Dasein's relation with world to the domain of sick subjectivities or to what he calls "*misglückten*," failed or false, Dasein. This practice is called "Daseinsanalysis," meaning an ontic, anthropological, but nevertheless phenomenological quest into "how" human beings have (or do not have) a world in contradistinction with Heidegger's ontological "*Daseinsanalytik*," which speaks in perhaps too lofty and exalted a manner of how the human being pertains to "Being" *überhaupt*.

Daseinsanalysis, for Binswanger, is

> neither ontology nor philosophy proper [. . .]. Only *phenomenological anthropology* accords with the matter at hand. Daseinsanalysis does not erect an ontological thesis about essential traits pertaining to Dasein, but issues ontical assertions, i.e. assertions about empirical discoveries of factical forms and images of Dasein.[2]

Whereas Binswanger's anthropology asks, "what is it, for the human being, to be," "ontology" in its Heideggerian vein asks, "what is being, considered from the fact that my being-there, Dasein as my own, is the only entrance in questioning what being in general might mean." Binswanger would completely agree with this distinction and would even assert the truth of Heidegger's ontological analysis, but he "will not admit that only this sort of resoluteness," ready for anxiety as it is, "would be able to produce the "proper truth of Dasein," for this truth lacks love, the original being-together"—*dieser Wahrheit mangelt die Liebe*.[3]

On this question of truth, then, Binswanger moves from the ontic and existentiell implications of Daseinsanalysis to a proper ontology of being-with and of what I will call here "loving togetherness" as a translation of Binswanger's account of human *Miteinandersein*. It might even be that the *crossing* of our ontic loves and its ontological signification will force us, just as it apparently did Binswanger, toward a new passageway from the ontic to the ontological realm or, more modestly, to admit that the facticity of love allows for another ontology than the somewhat grim picture of human being Heidegger painted in *Being and Time*. The simple presence of love, then, might point to a different ontology, if you like, to a different *presencing* of all beings to one another.

Binswanger, unfortunately, has not been frequently studied, although his name must have circulated in the philosophical circles of the day. His sanatorium, *Bellevue*, served as the meeting place of leaders of the artistic, psychiatric and philosophical world: Freud was a regular; Heidegger visited the place at least twice. Binswanger's fame extended rather quickly, and it is to be regretted that his work has not been confronted extensively.[4]

This chapter seeks to address Binswanger's understanding of love and relate it to other, more contemporary, philosophies while presenting other major themes in Binswanger's oeuvre. First, however, I will focus on Binswanger's peculiar take on poetry and language by addressing the ontology of greeting that is quite central to, even if it is only obliquely present, in the *Grundformen*.

Greetings from Being

Binswanger's philosophy needs to be placed in the wake of thinkers of dialogue and encounter, such as Martin Buber. The social ontology Binswanger presents, however, puts him on a par with the concerns of many of our contemporaries, such as Nancy and Levinas.

Toward an Egalitarian Phenomenology

Nancy, as I have shown, seems to have abandoned the long-fashionable cleft that sets philosophy apart from the very world in which the philosopher acts, lives and moves. Indeed, in Nancy's work, the ontic and the ontological realm are intertwined, mingled, and mixed to such an extent that it is hard to see why, for instance, Heidegger maintains such an utter separation of the ontological and the ontic everyday realms. In a certain sense, one can say that this problem of intertwining, of mingling, and of mixture is precisely Nancy's main philosophical question. This might also be the reason why his thought is centered on what one might call a *return to the world* or, more precisely, to our being-together-in-a-world, to our making sense of that world, and to the sense, if any, of that very world itself. Binswanger can be aligned to Nancy's endeavor through his acknowledgment that it takes *two* for there to arise something like signification and sense at all. In addition, he already attempts to unsettle the *hubris* of philosophy as detected in Schürmann's work, where the philosopher still thinks himself able to set himself apart from all things ontic and everyday.⁵

If, indeed, it takes two for there to be any meaningful experience—what I will call here a greeting and salutation in being—this would mean two things: first, that nothing is that cannot be communicated as much as, inversely, that which is not shared in this way does not yet attain to being. Secondly, such an ontological salutation means that here all hubris needs to be eradicated: I cannot experience anything other than what you would be able to experience. This would explain Binswanger's affinity with Merleau-Ponty, who beautifully described the presuppositions of phenomenological philosophy as "a familiarity of all human activity with all human activity."⁶

Let us return to Nancy's example of such an address and greeting in being. Take for instance the Cartesian *cogito*, a prime example of a "worldless" subjectivity: I can doubt the existence of others, I can even doubt the existence of the world, but never can I doubt the very fact that it is I who is doubting. Descartes's conclusion is that I am not certain that there are others at all, I am certain only of the fact that if I think and doubt, I must also be. Nancy comments: for such a solipsistic phrase to be true, it must presuppose that others, namely "each one of Descartes' readers": *even the experience of solipsism makes sense if and only if it can be communicated to others, which means that there is no such thing as solipsism.*⁷ In this regard, one might say that philosophy, for Nancy, communicates the impossibility of the ivory tower: it tries to understand just to what extent philosophy is immersed in everyday life, or, in more philosophical terms: how there is an address and a salutation to the other in all that is said, how—to use Nancy's terminology—being-with-other-beings constitutes the very being of "my" being and of all beings.

This makes for odd consequences when considering the phenomenologies of, for instance, Heidegger and Marion, when attending to the, often somewhat hidden, remnants of hubris in their thought. Consider for a moment Heidegger's infamous statement in *Contributions to Philosophy*—"No one understands what 'I' *think* here"⁸—along the following Nancyean lines: not only does such a sentence not "make sense," for the very fact of writing such a line implies that the addressee, that is, the reader, *is*, to say the least, able to understand it, but this sentence is guilty too of the age-old philosophical *hubris* that—wrongly—presupposes that the philosopher is "in the know" about something (whether it be death, *Ereignis*, the Ideas, or the Absolute Spirit) that others, that is, non-philosophers, do not and cannot know.

Marion's slip of the tongue is even more obvious. Recall that, for Marion, it is a matter of receiving that which gives itself of itself and as its self. The counter-experience is nothing else than the registration (as a clerk would do) of this showing up in phenomenality of the saturated phenomenon. Now consider the following rather peculiar opening lines of Marion's *Being Given*: "what this book [*Being Given*, JS] succeeds in saying remains far behind what was conceived without being able to formulate it. And what ended up being conceived itself remains well behind what was *seen*."[9] To the extent that such a phrase needs to be taken literally, it might be interpreted as communicating simply another form of the philosopher's *hubris*: although "I," that is, Marion, have done the utmost to communicate what I have "seen" and although my efforts to show to you what I have seen most probably will not succeed in making you see as well, you will have to take my word for it, that is, both for the fact that there *is* something to see that you do not (yet) see and for the fact that I—Marion—have, in fact, seen it. Nancy, then, might be interpreted as protesting against these kinds of mystifying (and mystical) propositions in contemporary philosophy: there is nothing that I see that you cannot see (and vice versa).

In this way, Nancy's and Binswanger's philosophies will make us want to reconsider the practice of phenomenology, not (or no longer) the *elitist* formulations and mystifying *play* in which someone is able to see what the other cannot or does not yet see, but rather a phenomenology that, faithful to its principles, aims to show and say that which is there for everyone to see and experience and what is *already* seen and experienced by everyone starting from the admission that what I, as a phenomenologist, see and experience is *hopefully* seen by you as well. In this regard, phenomenology proper would need to speak perhaps not only of the greeting in every experience, the greeting *to* the other, but also of the supplication if not prayer in all experiences: "by virtue of my experiencing, I am already committed and turned toward the other." What Binswanger initiated then is not only a fundamentally *egalitarian* phenomenology but also and no less importantly an originary *coram*: an always already being turned toward otherness. It is this "turn," which is by no means violent, which Binswanger will understand, with Von Hofmannsthal, as the enticement that is love, a love that always and already lures us toward the other.

Greeting Levinas

The brackets in the last sentences are paraphrasing Levinas. It is indeed Levinas who pondered, mostly in his later, mature writings, on the greeting and the salutation that are present in the responsibility toward the other, for the "response of responsibility [. . .] already lies dormant in a salutation, in the *hello*, in the *goodbye*."¹⁰ This is not only why this responsibility will at times appear as "*simple comme bonjour*," but one might even surmise that this greeting of the other lies prior to the accusative and the accusation that the other will eventually utter toward me. Indeed, there is a "benediction contained in the word *bonjour*. This *bonjour*, already presupposed by every cogito, would be the *first* transcendence."¹¹ *Before* then (a second?) transcendence awakens, awakens toward the full-fledged persecution and sacrifice for the Other, there is in a consciousness (that is not yet the cogito) a greeting, a consciousness that is barely awake but vigilant enough to acknowledge the other. Yet "the saying is a way of greeting the Other, but to greet the Other is already to answer for him."¹² All of a sudden, then, the order is reversed: the vocative recedes for the accusative. It is true that Levinas hesitates at this nevertheless quite central point, for one can also read: "the Other is not only known, he is *greeted* [. . .] The Other does not appear in the nominative but in the vocative"—it is *to you* that the greeting is addressed, and the greeting is possible only because of this fundamental *to* is distributed equally to all beings.¹³

How does this salutation work in Levinasian thought, and just how is this "saying" related to everything that is "said"? Just like Nancy after him, Levinas acknowledges that meaning is never present for one alone. Levinas interprets this *ethically*, in that meaning only ever arises to be addressed to the other. This is why, for Levinas, all that is and can be said (ontology, politics . . .) is meaningful only when it is oriented toward the other's benefit. The salutation then would be the moment in which in fact it is signaled that nothing would ever take on meaning were it not for the two (or more) of us, indicating that no "indication" or "proposition" would make sense without the presence of others. Hence Levinas claims that "a salutation [is] the giving of a sign signifying this very giving [of signs, JS]": it is a sign of the sense of all sense, the speaking of (un)common things in an (un)common world.¹⁴ In a way, then, the very act of salutations and greetings would not only attend to this particular other here but also to the very existence and possibility of sense and meaning *between* this other and me and a fortiori among all the possible others, for to what else would "the donation of a sign refer (a donation that is perhaps present in salutations)"?¹⁵ This salutation would be ontic as well as "ontological": ontic, in that the salutation is indeed nothing but the giving of a sign to another, as when raising one's finger or tipping one's hat; ontological, in that whereas this giving can do without "ontic" content—the salutation is no sending of determinate information—it does confide to the other the fact that it is through his presence (and those of others) that there can be information and signification in the first place.

Levinas never really explains why the simple vocative does not suffice and therefore why one could not simply remain with this "first" transcendence without the violence of the Other summoning me toward destitution and incapability of attending to him or her properly.[16] Nor does he explain why the "last" transcendence, the third party disrupting this private conversation between this Other and me, that is, comes so very late, to the point of missing the rendezvous.

The debate between Levinas on the one hand and Nancy and Binswanger on the other thus seems to be centered on just how many others are necessary to explain a thought, for whereas Levinas would stick to "only two," Nancy and Binswanger would no doubt say "all others." One may legitimately wonder whether this stubborn sticking to two parties in Levinas has to do with the fact that, behind the "authority" and the "power" of the Other over me, there stands already (and always) the authority of the Most High. Both "authorities" would need to be reconsidered and reconfigured as soon as the third party disrupts the quiet conversation of the souls.

Nevertheless, one would have done injustice to Levinas if one would not signal that it is from out of the facts of salutations that he conceives a passageway toward the divine, for, among those things accorded to life down here by the one who is Most High is in effect "the authorization of proffering the name of God when greeting a human person,"[17] as when one says "may God be with you" when someone is leaving. It is, as we know, from "the presence of the human face that the dimension of the divine shines forth" or, as the later texts have it, from "the word addressed to the other man [that] the first religious service, the first prayer, the first liturgy, the religion out of which God could first have come to mind [. . .] entered into language."[18]

In this regard, for those of us who would want to remain with this "first transcendence" intimated here, nothing much would be lost, and all the religious senses of Levinas's discourse might possibly be maintained without the violent variety that *Otherwise than Being* entertains.[19] Yet it must be remarked just as well that this first transcendence, in Binswanger at least, would be pre-ethical.[20] Love would rather be something like the transcendental and ontological condition of possibility of ethical (and, of course, therapeutic) practice. This existential of "togetherness" would "take on flesh," become "ontic," and "incarnate" as soon as it faces a factual other: only then it would become ethics proper. In this sense, this other would effect an "ethical reduction"[21] on me, but the sense of this reduction would not be exhausted by ethics alone. This is the existential but nonetheless existentiell and ethical meaning of therapeutic practice: an "entre-nous [. . .] remains the human horizon of every encounter [and is] a possibility that each human being carries in him. Therapy consists [. . .] in being toward the other that which the other for the moment cannot be."[22]

With Loving Regards: Binswanger

Let us turn to Binswanger's account of this greeting insinuating itself in being and between all beings. I noted already that a citation of the poet Van Hofmansthal features quite centrally in the *Grundformen*: the quote is found in the beginning of this monumental book and then only referred to obliquely, between brackets, throughout the book. Here is Von Hoffmansthal:

> But is certain that all the going and the seeking and encountering somehow belong to the secrecies of eros. It is certain that, on our wounded ways, we do not advance and push forward simply because of our deeds but are always drawn to and enticed by something [*gelockt von etwas*] that seemingly always awaits us somewhere yet is always veiled. There is something like a longing of and for love [*Liebesgier*], a curiosity of love in our striding forward even then when we seek the solitude of the forest [. . .]. All lonely encounters are intermixed with something very sweet, may it only be the encounter with a huge tree standing alone or the encounter with an animal of the forest which stops inaudibly and eyes us though the dark. As for me, it is not the embrace but the encounter that is properly decisive of the erotic pantomime. No moment when the sensual is more spiritual or the spiritual more sensual than in the encounter [. . .]. Here one finds a mutual aiming-for-the-other yet without lust [*Zueinandertrachten noch ohne Begierde*]. *A greeting is something borderless.* Dante dates his "new life" back from a greeting that was imparted on him. Wonderful is the cry of a great bird, the peculiar, lonely sound, prior to the world, loud at dawn from the highest evergreen, heard somewhere by a rooster. This somewhere, this indeterminacy which is already a passionate longing, this crying out of the stranger to the stranger [*diese Schreien des Fremden nach der Fremden*]

is what is awesome. The encounter promises more than the embrace can hold on to.²³

Everything that Binswanger's phenomenology of love presents us with is present here: the loving salutation extended to all beings, be they inanimate or animate; the odd encounter of the sensual and the spiritual or, in phenomenological terms, of *eidos* and *Faktum*, of ontological encounters and ontic embraces; the incarnation of the excess of the encounter, becoming flesh in the finitude of love that nevertheless will never contain this aspiration of the infinite toward the finite but will thus, by this greeting, be enticed to long for the more-than-finite that is glimpsed in love.

Binswanger repeatedly returns to these phrases of Von Hofmannsthal. His phenomenology might in effect be read as showing the passageway from the ontic embrace to the ontological universality of beings saluting beings. This passageway only comes to mind *phenomenologically*, for not only does it take two for there to be an embrace (or a kiss, or a hug—the figurations Binswanger will use to "imagine" this thought of love), but this universality stands in need of this ontic "you" whom I consider my love, for without "you," my love, I would not be able to know of this greeting extending toward everyone and his brother. Binswanger, however, will never lose sight of a sort of discrepancy between the ontological, originary *coram* (to you . . .) and the ontic "you" to whom my love is first addressed, although without such an ontic occurrence, in which the greeting of love is first of all factically experienced and "incarnated," we would never know of this originary togetherness. In Binswanger's terminology: without you, there would be no "We" (*Wirheit*), without your embrace no encounter (*Begegnung*), and without you no sense of this being-with of all beings (*Miteinandersein*). Yet similarly, this togetherness functions as the transcendental and ontological condition of possibility of the ontic embrace: without such a fundamental address of being extending to beings universally, the ontic embrace could not be differentiated from ordinary concern and care in which even human beings can be treated as mere objects-at-hand or beings ready-to-hand. For Binswanger, then, it is love that unites identity and difference, for the ontic experience of love is to be identified with the ontological salutation that is love but differs from it in many other respects too, as it is after all only seldom that this one, this one experience of love, with you, with her, will tell me all I need to know about love and could show what there is to love in an exhaustive manner.

Before delving into this ontology of love a bit further, it should be stressed that Binswanger is careful not to lose sight of how such an ontology craves, as it were, for the ontic, as if it needs a place, the world, where it is "phenomenally validated": love becomes flesh means that it does show up in phenomenality if one is to speak of it meaningfully. It is for this reason that Binswanger refers to the greeting as the primary instance in which the loving gaze, the look my lover and I give to one another, shows up ontically—"though still borderless"—as "the nudge, the shaking of hands or kisses."[24] This ontic greeting, then, somewhat diminishes the ontological essence of love, because this one image, this one *Gestalt* of love, obviously does some sort of injustice to the universal idea of love—though I can in principle greet everyone, and though it takes two for there to be a greeting and a handshake at all, the fact remains that, when shaking hands, it is just you I salute. Binswanger here is obviously dependent on the metaphysics of his time considering empirical events, language, and images as unfaithful instantiations of a prime essence. The fact remains, however, that Binswanger is more attentive than anyone else, perhaps, as to just how this essence of love is attested to phenomenologically and empirically. One therefore has to describe carefully the "unfolding"[25] of love from its evanescent essence to its downright empirical messiness and sexual embodiment. The *Grundformen*, then, proceed quite contrary to the habits of the postmodern mind, which, one surmises, would have started from this messy finitude of love rather than from an essence hovering above this finite world of ours only hoping to hint at a bit of ontic love: it is, however, in Binswanger, as if love *throws* itself on Heideggerian being-in-the-world in all of its thrownness and clothes it with a garment that, although it does not entirely suit it, it will never be able to dispel, for this aspiring toward concrete, factical imaginings is part and parcel of ontological love just as well.[26]

This originary *coram* then is, with or without *Deo*, to be seen as a fundamental salute to beings and of beings: "that which is enticed [*gelockt*] in this way, that which is lovingly sought and what one is on track of, both traced and tracing, is Dasein "in its entirety," that is, the Dasein in full possession of all of its possibilities."[27] The greeting, in this way, becomes a sign of the fundamental enticement taking place within being and between beings, of the fact of being drawn to one another the world over. It is this *Lockung* that makes for the primal encounter that is love and serves as the condition of possibility of the concrete encounter. Love is another name for "life greeting life": "the there of Dasein" is intimated in that it "is enticed [*lockt*] by another, nudges toward and greets one another, in that it looks toward the other and speaks with him, in that it embraces each other."[28] I come back to the fullness of being intimated thus below, but for now it is important to note that in this mutual attraction between beings Binswanger perceives the beginnings of love: love is "the never ending, never coming to an end, borderless or better infinite, thus never definitive, movement of drawing near [*Bewegung der Näherung*]."²⁹

This incoming of another Dasein is then experienced only in a concrete encounter with this other here in the world, for if love is not to be identified with a movement within the world, it takes place nowhere else than in the world.

Phenomenology of Love

Love, as I indicated, is to be attested phenomenologically in the concrete encounter of two lovers, for not only is there no meaning for one alone; there is neither embrace, kiss, nor greeting for one alone. Love "does not float in the air."³⁰ This is what Binswanger calls "*Überschwang*," a real though precarious excess over Heideggerian being-in-the-world, for we love in the world, in any case not elsewhere than in the world, but *why* and *what* we love is not (of) this world. It is through such ontic love, then, that Dasein experiences the infinity of love-without-borders, capable of extending to all beings without exception as it is, *in and through* Dasein's finite existence.

Binswanger's main target here is Heidegger. His phenomenology of love intends to show "what Heidegger did not show."³¹ For what exactly is love's place in the existential analysis carried out in *Being and Time* if it has a place there at all? Binswanger is looking for a *tertium datur* between the ontic preoccupations of everyday Dasein and the ontological heroism of authentic Dasein that faces (the possibility) of his or her imminent death. This is what he considers his "cardinal question":³² what kind of temporality and ecstasy pertains to Dasein when it loves if the loving Dasein is not solely in advance of its own future and its own death or if death is not the sole face of the future? Binswanger argues that the factical experience of love can be aligned to Heidegger's account of Dasein, in that surely the loving Dasein is an experience of ecstasy—it temporalizes, say, toward the future—but the future here figures—takes on a different *Gestalt*, a different *Gestalt* is in any case imagined—from out of a timelessness and infinity that are proper only to the experience of love.

Binswanger therefore does not dismiss Heidegger's analysis of Dasein altogether but considers it not to be able to contain the whole truth of Dasein (for the truth of this enticing—*Lockung*—cannot be contained in the first place, even though, as I will show, it can be conserved through love). For this, Binswanger's Daseinsanalysis "falls into" ontic "time" to see what shows itself, phenomenologically, in the experience of the two lovers. Obviously, there is no love for one alone. This, at least, explains Binswanger's rather formal definition of love: the "loving togetherness" is an "already being ahead of one another in the world of one another as being with each other [*der Welt des Einander als Sein miteinander*]."³³ The world worlds, one might say, from out of the horizon the two of us give to one another. The only concern I should have here is my anticipating your every move just as well as your anticipating the future that belongs to us. Love *deflects* Heideggerian care; it is "a curvature of intersubjective space"³⁴ that bends my finite space in such a way that my death is not what matters most here but rather the death of my lover, your death, which here substitutes itself for the end and ultimate aim of my Dasein—and ours.

Love, in this way, insinuates a different way of being-in-the-world than the somewhat solipsistic struggle of one Dasein with all other Daseins that Heidegger had in mind. Over and against the "*Hineindrängen*" of such a being-in-the-world, where I envy "your" space because it could be "my" space just the same and which is dominated by the concern for "what is yours and what is mine," Binswanger's love intimates an "*Einraümen*" that is proper to love, where we reserve a place for one another because there now is a place for us. This figure of the spacing of love's space is for Binswanger to be traced to Heraclitus, who had so described the *ontic* figure of *eros* as "the growth of having through giving"—*eauton audzoon*.³⁵ The loss of my space, then, makes way for the ontological *Heimat*, to which "we" belong, through "the remarkable phenomenon of a 'borderless' increase of my proper space through giving away my own space"—or where, if I am allowed to abandon the language of philosophy for a short while, "all that I have is all that you have given me."³⁶

Here Binswanger anticipates Marion's reciprocal giving that marks the erotic phenomenon, adding that it is from this back and forth *between* us that both of us receive independence. Therefore "you" become yourself in love because you give yourself as an "I"—the ego of and in "You and I"—to me while receiving my ego through my giving to you and thus receiving me—the you in and through "You and I": "It is from out of togetherness [*Wirheit*] that there first springs selfhood."³⁷

This movement of love requires for Binswanger its own space and time, similar, again, to the erotic reduction in Marion where love erects its own timing and spacing during the erotic encounter. Yet this space, for Binswanger, is not solely timeless but, in a certain sense, worldless. This forgetfulness of world happens precisely because loving togetherness temporarily overtakes the world: the space of us being together is, because of the particular "augmentation of being" (*eros*), literally limitless and borderless. Binswanger here relies on the sentiments of Rilke: "*Nur wo Du bist, ensteht ein Ort*"—so much "You" so much "space," one might say. It is important to consider that Binswanger argues for a negative as well as a positive interpretation. For this "*Ort*," this space between us, the "*Heimat*" or homeland of the lovers can be stated in terms of the bad as well as the good infinite. Negatively, then, this *Heimat* is borderless, limitless, endless, inscrutable, and inexhaustible, allowing for the fact that "my home is nowhere without you." Yet, positively, the *Heimat* makes for an actual, real infinite, "inhabiting all this negativity," allowing for the fact that no place is uncanny if you are there and that no matter how far away you are, you are always near. Love is thoroughly dialectic: it is the sole instance that can put "the power of the negative" to work.[38]

This is perhaps best made clear by the role the hand plays in Binswanger's *Grundformen*, for the hand is not only that which can heal and caress; it is also that which can hurt and hit you.[39] Love, then, is "worldless" in the very precise sense that it transgresses and transcends the borders of the world: it insinuates a "being-beyond-the-world-in-the-world," *über die Welt hinaus sein*. This *Heimat* for Binswanger transcends all nationalist and biological boundaries as well as the difference between male and female, for, although this difference is not denied by Binswanger, it is incorporated into a higher unity where what matters is first of all to be human and only afterward what it is to be "male" or "female." Ontologically, Binswanger points to the essence of being human as androgynous where what is "male" or "female" is distributed to all members of humanity.[40]

In this regard, the space of love is to be considered as the *conquering* of the world. It is beyond the world, in that it is not concerned with intraworldly beings at all but rather with the space that you give to me (and vice versa) so that "We" can show up in phenomenality. I speak of love's restriction to world later, but for now it is important to note that Binswanger relies here not only on poetry but also on ordinary language—*Umgangssprache*—stating that my love for you "deepened" and "widened" my horizon, and we reach the "highest" of our being. Love, for Binswanger, at least alters and modifies the basic tenets of Heideggerian *Besorgen* and the concomitant "deseverance" (*Entfernung*). The *Heimat* extends the world over: it *conquers* the world, in that "you" transpire through all things in the world, and the world becomes transparent and properly belongs to you and me: I am at home with you in the world, and it is in and through the world that I meet you.

Love shows itself again in its dialectical form here, because for Binswanger love, if it is to be meaningful is with *and* without world at the same time. Conquering the world means, positively, that I offer the entire world to you; negatively, that the world no longer matters if only I can be with you. Love, to be distinguished here from passion as well as sentiment, is with and without world at the same time. A love that would remain too much "with" world turns into a "care for love" (*Sorge um die Liebe*)—as, for instance, we worry about who will pick up the kids this evening—and a love that is too much "without world" turns into a being-in-love, *Verliebtheit*, that is concerned too little with the things of a world and becomes a *solitude à deux*. For Binswanger, then, it is Goethe who saw the unity of love and care in that love both needs and dispenses with world: "I see you in all things of the world" even though I cannot give the entire world to you. It is *from out of the world* that I will encounter you just as well as it is from out of your presence that I will be directed *toward the world* and this will serve as its primary orientation. Such a proportionality is a key feature of Binswanger's thought: we will encounter it again in his account of the "sick Dasein."[41]

It is in effect because of Binswanger's being concerned with all things ontic that such a restrictedness to world will show the phenomenon of love at its most remarkable, but now I need to show that this phenomenon alters not only the basic space of Dasein but its temporalizing as well. Love ecstatically gathers the present, the past, and the future.

Its *present* is not the being-with or *Sein bei* intraworldly beings. Loving Dasein does not fall into the world of concern, for they are not to be identified by what they do (in the world), but their respective egos only arise out of what they are together. The present of love is, for me, the experience of who I am when I am with you: there are no roles to be played here, and I can be properly, "fully," myself: *bei einander*. Love cannot be understood from out of its worldly *past* either, from out of the ontic occurrence that occasioned love, for instance, for loving Dasein is not to be identified from out of that which factically happened to it but rather as ourselves, as that which we are and have been with one another. In love, I do not return to myself as to "my past" but my self "selves" from out of our past: I return rather to just how my world took on meaning through your presence precisely as the past we share *Miteinander*. The *future* of love differs from the future threatening finite Dasein as well. Loving Dasein is not to be identified with two selves that are always already ahead of another, in advance of themselves until death, for this would mean that these Dasein could never properly meet, but they are ahead of each other and anticipate the future that is theirs: whatever happens will happen to the two of us.

Thus is intimated in Binswanger the ontological condition of possibility of an experience that lacks nothing (which does not know a regret of something in the past or of any fear for the future, for instance), and loving Dasein attains the highest possibility of its being.[42] Although this experience is effected only in and through time, as the three ecstasies show, time does not seem to affect this experience. This is why Binswanger considers the experience of love to be timeless and eternal: it can even stand the test of death.

In its very first moment, then, the ontology of love transcends all figures of being-in-the-world. In Heidegger's analytic, Binswanger writes, love "remained in the cold."[43] In this moment, this (Heideggerian) world is penetrated with the spirit of love, and the two of us experience the beyond of space and time *in*, precisely, space and time. Love is "beyond-the-world-in-the-world": this is the *überweltlichkeit der Heimat*.[44] Yet this moment of transcendence has to be (en)countered by this very ontic you whom I encounter in the world that we already share, for without greeting and kissing this particular other here I would perhaps not know about the borderless ontology of the greeting in the first place. There is no love for one alone.

Toward an Ontology Incarnate: The Fullness of Being

It is on this exact point that Binswanger can be connected to Nancy's "shattered" thoughts on love, because it is only "appropriate that a discourse on love [. . .] be at the same time a communication of love, a letter."[45] Yet on this ontic incarnation—in language, in poetry, in kisses—Nancy and Binswanger diverge, for Nancy, not unlike a great many postmodernists, insists on the antidialectical strand of love as that which can never be incorporated and recuperated by ontological discourse, be it one on love. Love, for Nancy, is always ambiguous: "it is the contradiction of contradiction and of noncontradiction": it escapes the dialectic while enabling it.[46] It is both too ontic to say anything meaningful about it (lest we be sentimental) and too ontological to ever coincide (and thus not contradict) with all these ontic things accompanying our loves. Love, for Nancy, is *exposed*. It presents itself to the world and to thought, as that which is destined to all of us but can never find a home. Love cannot *not* be in the cold: its letters never arrive, and neither do they return to the sender. Love "is" and it "is not": it borders on being, being exposed to its margins; it is what keeps us going while we never know where we are going.

In this regard, Binswanger's and Nancy's thought could be aligned, but the latter, just as I have shown in his account of language, again forgets the restriction to world precisely, to the fact, if you like, that my love is nowhere else than in badly written love letters, in mellow, all too mellow love songs and in those "classical figure[s] of romantic comedies [where even though] it is another at the rendezvous, [it] is love itself that is revealed thereby."[47] Binswanger, then, is much more aware of the back and forth of the ontic and the ontological and considers the former as the only legitimate passageway to the latter without one being able to dismiss the former completely.

Let us turn to how Binswanger considers the (ontic) restriction to world. Of course, lovers meet in-the-world and understand themselves from out of the concerns and preoccupations making for this very world. Yet "even when true love entertains a particular relation to such an existentiell process [such as the ontic occasion or the 'outer' impulse of falling in love, JS], its ontological essence does *not* lie in this."[48] Thus the ontic occasion of love is not to be confused with love's essence, although it does open to the more-than-ontic or at least other-than-ontic nature of love. What happens, then, when lovers meet if the only place where they can meet is called "world" considered from the fact that love cannot "pass over" the world?[49] Loving Dasein is not miraculously transposed and transported to another world. Its transcending toward the particular lover does not happen elsewhere than world. Yet this transcendence will transpire onto the world and turn its basic orientation around and will eventually make love come to terms with the world. With this, a new ontology, other than Heidegger's, is glimpsed in and through the experience of love.

The meeting of lovers is the crossing between (ontic) encounter and the (ontological) *Urbegegnung*, between our togetherness (*Wir beide*) and togetherness in general (*Wir überhaupt*) or, in terms of the previous section: it is my being drawn to you because of the universal enticement that rages through being and presences between all beings.[50] My "advancing toward the 'expected' yet indeterminate You, as a being drawn by you and 'your' seeking" is an ontic longing or *Sehnsucht* conditioned by this ontological greeting within being, the latter being conserved and first glimpsed in our very ontic encounters.[51] What happens when we meet?

Then another Dasein *answers* my longing just as my approaching toward you will answer you. In love, Binswanger's famous definition of the human being, as "the play of questions and answers of Dasein with itself"[52] and with being, is temporarily put out of play. No questions are asked. For what is disclosed in the coincidence of this ontic and ontological meeting is "the fullness of the spatiality of a determinate 'we' (in the sense of finding ourselves and choosing for another."[53] Yet "disclosive" how and of what? It, Binswanger argues, discloses "the borderless, inscrutable, inexhaustive [. . .] character of this determinate space [*bestimmte Raum*] only because the borderless, indeterminate Dasein as encounter, quest, and longing as such is here unconcealed and revealed."⁵⁴ This is why ontic Dasein may enjoy here a glimpse of its ontological makeup: "Dasein glimpses itself as *Mitdasein*"—there is no one who does not want to be loved as much as there is no love for one alone.⁵⁵ This is also why Binswanger speaks of an "empirical miracle" here and why this miracle, that is, the unification of mutual indeterminate longing with the love for this one here, can be experienced as an overwhelming *tremendum*.

Yet what is so united does not collapse all differences.⁵⁶ On the contrary, it is through my love for this one here that I notice a certain disproportionateness as well "between the degree of factical unlikelihood and the height of the evidence of truth," between the ontic questions of how this meeting came about at all and the consciousness that it could not have been otherwise.⁵⁷ When love overtakes the existential analytic, then, it "is" you and it "is not" you whom I love. It is you, because obviously and empirically it is you whom I love and it could not have been otherwise. It is not you, though, because factically I could have fallen in love with anyone else just as well, and, even when this is not the case, my love for you does not exhaust the essence of love—which stretches toward being/s in its entirety—and it is only because of this (ontological) presencing of love that you and I are able to love ontically at all. Love, rather, for Binswanger, unites identity and difference; it is the *unio as communio*: "our" love is the meeting of you and I with one another and, through this, a glimpse of the meeting of all with all. It prevents us from reducing the difference of love to an identity—as when one would lose track of that facticity that I could have loved someone else equally—as much as appropriating this identity of love to such an extent that different loves would no longer be possible—the danger of a *solitude à deux*. Binswanger argues that what reason and rationality can barely understand is the fact that in love there is "a coinciding of this *one* particular You and You-ness in general [*einen geliebten Du und 'Duhaftigkeit' überhaupt*]." And yet this is the "proper essence [of love], the life of love."⁵⁸

The marvel is in effect that I love love in loving you, that is, I love not only "you" as this ontic Dasein but neither do I love just the idea of love through loving you—one cannot love an idea, Hegel says. This means that here this ontic love—for you—serves as the particular passageway to the idea of love, to the love that extends to all beings. This love here, in its ontic variety, is extended to an ontology of love, as it extends the greeting to life greeting life, universally. The one Good that you and I share shares itself with all and everything that can be named "good."⁵⁹ This is love's principle: it cannot remain content with you and me alone. What is unbearable for a reason prone to seek metaphysical residues is that this is an ontology incarnate: the "infinity" of love presences in this ontic love "down here" and is conserved and preserved there, yet not contained. This ontic love, then, is capable of uniting the most empirical of empiricism—which seems to be bodily love for Binswanger: one, in any case, cannot *make* love with an idea—and the most universal aspects of rationalism in the borderless greeting of love insinuating itself only through our ontic dealings with one another. It is such a penetration of the body with the idea or the incarnation of the idea in the body that philosophy should seek to understand again, reminding ourselves, despite Derrida, that not all gathering and uniting is an unfortunate and improper metaphysical naming and appropriating.

Later, Binswanger turns to Husserl to understand this incarnation of ontological love in the peculiarity of my ontic lover. Whereas for Husserl it matters to see in the *Faktum*, in the ontic instance that is, that which the phenomenological gaze had already glimpsed of the *eidos* through imaginary variation (as when I recognize in this table here a table "in general" because I perceive a plateau with four legs), in Binswanger's phenomenology of love things change: not only, as is somewhat the case in Husserl as well, the state of the factum may have repercussions for the conception of the *eidos* (certain tables can alter my view of what a table is) but also and especially, because in love the *Faktum* is the exemplary basis for the glimpse of its essence, for only from out of the *Faktum* of my love for her and her love for me can the essence of love in an exemplary way be intuited, for here I do not only see (and think) its *eidos* but also love (ontological) love through loving you ontically.[60] This is close to the *avance* of the lover in Marion's work of love indeed: for, well before the particular encounter with my love, this advance is made "for nothing" for the sake of loving love.[61]

In Heideggerian terms, the ontic encounter between my love and me necessitates a different comprehension of being and of Dasein's *worumwillen* than Heidegger had provided. In Heidegger, in effect, my being is such that "being" is at issue in my dealings with world. Similarly, "my" being is at issue in my dealing with the beings of the world.[62] It is here that Binswanger most firmly disagrees: in love, what matters most is not this being that I in each case am and have to be but rather the togetherness that *we* always and already are, have been, and will be. The "for the sake of which" these Dasein are their being is therefore no longer its own being, whether it be fallen or authentically appropriated, but these lovers rather are solely and uniquely "for the sake of that which *we* are as Dasein (or this Dasein as *ours*)."[63]

It is thus that a fullness of being is intimated in the experience of love, which does not remain blind for "the power of the negative" but approaches negativity with eyes wide open too. For in Binswanger "the detour that is world"[64]—which seems to be what he takes from Heidegger's *Being and Time*—does not necessarily and ultimately lead to a most proper appropriation of what there is to (my) being. It is rather that the detour via our eternal love leads to an authentic togetherness: it is not that I need to seek how I can love *in* the world; it is rather that from out of our love we are led back to the world. Loving Dasein is not first experienced as a burden that I should assume at all costs; it is rather that, in encountering you, I too will experience the fullness of being. But this fullness is not experienced *despite* the void of being or the void that it at times can be and that has obsessed so many contemporary (antidialectical) philosophies. On the contrary, in loving togetherness, Dasein is very much aware of "its own nothingness as the nothingness of the foundation," but this nothingness need not be understood here as if one is being overpowered by it, that is, as guilt and a burden. Here rather Dasein receives its self through our togetherness precisely as the reception of not-having-laid-its-own-foundation. Here Dasein gives its self away to the *Heimat* it receives from its togetherness with this particular you *with and through whom* it is now "gifted," whereas that with which it is so gifted is the fullness of being out of which it understands itself as the rightful "giver of a gift."[65] In short: I give myself to you because I have first received myself from you, and vice versa because we have both received ourselves—as *us*—from out of the primordial opening of all beings to all beings, that is, from out of ontological togetherness that functions as the condition of possibility of us concretely meeting in the world: I give myself to you because we have given and received ourselves to and from *one* another. It takes two, in effect, for there to be gift.

What is it that is thus given? The fullness of being is in tune with the augmentation of being that accompanied the *Heimat* already: the lovers experience *wie sehr sie sind*—the phrase is from the poet Klopstock. This needs to be understood not only as the experiences of loving Dasein as "how much they are" but also as how much being they have received. The latter is a proper metaphysical experience, for it experiences beingness in its totality—recall the borderlessness of the greeting—the former is the concomitant ontic experience, because "what offers its hand here is the Dasein itself as a you":[66] the (ontic) embrace and the offering of a hand, to recall Von Hoffmansthal, can and cannot hold fast to the (ontological) encounter. But both "aspects" make for the wholeness of Dasein: at one with all beings through the hand offered by another being.

The marvel of this experience of awe is that it questions Levinas's dismissal of *thaumasein* as a lone, theoretical experience in which a worldless ego would wonder about being and beings[67] but also the manner in which finite Dasein, in Heidegger, "experiences" its being. Whereas Heidegger's retrieval of Aristotle's dictum that possibility always stands higher than actuality resonates with the way in which Heidegger conceives of the *geworfene Entwurf*, Dasein's projection of itself toward its future, in that certain possibilities are always withdrawn from this particular projection: more and other things would have been possible than what I actually experience. This is Dasein's finite, always finite projection: in everything that is happening, there is always something *not* happening. Possibility is therefore greater than actuality.[68] It is, however, precisely this withdrawal of other possibilities through the actualization of certain "preoccupations" that will vanish in the experience of love: here possibility equals actuality.

This reveals an experience from which nothing is lacking. On the contrary, one might be quite certain that if something were lacking, this experience would not be love. Love, then, is *not concerned* ("*nicht kümmert*") with other possibilities that might be projected.[69] Love, in a way, says no to the nullity that Dasein has to be in the mode of care. This is why love is, for Binswanger, ultimately an *affirmation*, a "yes" toward one's thrownness in being with the other and others. This is why love, too, asks no questions: it does not hope, it does not fear, and it does not judge, for there is here no "not-yet" that would pose questions or threaten the "risk" (*Wagnis*) that is love.[70] If anything, love "mocks" the laws of the world, for it knows not of anything absent from its present, and it is ignorant too of any loss to come.[71]

Conclusion: Faith in Love

What does this love risk? It risks a certain faith in being and beings: it is not that you need to have faith to believe Binswanger's phenomenology here; it is rather that without this belief (in loving togetherness) you will have no (religious or otherwise) faith.[72] For this belief is first a daring theory of the power of imagination—powerful enough to trigger the thought of Michel Foucault, for instance—and traces an "imaginative realization" which, through the "double wonder" of *our* love, as a mutual loving and being loved, glimpses a love of all for all.[73] This realization (which is also an awareness) *requires* the participation of the lover in what is thus glimpsed, not to make this glimpse "subjective" but rather to attest to the only objectivity possible in matters of humanity, the knowledge of a certain love that, were it not for my love of you, I would have never known or imagined. The passageway through the ontic is a necessary although not sufficient condition for this view of love: I can imagine whatever I want, but it is *in each case you*, as my lover, who offers and has offered the condition necessary for me to imagine love at all—love, in this regard, is *Ein-bildung* and *Bildung* at once, "imagination" and "formation."

"Without your answer" (to my loving advance), my ontological quest into what there is to love would in effect float in the air.[74] Yet what is imagined here is a possibility that is no longer higher than reality: everything that is imagined as possible is real here. And what is real is all that we had imagined. It is a love that lacks nothing, and even if it lacked anything (of the world), this lack will not be felt with the measures of the world (as a possibility to be realized sooner or later). The experience of the lack will not stand in the way of the fullness experienced: love conjoins deception—the shattering of fullness—and satisfaction—fullness before its shattering.[75] This is ultimately the "imaginative realization": if love is not all of this, if love is not all, it is not love; if love does not attain or aspire to reality in this way, there *is* no love either. Again, Binswanger's claim is an ontological one—it is this that has seemingly unsettled Heidegger.

So one is led to believe, if only for an instant, that it is in effect love that makes the world go round. For Binswanger, in effect, the imaginative realization of love is the source and origin of all "creativity," it—contra Foucault—craves images: love then is, as it was for Joyce, "the virgin womb of the imagination where the word is made flesh" (*Portrait of the Artist as a Young Man*). If for Heidegger there is an overlap between Dasein and world, for Binswanger Dasein overlaps with whatever it can imagine and whatever empowers this imagination, that is, love.[76]

9

The "Ends" of Love

Friendship, Death, and Care

Heidegger and Binswanger

The debate between Binswanger and Heidegger is a complex one and not always documented well. There have been some meetings and some letters between the two men, and it appears that whereas in the beginning their relationship was a friendly and generous one, Heidegger and Binswanger later entertained almost hostile relations with one another. The reason for this is, it seems, that Heidegger had found in Medard Boss a more faithful follower, one who would listen to the "voice of Being" only through what the voice of the "hidden king" narrated about it. Binswanger, so far as I can see, ultimately became disappointed in Heidegger and was, through the latter's interventions, less and less inclined to speak out in philosophical matters. He labeled his *Grundformen* in too humble a manner famously as "a productive misunderstanding" of *Being and Time*.[1] Whatever the case, it is no exaggeration to say that the debate between the two thinkers was, if anything, a "dialogue between the deaf" because in effect their pathways "crossed one another more than they would be opposed."[2]

Some sort of clash between these giants could, of course, not be avoided considering Binswanger's claim of a different ontology and a different form of being-in-the-world than Heidegger had advanced. Because loving Dasein might very well be, if only for an instant, "without world," it inversely cannot *live* without being preoccupied with world. Binswanger is very clear on this. Love and care are not unrelated. One might even say that Binswanger's quest for the "knowledge of Dasein" (*Daseinserkenntnis*) is the goal of the *Grundformen*: showing just how care can be *united* with love and how pedagogy and psychotherapy can be done *with love*. Yet the relations between world and love are more complex still, because Binswanger argues that "for love to be *there*, it needs to be 'at one' with care or, put differently, Dasein can only be 'there' in an infinite manner insomuch as it is finite!"[3] Love is restricted to world as much as any other experience, and Dasein is, in the best case, at once loving and caring—it needs to "assert [*behaupten*]" itself in the world.[4] Were it not for being-in-the-world and all of its adversities, we probably would not have imagined anything other than world in the first place. But, similarly, if to understand Dasein one needs to understand love as well as care, then it follows that Heidegger obviously did not understand Dasein.

Yet Binswanger's understanding of world is tainted already by his ontological understanding of love. It is for this reason that other ontic phenomena than Heidegger described come into view—the body and friendship, for instance—and that the ontic phenomena that Heidegger did depict, namely "the They," are also assessed otherwise. Let us first, however, turn to Jacob Needleman's interpretation of the relation between Binswanger and Heidegger. Needleman has argued that Binswanger's ontico-ontology is, in fact, not *an* extension "but the only possible extension to the ontic level of Heidegger's ontology," through "[taking] the ontological determined existentials [and bringing] them into the frame of concrete human existence."[5] For this, Needleman develops the notion of an "existential a priori," close to the practical a priori we have seen in Schürmann.

This existential a priori is "a priori" in the sense that for human beings universally there is world, and "existential" in the sense that each human being configures, constructs, and thus lives this being-in-the-world differently. One might say: there are as many worlds as there are Dasein, but each Dasein "has" world. For Binswanger the psychiatrist, then, this would mean that there are possibly as many maladies as there are Dasein, meaning that in each case Dasein and the concomitant construction of world has to be looked at individually: if all human beings are Dasein, not all human beings experience this "Da" in quite the same manner. What the "ontological anthropology" aims for then is the condition of possibility of each Dasein's ontic, often disturbed, experience. Sickness and malady, for Binswanger, are in effect to be understood as modifications (to the point of interruption) of being-in-the-world: false and failing Dasein cannot "assert" itself in the world properly. It goes without saying that this proper way of being-in-the-world will differ considerably from the heroics of *Being and Time*.

It is on this point that much of the debate between Binswanger and Heidegger (and followers such as Medard Boss) turns. For the latter two, in effect, the ontological "worldhood" is distributed immutably to all Dasein, whereas for Binswanger the ontic experience of malady (and of love) conditions as much as it is conditioned by worldhood. The ontic experience *conditions* worldhood in the sense that sick Dasein constructs (or fails to construct) a world still—it is *some* world that we experience when we are sick, but, obviously, not all the possibilities of *the* world are still present—yet is simultaneously *conditioned*, because no Dasein is, obviously, without world. It pertains to the psychiatrist then to *describe* phenomenologically how the world "worlds" in each given case.

In this way, Binswanger aims, not unlike many others coming to Heidegger through Husserl, to separate the *Da* from its "*Sein*" in order to speak of the "there" without being(-in-the-world).[6] One might indeed argue that there are *degrees* in Dasein's restriction to world. Binswanger, in this regard, speaks of the experience of sheer horror—*nacktes Grauen*—in which Dasein experiences a being *without* Da, that is, a being that can no longer ecstatically relate to its world—experience it as meaningful—and is haunted, frightened, and *taken over* by world to the point of collapse.[7] This horror is closer to Levinas's *there is* than to Heidegger's anxiety, which can *always and already*—not to say immutably—find an ecstatic evasion "most proper" to the experience. Sickness would then share with horror the fact that it is the experience of a *lesser "Da"*: simply the experience of an incapability of being-in-the-world. Although Heidegger would no doubt eschew such a separation between "*Da*" and "*sein*," it must be recalled that his own proposal in the *Zollikon Seminars* for the proper French translation, "*être le là*" or "being-the-there," at least hints at the possibility of a "not-being-the-there" that would not need to be equated with the talkative "They."

To understand how Binswanger configures this "Da" not yielding to "world," we must turn to his account of modern secularization and of the "loveless century" that is his.[8] Binswanger shows himself to be a modern thinker, well aware of the issues surrounding secularization and the fact that the self-realization of being human no longer lies immediately in his or her relation to God. In its stead, the human being has to reckon with an increasing muteness of being as to the question of humanity's *Worumwillen*. The questions of humanity now can no longer be solved by being or by cosmology, for being does not answer. It is for this reason too that Binswanger will turn to love and look for an answer to the question that is the human being in its relation to his and her fellows, to the ones answering.[9] This relation is not properly understood, neither in an ethical nor in a religious manner alone: "increasing secularization has made [modern thought] turn away from love and turn to ethics, instead of, despite its un- or anti-Christian tendency, seeking to understand this primal human phenomenon properly."[10] Yet because of this very tendency, the religious answer to human *Worumwillen*—I am "for the sake" of God—does not satisfy either, which leaves Binswanger (and us) in an awkward situation, because the question as to the sense of my Dasein remains even when the older answers are eradicated.[11] This might be the reason why one sees Binswanger develop what one could call a *phenomenological belief* in love, which could serve as the basis of religious faith. In any case, modernity uproots the human being considerably, that is, both ontologically and ontically. Ontically, it is the dawn of an increasing instrumentalization of the human being that is, for Binswanger, the genuine opposite of love and what he will conceptualize as *nehmen bei etwas* or "taking someone as something." Ontologically, the modern times are no less awkward—recall for instance this quote from our introduction:

> the problem of the human being needs a new solution. If we can no longer look for it in "the transcendent" or the eternal realm, then we will need to seek in the temporal and finite realm, in being and time, in being-in-the-world therefore. Yet in these realms alone not all accounts are settled. There remains a residue that does not befit finitude, the *yearning* [*Sehnsucht*] beyond the worldly finitude of Dasein for unification with infinite and eternal being.[12]

Dasein, then, does not dissolve in being-in-the-world: it is bothered and burdened by a longing that seeks beyond the established borders of the world. Of this longing, why would one assume that Heidegger said everything there is to say? This *Sehnsucht*, the passion for who and what is other, is for Binswanger primarily a longing "for oneness and wholeness" that will be satisfied only in the loving encounter where *one* is aware of and attuned to the fact of "how much *we* are," and all union has already passed through communion.[13] Yet prior to the encounter with this very empirical and ontic you that you are, *Sehnsucht* expresses itself primarily as a "dissatisfaction" with the ways of the world.[14] It is this *Ungenügen* that for Binswanger indicates a Dasein that is not crafted very well onto its world. And it is precisely this for Binswanger that "Heidegger did not show," namely "that Dasein [. . .] does not dissolve in being-towards-its-end and therefore in no way can be understood from out of its facticity alone, i.e. from out of the factuality of the fact of one's own Dasein."[15] This facticity lacks imagination, one might say; it knows nothing of the turn (not to say conversion) that love brings to one's Dasein simply because love, ontologically, is the being-turned of all toward all.

The "Unfolding" of Love in the World: Toward a *Liebende Sorge*

Binswanger is well aware of the frailty of the "there." Both when it comes to matters of sanity and in matters of love, he will therefore argue for the proportionality of a certain *phronesis*. Consider, for instance, the weal and woe of loving Dasein:

> The "true" relation between "love and world" shows itself neither in you and me retreating from the world nor in our dissolving in the world. Yet [the relation] is not a simple switch between both "movements" as in some sort of succession between "sufficing to one another" and "having enough of each other." It is not these "real" possibilities that are intended but the fact of the possibility of the permeation of the world of concern and solicitude with the spirit of love on the one hand and the transparency of the world of concern through this spirit on the other. Herein lies the dialectic of love and world.[16]

Love too will put itself at risk *in* the world. It aspires in this world a new possibility for being contending to be the "highest possibility" for the human being. Binswanger's ontology seeks to *cover* the world slowly but surely with the spirit of love and seeks the enactment of even the most ordinary of ontic experiences with love. For this, loving Dasein will need to balance between world and the isle of love, and try to inject worldhood with "the calmness of love," "the delight of its humor," and its "acquaintance with infinity."[17] This is, simultaneously, to return to the world with love—loving Dasein *asserting* itself in the world—as well as to turn to love those who are lost in world—for instance, the failed Dasein or the They lost in the crowd of fanatics. Even more than the ontology of love and the greeting in being, it is this that the psychiatrist Binswanger, although obliquely, presents as the outcome of his ontology, namely "knowledge of Dasein" that is "an entirely new way of being, a distinct rootedness in being. This way of being is not to be understood as the resignation of love in favor of the nullity of care [. . .], but rather as the 'elevation' of the nullity of care in its entirety into the 'positivity' of the encounter."[18] We have yet to see how this dialectic plays out.

For now, it is to be noted that this return to the world will be accompanied with a certain uprootedness: falling into the world will inevitably be lived as a loss of the *Heimat* or homeland of love, somewhat as a paradise lost indeed. Love lives both the experience of belonging and the experience of being expelled, for just as there is no love for one alone, so one does not live from love alone. If this homeland is such that it intimates the heart of Dasein or rather the Dasein as "heart," in my belonging to you and your belonging to me where my and your longing [*Sehnsucht*] turn into a be-longing to being because of this *co-longing*—such that love speaks, if it would speak, from heart to heart—then it takes this *swing* or *rhythm* of the heart to the world. Love, in this regard, is the ultimate, because it offers to Dasein the ultimate *sense of direction*: it turns the wandering [*Wanderung*] in the world into an alteration [*Wandel*] through the world, a *walking in-the-world* without alienation.

Yet this heart is nowhere if not in the unity of its pulse, uniting systole and diastole—the non-beating of the heart would still be a beating as much as its beating is in the non-beating—in the time of life, and this back and forth between you and me and the world.[19] The allusion to Levinas's "alteration without alienation" is deliberate, because the advantage of the phenomenon of the pulse is that it is a *"processus en troisième personne"* (Merleau-Ponty) and allows for an elevation "beyond" Levinas's ethical curvature of being with its focuses on "breathing" and "inspiration." Here too, of course, non-breathing would still be breathing (and vice versa) as the breath is the unity of inhaling and exhaling. Yet one's breath is still somewhat in one's control: I can hold my breath but I cannot stop my heart from beating.

In this regard, Levinas's curvature of intersubjective space oddly enough might be *too* intersubjective when compared to Binswanger's greeting at the heart of being, extending to dogs in the sun and stones as it does. It is not to be excluded then that such a pulse gives way to a *ruach* more divine (because its coming and going, beating where it wills, is even less localizable). Binswanger once again anticipates Nancy here, for whom "it is necessary that being have a heart, [that] being be a heart [. . .] being beats, [it] essentially is in the beating."[20] From this perspective, Levinas, *like* Buber, would be more prone than Binswanger to "objectify" the "you" of ethics to the "You" of religion, so underestimating its *pulse* (which can be neither located nor controlled). The pulse of being, then, is, because it is less localizable and less visible, less prone to one or the other "metaphysics of presence"—I can see your breath but I can only feel the heartbeat—but no less *present*. In the general conclusion, we compare it to the phenomenon of tickling.

The difference between Levinas's transcendence of the face and Binswanger's *überschwang* would not lie in the fact that the former thinks of a transcendence that cannot be conserved within being, for the face is where this transcendence ultimately "condescends" and where it apparently remains; the difference rather lies in the fact that the latter thinks of an intersubjective curvature where this transcendence is conserved just the same, but cannot be contained: it is therefore not to be *confined* to human transcendence alone.[21] Certainly, for Binswanger too, the divine "shines forth" from the face, but its splendor ultimately cannot be contained to the "après vous *Monsieur*" that Levinas glimpsed. This uncontrollable, barely localizable heart, one might argue, has been intuited well in certain Christian spiritualities, where it is stated that the bleeding heart of Christ for humankind cannot stop bleeding—a tradition stemming from Joh. 19, 34, where piercing Jesus's side with a spear "brings a sudden flow of blood and water," so intimating the sacrifice of the Eucharist and the new life received in and through baptism. One should note as well that, in Nancy, this pulse of love overrules being ultimately, because being and beings cannot theorize or grasp this pulse. Love, to refer to Marion, outwits being/beings. To conclude, some account of being in effect *takes a beating* here. But again: why would we assume that it is Heidegger who said everything there is to say *vom Sein*?

The heart of Dasein, one might say, *takes a beating*, too, once expelled from the homeland to the *Unzuhause* in and *Ungenügen* about the world.[22] It is, however, uncertain whether Binswanger consciously secularized some aspects of salvation history here, the fall from Eden for instance, although numerous citations could hint at such an attempt. This is in effect why the lovers experience not only a sense of belonging (to one another and to being) but also, as indicated earlier, an uprootedness once returned to the world, for "insofar We are expelled from the Homeland of our love, the ego becomes a stranger on earth."[23] Dasein is no less than a being in between: although in love where they uncover their destiny, the lovers are nevertheless destined to go to the world, where they have to take care even of love and while being well aware that the difficulty precisely consists in (a) loving care—*liebende Sorge*.[24]

This means that the essence of love cannot *but* unfold in the world. Love "as such" is destined to *exist* in loving Dasein, which also means, to Derridean ears, that love cannot but be "in the cold" when it comes to the ways of the world. Long before any "metaphysics of presence" became suspect or even detected, Binswanger perhaps succeeded in resisting its temptation. For even if one is suspicious about some sort of descent to the world from love's "original plenitude," which would then only be dimly present in the world as some sort of supplement to the originary fullness of love (so risking to declare ultimately the experience of "pure" love inexistent or a phantasm), Binswanger's unfolding of love in the world avoids this logic because of the difference it maintains between this very ontic you and "youhood" (*Duhaftigkeit*) and togetherness überhaupt (*Wirheit*). Although I pass from this ontic you here to the "carnal idea" of togetherness, this togetherness in turn cannot be identified with the love for this ontic you at all—other "yous" would have always been possible, and no single presence exhausts the idea of togetherness. In fact, for Binswanger, to consider this love between you and me as the ultimate and one love, fundamentally and originally incarnated, would in effect be a metaphysics of presence or, in his terms, a degenerate form of love. But, similarly, a love that knows of no particular you but simply loves *Duhaftigkeit* or *Wirhaftigkeit* in and of all things is not "love" either. If the former admits *too much* of the world, risking the dependency, most often sexual, of the lovers to one another, the latter admits *too little* of the world, which Binswanger sees happening in the religious-mystical fusion with the divine "in all things"; the former substitutes the you for the "we," the latter the "we" for a You.

The essence of love is to be neither entirely *beyond* nor entirely *within* the world; pure love, if there is any, is therefore *in* the world *beyond* the world. Love, for Binswanger, simply *is* not apart from the world even if this means that the fullness of being—the love without lack—can only be loved in and through being-in-the-world, through loving precisely the lack. Love *is* then nothing but its unfolding in being and between beings. This is why, Binswanger writes,

> we have to envisage a further basic trait of the *unfolding* of the pure *Überschwang* in the loving-caring structure of friendly being-with-one-another. *That which* succeeds in a differentiated unfolding [. . .] is spatiality, which here is no longer *solely* Heimat, but a friendly space [*heimatliches land*]. But temporality unfolds as well, from the eternity of its duration to the, through this eternity, "eternalized" doing and "eternalized" conversation. Such unfolding happens entirely *by reason of* and *in favor of* care.[25]

Love, then, admits of degrees. And "pure" love can, for Binswanger too, only be attained through admitting levels of impurity—it could perhaps not get more Derridean. Let us listen to Binswanger's account of love's unfolding once more:

> There are many varying degrees of completeness of such a knowledge of Dasein. From the sketched highest degree to that

degree, in which I lose sight of You and glimpse only the essence of you-ness, where you and the essence of you in general no longer coincide or cover one another [*zur Deckung gelangen*], there is everywhere transition. If finally the glimpse of you-ness is dropped then I no longer know in a psychological manner but only in an objectifying manner."[26]

Yet, on the other hand, Binswanger argues that between objectifying knowledge (in which the other becomes, in psychology, the object of experiments with no regard for our original belonging together) and the potentiality for Being or ability to be (*Seinkönnen*) of love, there are no "ontological borders and therefore no ontological transition."[27] How to understand this? Of this (Husserlian) "*zur Deckung gelangen*," Binswanger provides one negative but rather intriguing example. The "compulsive" "question of many young brides," for instance, "why this one and no one else, why now and not some other time, why at all and not never?" makes clear "the ontical fact" that "loving primal encounter and this encounter here have *not yet* coincided [*zur Deckung gelangt sind*]."[28] Binswanger argues for several reasons for such a non-coincidence: some pertain to the particular "you"—it might not be the right one; the bride may have some stress disorder that keeps her from affirming the "we"—others pertain to the primal togetherness—the loving Dasein as "We" cannot "pronounce" itself at all here; it does not "speak" to the lovers.[29]

What are we to make of such an example? First of all, so as to not upset female readers, it goes without saying that these questions pertain to almost everyone. Even apart from the context of marriage, it would be simply awkward if such questions were never posed. Philosophically, however, it is to be noted here that the non-coincidence is the rule rather than the exception and that Binswanger takes his cue here from Husserl rather than Heidegger.

Binswanger shows his preference for the later Husserl over and against the somewhat "ahistorical" earlier one here—one should not forget that Binswanger turned to Husserl's phenomenology well before *Being and Time* was published. This is evident from the indications of temporality: the lovers have *not yet* succeeded in the coincidence between you and me. But one might legitimately wonder whether such a coincidence ever *actually* occurs and whether it would not be more correct to argue, in the spirit of Derrida and a certain phenomenology, that it in effect takes a lifetime to coincide, which means simultaneously that in love this coincidence never "coincides" properly, that is, is never attained once and for all and that there is no guarantee that it will happen at all. It is this that Binswanger takes from the later Husserl: instead of a onetime and once for all analogical constitution of the alter ego through appresentation, here the other you is originally a living presence *all the time*.[30] The difference between such an "all at once" and "never once for all" is arguably immense: it means that it takes the world, if you like, to get to know one another and to learn to live with love.

Yet the fact that this love requires the world and allows a great many variations does not affect the unity of love in any way: it is the same love that lovers love through their love for one another. Such an "objective" unity of love is obviously (and fortunately) not the objectivity of science: one does not prove the existence of love just as little as I can prove my love to my partner. It does require not the "you without we" of objective experiments, but rather the "you with an eye to the we" of togetherness of all with all, that is, with an eye to the human being as the one who can never be reduced to just such an object (of experiments, of knowledge).

Here Binswanger comes close to some sort of *originary belief* in love (or an "elementary faith" that *is* love), and in a *particular stance* in the world where the contingency of our loves, the fact that it equally could have been some other whom I love, gives way to the fact that all could in principle be loved. In this regard, love again shows its dialectical essence: for the *negativity* of the care for love—the fact that I, like the bride of the example, doubt why and if it should be you—gives way to the *positive* if not actual infinity of love—it can and could have been anybody. It is, however, and this should not be underestimated, *from* this very ontic you whom I love and loves me back, from this back and forth from the heart, from the back and forth of the twofold of the two lovers, where "Dasein" first glimpses "*Mitdasein*," that love *unfolds* right up *to* the vision of the possibility of a love of all for all or at least that anyone and anything is worthy of love. This is, rather than an eidetic, Binswanger's *imaginative* (not imaginary) *variation* on the idea of love and explains why there is no phenomenological reduction here: this very ontic you cannot and should not be bracketed—he or she is what Lacoste would call "irreducible" and other thinkers "indeconstructible."[31]

It is then, for Binswanger, not death but rather love that appears as "the great leveler": it does not discriminate or distinguish between Dasein, nor are animate and inanimate nature entirely exempt of love. Such a belief, for Binswanger, is the *judgment* or *decision* on the essence of humanity: the decision for love intuits the original togetherness, if not fundamental equality, of all beings through glimpsing the shared fate and destiny of all beings—which Binswanger calls the *koinos kosmos*, a being-in-the-world-of-all-with-all. This judgment is not the scientific judgment, in which it is decided once and for all that snow is white if and only if snow is indeed white. Rather, this judgment pertains to the other as my lover as well as to me as her lover. In this way, it speaks of a judgment in which "the judge and the judged are equally concerned"[32] or a decision in which my choice for you concerns you as much as me and that which we choose and decide for is the *identity* or sameness of our love in order that this reciprocal loving may meet and succeed (more or less) in its encounter. The decision for my love is made in the name of *our* togetherness and belongs as much to the original and universal togetherness that decides for us. This decision for love, then, is a genuine *docta ignorantia* for Binswanger: a knowing that one does not know about the ultimate stakes of such an ultimate love. The "knowledge of love is precisely the knowledge that reveals that the deepest knowing of the understanding and of (theoretical) reason is a not-knowing."[33] This is, for Binswanger, its truly practical and existential stake: both the decisions for love and for this lover here are never made once and for all. Its greatness rather lies in the fact that it exceeds all fanaticism: the decision for love is never forced—"love does not reign,"[34] a phrase of Goethe—and the decisions I make for or against and about my lover can always be revised or retracted.

Love, Language, and Community

How does one know about this? In the best of cases: from experience. In all other cases: through language. In the first case, the problem with love is in effect that, from the perspective of the two lovers, their love is indeed a "hermetic phenomenon,"[35] one that cannot be communicated easily if at all and that in effect seems to allow for "no transition" between the world of love and the world of care. In the second case, the problem rather is that the phenomenon is always talked about somewhat inappropriately. It is for this reason that Binswanger proceeds to "a phenomenological account of the literature on love." I have indicated already that a lot of the theory Binswanger developed is distilled from the poetic writings of Schiller, Rilke, and Goethe, for instance. Love, then, for Binswanger is not the only transgression of being-in-the-world available, for poetry too "attempts to transgress [*Überschwingen*] the world of care through language."[36] Poetry, for Binswanger, is in effect the "self-articulation of love,"[37] the attempt of love to understand itself in the world and in the language of being.

Throughout his work, Binswanger is attentive to ordinary language and expressions as ways for Dasein to cope with and express its being-in-the-world. Love and poetry, one might say, "bathe in language." Language, for Binswanger, is, in a phrase he takes from Rudolf Schröder, a "poet prior to all the poets"; it is the medium in which "the conversation of humanity with itself" takes place.[38] It is in his thought of language, as the space where the question and answer-play of humanity takes place, that many, if not all, central features of Binswanger's philosophy converge. For if love indeed appears as the great leveler, it is an equally "democratic" leveling, as an equal participation in being of all with all, that is intimated through language. Similarly, it is through language that the therapist returns the patient to the world, which itself is no more than the speech all share with all, from out of its *idios kosmos*. If sick and failing, Dasein experiences an "interruption" or "improper modification" of his or her being-in-the-world to the point that melancholic Dasein constructs "a world of his own" and manic Dasein moves in a world that is continuously altered and calls for new decisions (and so cuts itself off from the "common" world). The task of the therapist, for Binswanger, is

> to awaken or increase the "divine spark" that can only [be done] through real communication from existence to existence, which heat and light [are] alone able to liberate the human being *from* blind individualization, from the *idios kosmos* as Heraclitus says, thus from the sheer life in its body *for* the being-able-to-participate in the *koinos kosmos*, in the life of real *koinonia* or community.[39]

It is for such a *koinonia*, as the equal share of all in being, that phenomenology is needed. Such a reference to Heraclitus is a constant in Binswanger's work since the 1930s and marks an early move away from Heidegger's separation between authenticity and inauthentic everydayness. In its stead, Binswanger differentiates between "unhealthy" Dasein, cut off from world through abstaining from world—melancholy and depression: *Ideenflucht*—and maniacal Dasein, moving from decision to decision, always and already "hovering above" the world, as it were, and proper Dasein "walking" in the world between the "too little" and "too much" of melancholic and maniacal Dasein, respectively. It is to Heraclitus, Binswanger argues, that we owe "the expression of 'cosmos' as an anterior style or a norm prior to all knowledge. The unity of this style [. . .] is given from out of the goal of *koinonia* within the *logos*, from out of the gaze toward the universal and toward the community that dwells [within the logos]."[40] Given that all human beings *are* "at once *idion* and *koinon*" and *exist* only as balancing between private and public *persona*, the "physician" can appear as "the wise mediator between the private and the communal world, between deception and truth."[41]

There are some profound similarities here between philosophical and therapeutic practice. And, after all, one should not forget the common roots of these disciplines back in ancient Greece. For Binswanger, one such similarity is of course that the human being (for philosophy) and "failed Dasein" (for phenomenological psychology) may never be seen as merely an object or some sort of mechanism that could be "fixed" and "restored" to its original state. This resistance toward objectification is, by the way, Binswanger's main disagreement with both Freud, in whom he suspected some sort of reduction of the human being to his or her drives and desires—the human being here would be nothing but *homo natura*, obedient to pulses "unbeknownst to him"—and the "objectivity" of the sciences of his day, substituting (Dilthey's) *Verstehen* for the causalities of *Erklären*. For Binswanger, both figures testify to the spell of "mechanization," and they fall prey to the "myth of the sciences of nature."[42] In phenomenology, then, Binswanger found an aid for his quest to go beyond the paradigms of his time (and ours). Quite revealing in this regard is his statement that it is his distance from Heidegger that is of significance for psychiatry too, because "the analysis of psychotic forms of Dasein has to take these alterations of Heidegger's doctrine even more into account, for what we see here is more often a disturbance of the transcendence [of love] than it is a disturbance of the transcendence of care."[43] If Dasein does not exist properly, it is due more to his or her failure to love than to his or her failure to respond to the call of an authentic existence. And indeed: one may well live without ever facing death anxiously and appropriating it, but one cannot live without love.

Nevertheless, if Binswanger found in phenomenology an aid for his quest to go beyond the subject-object split, which he once called the "cancer of psychology," it is because of this emphasis on speech that put him on track to a "cosmos" common to all: speech, in a way, is the sharing through which we come to be aware of the original, ontological sharing. It is such a sharing that is not even interrupted through death. It is this emphasis on speech as well that pushed Binswanger beyond Husserl, and his account of objective intentionalities, toward a non-positivistic *world* which is no longer "what is the case," but rather "what can be talked about," since in this latter world, phantasms are as real as the love here in front of me: the possible can, perhaps, approach the actual in many ways. What in each case matters is how Dasein *expresses* his or her being-in-the-world.[44] As for Heidegger, so for Binswanger too, there is "no giving prior to language,"[45] and language, in ways similar to love, *covers* the world. Unlike Heidegger, what is given through language is not solely "world" or "being" even, but the beyond of being in and through being, which is the communion through the unity and the (basic) unit of lovers. It is such a commonality that philosophy, as the wisdom of love, for Binswanger, seeks: every ontic communion, be it love or be it successful communication, can only take place because of the ontological communion through which all beings crave communion with other beings.

This is ultimately for Binswanger what one could call the goal of philosophy and what explains his praise for (Husserlian) phenomenology on the very last pages of the *Grundformen*: phenomenology showed that the general and the "in-common" "can be seen (and not only *thought*)" and offered a method and a way "which not only can be 'walked' by everyone but a way and a method about which everyone can explain him- or herself [*Verständigen*] to everyone else."⁴⁶ This *Verständigung* is close to the *entente* we have seen Nancy describing earlier, except that the latter was "without world" and the former suffers from only speaking from "within the world." It is, however, not certain whether one, as Coulomb argues, would find such an idea of community in Husserl.⁴⁷ For Husserl, in effect, there is something of an "original community" present, where "one being is intentionally in community with another being," but such an idea of community seems not to emancipate itself yet from an isolated subject whose intentionality can be frustrated with and/or met through other intentionalities.⁴⁸ In this regard, this idea of community, through which community arises out of the different directions of different intentionalities into a common world, is too close to the idea, so common these days, of one liberty being free only as long as it does not limit the liberty of the other. Such a community does not yet liberate itself from the "once and for all," that is, one-sided constitution of the alter ego through analogy: here objective intentionality is limited or interrupted only; it is not yet displaced. For Binswanger, one might suspect, such a community is too close to the conflicts pertaining to being-in-the-world. It does not reach the *ontological* communion, and the *ekstasis* of all toward all, through which these and other ontic conflicts would become first possible.

The "conversation of humanity with itself" is one long and lasting attempt of humanity to make sense of itself and of its world. It is to this that poetry obviously contributes, but here too it is love that is most meaningful. Love, for Binswanger, does not even speak. If lovers speak, it is always and already *about* something that they would speak, about something in and of the world, and they would no longer be lovers. This is why, one recalls, love for Binswanger is best imagined through the gazes and kisses that the lovers exchange. In fact, for Binswanger, the only "speech" that love endures is silence—the experience that one remains silent in the presence of one's lover, easier than in the presence of friends and fellows, testifies to this. Every speaking, every word is a limitation of love and fuels it with retreating possibilities or *Entzug*: every word spoken leaves other words unspoken. If love is pressed to converse, then what matters most is that it is the person who speaks rather than the content we speak about.[49] In this way, the conversation of lovers is but the vehicle of the revealing and the letting be of the selves to and of one another.

Yet love *is* not apart from the world, and speaking is part of its fate: in fact, considering that the *Grundformen* were written in a time of war, one might just as well argue that love, here, *could not* remain silent. It is to such an original sharing—its craving for communication—of love through speech that is intimated in poetry and friendship to which I now turn.

Phenomenology of Friendship— The Death of Friends and Lovers

Feuerbach once wrote that "the index finger is the sign pointing from nothingness to being." Binswanger agrees to the extent that this transition can be (heart)felt and not only thought. Feuerbach, he argues, still writes from out of a Greek perspective, where thinking equates being, and the transition between nothingness and being can be "held in" thought. Nothing of the sort happens in this phenomenology of love and friendship. Here the "signs" elevating the human being out of its nullity are, respectively, the kiss and the handshake, both of them participating in the endless greeting that is being. Whereas the index finger, for Binswanger, only shows the place "where you are" and "where I am," the kiss and the embrace of lovers show us our togetherness everywhere and anywhere, and the handshake of friends reveals "the hold" these friends have on one another.[50] Friendship is a further unfolding, be it limited, form of togetherness as a "taking part"—*Teilnahme*—in each other's life and being. Friendship, in this way, is somewhere between love and care; it is its "complexion":[51] friendship is less than the isle that love can be, but it is more than the simple sharing of a job or a task with co-workers and colleagues (*"Teilen-mit"*). Although such a sharing-with might be an occasion for the togetherness of friendship and might even be elevated to love, most often such a "sharing with" limits itself to a sharing of beings and things in the world. What is talked about here are in effect these beings, but only rarely *you* and *me* and the beings that we are. This is what differentiates it, according to Binswanger, from friendship that takes an interest precisely in you and eventually takes part in the other's destiny. This is what already distinguishes friendship from love: whereas we still are friends even when we are not together, the lovers are, in a sense, always together and so "tied" to one another even when this togetherness is merely temporarily imagined and realized. Friendship, in this way, allows already for more of an independent self than the "You and I" that springs from the cocoon that love somehow is.

"Friendship," for Binswanger, "is much more burdened, and wants to burden itself, with care than love."[52] It knows much better to combine life and "love" than love alone would. In this sense, friendship seems much closer to the "*liebende Sorge*" that Binswanger had earlier described as the summit of his phenomenology of love. The "taking part" in the lives of friends, then, is not a mere taking part of some-thing (of the world) in his or her life, but rather taking part in his or her life through these things of the world. Friends support each other rather than they simply endure the things of the world "together." If one friend, for instance, says to another, "I feel your pain," what is meant is not that I observe that I feel the same thing about the same thing, but rather that I take part in your pain and take this pain upon me as the "share" concerning *us* rather than you or me individually.[53] This is what marks the phenomenon of friendship for Binswanger: *taking part in each other's fate*. This "taking part" is obviously not a onetime act (of constitution), but rather a reciprocal and continuous giving to and receiving from one another: it is a taking part in *the fate that you are and have to be* as well as your taking part in the fate that therefore I am. This fate here is the one that befalls us passively and at times despite us as well as the one that is actively constructed from out of the (and as) world around us.[54] "Friendly being with" is therefore a "*Miteinander Schreiten*," a walking together, through a friendly land: friendship, too, covers the community of worldly beings with a layer of benevolence that is curiously absent from the world presented in *Being and Time*. This is one of the reasons why friendship for Binswanger remains tied to care: it does not exceed ontic situations (although these situations can, of course, occasion loving togetherness) and *is* only in the unfolding of the ontic and worldly histories my friends and I share. Here one finds a further fold of love or, if you prefer postmodern metaphors, of its splitting up and its shattering, for if there's only one whom I love, I can have many friends. This plurality of friends is, for Binswanger, every so many "wes" springing from out of ontological togetherness.[55]

Yet again this togetherness, in the mode of "friendly being-with," shows itself as something that cannot be confined to particular ontic borders: "friendly taking part in [. . .] reaches as far as encounter is possible: the possible circle of human taking part [in one another's fate] is therefore 'borderless,' since even if I cannot be friends with everyone, I can at least approach anyone in a friendly manner."[56] The difference with love is clear when Binswanger continues citing Chesterton: "[In] our friends the richness of life is proved to us by what we have gained. In the faces in the street the richness of life is proved to us by the hint of what we have lost," a possible friend or lover.[57] Both love and friendship, then, crave for community, and it is "only through taking part in [the fate of others, JS] that commonality or better community of world is 'constituted.'"[58]

Can such a community, not constituted by anyone, stand the test of the death of friends or of one's lover even? Can death be understood "from out of being-with-one-another"?[59] What indeed if there is no one left to embrace, the bed remains empty, her voice is no longer heard, and the "outstretched hand reaches 'in the void.'"[60]

Death, for Binswanger, undergoes a displacement: it no longer occupies the prime place as it does in Heidegger's existential analytic but receives its meaning as an "erotic phenomenon."[61] Such a phenomenon only shows itself as itself from within the loving encounter, from out of its "immanence in love."[62] This immanence is for Binswanger another reason to shy away from religion and the false comfort it often brings to the questions of finitude. Only love, and its uniting of finitude and eternity, is the mode of being that opens "the irreducible entrance to reality" and does not shy away from death's "unmasked horror."[63] The horror of death, however, differs in a remarkable way from other interruptions of love, such as infidelity, for if in such suspensions the love of lovers comes, more often than not, to a halt, the death of one of the lovers does not mean the end of the loving "we." Let us listen to Binswanger:

> Just as I received "my life" all new from your hands, so, dying, I lay my life back in your hands, I don't die a "painful death" as the death of an isolated "ego," but rather I part from you, aware that in this parting there is still some present. For this Dasein of the lover as the one-who-was-there is still a "there" as the "there of us."[64]

The death of one of the lovers, for Binswanger, does not end the loving togetherness of the "we." Quite to the contrary, one might say, because this "we," you and me, will have to be this departure as well. And even after your parting you will still be present as the "there," as the "you" necessary and *belonging to* "us": the one who once belonged to me *still* belongs to me—I don't die as the you belonging to you. The immanence of death in love is exactly this: death is not elsewhere, it does not happen from the outside to love as if it were an unexpected enemy, but presences as it were from out of love. It is this that death would share in common with every other departure of the lover: it is not we who are so abandoned, but "you" separate from me (and vice versa) in order to show your "*Da*," your being-the-there *of* us, even better.

However, even if death is inscribed in every parting, and so takes part in the horizon of love—which means, obviously, that one should understand death through love rather than love through death—it brings an even greater insecurity to the lovers than the "certainty" that Heidegger ascribed to death. This certainty for Heidegger in effect meant that no one is certain of the hour of his death, and is further rendered uncertain in turn by Binswanger through the unavoidable question that one of us will be the first one to go—a question "belonging" to love even though it betrays already the creeping in of a care for love. It is this question that rules out any "resoluteness" for Binswanger, for such resolution requires a future that itself is "certain" and a death that is the prime possibility, "not to be outstripped,"[65] of and for Dasein. Dasein, as in each case my own, heroically facing its upcoming death, is utterly incompatible with the self issued and brought forth by loving togetherness. If *jemeinig* Dasein still can find in its mortality something of which it can take hold, such a hold is all the more excluded by loving Dasein, whose "Wandel" in the world never accedes to a firm base and its "ekstasis" never to a "stasis": the self issued in love—*das vom Wir gewonnene Selbst*—is another self than the one arising out of "the They." There is a passageway from the former to the latter, but there is no path from the "authentic self" in Heidegger's sense to the selves springing from togetherness.[66] Binswanger continues: the "self" Heidegger envisions "may very well be active, heroic, philosophical and humane, it is not loveable."[67]

What kind of self is revealed in loving togetherness and in the parting of the lover? Binswanger here makes an interesting distinction between "loneliness" (*Einsamkeit*) and "solitude," where the latter may echo the egocentric if not solipsistic philosophies from Descartes and Kant up to Husserl and Heidegger. Loving togetherness makes possible "the 'being given' of loneliness through the reception of self"[68] through a love that has not laid the foundation and has no hold over that which occasioned it empirically and its subsequent history. In this regard, it is the "twosome" of love that first makes one lonesome. "Loneliness" then is the experience of Dasein that is not, or is no longer, alone: I can only be lonely if I am without you: it is through you and the unity of our love that I experience my self as the *one* who is in love.

It is precisely this gift of self—my "Da" for you as yours for me—that remains untainted by the death of one of the lovers. This is why death ultimately does not teach love anything new: it merely deepens the loneliness of the one left behind. This is for Binswanger the "gift of death" and one more example of how love gives something of its eternity to the finite realm in which love is lived. The death of the lover, in a sense, *perpetuates* our loving togetherness, because "not even death can jolt"[69] "you and me."

Your death is your gift of an even deeper loneliness to me [whereas] I give you the gift of being your loving self in the full sense of the word. Every exemplariness of the phenomenon of death and the full meaning of the loving self would consist in that the "twosome" of my being "lonesome" can no longer be fulfilled within-the-world [*Mitweltlich*], but now only "beyond the world." In other words: I become the *sole bearer* of our love. The erotic phenomenon of death therefore does not experience its exemplarity from out of love itself but rather from out of care, from out of being-in-the-world.[70]

One might argue that it is death that draws the lovers (and loving togetherness) toward the world. But, similarly, one might suspect that in so doing it is love that covers the world with a benevolence and grace even that are not solely "of" this world.[71] Within the world without you: your death leaves me in the world as the one who now can "for the first time appropriately" be "beyond the world" through a "deeper loneliness" and a "heightened longing."[72] The true test and work of mourning here are to both conserve and live on "after the fact" through the continuation of my loving Dasein and its ecstasy toward you. Here Binswanger argues for a profound continuity between my (or your) loving Dasein before and after your death, because this loving self "is not another self" from the one I already received from you during your lifetime and our living (our) together. In this regard, Binswanger mentions not only an immanence of death in love, but also an immanence of life in death: the parting that is death would in this respect in no way differ from any other departure we have experienced in our living together—and just as I die a little when you leave, so too your death leaves me as forever yours and you, similarly, as still living "with/in" me.[73] The death of the friend shows in a similar manner that there is no path from death to solitude: every parting of you, for Binswanger, will "when properly experienced lead back to you."[74] The being-there of the deceased friend and lover remain as long as my finite Dasein is "there" and as long as my loving Dasein loves, that is, is turned toward *us*, toward what we are and were as you and me.

The Self between Love and World

The question of "self-realization" is a central question in Binswanger's, certainly when Heidegger's authenticity, enacted and obtained *apart* from every fellow human being, in a resoluteness that concerns only me, is no longer valid. What kind of self springs from love, friendship, and one's dealings with the world if the path to the self is to be found from out of the unfolding of loving togetherness, in turn, in the world.[75]

For this, one has to recall the unfolding of love within the world, for which friendship now has somewhat become the norm: it is as if, for Binswanger, the *solitude à deux* of love has to be interrupted and is in need of the world. One might say that love *braucht* the world, close to Heidegger's infamous statement that Being *braucht* beings, is in need of beings (and it is certainly true that Heidegger II was in need somewhat of the world that preoccupied Heidegger I). Whereas the hermetic phenomenon love, for Binswanger, risks being "without world" and is in need of world, friendship is lived and experienced nowhere else than in the world. Friendship shows, instructed by love, how to love (in) the world. It reveals the commandment "thou shalt love" as taking place within the world and as having no other place than world. This ultimately explains Binswanger's wariness against the Christian religion: for Binswanger, Christian religion projects love onto God and so risks abandoning the world altogether. One might argue that whereas for Levinas, Christ's sacrifice risked abandoning and alleviating the responsibility of all for all "down here" in the world, for Binswanger, Christ's love for the world risks displacing the duty of the human being to love.

Binswanger puts it in this way:

> love knows no other duty [. . .] than being true to its own being, as a matter of life and death, that is to, despite death, "remain what *we* are: You and I." [This is not] an individual duty, it is *to live being-toward-death in the form of love*. But this means: it is to fly above Being and Time in the eternal moment of love from within the resoluteness toward death and the nullity of

existence. It is not love who lacks life here, it is life—time, life, care—that lacks love.[76]

Binswanger's thought of a *liebende Sorge* transcends even Heidegger's "ultimate" transcending toward one's own individual death. Everything in Binswanger happens as if the exodus of love *out of* the world were at the same time a mission toward the world and toward others. This is where Binswanger's dialectic needs to be situated. Whereas friendship happens within the world and within concrete histories unfolding there, love still in a sense *has to* happen within the world. It is so that friendship, instructed by love, in turns instructs love on just how it needs to happen. What is it that friendship shows to being-in-the-world? How, according to Binswanger, to conceive of the world?

It is here that Binswanger, deliberately, takes his distances from Heidegger. For friendship, in a sense, hovers already above "Being and Time" by insinuating a *tertium datur* between the anonymity of "the They" and the heroic authenticity of resolute Dasein. Heidegger, for Binswanger, knows only of a call of authenticity toward the inauthentic clutches of "the They," appealing to our conscience to come out of the everydayness of world, but disregards what Binswanger, with Löwith, calls "the authentic and positive possibility of togetherness"[77] within this very world, for which friendship stands as a paradigmatic example. In friendly togetherness, the friend serves as the norm for the self: the friend, in a sense, shows you how to live, whereas the lover lets the worries of life disappear to let the fullness of being appear: what love lacks, friendship supplements.

Friendship inserts freedom in the world. In this regard, it is to be distinguished from Heideggerian *Fürsorge* and solicitude. Whereas the latter is to be seen as a sort of one-way traffic from authentic Dasein toward everyday Dasein, friendship *is* only as a free "double passage" both *between* friends—from you to me as well as me to you—and *between* the world wherein such friendship is enacted in and through ontic histories and the sharing in each other's fate, which is friendship's (ontological) being and which taints it, so to say, with love.

Some have argued that Binswanger ignores Heidegger's solicitude, where one Dasein "leaps ahead" of another Dasein so as to open to the latter Dasein its ownmost potentiality for being.[78] This might indeed be the one case in which Heidegger comes close to a "positive togetherness" in *Being and Time*. But Binswanger's critique of Heidegger here plays on another level. Binswanger's concern is not how to reach one's ownmost, authentic potential for being; it is rather to show that underlying such potentiality is an (ontological as well as ontic) togetherness that alone can be called "authentic" and for which the *Jemeinige* modus of Dasein can only appear as deficient.[79] From out of the phenomenological ontology of togetherness, the problem of our "Being and Time" is not that being is finite (and in each case my own) or that finite time shows up at the horizon of being; the problem is that "being and time" appear only ever as *ours*, as "the conversation of humanity with itself," that is: the ontological question to be asked about "being and time" here turns into an "erotic problem of time and eternity" evolving around the meaning not of being, but of our loving togetherness longing for and lured toward infinity.[80]

Whether it is in the mode of the love of the lovers or in the friendship between friends, this positive *Miteinandersein* insinuates a fundamental freedom and equality in being and between beings. In fact, the world, for Binswanger, prior to its being covered with love is fundamentally a world where the will to power reigns and where one Dasein's will to power is only interrupted by the will to power of other Dasein. It is this that turns our world "first and foremost" into a "sad milieu,"[81] where the will to power turns *even* the human being into a being ready-to-hand. This is what Binswanger's analysis of being-in-the-world of *taking* something as something or even grasping someone as something is about: it shows the ever-present possibility of the "*Verumweltlichung der Mitwelt*"—the "with-world," *Mitsein*, is turned into an *Umwelt*, an environment at my disposal.[82] More than once, Binswanger turns to Kant to explain this world: it is dealing with the other man and woman not as an "end in itself" but as a "means to an end"—it's not who you are that matters, it is what you can do for me. The other here is in effect reduced to the role he or she can play *for me* rather than turning up as someone who might become a friend or, who knows, a lover. Yet Binswanger here distances himself from Kant and Heidegger considerably: even though this world is a "sad milieu," its description—which makes for half of Binswanger's *Grundformen*—is not to be considered morally or ethically but rather (a bit tragically) "beyond good and evil."[83] Here is Binswanger's aversion of modernity's turn toward ethics: for him, the Kantian *Achtung* making for a *Gesellschaft* of *Weltbürgers* is, as long as it is without love, but a coat of varnish. This respect may very well offer for some time some sort of respectability and faithfulness between civilians, it may even promise some sort of regulative ideal, but it is always threatened by one or the other Dasein breaking its word of honor. On this topic, Binswanger is close to the double bind of the promise/threat Derrida signals in the "nature" of things and even offers a word of warning, *avant la lettre*, to Levinas: "that responsibility is also just a role played, surprises only those who have not encountered irresponsibility."[84] Binswanger's attempt to go beyond ethics entails the recognition that such taking of the other as something is not and cannot be avoided. It is not, as a certain Heidegger would have it, to set apart the miserable world of *Das Man* from authentic Dasein or, as a certain Kant would have it, to wait teleologically for a utopia where all would be "an end in itself" for all other "ends in itself." It is rather to recognize that this world of concern and care needs to be filled with love because it "first and foremost" is contaminated with power: "Do all the things you need to do, but do them with love."

It is this contamination with power that Binswanger holds against Heidegger and that makes him wary of solicitude. For the world is constituted in such a way that its *Worumwillen*, its "for the sake of which" is in effect power, and it is, for Binswanger, just this that Heidegger's authenticity and solicitude seek to promote.[85] Solicitude, Binswanger argues, wants to make the other Dasein free and ready for its very own claim to power, but this liberation proceeds "without ever asking whether the other actually desires *such* a freedom."[86] This is the one-way traffic in Heidegger's existential analytic: authentic Dasein *returns* to inauthentic everydayness only in order to instruct everyday Dasein about its possible exodus, but authentic Dasein has nothing to learn in and from everydayness.

Binswanger, however, knows that there is no "beyond" such power but insists that it be filled and fueled by love. This is also why Binswanger's appropriation of Heidegger differs from that of Medard Boss: if, for the latter, therapy consisted in the "ineffable superiority [of the therapist] over the tormented and needy patient,"[87] very much like "the voice of being" seems to have resounded only in Greece, Germany, and, of course, Todtnauberg, no such superiority is found in Binswanger, who insists in a loving and friendly approach to his patients because of his belief in the fundamental equality of all beings. Binswanger's aim is not to hubristically instruct others about that which they do not yet know: it is not that he would know "more" about what it is for us to be, but rather, more modestly, to share that he knows as little as all others about what being means. This, as I will show, is the *nicht-wissende Wissen* that comes with love.

Such equality in effect prevails for Binswanger in the phenomenon of friendship, and this is what necessitates his critique of Heidegger on this point: "if there is one marker of friendly relations, [. . .] it would be freedom": friendship is not about becoming the "conscience of (the) other," but is the realization that you, as my friend, are my conscience just as I, as your friend, can be your conscience. In this way, and because friendship knows not of any borders, the *communio* of love—its *unio* as *communio*—extends to a union of the equal—a "*Vereinigung unter Freien*."[88] It is to be noted, finally, that if it is for this friendly gathering of all human beings and all creatures that Binswanger reserves the name of religion: it opens the possibility of a "religious gathering" of all beings.[89] It is here, in the communion and greeting between beings, that religions for Binswanger ought to begin and theology, it if it is to be trustworthy again, should begin.

How can the originary dualis of love, the fact that love plays "first and foremost" only between my lover and me, finally "extend to all people"?[90] By seeing, Binswanger argues, that love itself is a principle of being, that it *is* this unfolding and extension to the entirety of beings within the world, that it lets me turn *from* you to all the others who are in principle able to incarnate "youness," that youness cannot be reserved for you, my lover, alone. It is by turning to you—to *Du*—that I encounter love, but, in turn, it is through this encounter that I can turn *away* from you and see "youness"—*Duhaftigkeit*—incarnated in all beings. This is how Binswanger wants us to approach the other: not as the one who needs to be prepared for his or her ownmost death, or as someone who plays such and such a role, but as a human being (beyond such roles) in which in each case the (possible) coincidence between you and youness is (actually) met.[91] Far from a sterile bifurcation between the non-essence of the human being and the representations and roles that obfuscate such a non-essence, as I have shown earlier in Marion and Nancy, Binswanger tries to retrieve phenomenologically the "beyond" or otherness of the human being from "within" these roles precisely.

Where does this leave me (or you), then? What is the self for Binswanger? My self is caught between the self I receive from my lover and the self that arises out of the pressure of the roles I need to play within the world and that others force upon me.[92] It is from out of the unfolding of love in the world that one needs to understand how "the with-world [*Mitwelt*] relates to my own world [*Eigenwelt*]" and how the "one-time only" of my singular being is to be conceived.[93]

It is here that the turn from love *to* life and world is for Binswanger also a turning *away* from love. But, by the same token, this exile of love within the world is the occasion through which life and world can be loved and the subject of a *liebende Sorge*, which uplifts what Binswanger calls with Hegel "the power of the negative"[94] and puts it to work. For this, one needs to better understand love's turning to life and world. Binswanger is quite explicit that love's turn to the world entails an "*Abwendung von Dir*," a turning away from you for me "to be" in the world. Such a turning away from love first takes place in friendship. For the friend offers me a self that is, although only ever within-the-world, not "of" this world: it concerns a self that is enlightened by love and is so enabled (perhaps empowered) by love. Friends, one recalls, become the norm of my self and show me to myself (as well as to others).[95] And because every friend relates me to my self in a different way, Binswanger argues, I can only relate to my "lonely" self "by neglecting and turning away from the taking part in friendship and by turning to a free affirmation of my own fate. But this means: I have to become my own friend."[96] Binswanger insists that the arising of the ego happens through a turning away not only from friendship, but also from love. I only become a question for my self, if you like, once my love and my friends send me into the exile of world. Only then I attain and attend to the principle of being in my own way (although still through others), and I query, from out of my singular being, for my *Sein zum Grunde*: "*Grund* [what is fundamental, not what is 'foundational,' JS] means here that principle of being (which is also a principle of truth) through which the self relates as to a hold and understands itself, when this self turns off [*Abhebung*] with-world and its environment and turns away [*Abwendung*] from you as my lover."[97] It is therefore by turning away from love and friendship that I can turn to and question the principle of being (which is the principle of love and truth). But this means that, in a sense, I can only see and understand the truth of love from out of the world, from out of that which, first, keeps love at bay. It means that love, although it cannot *be* in the world, cannot do without world either for love to be truly, and thrive there: love's restriction to the world is *simultaneously* the chance of the world.

This is, if you like, Binswanger's version of what happens in Levinas when the third party comes to trouble my responsibility for the singular you over and against me. Binswanger's version might even be an earlier version of this arising (and arousal) of "weighing, objectivation and comparison," earlier that is, both *historisch* (ontically) and *geschichtlich* (ontologically). This moment might be, for Binswanger, the "birth of philosophy" as the "question of the question" (Levinas), considered from the fact, as Derrida has it, "the principle of philosophy is not philosophy,"[98] it is the "first kiss," the body and the matter that accompanies all our representations: philosophy comes "after the fact," after a certain thrownness in life and falling in love. For this is the moment in Binswanger where the love that plays between my lover and me is interrupted and brought to a halt by precisely an awareness that there are others besides this very ontic other, whom I love, here. Here, for Binswanger, the awareness arises that I am not only responsible for all, but that my love for this very ontic you possibly in injustice done to all others whom I could (and perhaps should) love. Love needs the world because it is the only place where it can take place precisely. And the world needs love only to show this world that other principles than power might play there.

This is the ordeal that the self undergoes when it is "in the world beyond the world," when it comes to the world in and through that which is not "of" this world, namely love. Binswanger preserves a taste for the tragic here, since this *Sein zum Grunde* never receives an answer: there is no ontotheological cyclope in this city of the blind. Rather, this self that falls out of the world as much as falls "out" of love, lives the "drama" between its diverse roles, between these roles and its love, knowing fully well that it is no longer "in love"—love does not ask anything: it is the triumph over the "why question"[99]—when it asks for the for-the-sake-of-which, for the *worumwillen* of its being-in-the-world. It is to be noted that the *Sehnsucht* and *Ungenügen*, which puts us on the tracks of love is neither alleviated nor undone with love. For, in love, no questions are asked, but similarly no ultimate answers and final solutions are offered.

So the loving self is firmly placed within the world. Yet it is from out of the "experience" of love that it queries for the "foundation" of being: it is the being of love that *grants* the self the opportunity to envision being otherwise. For this *Sein zum Grunde*, as the question toward my lonely fate and destiny within the world (considered from the fact that my "loneliness" too is a *gift* received from my lover), is not a dialogue: it happens when I am and exist in the world without you. It is not a dialogue because, in our modern times, this "ground" is no longer to be equated with God—with whom the believer "converses" through prayer—but rather remains mute: "the ground does not answer, but remains—mystery. This is why the question of being can only be a question and can only be expressed in ever new questions."[100] It is, for Binswanger, the question that love raised against and within being: "the question of my origin, my destiny, my 'natural' being, my suffering, my guilt and my death. The more seriously I ask this question, the more hold I find on my ground, on the mystery of my existence"[101]; the more firmly I get a grip on and am gripped by the foundation of being. Yet the *Grund* remains *unergründlich*: it is a principle of reality and of being as long as we realize that this "reality" is, although thoroughly historical, not man-made.[102] The foundation and ground of being can only be apprehended but it cannot be comprehended: it no longer turns into a "highest" Ground of being—what is fundamental is not available for foundationalist thinking. Yet it is not, as Heidegger and certain Derrideans would have it, an *Abgrund* or abyss either: it is rather the recognition that "there is" ground (a sort of "*Es gibt Grund*"), but that no one can take possession of such a foundation once and for all.

Such "authentic questioning" for Binswanger is a lifelong task and is therefore never acquired once and for all. It is the ever-new arising of a loving self, out of the changed circumstances and changing situation offered to me through being-in-the-world and the roles played there and taking place (or touching ground) as the steadiness of existence—Binswanger more than once points to Heidegger's authenticity as "*erstreckte Stetigkeit*" here. As such, this questioning is for Binswanger the counterpart of fanaticism, "which does not question anything, but rather already knows everything."[103] On the contrary, "the truth of the self, the being-toward-the-ground as mystery, is based in the mystery and remains "surrounded" by the mystery. This is why [this questioning] is modest and a *knowing of not-knowing*."[104] It is no more than the marvel at being from out of the presence of love which, itself, ventures "beyond being" (or at least "sidetracks" being-in-the-world).

Binswanger's reference to Heidegger's account of authenticity should, however, not mislead. Binswanger regularly insists that one can get from the self "gained from" togetherness to the *stetige* self that Heidegger prescribes but not the other way around: the heroic Dasein of Heidegger may very well act and acquire a "standstill" in the world; it does not know of love and is not loveable.[105] Heidegger's Dasein may very well engage in the "collective task of a people"; it knows nothing of the conversation and community of humankind that dawns upon us as a task and a duty through love. Heidegger's Dasein may very well come to grips with its own death and succeed occasionally in attending to its mortality in a proper way; it cannot succeed in being-toward-death in a loving way.

For this, it needs to be recalled that Binswanger's starting point, although it is still existence-in-a-world, differs from that of Heidegger. For Binswanger, this starting point is not the anonymity and the fanaticism of the They, but rather our always and already being-thrown-into the horizontality of a determinate world, of a very particular situation in which one finds oneself. All these particular situations are ever so many occasions to "project" oneself in the world and to arise as a loving self out of this world. This, then, for Binswanger, is not to be seen as some sort of Heideggerian "*Verfallen*," or fallenness into a world, but rather as a being immersed in society and "worldly situations."[106] Here one is not being thrown in the turmoil of the they, but in a stepwise succeeding of ever so many situations, in what Binswanger beautifully calls the *"Geworfenheit des Schreitens"*—a striding from situation to situation.[107] The self that is present in and to such a situation is no longer the "non-self" that is immersed in everyman's everydayness, even though it may not yet be the resolute Dasein that Heidegger has in mind. The latter, for Binswanger, remains significantly only a "limit-case,"[108] which is neither to be desired nor to be loved. Two reasons can be named for this: first, this "resolute Dasein" is, for Binswanger, too closely tied up with a question of power (whereas love "does not reign") and it too easily forgets the body, as the condition of possibility, of being thrown in *this* situation rather than *that* situation in the first place.

The question of embodiment is central to Binswanger, for one should not forget that, as is the case with everything in Binswanger's phenomenology, this phenomenological ontology has to be *put into* (therapeutic) *practice*: it strides with and turns to the other from the very beginning to the very end. This is why Heidegger's *Eigentlichkeit* turns into a limit-case: the thought that being authentically human is to be defined as a decision for a certain kind of resolution can only pop up for someone whose body poses no question. Heidegger's "ontology" of existence does not take into account "sickness, exhaustion, and tiredness": as much as it forgets about love, it forgets that "vegetative" existence for instance is part of being human too.[109] In short, Heidegger forgets about those who in this world receive little or no love.[110] This is also why Binswanger distances himself from the powerful and firm hold on existence that Dasein is allotted in *Being and Time* and insists on what I have termed the "irresolution of the resolution" or, with Derrida, the indecision in every decision, in the introduction to this work. The dignity of Dasein lies not in the holding onto the decision about this or that situation, but rather in the possibility of "taking [the resolution] back," in changing one's mind, in positing that there are, because of the ever-changing circumstances within the world, no final position and solution available to us.[111]

This is how, in and through the situations within-the-world, authentic togetherness, the community of humanity in its entirety, is possible only when, through love and friendship, a *"grenzenlos unfanatisches Selbst"* and a *"grenzenlos unfanatische Welt"* come together.[112] But it is *in the world* that such a borderlessness can only ever be imagined, just as it is in the world that the fanatical individual sticks with one take and one interpretation of the situation, and the "loveless" fanaticism of the masses runs aground in, for instance, just one accidental decision and in one final solution of a "hatred of all otherness [and] of all others"—it is clear that one cannot read Binswanger without sensing the presence of the war on these pages.[113]

Conclusion: Loving Life and Living Love

How does one come to love life? How does it come about that one writes a 600-page treatise on love in a time of war? Because love only ever happens *in spite of* the adversities of life: "this yes-saying is not possible, if the 'spirit' does not put the negativity of the misery to work and does not have the power to endure this."[114] It is this conjoining of the negative and the positive, of saying "yes" in the face of all the "nos," that, according to Binswanger, will lead to an ever "deepening of the knowing of not-knowing" and finally opens a new potentiality for being, a *sein-können*, that knows how to love within the world as well as live in the world with love.[115]

This *sein-können* allows to see in our fellow human being a "youness" that turns everyone into a possible friend (if not lover) and so succeeds in the overcoming of the *Widerspruch* between love and care. This "knowledge of men" has to proceed out of love and return to love. But this procession and return here is obviously not the movement of the neo-Platonic One, for it takes place nowhere else than in the world and between human beings. It is, for Binswanger, to see love as the condition of possibility of all knowledge, for love moves within (the negativity of) the world to the beyond of world that is love and the "positivity of encounter."[116] Such a knowledge of men and women knows of a "love" that "lives,"[117] that is, it encounters the human being from out of the world (as a being always on the verge of being taken ready-to hand) and from out of love (as a being that is always other and more than *Zuhanden* and *Vorhanden*): a love that is all these things at once.

To think this, philosophy itself must for Binswanger turn into a "thinking that loves"—*liebend Denken*: philosophy must both see the *Faktum* and the *eidos* and conjoin negation and affirmation in a loving way, that is, it must move from the concrete you (even if not immediately loveable) to youness, *and* it must see the possibility of such "ideal" youness being incarnated in every very ontic you we encounter (even and especially when it is not loveable). *Liebend Denken* needs to live in the world and endure the world with love. This new anthropological mode of being thus needs both to risk "rescuing of love whatever is possible for care and risk leaving to care what can be given to it through love—*überwunden ist der Gegensatz von Liebe und Sorge hier insofern, als von der Liebe gerettet ist, was von der Sorge aus möglich ist* [. . .] *und daß der Sorge zu überlassen gewagt wird, was von der Liebe geschenkt oder gegeben ist.*"[118]

10

From Love to Life (and Back Again)

From Love to Life (and Back Again): this would be the overall thesis one can gather from Binswanger's work. In this tenth chapter, I want to trace, inspired by Binswanger, three central guidelines that feature in his work. First, there is what I would like to call the phenomenological return of the human being to its existence in a world. Second, there is the need to reconfigure the phenomenological method into a full-fledged empirical-transcendental phenomenology. This method should do justice to both the transcendental as well as the empirical aims of phenomenology. Third (as previously announced in the introduction), I want to focus on a contemporary phenomenology of religious life.

The Knowledge of Love

Binswanger's pathway indeed comes as a surprise. A phenomenology of love that only shows its true stakes once it turns into a phenomenology of friendship? How can this degradation be simultaneously an augmentation? A phenomenology of friendship that amounts to a phenomenology of my singular being? How can this phenomenology of togetherness, of a fundamental and ontological togetherness, feel the need for a phenomenology of the singular ego? Is it possible that both Heidegger and Levinas—and Theunissen, for that matter—are right after all when observing that Binswanger at the end of his *Grundformen* had succumbed to a transcendental philosophy (that thinks the ego but knows not of any world)?[1]

How then can one understand a phenomenology of love whose last word is to turn away from love, toward a lonely ego thinking love, in an exodus that is clearly an *Abwendung* from the one the ego loves?

Had Heidegger (and Levinas, who too easily compares Binswanger with Buber) actually read the *Grundformen*, he would have noticed that such an *Abwendung* toward that which is not loved is not a *Rückfall* into transcendental philosophy but rather a fall into the world that is not to be described as (Heideggerian) fallenness. Furthermore, he might have noted that this *Abwendung* is a turn to the world precisely (in and through turning to the thinking ego that thinks being-in-the-world) and in no way an "*Abdankung der Liebe*," a resignation of love, of togetherness-in-the-world.[2]

On the contrary, in this turning away from love, there is revealed Binswanger's fundamental ontological aim, which both recognizes that "in transcendentalism, it is idealism that must be overcome," and that a phenomenology of love has "to end there where care begins," namely in the thinking of (my) singular being, of an ego, which, despite love, knows of a *Sehnsucht* and longing that remain even "after" being-with-this very ontic you in love.[3]

What has been mistaken for a transcendental turn of Binswanger is in fact Binswanger's acknowledgement that a phenomenology of love needs to do more than simply point to the fact that, more often than not, thinking, acting, and willing begin with this ontic you whom we love. And even though it may well be "love that makes the world go round," the world, of itself, claims the singular being of lovers in ways that ultimately have little or nothing to do with love. This is why Binswanger's aim, when "turning away from love," is universal, ontological, and transcendental. Love is erected as the fundamental condition of possibility of knowledge, stemming from the recognition that love itself *aspires* to the idea (in its Platonic sense) and transcends these very ontic figures and ways with which we love (and sometimes love badly). "In this, namely that in the You of all true love, the pure form and the 'essence of love' are lit up phenomenologically and [are] co-loved, that love as such is already Idea as well, this is the essence of imagination."[4] A *loving* thinking therefore is a loving *thinking*: the thinker who thinks love, has to love what he so thinks, which means: he or she is no observer ("*nicht nur schaue*") of what he thinks, but takes part ("*Teilnehmender*") in what he thinks. In a sense, it is through this very ontic you whom he (or she) loves that the thinker becomes what he (or she) thinks when thinking love. Loving thinking, therefore, can only be done by lovers. Lovers, however, do not rest with their lover but transcend the very ontic dealings with their lover in order to reach the world of care and touch these with a tint of love. What the world lacks, love may provide; but what love lacks, precisely, is being-in-the-world.

The *Grundformen* is therefore about the *Erkenntnis* of *menschlichen Daseins*. It seeks to develop an ontology of that which a "loveless" soul would call epistemology. And, by virtue of the intertwining of the empirical and transcendental, for Binswanger what is most spiritual belongs to what is most sensual. Here one can reiterate the principle of Binswanger's phenomenology (almost) against Binswanger himself when he writes of the togetherness of *Wirheit*: "there is never something 'in the spirit' that occasionally would also appear bodily. [On the contrary] to the being of togetherness belongs essentially its appearance, like with beauty, where essence and appearance belong together as well."[5] This intertwining is articulated in an exemplary manner when it comes to knowing the human being:

> The judgement of human character" [*Menschenkenntnis*], which purely arises out of being-in-the-world as care, only becomes knowledge "of men" if it is based on love, that is, when it in others or in being-with not only "sees" but also "meets" the human being as the coincidence of you and youness in general.[6]

Binswanger thus tries to point out that in order for us, thinkers, to know the human being we must first love the human being. But to love the human being one must *be* with the human being within the world, know of the "nullity" of care and put its negativity to work. In short: one must venture beyond the power play, the "*Kräfte-Spiel*,"[7] between Dasein to arrive at the *Frage-Antwort Spiel*, the "conversation" that humanity has with itself throughout the various epochs of thought. Binswanger's epistemological claim thus unfolds as love itself unfolds: first the world, then love, and finally a "return to world."

To think such an exodus philosophically—out of the world into love only then to return to the world *out of* love (in all of the senses implied)—Binswanger has repeatedly pointed to art and the self-realization of the artist, for art's exodus is similar to that which is accomplished in and out of love. Here it becomes clear that the conversion of the human being plays more in the "return" from love to the world than in the exodus out of the world to being-in-love. What matters is not the *solitude à deux* of the lovers, but the lovers' return to that very world while being *transformed* through this love.

And in the world, even the lover is alone, although he or she no longer knows of any "existential solipsism"—not even of the Heideggerian kind. One can best take Binswanger's transformation of Heidegger's "being-in-the-world" to an "existence in the world" in a literal fashion: "first and foremost," one does not ask the question of being. But this, in turn, need not mean that people are always and already fallen in the world, as "the They" would do. "First and foremost" one simply is in the world and one "goes about one's business": getting one's job done, making sure the children are picked up from school, having a few errands to run, and so forth. Things of everyday life, for Binswanger, are not to be considered as a somewhat inauthentic dealing with entities-within-the world but are rather, as we have seen, closer to the "authenticity" won *from* togetherness. Such is what Binswanger has in mind, in contrast to Heidegger's disdain for everything ordinary and for all things nonphilosophical. Why? Because these everyday things are "first and foremost" done, even while alone—my lover is not present in my work space, for instance—with a view to (my) love and its perpetuation in the world. "After" the *Heimat* with one's lover, in and through this *Heimat* rather, the human being seeks to find its place and space within the world. Obviously, this means that while the lovers acquire a taste for a *Wandel* or walking in the world (as Adam and Eve walked through Eden), this does not end one's *wandering* within the world.

Body and World: Onward and Upward

It is for such wandering, such *Fortschreiten* in the world from situation to situation, that Binswanger uses the term "*gestimmte Raum*": the space of a world that forms around my mood as well as my mood forming this space in which I for the moment exist. The concept is close to how English speakers use the term "personal space," even though this space here takes on the dimension of the world. For this personal space arising from out of my mood knows, according to Binswanger, several *Bedeutungsrichtungen*. Like any other space, it is constituted by height and width, but these are experienced here rather subjectively, stemming from my particular mood in a given situation. For the one walking through the world "first and foremost" receives meaning (*Bedeutung*) from this world—like a job has to be done at this particular place rather than another—and of which the singular being "has to make" sense in the particular space granted to him or her. The projection of world (Heidegger's *Entwurf*) here takes place within the thrownness in a particular situation. Binswanger is particularly close to Nancy's rephrasing of Heidegger in his reconfiguring of the resurrection here, as taking a stance against death within life. For Binswanger, it is clear that these *Bedeutungsrichtungen* are received (just as well as made possible) by our embodiment: it is by virtue of our body moving within particular spaces that these spaces and situations grant meaning as well as can be given a particular meaning.[8]

This wandering is not without its reminiscences of Derrida's destinerrancy. For Binswanger too, this wandering is, once fueled with the knowledge of love, turned into a *Wandel* as long as the latter remains aware of its *nicht-wissende Wissen*. In this sense, for Binswanger, one proceeds in the world very much like Derrida's blind men (and women). Here is Caputo's and Derrida's vision of such blindness:

> Blindness makes for good communities, provided we all admit that we do not see, that in the crucial matters we are all stone blind and without privileged access [. . .]. We need [. . .] to proceed on faith [. . .] by feeling ahead warily with our stick. "Like all blind men, they must *advance*, advance or commit themselves, that is, expose themselves, run through space as if running a risk."[9]

For Binswanger, it is from our bodies that there transpires world. This bodily wandering and walking in the world natively knows of both horizontal and vertical directions. Horizontality is a character of space and as such it is to be redirected to the world as a "'horizontal' leeway."[10] This horizontal directionality, which opens up a space within the world—I am here rather than there—as much as it is opened up by the space that is world—I am here because of the "there" of world prior to my being "here"—is what Binswanger *grosso modo* takes from Heidegger, although this directionality allows for more possibilities for the human being than Heidegger's "choice" between authenticity and inauthenticity does.

Where Binswanger differs from Heidegger is in what the former calls the "vertical directionality" of human existence in the world. As such, this vertical directionality of existence pertains to time: one does not know, when walking from situation to situation, what one is ultimately heading for, just as little as one knows what is coming our way. The horizontal dimension—our bodies pulling us in a sense toward the earth—stands for our ecstatic temporality toward the past and the present. The past "presents" upon our bodies in such a way that, for example, scars represent the past on our present body. The present is present because, obviously, one cannot *not* walk in the world: I am where my body is. The vertical, spiritual dimension is our ecstatic openness toward the future, a future that as such is always unknown.

The Art of a Difficult Existence: Binswanger's *Ibsen*

In the *Grundformen*, Binswanger thinks this verticality as an ever deeper "ripening" of the self, as (a somewhat teleological) better knowing of the fact that the human being ultimately does not know.[11] Shortly after the *Grundformen*, notably in his *Henrik Ibsen und das Problem der Selbstrealisation in der Kunst* (1949), the vertical dimension is identified with a "rising," a rising upward toward the dreams and aspirations of humanity as revealed through art. As such, this "height" of the human being is close to the possibility of the "fall" of the human being. Binswanger, for instance, analyzes Ibsen's character Sollness the constructor, an architect that delivers a building that is so high that he is afraid and ultimately *unable* to get down and crashes—"he builds higher than he can climb," as Ibsen has it.[12]

It is this inability to exist in the world that is of obvious interest to Binswanger as a psychiatrist. But, as a philosopher too, this is what will differentiate him from Heidegger and the latter's assumption that Dasein is always and everywhere healthy and powerful—if Levinas could write that "Dasein is never hungry," Binswanger would write that "Dasein is always healthy"—and why courageous, heroic Dasein, open for the *Ganzheit* of its being from out of its readiness for anxiety, is for Binswanger merely a limit-case with little traction in existence-in-the-world. In fact, one might wonder whether Heidegger's idea of authenticity would for Binswanger not rather be an unattainable (if not undesirable) ideal. Its utopia, that is, the awakening of all to their respective Dasein, will never have been Binswanger's mission. Heidegger proceeds—as does Schürmann somewhat in his utter separation of philosophy from all things everyday—as if the human being is not fully human as long as he or she does not philosophize.[13] On the contrary, the "highest" dream of and for humanity comes for Binswanger from the artists and the poets rather than the philosophers and is dreamt with a view on what is best for humanity rather than what is possible for the individual, solipsistic Dasein. For such a dream and imagination, then, it matters less what is possible for this or that Dasein.

Rather, what matters is the recognition that each of these Dasein, even the philosopher, somehow is unable to live in the world properly or rather is having difficulties existing in the world. More positively, this means for Binswanger that each Dasein shares a fundamental ignorance about what it is to be in the world. Each Dasein faces what Binswanger will call "the fall" into the world. If Levinas wrote "difficult freedom," then Binswanger could have written a book called "difficult existence." Unlike Heidegger, what matters for Binswanger is not how to avoid the fall and jump into a somewhat "imaginary" authenticity. Rather, one might situate his position as a tending to the fall of each and every Dasein into its most particular world where it is its being with others. One might say that if it was Heidegger's aim to reconcile *one's* being with *one's* time, then Binswanger's goal is to show how to love *our* being and *our* time.

Even the lovers are alone in the world and in their respective worlds. In fact, they experience what Binswanger calls "the deepest fall" the human being must endure, namely the fall "from out of the graceful height, [and] out of the hold on being in and through grace into the being as care, [into] finite possibilities for being."[14] It is here that each Dasein, for Binswanger, must "seek its way." This seeking, then, starts with what Sloterdijk has called Binswanger's uncovering of "the basic phenomenon of existential directedness."[15] Let us listen once more to Binswanger on this directionality of life: "in the practical directionality of life, [self-realization] is to be executed from out of the directions of sense that are narrowness and of width [*Enge und Weite*], self-realization through art is executed from out the directions of sense that are depth and height [*Tiefe und Höhe*]."[16] Binswanger accords a certain priority to the latter when arguing that the "width," the horizon of one's being-in-the-world if you like, receives its meaning and "its direction from out of height."[17] In this way, it is "love, art, religion, philosophy and so on" that tend to the fall of Dasein and so assist Dasein in its self-realization, which turns the *Bedeutungsrichtungen* into a *Lebensrichtung*: a life that receives a direction so as to make it worth living.[18]

The horizontality of existence in the world, and the sense encountered there already, receives its depth from out of the verticality of existence. A "healthy" Dasein is the one who keeps these dimensions in check and in the "right proportion": *misglückte Dasein* suffer from not being able to keep this right proportion. Manic Dasein, like Sollness, revels in verticality and ultimately falls to the earth. Or, in terms of the previous chapters, manic Dasein is the one who constantly changes his or her mind, permanently makes new decisions and resolutions, and so is unable to have a proper hold on the horizontality of world. Melancholic Dasein, on the other hand, revels in a decision once taken, is unable to change his or her mind, and so cannot find any footing in his or her present world.

One might interpret Binswanger here not as overcoming Heidegger's heroic distinction between authenticity and inauthenticity, but rather as overthrowing this distinction (like one overthrows a regime). For, just as Dasein is never permanently healthy and might be manic in one respect and melancholic in another respect or, more simply, might not always be able to keep the right balance between horizontality and verticality, so too the fate of Dasein might not be to choose between authenticity and inauthenticity once and for all. It might rather be to recognize that it could be more authentic in one respect and less authentic in many others, like I might be (more or less) authentic when talking and writing about philosophy but would proceed rather inauthentically if I were to go on and speak about astrophysics, for example. Let us, then, turn to phenomenology.

Sloterdijk, who discusses Binswanger's *Ibsen* in his recent book, is correct in pointing out that Binswanger, in quite the classical metaphysical manner, somewhat prefers the vertical dimension over the horizontal dimension of existence in the world. The fall into world and time shows itself only in the tragic verticality of Sollness, Icarus, and the like. Yet, Sloterdijk argues, there is a fallenness and a tragedy on the horizontal level as well: one might think of the wandering Jew and the flying Dutchman.[19] For Binswanger, indeed, there is no *Schwindel*, no dizziness or vertigo, on the horizontal level, but merely the *Hineindrängen* of our bodies moving about in the world.[20]

Yet from out of the *Grundformen* and "the sad milieu" of the practical and horizontal being-there-together it depicts—where, because of the power play between Dasein, the space of the other is always on the verge of becoming a "waste of space"—it is awkward to see Binswanger settling here for the tragic vertical dimension. In *Ibsen* he argues indeed that on the horizontal level the road taken, the walk walked, the horizons explored can always be "walked back," thereby excluding the genuine possibility for the human being of *being lost*, where the way back no longer coincides with the road taken to get there. The fall, for Binswanger, only plays in the vertical dimension, where the possibility of such a *return to others* is entirely suspended.

And such a return to others is exactly the aim of Binswanger's musings on art and philosophy. The aim of these latter two is not to awaken the sense of philosophy in others as Heidegger would have it, but rather, and more modestly, the fragile attempt to make sense of the world into which one is thrown. For Binswanger, one is thrown into world like one is *up* (or not) for a certain task—this is how the horizontality of world for him merges with its verticality. The aim of this phenomenological philosophy does not lie in seeing what others cannot (yet) see, as the know-it-alls Heidegger and his follower Boss have it, whose psychiatrists again pretend to "know more of Lucien than Lucien knows of himself" (Sartre). But rather in making clear what there is, in principle, for everyone to see. The *worumwillen*, the "for the sake of which" of Binswanger's phenomenology is, if you like, entirely for-the-sake-of-others.

In this regard, it is closer to Merleau-Ponty, who, we recall, wrote of a "familiarity of all human activity with all activity," and to Levinas, in whose work Jean-Marc Narbonne rightly noted "the idea of a missionary and fraternal philosophy," than to Heidegger ("no one understands what I am saying here") or Marion for that matter ("no one has seen what I have seen here").[21]

Such a mission, as concern for others, is what Binswanger reveals in his phenomenology of the artist Ibsen:

> once he [Ibsen] was at home and at peace with his art [*beheimatet in seiner Kunst*], he no longer circles around the rising in the aesthetic sphere and the clarification of the existential peculiarity [of the artist]. Now the interest of the dramaturge for the questions and difficulties of his time emerges. Herein lies the *back-to* his fellow human beings, in the sense of a higher, namely spiritual, *communication* with them. This bridge [to the other] does no longer lie in this or that artistic form, but in the collective task of dealing with the questions of one's era present in the artwork.[22]

Just what is to be communicated in this way is, as I will show, for Binswanger a collective not-knowing or lack of knowledge about what I would now call "the event of world" and its coming to pass (as Schürmann calls it). This spiritual communication would for Binswanger, however, be "for the love of truth and the good"[23] and is to be communicated *to* the world because the world, in his curious dialectic, shows the need for love more than love itself does. The world, for Binswanger, is (and has to be) designated by its lack of love, because the world is the space where one is only as turned-away from you (*Abwendung*). There is no *telos* that will suspend or otherwise alleviate this lack. Binswanger points to the fundamental historicity of the event of world *out of love*, of an *Abwendung* that is not an *Abdankung*, that is, it is love that will differentiate between what is *ungeschichtlich* or ahistorical and what is *geschichtlich* and comes to pass.

Before the artist is at home and at peace with his or her art, he or she, for Binswanger, experiences the *Sehnsucht* that could not be recuperated through love. The artist's experience of Dasein is one in which "the world becomes too narrow [*eng*] and too dark, not enlightened enough."[24] The world for the artist is like a piece of clothing that does not fit: his or her ideas seem *unfit* for the world. This narrowness is nevertheless a clear reference to the horizontal and bodily dimension of existence. Something similar is experienced by the phenomenologist when he or she has to endure the fact that it is from this experience of world here—this small bit of world that is Belgium in my particular case—that all generalizations of experience conferred to others necessarily takes place.

How does the artist, in Binswanger, experience his or her world? He or she experiences a certain *Bedrängtnis*, a sort of suffocating, instigated by the world. One must, first, recall that the artist for Binswanger, even though art and poetry are close to love, experiences being-in-the-world first and foremost as a lack of love, as lacking love. Second, one is reminded that even the experience of love, although it alleviates *Sehnsucht* for a moment—love is the moment where the lover "has nothing to do, desire, or ask for" simply because the lovers here dwell together—is not the end of such *Sehnsucht*.

This is why the artist will seek a way to be at once in love and out of love (in the world). It is important to note that the dialectic Binswanger has in mind (but which also "appears" to be the case), the "overcoming" of the contradiction between love and care, is one of *simultaneity* rather than one of succession. Instead of viewing, as historians would do, from the synthesis, the thesis and the antithesis, all these things here happen at the same time, like when one can be authentic and inauthentic with certain things *at the same time*. Even if the world, of itself, knows too little of love, the lovers experience both "too much" of the world—a "fall" proper to love where the lovers become "just friends"—and a "too little" of world, where the lovers find no footing in the world and cannot extend their love to the dealings proper to being-in-the-world.

The "*Da*" of the artist, if you like, is neither the *Da* of what Binswanger calls horror—which is the experience of mere *Sein* without any *Da* to witness it—nor the "*Da*" of anxiety that authentically experiences "world" and seeks to perform, enhance, and affirm its "Da" in the *Sein* of world. The *Bedrängtnis* or distress is, almost contra Binswanger, as much horizontal as it is vertical: the "narrowness" of world appears as something that cannot be overcome (my being will remain limited by the particular place of my body), and this impossible overcoming may be experienced as the doubt over whether love and beauty will ever find a proper form within the world. This is why Binswanger prefers artists, doubting and lamenting the insufficiency of both their native ground (in *Ibsen* he mentions Ibsen's quest for a liberation of his family, his native country, and his contemporaries) and their art as well as how they are always on the verge of concluding that it might be better "to burn out than to fade away."[25]

Binswanger, Art, and the Phenomenology of Religious Life

In and out of love, the artist experiences in his or her own way the moments we have mentioned as essential to the phenomenology of religious life:

exodus out of world, conversion, and mission to the world. Let me briefly consider these moments from out of Binswanger's phenomenology of the artist (which is a phenomenology of love).

> Distress threatens our being at home in the world, insofar it questions our world-projection [*Weltentwurf*] and, which amounts to the same, our self [*Selbstentwurf*] until now [. . .]. In distress the decision is made, whether we are genuinely at home in our world-projection, whether we are in this projection all too steadfastly or whether we are invited, in order to regain our freedom, to *depart* from this "home" and commence, homeless, our wandering and so find a new being-at-home in a new world-projection.[26]

The artist, once departed from and fallen out of the comfort-zone that his or her world can be, experiences a sort of cleft between his or her being and the world in which this being takes place. Such an exodus is the experience both of the meaningfulness of world and of its meaninglessness. It is the awareness that "without world," without the hold that the self has in and on his particular world, there would not be anything meaningful. *Simultaneously*, it is the recognition that this particular meaningfulness of this/my world here is not the meaning of world and being in its entirety and can even be that which turns the self away from other meanings (if not the meaning of others). In fundamentalism and fanaticism, for instance, *my* (take on) world becomes *the* (take on) world.

In short, the artist is so called toward an experience of what Binswanger, along with Von Hofmannsthal, names: "*die unausdeutbare Deutbarkeit der Dinge*," the inexhaustible capacity of world to receive meaning even if no meaning would ever exhaust the meaning of world and being in its entirety. The gaze of the artist and of the phenomenologist here is attracted to the discrepancy between several meanings: between my old world, which I've left in and through distress, as well as between "my" horizon of meaning and the horizon of the other, and so forth.

In this way, "the departure is not simply a farewell to being-at-home, but at the same time, a *going, seeking* and *meeting* of novelty."[27] This departure, then, is a quest for what is new, what is different. It is—Von Hoffmansthal again—"the curiosity of love," an incitement [*gelockt*] and excitement belonging to the "mystery of eros."[28] The philosopher and the artist, then, are those who "within the inexhaustible capacity for meaning of things make possible new meanings and a new home": what so causes distress, is the infinite and borderless spaciousness of the *"unausdeutbare Deutbarkeit."*[29] If there truly is no meaning for one alone (Levinas), then even this meaning between the two of us endlessly varies and infinitely carries on between each member of humanity. The dream and the conversion of the artist (and the phenomenologist) is not a utopia but is dreamt with a view on humanity and a "loving encounter with what is in general—*mit dem Seienden im Ganzen.*"[30] The poet and the artist, then, in and out of love, want to show (to others) what *is* and *exists*, but in and through the beauty of their artwork, they simultaneously show the beauty of what so is and exists. This beauty (or goodness and truth) here does not lie in this or that particular form, but rather in what I call "the event of world." This is: in the fact that "there is" meaning and that the "there is" of this meaning extends infinitely, though even only historically. The ultimate aim of such a conversion (in and through art) for Binswanger seems to be that the artist so extends the (spiritual) wandering, the feeling around for the "there is meaning" (of being) into a love for the beauty of what, *überhaupt*, "is there" (of beings). Binswanger's stress on beauty should not be misleading here. If contemporary art, for instance, turns even the ugliest and most meaningless things into art, it shows precisely that *even these things* can "receive meaning" and thus are worthy of art and ultimately of love.

This, finally, is art, philosophy, and love's mission and shows its "essential trait of togetherness [*Wirhafte Zug*]": the poet feels around with "a warm heart" for humanity, for "those suffering, the unhappy ones [and] the blinded."[31] Poetry, as was philosophy at its inception, is a medicine, a means for the treatment of humanity. Here the phenomenology of love turns into a phenomenology of compassion.

There is, of course, no guarantee that this dream for humanity will ever aspire to reality: recall that the hope for unfanatical self amid an unfanatical world only shows up in and through friendship, that is, when love is *already* falling toward world. There is no way to tell whether such an *Erziehung des Menschengeschlechts* (Lessing) is not merely in the philosopher's or the artist's imagination; whether the *Ein-bildung* is not merely a fantasy and wishful thinking. On the contrary, it is quite likely that such a dream for the end of fanaticism operates according to the logic of Derrida's primacy of bad conscience: anyone who thinks that he or is not fanatical at all is likely to be just that.

Yet what Binswanger achieves in his phenomenology of the passion of the artist[32] is precisely the possibility of a passageway from the ontic toward the ontological (through the ontic) or what he calls the *Überstieg*.[33] A transcendence within the immanent plane of world, which here is configured as the passage from an ontic question "what is best for me" toward an ontology of what would be best for all, from what is most particular to what is universal. It is this *Überstieg* that, first, unites love and world and so combines what is most singular (my love for this very ontic other) and what is common to all and therefore transcendental (our being-in-the-world), while, second, this *Überstieg* leaves room for a self that is at once in and out of love. Art and love aspire for Binswanger to a "liberation" of the self in (its fall to) the world.[34] Such a liberation is in consequence of the *Wandel* of love and ventures toward "a transformation of the whole of Dasein" from out of gazing at the finitude of all forms in the world.[35]

Conclusion: From a Finite Life to the Infinity of Love

The artist and the lover are the ones who maintain an infinity of sorts within the finite realm. Binswanger relies on Wilhelm Dilthey here and insists that the "realization" of the self issues from out of the awareness of the *Geschichtlichkeit* or fundamental historicity of all beings. "The human being reaches his independence or, in Dilthey's terms, his liberty or sovereignty, in the 'historical consciousness' of the finitude of all historical appearances, of all human and societal circumstances. In short: from out of 'the relativity of all beliefs.'"[36]

Binswanger stresses a similar fundamental insight in his phenomenological account of Ibsen, adding, importantly, that it is precisely from out of this fundamental historicity that the artist, like the lover, reaches for what is eternal, infinite, or at least "omnitemporal." Such an infinity is, for Binswanger, who is a "modern thinker wary of modern times," obviously no longer the infinity proclaimed and prescribed by the religions, but an infinity measured against the fate and destiny of humanity. (Almost) contra Derrida, Binswanger would in effect argue that the "destinerrance," the fact that humanity has no goal or *telos* to attain, does not make for the fact that one should not concern oneself with the fate and destiny of humanity from within this small bit of world and history that is granted to us.

In *Ibsen*, Binswanger answers the question of art's omnitemporality in the following fashion: "This question is only denied by those [. . .] who are shortsighted, the ones who fall in our time. Over and against these, Ibsen is again the hyperopic one [*der Weitsichtige*], that is, the one who keeps the changeability and the transitoriness of all historical forms and problems in sight."[37]

This does not mean that the artist (and a fortiori the philosopher) should remain with this endless finitude of all things. This is what separates Binswanger from Dilthey and also from the paralyzing tragic feel that

Caputo has mentioned. Precisely because of his awareness of the finitude of world and being, Binswanger detects in Ibsen an aspiration for the "omnitemporal condition of possibility, [that is] for the *a priori* trait of the human being and its problematic."[38] Binswanger explains:

> If in effect we are only *human beings* of our time—and not just human beings "*of our time*," as an inhuman [*Unmenschen*] *falling* into the needs, anxieties and dangers of this particular time—if we are beyond our time, as *our* (transitory) historical situation, and see the human condition as such. The immanent task of this human condition, to give direction, measure and form to all possibilities of our being, remains the same, independently of the given historical situation [. . .]. As long as humanity knows of a highest possibility of being, a possibility which gives direction, measure and form to all other possibilities, therefore as long as humanity deserves the name humanity [*solange sie also den Namen Menschheit verdient*], that long Ibsen will have "something to say" to humanity.[39]

It is important to note the passageway from finitude to some sort of omnitemporality: everything happens as if the one who is aware of the transitoriness of all things is simultaneously the one who will become aware of things that do not pass. It is in and through love, then, that the artist (or the philosopher) will learn to differentiate what is merely historical from that which is—while only ever showing up as historical—*ungeschichtlich*. The a priori task of humanity is, in a sense, to remain human (considered from the fact that—this is written in 1949!—humanity "first and foremost" is insufficiently human). It is *through* love's transformation that the artist can dwell in what is *geschichtlich*, being-in-the-world as care, and in what is *ungeschichtlich*, identified by Binswanger as "being-in-the-world-beyond-the-world" which thus is also a "being-in-time-beyond-time."[40]

The human being who is able to conjoin both modes and possibilities in being, for Binswanger, is the passionate human being: the one who was affect*ed*—*passio* in its passive sense—by the problematic and the question of one's time simultaneously reaches out for the "beyond" his (or her) being and his (or her) time and so "produces" works that form (*bildet*) humanity and represent it to itself. This, finally, is what separates Binswanger from Dilthey. Dilthey, for Binswanger, misses the productive and creative aspect of the human being and somewhat remains confined within the tragic paralyzed subject. A subject, who, because of the endless finitude, does not *do* anything.[41] Binswanger's preference for the creative artist, then, can be explained thus: he or she is the one who believes that things *can* change because, basically, things *are* change, or the one seeing that in and through all perishing there is also renewal.

Conclusion to Part 3

How is love able to discriminate between what is merely historical and that which is beyond history? Because love is lived nowhere else than in the world and in history. Love, of itself, is the meeting point of the historical and what is a-historical, and is what rightly passes here for the a priori trait of the human condition, close to what I named the "minimalistic universalism" of philosophy in our general introduction.

But first note that, even if Binswanger's is an ontology incarnate, and at times personal, the phenomenology of religious life sketched here with Binswanger is not a theology: it is a *salut sans salvation*. There is no theology here, in that there is for Binswanger no arrival of Christ in the world that would once and for all light up and consecrate this world somewhat with a definitive meaning. At best, Binswanger's phenomenology might be the condition of possibility of something like a theology or, who knows of, a secular phenomenology of religious life.

Let us, on this separation between history, finitude, and that which might insinuate itself there, listen once more to Binswanger:

> Evidently, love lives from out of a self-understanding and projection of love that is [historically] passed on to us. We live love "today" differently than in the time of the Renaissance [. . .]; yes, every generation lives love differently. The fact of the historical changeability of "love-experiences" in no way contradicts the unchangeability of the phenomenological-anthropological [. . .] essence of love [. . .]. For to this essence there belongs just as well that Dasein as love [. . .] does not take the self-understanding of love exclusively from out of the tradition [*Überlieferung*].[1]

Here one again senses Binswanger's primacy of the ontic or, if you like, love's "entrance in history" (Sloterdijk). It is from our own experience of love, that is, from out of my love for this very ontic you, that we glimpse (but not only glimpse) what there is (essentially) to love. This experience is here or there obviously colored by our time or by our traditional readings of love, but this does not constitute what is essential to this love. The "essence" of love, one might say, lies in its "existence." It is for this reason that the love Binswanger has in mind displays a fundamental openness and is opposed to all fanaticism. For this love, essentially, *includes* new and other forms of love rather than it would *exclude* these: one can love in many ways, and ontic forms of love might contribute to its essence and its ontology.[2] Binswanger's rehearsal of what I have called in this work "the event of world," and the concomitant distinction between "deconstructible" historical configurations and the indeconstructible event of world that escapes all construction and making, finds in love a way to dispel all misplaced moralisms that come to us through (most often) religious institutions.

We are back, here, at the starting point of Part 1, for Binswanger, like Sloterdijk and Nancy, allows no dictatorship of the tradition and accords a certain priority to life as it is lived today in order to see how one passes "beyond" our being and time (with or without the tradition). This primacy of life as it is lived and, as such, is "ahead of" yet also "prior" to theory and tradition is accorded by Binswanger only insofar this phenomenon of life is greeted with love. This is also why, just as Levinas's ethics does not offer any ethical guidelines, Binswanger never tells us just how to love.

General Conclusion

Phenomenology of Religious Life

An Empirical-Transcendental Phenomenology

Before turning to "the event of world," as the recognition of a *world* that is finite through and through, and its *event*, which itself cannot easily be reduced to finitude, it is perhaps worth exploring whether phenomenology itself, as a theory wary of theory, does not repeat, in its own way, the structural moments of exodus and mission, as one could note in Binswanger's phenomenology of love.

The very practice of the phenomenological reduction might in effect be construed according to these three modes. The famous bracketing of the natural attitude, the suspending of sayings such as "there is and exists this or that," is precisely a sort of *exodus* out of this very world. To where? What does the reduction reduce to? The phenomenological reduction functions by reducing us to a sort of gaze. It withdraws from the natural attitude only to better see the thing as it gives itself in the very act with which it gives itself. Husserl at times might have thought that the reduction would be to some sort of primary ego that would remain "identical" amid all of its constitutions. Or, at other times, an ego that would participate somehow in the union and communion that is transcendental intersubjectivity and from whence it would gain its force to constitute in the first place. Be that as it may, a certain Derrida would say that, for all that, the very practice of the reduction, the *fact* of Husserl constantly rewriting, readdressing, and so reassessing the phenomenological method, somehow already undermines Husserl's hope to find some instance "identical to itself" in the act of the reduction.

It might be better to state that the reduction therefore reduces to a sort of gaze. What does this gaze see? It sees the given to consciousness as it gives itself to consciousness—it sees what so appears. What I thought was a table, a plateau with four legs, now appears inchoately as a "thing" that stands on two legs or three legs, if only I adjust my body (and thus my gaze) somewhat and make different adumbrations. What does this gaze see and sense, then? It sees no table, but it senses that to this sight—the two or three legs—somehow something is added: to intuition there is added signification. This then is constitution: the (perhaps erroneous) attribution of meaning and sense to what I glimpse only partially in intuition. Here then the concept of "table" is thus constituted. To this perception here, I add through comparing with *other* tables I have seen the full notion of a table. I add to the fallible perception through discerning what is missing from this table here (in the act of reduction) and what cannot be missing for it to add up to the idea "table." It would not be a table if it had not four legs, and therefore I add the missing leg from what is given to me through gazing phenomenologically. Yet this arising of meaning, out of what one sees and what one has seen, remains fallible just the same. This is where something like "conversion" comes in. For the phenomenological reduction allows one to see the discrepancy between the "concept" (essence or idea) and the thing itself. If the concept indeed dictates that a table is a table if and only if it has four legs, then this dictate, for instance, cannot admit that certain things can function as tables even though they are usually not used for this and do not correspond neatly to the essence of a "plateau with four legs" or even that certain designer tables prove to outwit the essence of this thing "table" entirely.

The path from intuition to signification—what I see in this given to consciousness is not exactly a table (from "realism" to "idealism": I need to "add" to the given and so "create" an essence)—or from signification to intuition—I cannot constitute this designer table here exactly as a table (from "idealism" to "realism": I cannot add to the given or added wrongly)—is therefore not a one-way street.

The aim of the phenomenological gaze is not, as Binswanger has it in *Ibsen* (forgetting for an instant everything that the *Grundformen* had accomplished), to transcend the *Faktum* or intuition in order to see the *eidos* and signification, as that which "founds [and] makes possible"[1] the *Faktum*. It is also to realize that the *Faktum* not only "concretizes" a pre-existent ontological condition (Levinas) but at times also creates new possibilities for essences, like the reduction of the "thing" table can at times confirm my "idea" of a table but at times alter this idea. Phenomenology, in this regard, comes "after the fact": it *follows* things and their way of being. It observes (by taking part in) the transformation (if not historicity) of essences in this finite world of ours. It is therefore precisely this discrepancy between *Faktum* and *eidos* that the phenomenological method allows us to measure: both signification arising out of intuition and intuition giving way to signification. Phenomenology, if it is allowed to go beyond "the final state of metaphysics [which is] realism and idealism,"[2] is a witness to the place and space where meaning originates. This is why, in any case, phenomenology allows one to see things differently and, thus instructed, will *return* to the world of the natural attitude if only to see things better there. Or, at least, to see there that things can change because they are change.

The discrepancy between these empirical developments and their essence is one that cannot be overcome. This is how phenomenology attends to the finitude of "what appears" in order to so see "the appearing of appearing," which, of itself, seems to harbor an omnitemporality, ahistoricality (Schürmann), a tendency for change and renewal (Sloterdijk), and a transcendence (Levinas/Derrida) if not infinity of sorts (Caputo/Nancy). The constitution of ideality here is itself historicized, for even the "idea" of a table, or the "idea" of love, is dependent on a common history in a common world where autonomous (phenomenological) constitution of things always and already is invaded by prior shared histories. However, the very fact that there *is* such intertwining of the empirical and ontological is not of our own making. In this regard, Coulomb is right to point out that Binswanger never "offers a transcendental theory of such a "constituting togetherness" [*nostrité constituante*]"—but, then again, is there such a theory even today?[3]

One will need to mind the gap between what is possible and what is impossible or between what is conditional and unconditional (contra Caputo's critics). On the other hand, this work has shown that Caputo stretches the distance between these two orders, between the transcendental and the empirical if you like. In this way, just as much as Derrida advances against Nancy that the latter neglects (or is cured too easily from) a "quasi-transcendental dizziness," it can also be advanced against Caputo.

The quasi-transcendental *Verflechtung* of empirical events and what conditions them is such that there is a constant back-and-forth between the two orders, so that—in phenomenological terms—the one doing the constituting (and actively seeking for the "pure" transcendental ideality that functions as the condition of possibility of the empirical given) finds him- or herself constitut*ed* by what he or she is actually constituting (and so always and already passively marked and stamped by what he or she actively seeks to constitute). According to Derrida, such a dizziness would be truly aporetic: it is not sure whether the empirical given lies prior to its transcendental condition of possibility (and so renders it inoperative by condition*ing* the condition of possibility) or whether the transcendental condition of possibility would lie prior to empirical reality and in effect condition*s* what can appear in reality. It is, in short, not sure whether one travels from the empirical to the transcendental or the other way around, from the transcendental to the empirical.

It is such a "double passage" that Caputo at times seems to neglect by stretching the distance between what is conditional (what is made "merely" possible by the conditions of possibility) and what is unconditional (what makes even the impossible possible through undoing all conditions of possibility). On the one hand, Caputo shows himself at his most empirical by stating that this mixture and respective contaminations between what is conditional and what is unconditional are *really* all there is and that one will therefore have to deal with all the various hospitalities and Christianities as ever so many givens (for, although there is surely something "beyond" these givens, this "beyond" never shows itself in reality). On the other hand, however, Caputo shows himself at his most transcendental, and this "beyond" turns out not to be part and parcel of a "hauntology," but rather shows itself very much as a noumenon would do (thus not showing itself). For, to mediate and mitigate between these various hospitalities, a sort of vantage point is erected from which such mediation can after all be effected, and the entirety of hospitalities is reduced and bracketed (in the phenomenological sense) without taking into account how the "idea" of hospitality only ever arises out of the diverse hospitalities. Our point is that this is in effect a stretch: a quasi-transcendental dizziness means that one cannot have it both ways, for there is no such stretch between the empirical and the transcendental—if a pun would be allowed: one *must* have it both ways, just not separately (as Caputo has it) but simultaneously.

The dangers of such an empirical-transcendental phenomenology are, obviously, multiple. It can mistakenly interpret the empirical material substrate of thought as a simple stepping-stone for a full-fletched ontology (Heidegger's ontologism). Or it might just as well revel in the ontic and never really attain to the universality of the transcendental (which figures today in a hermeneutics according to which "everything is interpretation"). On this score, one should remain with the quasi-transcendental dizziness, and the concomitant "double passage" between the empirical and the transcendental, that Derrida prescribes.

Let us apply this once more to the idea of love. Binswanger's distinction between this very ontic you whom I love and the transcendental imagination of love of the idea of "youhood" (*Duhaftigkeit*) and togetherness überhaupt (*Wirheit*) is helpful here. Although my love for this very ontic you puts me on the track of the idea of a love and *Wirheit* of all for all, it does not present us with a "clear and distinct" idea of such togetherness. On the contrary, because of the fact that this ontic you here might always be substituted for an other you (and this is what most often happens), the idea of togetherness in a sense always and already is *insufficiently incarnated*. It does not attain the rank of a full presence, and its referent in any case cannot be located as high as one would want. But, similarly, the idea of such togetherness cannot do without a bodily incarnation in the union of the two lovers either: its ideality only ever presences in and through this very materiality. It *is* nowhere else than in this incarnation of love within the world. This ontology cannot do without the ontic, just as much the ontic craves a concomitant ontology. This idea of love, then, only ever exists as incarnated in the world where it presences only ever insufficiently: no ontic love will, for instance, exhaust once and for all what there is, ontologically, to love, just as no ontology of love will ever exhaust all new ontic forms of love "to come." Yet it is from out of this "simple" ontic presence of love in the world that one arrives at the event of love's presencing in the world, which, for Binswanger as for us, is and remains mysterious.

Of Authoritative Places and How Not to Occupy Them

Binswanger has presented us with an existential version of the problem that has occupied us in this work, the problem of the "deficit in Truth" or, in this case, the deficit in the idea: the fact that the idea of love does not even attain to the status of "ideality" if it does not pass through the very materiality of love and the concomitant problem that this material substrate of love does not once and for all answer for the idea of love (as traditional theories of transcendental thinking would have it).

This deficit of truth has occurred in this work more than once. It is present, for instance, in Caputo's and Derrida's claim that the truth of a system does not lie within the system, making for the fact that "religions with religion" (even though they decide more often than not for Truth, a truth that would correspond exactly with their own particular system) have to be haunted by an impulse and passion for truth from without. It is present, for example, in Schürmann's claim that not one "economy of presence" exhausts and coincides with the event of presencing. It is in turn present in Sloterdijk's and Nancy's idea that the exhaustion of the matrix of monotheism leaves us with and in a void of "sense" that no longer can (or should) aspire to metaphysical Signification. Last, it is even present in Marion's idea of the human being as "without being" or essence that should not be "filled in" with a particular being or essence.

Such a deficit in truth is obviously a consequence of the end of metaphysics and the corresponding withering away of the *arche* and *telos* for humanity. As mentioned earlier, it was Heidegger who foresaw such a deficit and lack in and of "truth":

> if God [. . .] has disappeared from his authoritative position in the suprasensory world, then *this authoritative place itself is still always preserved*, even though as that which has become empty [. . .]. What is more, the empty place *demands to be occupied anew*.[4]

If a great many of contemporary philosophers today agree that in effect the place of truth has become empty, not many have dedicated their work to Heidegger's second thesis here, namely that the empty place demands a new occupation and is always preserved—although one might argue that the work of the later Derrida on sovereignty was concerned with exactly this. The studies in this work therefore have tried to take up this problem—namely, that even this deficit of truth can be recuperated in ways reminiscent of the question concerning ontotheology and that it is quite likely that such a reoccupation indeed is what will happen. Schürmann's depiction of the "natural metaphysician"—as a metaphysics and ontotheology that comes naturally to us—has gone a long way to sketch this problem. Such a metaphysics, which is the "want of a hold" on being from out of one single phenomenon that it sees as exemplary for all other phenomena and that serves as the norm and criterion with which to judge these phenomena, might prove to be ineradicable. It seems to return even in Schürmann's utter separation of philosophy and everydayness. For this separation repeats the posture of the philosopher hovering above all things ontic (and so depreciating these) as much as the metaphysics Schürmann supposedly overcame. In a sense, in Schürmann, it is philosophy itself that occupies the authoritative position and that "sees what other[s] do not and cannot see."

Yet similar modes of procedure can be detected in Nancy's and Sloterdijk's works. Both see the present situation as the norm and criterion with which to judge the tradition of metaphysics, and both seem to think that this tradition can be abandoned in one stroke. Both thinkers forget what I have called above the historicity even of essence(s) and the slow transformation that so pertains to being and its event. In Caputo, the exodus of the "without religion" is what aspires to permanence, so forgetting the authoritative claims that this utters toward "religion with religion." "Religion without religion" would only be possible if we were not naturally metaphysicians. This is why we, philosophically, have argued that Caputo stretches the distance between what is historical and what is transcendental, in his case "the event" *tout court* to the point that, well, it is a stretch: "religion without religion" allows for no ontic incarnations that would at least point us or put us on the track of this "event." It disregards both the fact that, once there is religion, there is always religion with religion as well and the fact that, if religion without religion is not to remain without traction in the very historicity of things it seems to presume, it should be more than this ghostly, vitalistic force that no one can really see, experience, or live. Furthermore, it might need to be taken into account that, if it were to find such traction and to be "inscribed in a name" (Žižek), it is quite likely that such inscription happens according to ontotheology's prescriptions.

In Marion's work on love, finally, the usurpation of being-in-the-world through one single experience, the love without being (a very theological experience at that) may be obvious: love, "the transcendence par excellence," for Marion is both the origin and end-all of our existence in the world. Love, for Marion, is the one transcendental worthy of the name. However, because the lovers in Marion are without being as much as they are without world, there remains in the end very little to love.

The chapters on Binswanger serve somewhat as an antidote to this anti-incarnational, anti-matter tendency present in Caputo, Marion, and Nancy. This is so because Binswanger focuses both on the *exodus* of the world through the *Heimat* of the lovers *and* is keen to see the fullness of the phenomenon of love only in its *return* to the world, where love is lacking: that is, in their *mission* to be *with* others what they are together.

Binswanger's phenomenology of love only ever distinguished love from Heideggerian care in order to fill this care with love. It is to a new *Seinkönnen* in the world that Binswanger tries to point, a sort of doing the things we do with love. Caputo's position on our love and passion for (impossible) justice, although at first sight attractive, cannot be maintained. The attempt to distinguish between "religion without religion" and "religion with religion" seems in effect to be but one more version of a "Christmas-projection" (Nancy) and dissolves as it were from within. On the one hand, one might argue, with Heidegger, that one does not pray to, kneel and sing for an abstract appeal of "justice"—that is, the appeal to construct the least unjust world through deconstructing all structures and patterns of injustice—no matter how "indeconstructible" it may be. On the other hand, Caputo seems again to construct these unconditional and "indeconstructable" appeals *at the expense of* all conditional and "constructable" patterns and structures. This is why both Caputo and Nancy share a certain set of axioms: both disregard what I would call "the politics of being," that is, the minute, meticulous and phenomenological assessment of the concrete differences between particular traditions, be they religious (Caputo) or ontological (Nancy).[5] In both cases, a particular and singular account of belonging to a tradition or a community, however troublesome, is substituted for an abstract, universal account of an appeal to justice or to community hovering over the human being in ways that appear entirely untroubled with the human's concrete condition.

Yet the problem is not that they give a universal account of the human being (or even that it would be abstract). The problem rather is that both deconstructionists do not show just how one arrives at such an unconditional appeal *from out of* the conditional structures structuring our very world. Here, of course, the practice of phenomenology proves to be fruitful in order to return deconstruction to its mundane roots. Phenomenology, which I would like to see affirming a sort of minimalistic universalism that still connects with "world," could aid deconstruction when the latter still opts to "locate its referents up high" (Schürmann). Something similar is present in Marion's account of the erotic phenomenon of love. Here again a remnant dualism between an "unworldly" "love without being" and, if you like, a "being-in-the-world-without love" seems to be erected, and the mundane and worldly conditions in which these experiences first of all occur is forgotten. This is why we have preferred the not so contemporary philosophy of Binswanger, who, from out of his interpretation of the essence of love, settles for the existential weal and woe of love within the world and history. The "dualism" or "contradiction" between love and world (or being) here is simple and almost self-evident: love is not the world and the world is not love. But love, similarly, has no other place than world: if love lacks world, then, this is so because the world lacks love.

Of Love, Power, and Anarchy within the Event of World

Perhaps here is the place to settle the dispute about the anarchistic tendencies in contemporary thought. Whether it be Schürmann's ontological anarchism, resorting to the sovereignty of the philosopher overseeing the turmoil of everydayness or Caputo's sacred anarchy, unable to escape the sovereign God lurking behind and subtly controlling the Christian reversal of values, the lesson to be drawn here is perhaps that nothing is easier than turning the an-archist strand of thinking, and its thinking *without* principle into a principle after all. This is, in effect, what the chapter on Schürmann might have shown and what we have elsewhere concluded with regard to Lacoste's latest work: the trouble with anarchy is that anarchy means trouble. Its being "without principle" all too easily resorts to a somewhat gnostic counterprinciple, where it is construed as an effort and struggle against the injustices and evils of institutions and powers.[6] Here again one might opt for Binswanger's view of love and its subtle disruption of power within the world (and therefore not against it), where it is through love that one is guided toward the mysteriousness of the event of being happening regardless of principles, arches, first causes, and what not. Let us listen to Binswanger one more time:

> When we ask which "idea" underlies the projection upon being [*Seinsentwurf*] of Dasein as *love*, then this is surely not the idea of power. Love does not want to reign and it does not want to take hold of itself, our own Dasein, nor yours or ours. Surely love *wrestles*, and surely the happening of this wrestling has its (worldly) history; yet what is going on in this wrestling and becomes historical, is not love itself. It is care struggling for the survival and the rescue of a finite love. Surely love *suffers* and the happening of this suffering has its (worldly) history. But who is suffering in love and enters into history, is yet again the human being as caring, as caring for the finite continuation of love.[7]

All of a sudden one is reminded of Levinas, for had not Levinas himself written that "anarchy does not reign" and "cannot be a sovereign"?[8] Yes, but here one needs to recall that Levinas's interpretation of ontotheology's inevitability (which I traced at the end of Chapter 5) has also shown that, in being and in world—the advent of the third party—the anarchist truth of that which lies outside the system will *always* be recuperated by that system. Today there is a *market* for anticapitalist works as well. It might be, finally, that love's subtle subversion of power might escape from such recuperation and resist it more than Levinas's anti-ontological anarchy would do. Love, in the last resort, might be a name for what is "otherwise than being."

But just as "the" otherwise than being inevitably shows up in being and will be "managed" there, so too love incarnates in the world by "showing up in being." How to configure the event of love within the event of world, or, in other words, love's unfolding in the unfolding that is world? Nancy's thinking of the event is as follows:

not [. . .] the thing *which* happens, but [. . .] *the fact* that it happens, the event-ness of it event. [This] event-ness, insofar as it is conceived in terms of the truth of the thing, is distinguished from the phenomenon: [it is] the nonphenomenal truth of the phenomenal itself.[9]

The event of world, then, can be understood as an *extension* of Husserl's "originary nonpresence" of the otherm and so extends, à la Derrida, "a phenomenon of a certain nonphenomenality" to the very event of world and all that happens there.[10] "Appresentation" then would no longer concern only the other but rather the world as such. The world therefore "worlds" beyond me, "with" and finally *without* me. It would not be the mind that "accompanies all of our representation"; it would not be the body that accompanies all perception (leading to what Derrida calls "a globalization of flesh",[11] seeing the immediacy of flesh even there where it is not); it would rather be the "worlding of world" or the event of world that accompanies and makes possible all of our constitutions. In a sense, then, this event of world would be the machine-body that Derrida has in mind, conjoining the muteness of matter with the seeing and the sightings of the mind, so disrupting our desire for full-presence from within. This transcendental historicity or archifacticity is in a sense Derrida's version of "a phenomenology of the unapparent" (Heidegger). For Derrida, one recalls, the "originary nonpresence" pertains not only to the other but also to the self. Even the most immediate of immediacies—me touching my hand, for instance—would not give and present us with a "presence of self," for what I am so touching, my hand, is not the transparency of the flesh (*Leib*) but already a muteness and blindness pertaining to the body. When I touch my hand, I *simultaneously* touch what is no longer me: the flaking away of skin and sweat, for instance. The most pure presentation of my self to me occurs through what is not myself. In the non-phenomenality of the other, this is even more obvious.

Such non-phenomenality might best be elucidated by the phenomenon of *tickling*. It is well known that one cannot tickle oneself. Only the other's tickle causes me to laugh. What happens here, phenomenologically speaking? It is the *presence* of the other that presents me with something I cannot present or give to myself: it is the presence of that which can never be made fully present to the self. The tickling so symbolizes the non-phenomenality of phenomenality or, in Heideggerian terms, the presence of presencing that has come about despite myself. One might surmise that love's happening in the world from without the world, its unfolding, in this way represents something like *the tickling of being*: something makes one live, love, and laugh, one knows not what.

A Phenomenology of *Religious Life*

Of Being in Default

In these final sections, my aim is twofold. On the one hand, conceding to Martin Hägglund that in religious matters indeed one has most often desired to overcome the "lack of being" (finitude, changeability, mutability) by positing an instance that would be *immune* to the fate of all things finite, I argue that such a lack of being is in no way hostile to a contemporary phenomenology of religious life.[12] Quite on the contrary: it might include rather than exclude a religious stance, in the same way that Binswanger's phenomenology of love sought to include new forms of love rather than excluding them. On the other hand, I want to give some ontological relief to Binswanger's phenomenology of the greeting and the concomitant "conversation of humanity with itself" through sketching the debate between Heidegger and Levinas on the question of speech: where for Levinas speech is what attends to the height of the Other, for Heidegger it is exactly what pulls us toward being and beings, toward being-in-the-world-with-one-another, that is.

In this work, such a lack in being has revealed itself in a double manner. On the one hand, one needs to think of Binswanger for whom the world shows itself to the loving gaze as the lack of love. On the other hand, one must recall here Derrida's primacy of bad conscience, which I advanced against Caputo's overly optimistic "religion without religion," which forgets the pull of the "with." The primacy of bad conscience, in Derrida, is such that whoever thinks he or she is open to the other sufficiently is likely to be not open enough. In this way, Derrida extends Levinas's complaints about the subject's complacency about its being. If being is "evil" (Levinas) or "injust" (Derrida), then the primacy of bad conscience means that, for Levinas one cannot be, in being, good enough or, for Derrida, that one is always and already insufficiently just. If being unfolds with lacks, gaps, and holes (Heidegger), then it not only falls to the human being to "endure" (*Aushalten*) such ontological insufficiency; it also *is* such a lack. The human being, I suggest, *is* in default, like one can be in default when one fails to pay back a loan or return a borrowed item. If, for Binswanger, the world is what lacks love, this is so because the human being fails to love properly (just as Heidegger's Dasein most often fails to be authentic). If, for Derrida, the human being fails to do justice to the law of being-in-the-world, it is because the human being only ever is *insufficiently* dealing with the laws mitigating the law of justice. Whoever would think to be able to do enough for the other would, in this regard, once again desire to overcome the lack that is (in) being and fail to be in default "properly": it would be to strip being from its being stripped of all *arche* and *telos* and once again supply being with a (metaphysical) Signification.

This is also why this *being in default* may not be confused with pessimism. For, if Binswanger, for instance, mentions the risk of turning away from love in such a way that one might turn out to be inhuman and speaks in this regard of a humanity that no longer deserves the name humankind, then this means that what we share in common is most often a failure to live up to what it means to be human. There is a positivity to this failure, for if no one is to be excluded from such a primacy of a bad conscience, it likewise means that all are included and no one can make an exception of him- or herself. It might be in this way that one positively guards oneself from excluding others and attends more properly to what Binswanger termed the dream of an *unfanatische Welt*. If, for instance, the human being, more often than not, turns out to be not so much a "rational animal," then this obviously would mean that he or she would share such a lack with animals, for example.[13] What human beings share, then, is not some sort of fullness and plenitude in being; rather, we share a certain lack. This is our *being in default*: what we share is not so much our capacity for love, but rather our lack of love.

There is a philosophy of incarnation here, in that meaning arises out of matter (out of signs, out of greetings, out of communication and community). There is meaning, then, but this meaning will never exhaust, definitively "reveal" the sense of materiality: there remains a muteness, after metaphysics, to being and world, as if something refuses to be signified. Failing to deal with such a muteness, so jumping to metaphysical conclusions, is what Binswanger warns us for: it is to forget that *zunächst and zumeist* we lack love, that we do not know and that being itself does not answer; it too remains in default.

Binswanger here is close to Derrida's primacy of bad conscience: everyone pretending to know, to be just, and to love is likely to know nothing, to be unjust, and to lack love. This is perhaps what needs to be done at the end of metaphysics: recognizing that we know that we do not know and that we most often fail to love properly. The human being is a being in default: its ambition surpasses its ability. Coming to terms with such a being in default may be the adequate response to the end of metaphysics: it is to recognize that we all share in this default and this lack and that this "knowing of not knowing" is what turns philosophy, as the love of wisdom, into a wisdom of love: not to overcome the lack, but to love even the lack (of rationality, of ultimate meaning).

Again, philosophy may very well wonder about wonder. It begins in love. Unlike wonder, love ventures "beyond" being: it all starts with this very ontic you whom I love; from there it risks the passageway to the totality of beings and their possible communion on the fragile basis of love; then to being in general, which seems sparked by love, to, perhaps, that which is "beyond" being while remaining within the restrictions posed to us by being-in-the-world.

Of a Common Lack in Being and How Not to Speak

Yet nothing is more human than the desire to overcome such a lack and to explain away its finitude, irrationality, and at times inhumanity. The question concerning ontotheology, on these terms, can be seen as being in default against this being in default: it is to erect an instance that occupies and overcomes the lack of being whereas, as such, there is only this lack. It is here that a discussion between Heidegger and Levinas is helpful. If Levinas, rather late in *Otherwise than Being*, asks whether his stress on the other is not still determined by metaphysical residues and wonders whether he has "eliminated from signification [of the face, JS] the idea of lack and want of presence?,"[14] Heidegger, as one will see, will reply in the negative, for it is impossible to eliminate the idea of lack, just as one cannot eradicate the want of presence or the want of a hold of which Schürmann spoke.

The problem, for Levinas, is whether the face's invisibility is not, instead of pointing toward the invisibility of the Infinite, merely lacking the visibility every other object in the world has and whether he might be simply positing its invisibility as an ontotheological extrapolation of all things visible obtained through negation. Whereas Levinas answers this question, obviously, affirmatively—the face's invisibility is not analogous to worldly invisibility—Heidegger would respond in the negative because, for Heidegger, there is nothing outside the visibility of worldly phenomena, and Levinas's "otherwise than being" would be, for Heidegger, one more improper attempt to escape being and posit an instance "over and against" the immanent presencing of beings.

Levinas, however, distinguished between "saying," speech, and the said. The extra-ontological "saying" is the commonality of speech that underlies all objectivity and all objectification and makes for the fact that "an explanation of a thought can only happen among two": it is because of your presence in the world that something of this world can be talked about in the first place. This is Levinas's version of the "elementary faith" of which Derrida speaks. Speech and saying are, for Levinas, "attention to something because [they are] always attention to someone."[15] Levinas's point, however, is that this peculiar relation to the other in and through speech exacts objects and objectivity in order to be able to welcome the other not with empty hands. Husserl's stress on objective intentionality is countered here by retrieving the condition for the activity of representation and ontological constitution: it is not because there is ontology that we speak, it is rather because of our speaking to one another that there is ontology.

In the words of *Totality and Infinity*, one "can formulate it in this way: the consciousness of a world is already consciousness *through* that world."[16] For Levinas, it is not the I or ego that constitutes the whole of reality, but, on the contrary, it is the subject that finds itself constitut*ed* by the reality in which it finds itself constituting. Levinas thus retrieves "the antecedence of what I constitute to this very constitution."[17] Representational knowledge thus finds its proper function in attending to the other; it is what allows us to approach the other, not with empty hands, but rather to have *something* (objects and beings) to give to the other. And it is, again, through language that we encounter objects: in and through language the subject can speak both *about* something and give *something* to the other. "Objectivity [. . .] is posited in a discourse, in a conversation which proposes the world."[18]

It is this objectification—which is the very existence of predicative language—that finds as its condition of possibility the other's revelatory speech: "the world is oriented, that is, takes on signification. In function of the word, the world commences [. . .] the world is said and hence can be a theme, can be proposed."[19] Saying is, therefore, not a mere saying something about something—predicative speech or the "*logos apophantikos*"—but a seeking for "the condition of communication"[20] that accounts for the fact that there is communication—predication, knowledge, science, and so forth—in the first place. Saying is subjectivity, that is, in each case mine, and in each case my responsibility. It is not a "giving out of signs" but rather the sincerity of the one who "makes signs to the other of the very giving of signs,"[21] the sincerity of the one who knows, therefore, that there is a salutation to the other in everything that has been said, that is said, and that is going to be said. Were it not for the other, nothing at all would be said, and absolute silence would reign.[22]

The problem, however, is that this Levinasian account of language is very close to Heidegger: for Heidegger, too, the world commences in and through the word. Levinas perhaps too quickly resorts to the extraontological otherwise-than-being here, for it might be precisely this that Heidegger foresaw when criticizing, say *par avance*, Levinas's account of the Saying. For Heidegger, language is the way in which things come to presence through the ways in which we name and speak of them.[23] One might say that for Heidegger all speech is a form of showing, and that the possibility of showing something to someone arises from the more fundamental fact of speech through which all showing (appearing, revealing) is always and already a speaking. Just as Levinas tries to understand the fact of the sciences and of ontology from out of their relation to the Saying, so too for Heidegger the ontic discourse of the sciences arises from out of the hold that language has on human beings.

Heidegger thus hints at the disclosive nature of the word, both in "what" the word discloses and "how" the word discloses. However, the fact that speech discloses is not one of our own making; it is rather our own making that is itself rooted in the disclosure that is named "word" or "*legein*."[24] The word discloses the world, and the world only, but this "being held by the world" is not of our own making. Whereas Levinas points to "saying" and the word as the condition of possibility of the (shared) world—the said—Heidegger points to that very world itself as the condition of possibility of the word's disclosing. The world itself is that which is disclosed in every word and so is what is obliquely present in everything there is being said. Thus Heidegger says that the sound of the word—*phone*—is not itself showing, but rather that this sound is a "structural moment which in the spoken communication, as a self-expression to another about something, is indeed invested."[25] Heidegger then distinguishes three versions of correlations between the word and the world, as ever so many orientations toward otherness.[26] The first is that all speech is a form of showing, because of the intertwining of the word and the being. A particular being shows itself only in the ways with which we speak of them, and the word is not a *doublure* of the entity, but rather is already intertwined with or "in-formed" by how this particular being demands to be shown. Perhaps an example will make this clear: when I say to you "Look! Over there!," your attention to this or that particular being or event over there is drawn, but the way in which my utterance is stated, be it loud and anxious or quiet and smiling, will determine just how this or that particular being over there demands to be seen. The second is that of the nature of the "*logos*," of speech. Heidegger argues that just as consciousness is always and already consciousness of . . . something determinate, so too speech and speaking is always and already speaking about . . . something determinate.

This relation thus concerns thus the intertwining of the "*logos*" with the "*on*," a being. This speaking about . . . something must, according to Heidegger, not be taken as something present-at-hand. Most often, indeed, it concerns the preflexive and "pregiven [. . .] unity of a being."[27] This relation between language and some particular being is what accounts for the fact that when I hear a car outside I do not represent to myself, first, its sound, in order to then attribute this sound to the sound of a car starting too fast. Rather, when I hear this sound, I at the same time know that a car is leaving. In short, I do not hear a sound that I, after the event, link to a car, I hear (the event of) the car starting through which the being, that is, the car, appears. Heidegger concludes: this relation shows that speech is always speech of something, namely "the whole, present, givenness"[28] of the world, and at the same time speaking about something, namely the being that makes an appearance from out of the horizon of givenness, which is to say, world. It is from out of this givenness of world that human beings are able to see something as precisely some thing *in particular*.

This last statement already intimates the third relation to the otherness of the world. Heidegger calls it the delotic and "intentional *koinoonia*."[29] This relation resembles that which Levinas would term "thinking" or "reflection"; it concerns the reflection on speech or "*logos*" as a being itself, or better: on the being of speech. This reflection, according to Heidegger, shows the two fundamental possibilities of speech: either one speaks truly or not—one speaks of the being as it is and shows itself or one does not. To speak truly means that we bring a being to speech as itself and show it "to the other" as the same being it is and was. In other words, it is in and through the reflection on speech that, to use Levinas's words, "the same train" can appear as "the train that leaves at the same hour."[30] It is from out of the givenness of world that human beings can speak (more or less) of the same beings in (more or less) the same manner. More or less, for the speaking of "*tauton*"—the same—is inevitably intertwined with the "*heteron*"—the other: accordingly, a being can appear as other than itself (when, for instance, the car I think I hear turns out to be a sample on a radio that is playing loudly).

One might already surmise just what Levinas shares in common with Heidegger here. The entire reduction of the said to the Saying may indeed be Heideggerian in nature; for if beings, in and through representational thinking, acquire "a name," a "fixity," and "an identity," this can only be the case because, prior to this shared world (Levinas), we *already* share, and are held in, speech (that is: we can speak about and from out of the sameness of a world, the world we always and already share) to the point that one might risk the concept of a shared facticity here.

Yet there are some important differences to be noted. These differences will allow us to nuance Levinas's utterances about "the" otherwise than being. Already in Heidegger's account of "*phone*," a tiny difference with Levinas might be noted, because whereas for Heidegger the sound of the word contributes to the way with which the being shows up, such an empirical said would for Levinas be nothing more than "the babbling utterance of a word."[31] Levinas thus would relegate such sounds to the realm of the said, which, at least according to Levinas, does *not* contaminate the "pure Saying," namely the "saying without the said."[32]

At issue here is thus speech ("*legein*") itself and whether something can be spoken of "without being," without (anything being) said about something ("*legein ti*"). Remarkably, Heidegger has responded, with a peculiar foresight as it were, to Levinas's and Marion's enterprise. Heidegger indeed shows that there can be no speech that is not the saying of something to someone: there is an overlap between the world and the word. There is no "Saying" that lies prior to the said, or that is *uncontaminated* by the said. Let's listen to Heidegger:

> There is no modification of "logos," that does not modify it as "*legein ti*"; i.e. every modification of "*legein*" is a modification of it in its character of revealing. Through such modification, the "*déloun*" [revealing, letting be seen, JS] does not [. . .] come to nothing [or] to a total lack of disclosure but because the "*legein ti*" is a constitutive structure [and] is necessarily preserved in every modification of "*logos*," "*logos*" can only be modified into a non-disclosure only in the sense of concealing, distorting, obstructing, not letting be seen.[33]

The idea of a "saying without said" would be, according to Heidegger, nonsensical, because it has not taken into account the inevitable character of metaphysics' mode of procedure: such a saying without a said, for Heidegger, would, as a modification of the "*logos*," not only still be part of the said—that is: it remains a "*legein ti*" and as such a discoveredness of world—but it also would be configured in a negative, privative way: the saying without said would merely be a non-showing of that which, properly speaking, belongs to that which, all in all, shows itself, namely being, the world, and being-in-the-world.

For Heidegger, it is impossible to say "the beyond of being" not only because thought installs a cleft between its statement and the condition of this statement but also, and simply, because "*es gibt kein Anderes als Sein.*" Every modification of the primordial logos can only be construed in a negative manner, that is, it will run into the problem of the lack (whether it lacks visibility, presence, etc.) simply because it is impossible to eliminate the idea of lack. It is impossible to eliminate the want of presence, precisely because everything that tries to "escape" or "overcome" the "*logos*" as "*legein ti*" will configure this escape in a privative manner, that is, as a non-appearing of that which, properly, ought to appear. Heidegger's account of this modification, of the absence of visibility with regard to the face, for instance, turns Levinas's question whether he had eliminated the idea of lack and the want of presence into a *rhetorical question,* which has to be answered in the negative: this absence of visibility still pertains to the world, and all other ways of making it signify from a "beyond" of being will be construed ontotheologically as a lack of visibility that is overcome from without (being). For Heidegger, the Levinasian face cannot attain to the not-appearing, to an invisibility sui generis, simply because its non-appearing would still have to be thought from out of the realm of the visible that appears: the face's invisibility would not differ from the invisibility proper to every object in the world. Its invisibility is not a sign of excess, but rather of the lack proper to every appearing (as when I have to constitute the back side of the table and make adumbrations of it). The "originary non-presence" would pertain here to the being and the event of the world. In short, for Heidegger, Levinas's construal of the saying without said would merely point to a refusal to let the world appear through speech: there is no disclosure that would not be a disclosure of world, because every modification of the "*logos*" will forever remain bound, even when "non-disclosing," to the finite world. Therefore, Levinas's modification of the "*logos*," as a "saying without a said," will, for Heidegger, nevertheless point in the direction of the "said," of the world and its finite properties.

Heidegger's account of the commonality of speech and world, this intwining of world and world, offers some important indications about our restriction to world. First, because of the intertwining of the "*tauton*" and the "*heteron,*" the possibility that one errs about being and beings is as essential as it would be to speak about these properly (and according to the later Heidegger and certainly Derrida even more essential). The possibility of deception and of erring therefore is co-given with being: to be is equal to be in default. Second, Heidegger, in a way, explains why even Binswanger's take on love remains restricted to being and why it cannot be anywhere else than being or in the world. There is no speech and no being that would not pertain to the world. Ontology, ethics, and love boil down to a speaking about and existing in a shared world, to a participation in the "conversation that humanity has with itself," and Binswanger's "detour of the world" is no detour at all: it is the only way ahead. Third, because the intertwining of the sameness and otherness and because the commonality of word and being is such that one cannot "jump over" being-in-the-world, the ontological greeting that Binswanger seeks to make clear *must* always be incarnated in and through the embracing of beings-in-the-world: there is no ontology that does not pass through the ontic. Here is how Binswanger could be aligned to Heidegger more than to Levinas. For the greeting in and of being cannot be elsewhere than, to use Levinas's words, in the said. All that is available and that we have access to are every so many presences that never attain to a full presence, every so many lacks without a *plenum*. But even if there is no clear and distinct way of seeing things, there is at least available to us still a way of seeing things, through speech and showing and sharing with one another: even if there is no "the" way of seeing things, we at least have "a" way of seeing things. This is why the shared facticity I pointed to, in Heidegger, must be extended to Binswanger's phenomenology of the salutation in being. Contra Levinas, the "to the other" of speech must be incarnated in the works and in the said, just as the (ontological) greeting is, though not contained, then at least conserved in ontic works and embraces.[34] But, both positively and negatively, the fact remains that such a commonality concerns what is most ultimate in and of being: it points to a sheer vocative that, in turn, points to a fundamental community of beings in being and in the world.

Of Being in Default in Philosophy of Religion

Tying these ontologies of lack together: the possibility of failure (Heidegger in *Being and Time*), the indecision of decision (Derrida), the irresolution of resolution, and the lack of love in the world (Binswanger's *nicht-wissende Wissen*), one may then ask what this might mean for our religious and spiritual condition. The first answer that comes to mind is that, especially in religious matters, one does not know about the ultimate. The lack of such knowledge is what gathers and opens onto others who, equally, share such a lack. It is here that the lack of being in default might give way to a joy and an affirmation, obviously, because it entails the joy of a humble recognition that no one really escapes such being in default. We all have an equal share of not-knowing.

It is here finally that we can turn to Heidegger's *Phenomenology of Religious Life*. It is well known that these early lectures on Saint Augustine and Saint Paul served somewhat as a prelude to *Being and Time*.[35] One can, however, find here some important indications for a contemporary Christianity—if I am allowed for a moment to speak from within Christianity—that would want to hold fast to a certain ignorance about salvation and redemption. This is what I would call here a "theological agnosticism": it is of God that *one knows nothing* (agnosticism) but it is just as well *of God* that one knows nothing (theological).

In his work, Heidegger describes how the early Christians held fast to such an ignorance, which was an ignorance about the exact nature of God's coming. They would not doubt the fact that "God will come" but confess their ignorance about the hour (which only God knows) and the mode of such a Second Coming. These early Christians, according to Heidegger, "lived" the certainty of this coming amid the uncertainty of the duration of this wait and the hope for God's parousia. Yet what Heidegger here and elsewhere laments[36] is the continuous attempt to safeguard the "When" of this coming. Such a safeguarding of redemption is, as I will show, remarkably close to how Heidegger in *Being and Time* understands the reverting of ready-to-hand to present-at-hand, with the difference that here it is our salvation that becomes *vorhanden*: it becomes a matter of instrumentalized, objective time. Redemption here is no longer dependent on "a how" and a way of life but becomes entirely a matter of the "When," and it is reduced to the time of clocks: if I do so and so before God's coming, I will certainly be redeemed.

This safeguarding of redemption, moreover, resembles the comportment of "the They" over and against death. Just as "they" fall in the world as some sort of "tranquilization" over and against death, so too the Christian safeguarding his and hers redemption knows not or no longer of any "reason for disturbance."[37] Such a tranquillization features in *Being and Time* as the "idle talk" about, and the "curiosity" of, the They for the "next big thing" through which "they" evade the question of one's finitude. This is why authenticity, for Heidegger, does not mean so much a *memento mori* of sorts, but rather already points to displacement and decentering of Dasein. A decentering (which would be Heidegger's version of a "positive failure" of Dasein to "assert" itself in being) through which the few years of being-in-the-world granted to us could be experienced as a favor or gift granted by being. "My" being and "my" time then appear not so much as a good to be appropriated but rather as somewhat of a "borrowed item." In this regard, I pointed to Houellebecq, who mentioned the Jewish saying "tonight is the night that your life will be reclaimed."

Something similar could finally, with Heidegger, be developed in a theology that does not shy away from the question of finitude and that, through the historicity of the event of the world, would dare to differentiate between what is merely historical and what is necessary. The similarities between Heidegger's analysis in *Being and Time* and *Phenomenology of Religious Life* are indeed daunting. The early Christians, for Heidegger, lived from and with the expectation that Christ would soon return. This return, and its concomitant temporality, is of such a peculiar kind that in a sense this "return" is always and already present even thought its precise "hour" is unknown, just as death in *Being and Time* is present in a "now" (or *Augenblick*) that, because of its ever-present possibility, spans the entirety of my life. This Second Coming, for these early Christians, served as the horizon out of which the Dasein of the Christian would appear: their "having become" Christian in a world that was quite hostile to Christianity made up for the entirety of their being. This being-there as being-Christian, their Dasein if you like, was nothing but the enduring of the wait and the vigil for God's coming.[38] Heidegger maintains that the ignorance about the hour of this parousia is essential for this experience of these early Christians and can in no way be interpreted as a foretaste of a certainty and redemption to come. This is also why Heidegger describes this faith as a "burden," just as "being" for the Dasein portrayed in *Being and Time* is a burden. This faith, for Heidegger, is always and already on the verge of despair, for it is always possible that I am unable to endure this wait and hold fast to this faith until "the last day."

Yet, and this is my point, Heidegger notes various possibilities for the tranquillization, if not sedation, of the uncertainty pertaining to this vigil, just as Dasein can always flee from death into the busy-ness of everyday preoccupations. In the case of the early Christians, the "hour" of God's coming, the time of salvation, soon turned into something present-at-hand, a matter of calculations and efficiency. The "hour" became part and parcel of "objective time." Its "now" was no longer a matter of the instant, but was postponed to the "end of time," just as death in *Being and Time* will surely happen to me sometime but is, first and foremost, something that will not happen now. This is what allowed the first Christians to "go on with" their lives as if nothing happened (and as if nothing will happen). Faith becomes present-to-hand: it so becomes more a matter of assent to this or that creed rather than a matter of living what one believes. The Christian, we would argue, flees from uncertainty as one flees from one's unredeemedness.[39]

As already noted, such a sedation of the ignorance and uncertainty regarding redemption, for Heidegger, most often takes place through ascertaining salvation. Yet one should note that such a critique of the assurances regarding salvation is certainly not foreign to the Catholic tradition. The Council of Trent, for instance, still knew of the "sin of presumption"—which was the Council's reaction to the Protestant "salvation by faith alone." This sin of presumption, then, is what one can call the theological version of Derrida's primacy of bad conscience. It states that whoever thinks that he or she will be saved is likely not to be saved. Obviously, this does not mean that such a false certainty with regard to redemption could not and will not occur in the Catholic tradition as well. Lacoste, for instance, has stated that the "liturgical experience," because of its emphasis on rituals and celebrations, always runs the risk of holding only God "in high regard" and so disregard one's neighbor.[40]

Heidegger, however, is critical of all instrumentalizations when it comes to the question of salvation and never neglects to point to the intimate bond between the Christian way of life and a possible redemption. One might legitimately argue that this bond is what put him on the track of the "existential analytic" that would become *Being and Time*. The exit-strategy toward an "inauthentic" Christianity for Heidegger seems to reside in a setting apart of the "wait for God" from the concrete and real unrest that disturbs the Christian. It therefore reveals itself first and foremost negatively, as the fear of being unable to endure the wait and of not being granted one's salvation. The sedation with regard to redemption, for Heidegger, mainly seems to consist in no longer realizing that the possibility of not being saved, of not being redeemed, pertains to me and me only and is so deferred to something that will happen to others. This is the reason why such an "inauthentic" Christianity judges others more frequently than it would bear the judgement on itself. The tranquillization, in Christianity, is of such a sort that it will strictly differentiate between those saved and those damned, where the first are the ones who assent to this or that and the latter do not. Nothing, in fact, is easier, one might say with Derrida, than to make an exception of oneself. The distinction between the "safe/saved" faith and the "unsafe/unsaved" faith here becomes a perfectly controllable "present-to-hand" distinction.

In this regard, it seems safer to hold onto to an ontological unredeemedness and be reluctant to all "ontic" exit-strategies. For such an unredeemedness might square well with the humbleness and the modesty that the phenomenology of finitude of this work prescribes. Such an ontological unredeemedness takes into account that the Christian—and this is what the Christian would *share* with the heathen—always and already is insufficiently Christian and is likely to be destined toward sin rather than to salvation. Salvation is, if it is, an uncertain business (if it would be a business). This is what the primacy of bad conscience means for theology: it recognizes that each and everyone, first and foremost, is "insufficiently Christian" and whoever thinks he or she is sufficiently Christian is likely to have strayed from the right path. This is why such an unredeemedness is wary of all historical and ontic figures of salvation that have been passed on to us, simply because, as one could note in Binswanger, the event of world might pass things on to us to which the tradition has no adequate response, and there is thus no need to substitute what is merely historical for what it is necessary.

This is also why such ontological unredeemedness seeks to recover the spiritual seriousness of (Christian) ethics. Such an ethics will endure the fact that one is always in default when it comes to the Christian reversal of values (as Caputo advances) and realize that, in all things theological, it is more likely to be in default *even against* being in default than the other way around. It humbly seeks recognition for the fact—although it resists and rebels against all ontic coagulations of redemption and against all illusionary assurances—that each and every person who attempts to be Christian is first and foremost insufficiently Christian and, at best, "faithful in an unfaithful way" (Pirjeri).

Positively, this, however, is exactly what the Christian shares with the pagan and what would make of the "pagan residue in Christianity" (Nancy) an advantage rather than a disadvantage. For it is such otherness that might precisely open up to other points of view that, in view of the commonality that is being, share more in common with us than they would be at a distance from our own. Yet, for reasons internal to Christianity, a sort of inversion of Pascal's wager is at issue here: as much as, for Pascal, the heathen has everything to gain from his or her conversion, so too the Christian, because of the ever-present possibility of not being saved, has everything to lose.

Again, one would be wrong to confuse this Christian version of the primacy of bad conscience with pessimism. For this work hopefully has shown that it is impossible to eradicate all instrumentalization when it comes to the question of the divine. The human being is likely to be in default against being in default. This is what our repeated reference to Paassilina's character Pirjeri, and our imagining Derrida as a natural ontotheologian, hopefully has shown. No one is able to avoid all instrumentalization (and so ontotheology) altogether. And yet it is this point that the Christian shares in common with the heathen and a beginning can be made with a dialogue between the various Christianities specifically and the various beliefs in general, so taking the "conversation of humanity with itself" seriously again. If all are "faithful in an unfaithful way," ourselves not even excluded, then one can have nothing but compassion for and mildness toward the other's point of view (and toward one's own). The task of theology, just as the task of the phenomenology of love, is indeed to include rather than to exclude, without ever being certain that one is oneself included when it comes to love and salvation. As the event of world, happening despite and even without myself, so too, perhaps, the event of salvation happens despite and unbeknownst to myself.

Notes

General Introduction: Toward A Contemporary Phenomenology of Religious Life

1. The first two concepts are from Christopher Watkin, *Difficult Atheism. Post-Theological Thinking in Alain Badiou, Jean-Luc Nancy and Quentin Meillassoux* (Edinburgh: Edinburgh University Press, 2011), e.g., pp. 46–47. For Hägglund, see his "The Challenge of Radical Atheism: A Response," in *The New Centennial Review* 9 (2009): 227–252, 228–229. See also John D. Caputo's review of Watkin's book online at *Notre Dame Philosophical Book Reviews* (June 10, 2012).

2. See Aaron Simmons and Stephen Minister (eds.), *Reexamining Deconstruction and Determinate Religion. Toward a Religion with Religion* (Duquesne: Duquesne University Press, 2012).

3. Caputo, *Deconstruction in a Nutshell. A Conversation with Jacques Derrida* (New York: Fordham University Press, 1997), p. 164.

4. Michael Naas, *Miracle and Machine. Jacques Derrida and the Two Sources of Religion, Science, and the Media* (New York: Fordham University Press, 2012), p. 352 n.17.

5. Ludwig Binswanger, *Grundformen und Erkenntnis des menschlichen Daseins*, in M. Herzog and H. J. Braun, *Ausgewählte Werke 2* (Heidelberg: Asanger Verlag, 1993), p. 6.

6. Cf. ibid., p. 110.

7. Ibid., pp. 218–219.

8. See ibid., pp. 347–348 and p. 384, respectively.

9. Ibid., p. 356.

10. Ibid., p. 229.

11. Ibid., pp. 367–368.

12. Ibid., p. 407.

13. Heidegger, *Einführung in die Phänomenologische Forschung* (Frankfurt a. Main: Klostermann, 2006), p. 226.

14. Hägglund, *Radical Atheism. Derrida and the Time of Life* (Stanford: Stanford University Press, 2008), p. 110 and p. 109, respectively.

15. Ibid., p. 96.

16. See Kevin Hart, "Without," in M. Zlomislic and N. DeRoo (eds.), *Cross and Khôra. Deconstruction and Ethics in the Work of John D. Caputo* (Eugene: Pickwick Publishers, 2010), pp. 80–108, p. 96. See also Caputo's response to Hart, pp. 109–117.

17. Caputo, "On Not Settling for an Abridged Edition of Postmodernism. Radical Hermeneutics as Radical Theology," in Simmons and Minister (eds.), *Reexamining Deconstruction*, pp. 271–353, pp. 292–293.

18. Ibid., p. 337. I italicize "no injury."

19. Hägglund, "The Radical Evil of Deconstruction," p. 144.

20. Cf. Caputo, "On Not Settling," p. 302.

21. For these quotes, see Caputo, "The Chance of Love. A Response to Olthuis," in *Cross and Khôra*, pp. 187–196, p. 193.

22. See Caputo, "On Not Settling," p. 342.

23. For Naas, see "An Atheism That (*Dieu merci!*) Still Leaves Something to Be Desired," in *The New Centennial Review* 9 (2009): pp. 45–68, p. 52. See also p. 53, where Naas rightly writes, "we need to give an account of this *compulsion*."

24. Caputo, *The Prayers and Tears of Jacques Derrida. Religion Without Religion* (Bloomington: Indiana University Press, 1997), p. xix, p. 122, and p. 334.

25. Jean-Luc Marion, *Being Given. Toward a Phenomenology of Givenness*, trans. J. Kosky (Stanford: Stanford University Press, 2002), p. 36.

26. Caputo, "The Return of Anti-Religion: From Radical Atheism to Radical Theology," in *Journal of Cultural and Religious Theory* 11 (2011): pp. 32–124, p. 47, and p. 124.

27. Nancy, *Dis-Enclosure. The Deconstruction of Christianity*, trans. B. Bergo, G. Malenfant, and M. B. Smith (New York: Fordham University Press, 2008), p. 102.

28. Hägglund, *Radical Atheism*, p. 133.

29. Derrida, "Faith and Knowledge. The Two Sources of 'Religion' at the Limits of Reason Alone," in G. Anidjar (ed.), *Acts of Religion* (London: Routledge, 2002), pp. 42–101, p. 84 n. 30. For a commentary, see Naas, *Miracle and Machine*, pp. 66–67, locating the "essence" of religion, the first source, in the erection of the unscathed, stemming from an experience of the unscathed of sorts, close to the experience of shame: the step back from something shameful, as when one does not want to be rendered impure. The second source would rather be "a milieu of the religious," "a kind of elementary faith [. . .] *before* any particular religion."

30. Hägglund seems to miss this point of Derrida entirely; see, however, Derrida, "Faith and Knowledge," p. 68, problematizing "the "proper and constant" usages" of the word religion that Benveniste tries to detect, while for Derrida these are precisely "chasms over which [this] great scholar walks with tranquil step": Benveniste *and* Hägglund, I would add, "presuppose thus an assured meaning of the word religion" (p. 73 n. 22).

31. See Ibid., p. 69, p. 76, p. 90, p. 93, p. 112, p. 116, p. 118, and so on and so forth: the list is not exhaustive!

32. See especially Derrida, *On Touching—Jean-Luc Nancy*, trans. C. Irizarry (Stanford: Stanford University Press, 2005), pp. 277–278, p. 199.

33. Ibid., p. 220mod., italics in last sentence are mine. One should not, of course, forget Derrida's deconstructions of Heidegger as examples of a discourse *being deconstructed by* Christian thought and traditions; see *Of Spirit. Heidegger and the Question*, trans. G. Bennington and R. Bowlby (Chicago: University of Chicago Press, 1989), esp. pp. 109–113.

34. See Derrida, *Rogues. Two Essays on Reason*, trans. P.-A. Brault and M. Naas (Stanford: Stanford University Press, 2005), p. 110 and *Of Grammatology*, trans. G. Spivak (Baltimore: John Hopkins University Press, 1997), p. 323 n. 3; on the "theological prejudices" of metaphysics amounting to, for Caputo, a "theology of atheism," see Caputo, "The Return of Anti-Religion," p. 117.

35. Derrida, *On Touching*, p. 279.

36. Ibid., p. 279.

37. Caputo, *On Religion* (London: Routledge, 2001), p. 31 and p. 117.

38. Derrida, *The Animal That Therefore I Am*, trans. M. Millet (New York: Fordham University Press, 2008), p. 47.

39. Derrida, "Faith and Knowledge," p. 68.

40. Hägglund, *Radical Atheism*, p. 126.

41. See, respectively, ibid., p. 128 quoting Derrida's *Rogues*, p. 114.

42. Ibid., p. 128, again quoting *Rogues*, p. 114.

43. Ibid., pp. 128–129, quoting Derrida's "Dead Man Running: Salut, Salut," in *Negotiations: Interventions and Interviews, 1971–2001* (Stanford: Stanford University Press, 2002), pp. 257–292, p. 258.

44. Derrida, *Rogues*, p. 114.

45. Ibid., p. 114.

46. Hägglund, *Radical Atheism*, p. 97.

47. Levinas, *Otherwise Than Being, or Beyond Essence*, trans. A. Lingis (Duquesne: Duquesne University Press, 2002), p. 92, "under the eye of another, I remain an unattackable subject in respect."

48. See Christina Gschwandtner, *Postmodern Apologetics? Arguments for God in Contemporary Philosophy* (New York: Fordham University Press, 2013).

49. One might turn to Derrida for support here: "the question of the living and of the living animal. For me that will always have been the most important and decisive question," *The Animal*, p. 34.

50. I have developed these "moments" in *Ontotheological Turnings?*, pp. 25ff.

51. One can argue that this stress on uncertainty and anxiety was in direct consequence of Heidegger's conception of "transcendental history," for which Descartes's drive toward certainty was a successor of Aquinas' craving for the *bonum*: just as, for Descartes, certainty was the primal transcendental virtue—it had to be erected always and everywhere—just so, for Aquinas, it needed to be shown that the *bonum* was always and already there, even conquering evil. Recall that, for Heidegger, Aquinas was the first modern thinker. Note, too, that what will separate Heidegger from Derrida here is that whereas the former clings to a "transcendental history," in which it is "being" that is distributed (permanently) to all the diverse epochs (differently), for the latter no such transcendental vantage point is to be found and one needs to settle for a "non-empirical historicity," therefore a "transcendental"

historicity. The difference is immense: for Derrida, no "grand story" of being can therefore be written—there will always be some matter, some material substrate that does not lend itself to being signified. For Derrida, see *Edmund Husserl's Origin of Geometry. An Introduction,* trans. J. P. Leavey (London: University of Nebraska Press, 1989), p. 42 and p. 107. *On Touching* speaks in this regard of a "historicity of transcendental archifacticity," p. 243.

52. It is to be noted that Heidegger uses *Beruhigung,* both for the comportment of "the they" toward death as for the comportment of the metaphysical tradition against uncertainty and historicity, the latter trying to stabilize and make permanent that which cannot, in any way, be made permanent or stable. This is what the question of "foundation," improperly, amounts to in ontotheological endeavors. Note too that this would lend support to the link Schürmann sees between the metaphysical tradition and his existential analytic of ultimates. For Heidegger, see *Being and Time,* trans. J. Macquarrie and E. Robinson (San Francisco: Harper and Row, 1962), p. 298 and *Einführung in die phänomenologische Forschung,* p. 226 on the "Sorge der Beruhigung."

53. Heidegger, *Being and Time,* p. 151 and p. 150, respectively.

54. Ibid., p 164.

55. Ibid., p. 217.

56. Ibid., p. 213.

57. Ibid., p. 232.

58. Ibid., p. 340.

59. See, for this "breakdown" of Dasein, especially ibid., p. 188, p. 213, p. 218, and 222 on "the possibility of genuinely foundering." Compare also with Heidegger's *own* admissions of such foundering on p. 276 and p. 284, "once again the attempt to make Dasein's being-a-whole accessible [. . .] *has broken down."*

60. François Raffoul, *A chaque fois mien. Heidegger et la question du sujet* (Paris: Galilée, 2004).

61. Heidegger, *Being and Time,* p. 308.

62. Ibid., p. 344.

63. Ibid., p. 344.

64. I am alluding to ibid., p. 173, "the pure "that it is" shows itself, but the "whence" and the "whither" remain in darkness."

65. Ibid., p. 345.

Chapter 1. Anarchistic Tendencies in Contemporary Philosophy

1. Reiner Schürmann, *Heidegger on Being and Acting. From Principles to Anarchy,* trans. C.-M. Gros (Bloomington: Indiana University Press, 1987), p. 191.

2. Reginald Lilly, "The Topology of *Des hégémonies brisées,"* in *Research in Phenomenology* 28 (1998): 226–242, p. 231.

3. Schürmann, *Heidegger on Being and Acting,* p. 182.

4. Ibid., p. 38.

5. Schürmann, *Broken Hegemonies*, trans. R. Lilly (Bloomington: Indiana University Press, 2003), p. 345.

6. Schürmann, *Heidegger on Being and Acting*, p. 155.

7. Peyman Vahabzadeh, "Review of *Broken Hegemonies*," in *Journal for Cultural and Religious Theory* 5 (2004): 51–56, p. 55.

8. Schürmann, *Broken Hegemonies*, p. 629.

9. See also Schürmann, *Broken Hegemonies*, p. 35, "the order established by hegemonic fantasms *is conquered* each time. By what? By the nameless abyss where we are devoured by negative experience (the experience of the unjustifiable, of evil, [. . .] and of death. Fantasmic consolations and consolidations work against that experience."

10. Schürmann, *Broken Hegemonies*, p. 624.

11. Schürmann, *Heidegger on Being and Acting*, p. 106.

12. Ibid., p. 197. Italics are mine.

13. Respectively, Schürmann, *Heidegger on Being and Acting*, p. 204, p. 252, and p. 226.

14. Ibid., p. 287.

15. Ibid., p. 237.

16. Ibid., pp. 236–245.

17. Ibid., p. 237 and p. 238.

18. Ibid., pp. 238–239.

19. See, for instance, Marion, *Being Given. Toward A Phenomenology of Givenness*, trans. J. Kosky (Stanford: Stanford University Press, 2002), pp. 282–319, esp. pp. 306–307, where the primacy of praxis gives way to a priority of a supposedly extra-moral "willing" over "thinking," which is a reversal of the medieval adage stating that "acting follows being." Consider also Marion's contention that it is no longer a matter of representational thinking, but of "aiming in the direction of . . . of relating to . . . of comporting oneself toward . . . of reckoning with . . ." whatever gives itself in his *In Excess. Studies of Saturated Phenomena*, trans. R. Horner and V. Berraud (New York: Fordham University Press, 2002), pp. 144–145. For Levinas, see *Otherwise Than Being*, pp. 144–153, esp. p. 149mod. "the appeal is heard in the response."

20. See also Levinas, *Totality and Infinity. An Essay on Exteriority*, trans. A. Lingis (Duquesne: Duquesne University Press, 2002), p. 154: "How would a total reflection be allowed [to] a being that never becomes the bare fact of existing, and whose existence is life, that is, life from something?" Life from something, that is, according to Levinas's thesis of enjoyment as concrete as the drinks that we drink, the food we eat, and the men and women we entertain and encounter in our houses. Consider also the anti-metaphysical (yet theological) statement that "life is not comprehensible simply as a diminution, a fall [. . .]. The individual and the personal are necessary for Infinity to be able to be produced as infinite," Levinas, *Totality and Infinity*, p. 218. Note finally that Marion, however, at one point claims to have found such a priority of praxis in Levinas's thought. Cf. Marion, *Being Given*, p. 287 and Marion, *Reduction and Givenness. Investigations of Husserl, Heidegger, and*

Phenomenology, trans. T.A. Carlson (Evanston, IL: Northwestern University Press, 1998), pp. 185–186.

21. See for instance, Levinas, *Otherwise Than Being*, p. 144: "[Sincerity] is not an act or a movement, or any sort of cultural gesture." In Heidegger, the call of conscience opens onto the condition (?) of "possibility of taking action" precisely because this call "fails to give any [. . .] 'practical' injunction" or maxim, see Heidegger, *Being and Time*, pp. 340–341. Though Levinas would perhaps agree with the ontological nature of such a practical a priori, it remains to be considered whether he would concur with the extra-moral sense Marion tries to give to it; see Marion, *Being Given*, p. 314, "If this willing can abandon the given to itself, [this] abandon does not belong to the moral [. . .] disposition."

22. Schürmann, *Heidegger on Being and Acting*, p. 257.
23. Ibid., p. 57.
24. Ibid., p. 160.
25. Ibid., p. 257.
26. Ibid., p. 211.
27. Ibid., p. 211.
28. Ibid., p. 213.
29. Ibid., p. 270.
30. Ibid., p. 258.
31. Ibid., p. 57. This sobering up is best contrasted with the optimism of theology; see ibid., p. 159: "Heideggerian 'philosophy' would oppose, point for point, all that the theologizing readings praise in it: instead of Subject of history, the raw positivity and the irreducible contingency of facts; instead of a Doctrine, inventory."
32. Ibid., p. 57.
33. Heidegger, *Plato's Sophist*, trans. R. Rojcewicz and A. Schuwer (Bloomington: Indiana University Press, 1997), p. 415, translation modified because the German has, respectively, "der 'logos' [. . .] hat zunächst vorgegeben eine unabgehobene Einheit eines Seienden," and "die ganze vorliegende [. . .] Gegebenheit." See Heidegger, *Plato's Sophistes* (Frankfurt a. M.: Vittorio Klostermann, 1992), pp. 599–600.
34. Schürmann, *Heidegger on Being and Acting*, p. 76.
35. See also ibid., p. 153, "the unity does not rest on any ground, endowed with permanence, be it substantive or subjective."
36. Ibid., p. 76.
37. Ibid., p. 273.
38. Ibid., p. 158.
39. Ibid., p. 159.
40. Ibid., p. 158. See also Schürmann's reading of this into Heidegger's *Contributions to Philosophy*, in Schürmann, *Broken Hegemonies*, p. 519.
41. The expression is taken from Véronique-Marion Voti, *Epochal Discordance. Hölderlin's Philosophy of Tragedy* (Albany: State University of New York, 2006).
42. *Heidegger on Being and Acting*, p. 25 and p. 59.
43. Ibid., respectively p. 47 and p. 59.

44. Heidegger, *Being and Time*, p. 173.
45. Schürmann, *Heidegger on Being and Acting*, p. 281.
46. Ibid., p. 84.
47. Ibid., p. 242.
48. Ibid., p. 93.
49. In this respect, the parallel Schürmann draws between the Heideggerian "step back" and the phenomenological reduction is noteworthy: not only is releasement or letting-be "the properly phenomenological attitude" (ibid., p. 212) but the phenomenological reduction is also the method according to which the "double step backwards" "from the situated or manifest entities toward their site [then] to the self-situating, the self-manifesting as such" (Ibid., 19–20, also 79–81) is possible. Because it is a form of the phenomenological reduction, Lilly's statement that "one finds no delineated method" in Schürmann's work thus has to be nuanced; see Lilly, "The Topology of *Des hégémonies brisées*," p. 230.
50. Schürmann, *Heidegger on Being and Acting*, p. 281.
51. Ibid., pp. 321–322.
52. Ibid., p. 148.
53. Levinas, *Totality and Infinity*, p. 294.
54. Levinas, *Time and the Other*, trans. R. A. Cohen (Pittsburg: Duquesne University Press, 1987), respectively p. 42 and p. 75.
55. This duality appears, for instance, in Levinas's description of solitude in Levinas, *Existence and Existents*, trans. A. Lingis (Pittsburgh: Duquesne University Press, 2001), p. 90: "The solitude of a subject is more than the isolation of a being or the unity of an object. It is, as it were, a dual solitude; this other than me accompanies the ego like a shadow."
56. Levinas, *Totality and Infinity*, p. 294.
57. Ibid., p. 35.
58. Ibid., p. 294.
59. Schürmann, *Heidegger on Being and Acting*, p. 72.
60. I am alluding here to Levinas's statement that the manifestation of the face "consists in a being telling itself to us independently of every position we would have taken in its regard," Levinas, *Totality and Infinity*, p. 65.
61. Derrida, "Violence and Metaphysics. An Essay on the Thought of Emmanuel Levinas," in *Writing and Difference*, trans. A. Bass (Chicago: University of Chicago Press, 1978), pp. 79–153; respectively, p. 142 and p. 148.
62. Levinas, *Totality and Infinity*, p. 293.
63. Derrida, "Violence and Metaphysics," p. 143.
64. See, for this Levinas, *Otherwise Than Being*, p. 194 and also Miguel Abensour, "Savage Democracy and 'Principle of Anarchy,'" in *Philosophy and Social Criticism* 28 (2002): 703–726, p. 723.
65. Levinas, *God, Death, and Time*, trans. B. Bergo (Stanford: Stanford University Press, 2000), p. 193. Echoed in Levinas, *Otherwise Than Being*, 147, "the anarchic infinite"
66. Levinas, *Otherwise Than Being*, pp. 122–123.

67. Ibid., p. 151.
68. Levinas, *Totality and Infinity*, p. 214.
69. Levinas, *Otherwise Than Being*, p. 122 and p. 152.
70. Levinas, *Totality and Infinity*, p. 290 and Schürmann, *Heidegger on Being and Acting*, p. 346.
71. Levinas, *Otherwise Than Being*, p. 59.
72. Abensour, "Savage Democracy" and "Principle of Anarchy," p. 723.
73. Jacques Rolland edited and annotated the French edition of *God, Death, and Time*. These notes are translated in the English edition as well; see Levinas, *God, Death, and Time*, 277 n. 1 and 283 n. 7.
74. Jacques Derrida, *Margins of Philosophy*, trans. A. Bass (Chicago: University of Chicago Press, 1982), p. 135 cited by Schürmann, *Heidegger on Being and Acting*, p. 362 and *Broken Hegemonies*, p. 14. Schürmann cites another passage in which Derrida presumes to go "beyond" metaphysics, see Schürmann, *Heidegger on Being and Acting*, p. 311, where Schürmann quotes Derrida, *Of Grammatology*, p. 4 stating that "the world that is ineluctably to come and which proclaims itself at present, beyond the closure."
75. Schürmann, *Broken Hegemonies*, p. 14 and p. 634.
76. Schürmann, *Heidegger on Being and Acting*, p. 371.
77. Dominique Janicaud, "Riveted to a Monstrous Site. Reiner Schürmann's Reading of Heidegger's *Beiträge*," in *Graduate Faculty Philosophy Journal* 19 (1997): 287–297, p. 293.
78. Schürmann, *Heidegger on Being and Acting*, p. 241 and p. 270.
79. Derrida, "History of the Lie. Prolegomena," in *Graduate Faculty Philosophy Journal* 19 (1997): 129–161, pp. 156–157.
80. Schürmann, *Heidegger on Being and Acting*, p. 360.
81. See for this Schürmann, *Heidegger on Being and Acting*, pp. 352–353 and pp. 361–362. Schürmann cites Derrida, *Margins of Philosophy*, p. 22, p. 132, p. 135, and p. 281.
82. In this sense, Schürmann's insights might nowadays most forcefully be perpetuated by Nancy, who, on several occasions, has shown himself to be sympathetic toward Schürmann's anarchistic project. A few passages in Nancy's work are noteworthy: Nancy, *The Experience of Freedom*, trans. B. McDonald (Stanford: Stanford University Press, 1993), p. 13 and p. 30 (on the anarchy of existence) and p. 187 (on his "community" with Schürmann); *Être Singulier Pluriel* (Paris: Galilée, 1996), p. 69 (again: anarchy). See also Lorenzo Fabbri, "Philosophy as Chance. An Interview with Jean-Luc Nancy," in *Critical Inquiry* 33 (2007) 427–440, p. 435: "one must reinterrogate from top to bottom the theme of the 'arche' in general—the an-archy of the 'arche,' in the sense that Reiner Schürmann spoke of a principle of anarchy."
83. See Schürmann, *Heidegger on Being and Acting*, p. 362 and Derrida, *Writing and Difference*, p. 281.
84. Schürmann, *Broken Hegemonies*, p. 626.

85. Rodolphe Gasché, "Hegemonic Fantasms," in *Research in Phenomenology* 35 (2005) 311–326, p. 320 and p. 323.
86. Ibid., p. 315.
87. Ibid., p. 325.
88. Schürmann, *Broken Hegemonies*, pp. 624–625.
89. Derrida, "History of the Lie," p. 154.
90. For Rolland's argument concerning the Levinasian without "principle," see Levinas, *God, Death, and Time*, p. 283: "Levinas confirms the *anarchists'* sense of anarchy. We should not forget, in effect, that 'they are without principle' was Stalin's fundamental charge against those situated to his left." I take the second point from Mitchell Verter's essay "The Anarchism of the Other Person," in Nathan J. Jun and Shane Wahl (eds.), *New Perspectives on Anarchism* (Plymouth: Lexington Books, 2010), pp. 67–83, which shows Levinas's meditation on the "revolution" of 1968 in Paris.
91. Schürmann, *Heidegger on Being and Acting*, 91 and *Broken Hegemonies*, p. 679.
92. Schürmann, *Broken Hegemonies*, pp. 523–528.
93. Schürmann, *Heidegger on Being and Acting*, p. 182. This passage echoes *Heidegger on Being and Acting*, p. 35, where Schürmann, while pointing to the public dimension of the "principle" of an epoch, notes that "not all cultural facts have an equally revelatory value. For Heidegger, the most revealing traces of past historical fields are preserved in philosophical works."

Chapter 2: What Comes after Christianity?

1. Jean-Luc Nancy, *Le sens du monde* (Paris: Galilée, 1992), p. 91. Nancy's earliest confrontation with religion is his "Of Divine Places," in *The Inoperative Community* (Minneapolis: University of Minnesota Press, 2006), trans. M. Holland, pp. 110–150. This text was first published in 1985.
2. Nancy, *La communauté désœuvrée* (Paris: Christian Bourgois, 2004), p. 222.
3. Nancy, *Being Singular Plural*, trans. R. D. Richardson and A. E. O'Byrne (Stanford: Stanford University Press, 2000), p. 10.
4. Nancy, *Dis-Enclosure*, p. 24, trans. mod., since the French has "le monothéisme contrarie le régime du principe . . ."; see Nancy, *La Déclosion. Déconstruction du christianisme* (Paris: Galilée, 2005), p. 39. "Principle" most likely refers to Schürmann's thought. Nancy uses monotheism and Christianity interchangeably, although he most often prefers to speak of the latter; see *Dis-Enclosure*, p. 33. Helpful in this regard are Nancy's definitions of the world religions in "Of Divine Places," in *The Inoperative Community* (Minneapolis: University of Minnesota Press, 2006), pp. 110–150, p. 147.
5. Nancy, *Dis-Enclosure*, p. 141 and p. 149. See also Nancy, *Le sens du monde* (Paris: Galilée, 1993), p. 91 n. 1.

6. Ibid., pp. 142–143.
7. Nancy, *The Creation of the World* or *Globalization*, trans. F. Raffoul and D. Pettigrew (Albany: State University of New York Press, 2007), p. 41.
8. Ibid., p. 123 n. 24.
9. Nancy, *Being Singular Plural*, p. 17.
10. The expression is Schürmann's, see *Heidegger on Being and Acting*, p. 197.
11. Nancy, *The Creation of the World*, p. 71.
12. Nancy, *Noli me tangere. On the Raising of the Body*, trans. S. Clift, P.-A. Brault, and M. Naas (New York: Fordham University Press, 2008), p. 14. For Nancy, see also *La visitation (de la peinture chrétienne)* (Paris: Galilée, 2001), p. 44ff and also *Dis-Enclosure*, p. 144. For Derrida, see *On Touching*, pp. 100–103.
13. Nancy, *Dis-Enclosure*, p. 39mod.
14. Nancy, *Being Singular Plural*, p. 26 and p. 204 n. 81, respectively.
15. Nancy, *The Creation of the World or Globalization*, p. 73.
16. Heidegger, *Being and Time*, p. 155.
17. The most lucid entry into this debate between Heidegger and Nancy is the latter's "The Being-with of Being-there," in *Continental Philosophical Review* 41 (2008): 1–15. One should note, however, that Heidegger has rejected this interpretation of his thinking, which always leans to a perhaps too straightforward incorporation of his thought into National Socialism; see his *Parmenides*, trans. A. Schuwer and R. Rojcewicz (Bloomington, Indiana University Press, 1992), p. 137, where Heidegger indicates that such a conception of the people ("*Volk*") rests on an entirely metaphysical understanding of subjectivity. Nancy's counterargument might be *A Finite Thinking* (Stanford: Stanford University Press, 2003), p. 184, stating that whenever a guarding of the open is needed, emphasis will sooner or later be on the quality of the guardians rather than on that which is to be guarded.
18. Nancy, *Being Singular Plural*, pp. 5–10.
19. Nancy states that "it is too contemptuous to represent humanity to oneself as though the immense majority of our peers [misunderstood] the intractable real that is dying"; see Nancy, *Dis-enclosure*, p. 102. Such a moralizing interpretation of *Being and Time* would state that whereas "inauthentic" Dasein would know not of death, "authentic" Dasein would have the courage to face death. Such an interpretation is, however, not entirely correct, see for this Heidegger, *Being and Time*, pp. 298–299, which states that "the 'They,'" although (in fact: precisely because it is) fleeing for death, *already* knows about Being-toward-death.
20. For Nancy's most extensive confrontation with Levinas, see "Hors tout," in D. Cohen-Levinas and B. Clément, *Emmanuel Levinas et les territoires de pensée* (Paris: PUF, 2007), pp. 382–392.
21. See "'L'éthique originaire' de Heidegger," in Nancy, *La pensée dérobée* (Paris: Galilée, 2001), pp. 85–114.
22. Nancy, *Being Singular Plural*, p. 11, italics are Nancy's.
23. Levinas, *Totality and Infinity*, p. 173 and p. 172, respectively.
24. See for this Nancy, *Being Singular Plural*, pp. 17–18, also p. 76.
25. Derrida, "Violence and Metaphysics," p. 127.

26. Nancy, *Being Singular Plural*, p. 43. Nancy's italics.

27. See Nancy, *Being Singular Plural*, p. 31 and also p. 66. In this regard, it is important to note that Nancy names Bataille here as formative for his thought; see Nancy, "'Our World': An Interview," in *Angelaki* 8 (2003) 43–54, p. 45: "the impossibility of a meaning "for one alone" (Bataille). This insight is also fundamental to Levinas's thought, see, for instance, his *Totality and Infinity*, p. 100mod., "the explanation of a thought can only happen among two." The debate between Levinas and Nancy thus seems to be centered on just how many others are necessary to explain a thought, for whereas Levinas would stick to "only two," Nancy, perhaps, would say "all others." In this sense, the debate between Nancy and Levinas repeats the one between Sartre and Merleau-Ponty; see Maurice Merleau-Ponty, *The Visible and the Invisible*, trans. A. Lingis (Evanston, IL: Northwestern University Press, 1968), pp. 78–85, esp. 81 n. 14: "Perhaps it even would be necessary to [. . .] say that the problem of *the* other is a particular case of the problem of others, since the relation with someone is always mediated by the relationship with third parties."

28. Compare Nancy, *Dis-Enclosure*, pp. 142–143.

29. Ibid., p. 136 and p. 177 n. 15.

30. See Heidegger, *Letter on Humanism*, in D. F. Krell (ed.), *Basic Writings* (London: Routledge, 1993), pp. 213–265, pp. 233–234. For Nancy on this height, see *Dis-Enclosure*, p. 19 and p. 28. Also *Being Singular Plural*, p. 70mod.: "we are not up to the height of the we." One might even contrast Levinas's statement that "by virtue of the human body raised upwards, [it is] committed in the direction of height" with Nancy's thinking of the "raising" of the body, which simply (?) opposes the verticality of the human body with the horizontality of the dead; see especially *Noli me tangere*, pp. 17–18. The raised body is, for Nancy, the body of the one for whom the boundary between life and death has been blurred; that is, the one who "sees life in death because [he or she] has seen death in life" (42) and is still "standing upright" (18) while knowing that his or her existence is nothing but the lament for and the unrest of "crossing through life for nothing," see *Dis-Enclosure*, p. 103. Citation of Levinas, is *Totality and Infinity*, p. 117.

31. Nancy, *Dis-Enclosure*, p. 138 and *The Experience of Freedom*, trans. B. Macdonald (Stanford: Stanford University Press, 1993), p. 71.

32. Nancy, *Noli me tangere*, p. 48.

33. Nancy, *The Creation of the World*, p. 60 and pp. 68–69.

34. Nancy, *Dis-Enclosure*, p. 10.

35. See Nancy, *The Creation of the World*, pp. 60–61. See also Ian James, *The Fragmentary Demand. An Introduction to the Philosophy of Jean-Luc Nancy* (Stanford: Stanford University Press, 2006), pp. 235–236 and Raffoul's and Pettigrew's lucid introduction in Nancy, *The Creation of the World*, p. 25.

36. Nancy, *The Creation of the World*, pp. 60–61.

37. For this difference between "sense" and "signification," see Martta Heikkilä, *At the Limits of Presentation. Coming into Presence and Its Aesthetic Relevance in Jean-Luc Nancy's Philosophy* (Frankfurt: Peter Lang, 2008), pp. 33–34 and p. 159.

38. See also Ignaas Devisch et al. (eds.), *Re-treating Religion. Deconstructing Christianity with Jean-Luc Nancy* (New York: Fordham University Press, 2012).

39. Nancy, *Dis-Enclosure*, p. 30. See also his *Adoration. The Deconstruction of Christianity*, II, trans. J. McKeane (New York: Fordham University Press, 2013), pp. 18–20.

40. Ibid., p. 143.

41. Ibid., p. 142.

42. Ibid., p. 71.

43. Ibid., p. 10.

44. Ibid., p. 144.

45. Ibid., p. 148.

46. Nancy, *Noli me tangere*, p. 108 n. 4.

47. See for this Nancy, *Dis-Enclosure*, pp. 23–26.

48. See for this also Watkin, *Difficult Atheism*, p. 116.

49. Nancy, *Dis-Enclosure*, p. 34.

50. See for instance *Gaudium et Spes*, no. 41: "[The Church] knows that man is constantly worked upon by God's spirit, and hence can never be altogether indifferent to the problems of religion."

51. Cf. Hans Blumenberg, *The Legitimacy of the Modern Age*, trans. R. Wallace (Massachusetts: MIT Press, 1985), pp. 65–75.

52. Nancy, *The Creation of the World*, p. 44 and p. 51. Also *Adoration*, pp. 44–45.

53. See Nancy, *The Creation of the World*, p. 44.

54. Nancy, *Dis-Enclosure*, p. 77.

55. Ibid., pp. 23–25 and pp. 147–148.

56. Ibid., p. 31.

57. Cf. ibid., p. 140.

58. Ibid., p. 34.

59. Nancy, "Of Divine Places," p. 113.

60. Ibid., p. 112–113. Next quote is p. 120.

61. Nancy, *The Creation of the World*, pp. 50–51, p. 120 n.23 and also Nancy, *Dis-Enclosure*, p. 18 and p. 88.

62. Nancy, *Dis-Enclosure*, p. 17.

63. Nancy, *Dis-Enclosure*, p. 18.

64. Nancy, *The Gravity of Thought*, trans. F. Raffoul and G. Recco (Atlantic Highlands, NJ: Humanities Press, 1993), p. 48. This end of significations likewise dawns upon us as a task; see p. 67: "there will certainly be other significations, other tasks than signification. But to discover them we must first make ourselves capable of wondering about this: that signification had a history, that this history has been completed, that this completion is an event, and that we are already, whether we know it or not, whether we want it or not, engaged by meaning and in the meaning of what happens to us in this way."

65. Nancy, *The Gravity of Thought*, p. 63.

66. Citation is Heidegger, *Being and Time*, p. 129. For ready-to hand beings, see *Being and Time*, pp. 95–122.

67. Nancy, *La communauté désœuvrée* (Paris, Christian Bourgois, 2004), p. 231, taken from "De l'être en commun," a text not taken up in the English translation.

68. Nancy elaborates on this in *The Experience of Freedom*, p. 87, p. 89, and pp. 102–103; *The Creation of the World*, p. 49; *Being Singular Plural*, p. 55 and p. 76.

69. Nancy, *Being Singular Plural*, p. 83 and *The Experience of Freedom*, p. 103.

70. See Heidegger, *The Fundamental Concepts of Metaphysics. World. Finitude, Solitude*, trans. W. McNeill and N. Walker (Bloomington: Indiana University Press, 1995), pp. 176–178 and pp. 196–199. Nancy comments on this in *Le sens du monde*, p. 92 and pp. 99–104.

71. Nancy, *Le sens du monde*, p. 100.

72. Nancy, *Being Singular Plural*, p. 118.

73. Nancy, *The Creation of the World*, p. 73.

74. For Nancy on this distinction, see his commentary on Hegel's distinction between *Geschehen* and *Geschichte* in *Being Singular Plural*, pp. 161–165. For Schürmann, see *Heidegger on Being and Acting*, p. 76 and p. 273. For this distinction in Heidegger, see e.g. *Parmenides*, p. 72.

75. Derrida, *On Touching*, p. 262.

76. Nancy, *Being Singular Plural*, p. 95.

77. Cf. ibid., pp. 94–95.

78. Nancy, *Dis-Enclosure*, p. 34.

79. Derrida, *On Touching*, p. 59 and also p. 64.

80. Nancy, *The Creation of the World*, pp. 60–61 and *Dis-Enclosure*, p. 149 and p. 217.

81. For Derrida, on a "non-empirical historicity," therefore a "transcendental" historicity, see again his *Introduction to Husserl's Origin of Geometry*, p. 42 and p. 107. *On Touching* speaks in this regard of a "historicity of transcendental archifacticity," p. 243.

82. Derrida, *On Touching*, p. 220 and p. 244.

83. Nancy, *Dis-Enclosure*, p. 10mod.

84. Ibid., p. 176 n.12. Compare with Nancy, *The Creation of the World*, p. 40, pp. 46–47, and *Dis-Enclosure*, pp. 75–80.

85. Nancy, *Being Singular Plural*, p. 168. See also *The Creation of the World*, p. 65.

86. Nancy, *Dis-Enclosure*, p. 62.

87. Ibid., p. 66–67.

88. Ibid., p. 67. Nancy is here quoting Granel's "Far from Substance. Whither and to What Point?" which is taken up as an appendix to *Dis-Enclosure*, pp. 163–174.

89. Ibid., p. 86 and p. 110, respectively. For Heidegger, see pp. 104–105. Nancy might be right here with likening Levinas to Heidegger, for has not Levinas written that the enigma of the alternation of meaning—"the" otherwise than being

that always can be interpreted as (a) mere being—"is the very pivot of revelation, of its *blinking light*"?, see Levinas, *Otherwise Than Being*, p. 154, my italics. See also Derrida, *Introduction Husserl's Origin of Geometry*, p. 149: "the Absolute is Passage," not the stable and constant presence of a highest being, but rather the coming and going of days and nights, for the time of a life: of a world that worlds for all of us (if only for a while).

90. Ibid., p. 113.
91. Ibid., p. 114, translation modified.
92. Ibid., p. 111.
93. Ibid., p. 72, last line is again citing Granel. Nancy goes on: "God [. . .] empties himself of substance and the divine [. . .] becomes the measure of the dividing of light and shadow, of the seeing and the visible."
94. Nancy, *Being Singular Plural*, p. 16, translation modified.
95. Nancy, *Dis-Enclosure*, pp. 24–25, translation modified.
96. See for Augustine's interpretation, for instance, Marion's account in *In the Self's Place. The Approach of Saint Augustine*, trans. J. Kosky (Stanford: Stanford University Press, 2012), pp. 243–249. A difference between Nancy's account of *creatio ex nihilo* and Augustine's *de nihilo*, however, is that Nancy argues that no supreme being could incarnate or assume, so to say, the being of the withdrawal or of the retreat and its nothingness, whereas Augustine and Marion need to take on the strange position that "the created *is* its nothingness [because] God gives nothingness to it." See for this Marion, *In the Self's Place*, p. 246.
97. Nancy, *Noli me tangere*, p. 14.
98. Ibid., p. 15.
99. Ibid., p. 28mod.
100. Ibid., p. 28.
101. Ibid., p. 46.
102. Ibid., p. 45mod.
103. Ibid., pp. 47–48.
104. See for this Nancy, *Dis-Enclosure*, pp. 124–125.
105. Ibid., pp. 126–128, e.g., p. 127, "Sex [. . .] is the sense of the senses."
106. Ibid., p. 54.
107. Ibid., p. 48.
108. Ibid., p. 96.
109. Nancy, *Adoration*, p. 92mod.
110. Ibid., p. 116 n.28, trans. mod.
111. Derrida, *On Touching*, p. 269.
112. Nancy, *The Creation of the World*, p. 61 and also p. 47.
113. Nancy, *Being Singular Plural*, p. 140.
114. Nancy, *Dis-Enclosure*, pp. 159–160.
115. Ibid., p. 160 and p. 161.
116. Ibid., p. 161.
117. Nancy, *The Creation of the World*, p. 1.
118. Derrida, *On Touching*, p. 220.

119. See the metaphors Nancy employs in *Dis-Enclosure*, p. 65.
120. Ibid., p. 9.
121. See Derrida, *On Touching*, p. 310, "'to you,' Jean-Luc Nancy, "a benediction without any hope for salvation [. . .]. Just *salut* without salvation."
122. Ibid., p. 181.
123. Ibid., p. 253.
124. Ibid., p. 129.
125. Ibid., p. 288.
126. This is also the reason why Derrida reproaches Nancy for the very same thing for which he once criticized Levinas: empiricism. See Derrida, "Violence and Metaphysics," pp. 151–153. The question of empiricism and realism pops up regularly in *On Touching*; see p. 46, pp. 116–117, but esp. p. 287. Derrida nuances his "reproach," however, at p. 307.
127. Derrida, *On Touching*, p. 232.
128. Ibid., p. 181.
129. Levinas, *Totality and Infinity*, p. 147.
130. A similar thought in Merleau-Ponty, *Signes* (Paris: Gallimard, 1960), p. 117.
131. Nancy, *Dis-Enclosure*, p. 12. "Belief" for Nancy is "a weak form of knowledge," through adhering to one or the other postulate—one can think of the dogmas of Christian faith—which allows the "believer" to "suppose within the other a sameness which allows him or her to identify itself with them and be comforted"—my belief in these dogmas is what will save me. Citations are, respectively, *Dis-Enclosure*, p. 52 and *Noli me tangere*, p. 19. Christianity, for Nancy, is an exceptional religion because it eradicates all forms of "belief" and myths.
132. Nancy, *Dis-Enclosure*, p. 48 and p. 153.
133. See Levinas, *Totality and Infinity*, p. 100 and also Nancy's *Being Singular Plural*, p. 27.
134. James K. A. Smith, *Speech and Theology. Language and the Logic of Incarnation* (London: Routledge, 2002), pp. 167–168.
135. Derrida, *On Touching*, pp. 287–288.
136. Ibid., pp. 287–288.
137. Ibid., pp. 287–288.
138. Levinas, *Otherwise Than Being*, p. 189 n. 21. Derrida has, moreover, commended a similar thought to Nancy, see *On Touching*, p. 117.
139. Levinas, *Totality and Infinity*, p. 173.
140. Ibid., p. 139.
141. To be sure, Nancy advances his thought as an "ontology of the address" and knows that "being is communication," but the address never occurs, according to Levinas at least, without something being addressed in the first place, always and already the one *with* the other. Citations of Nancy are *Being Singular Plural*, p. xvi and p. 28.
142. The reference to Heidegger's thrownness is deliberate; see Heidegger, *Being and Time*, p. 264: "Dasein [. . .] is already in a definite world and alongside a

definite range of definite entities within-the-world." Note also, on this topic at least, that Levinas and Heidegger are quite close; see for instance Heidegger, *Einleitung in die Philosophie* (Frankfurt a. M: Vittorio Klostermann, 1996), p. 139: "every being uncovered of present-at-hand entities is therefore also *already given away and shared*, since the disclosing of Dasein, that is being-there, is necessarily being-with." My translation and italics.

143. Derrida, *On Touching*, p. 54.
144. Ibid., p. 287.
145. Nancy, "Hors tout," p. 387.
146. See *La création du monde ou la mondialisation* (Paris: Galilée, 2002), p. 86, in the English translation, p. 67.
147. Derrida, *On Touching*, p. 184 rightly remarks the following: "Merleau-Ponty: Nancy does not cite him often." Derrida comes up with *one* reference. Compare Merleau-Ponty, *The Visible and the Invisible*, trans. A. Lingis (Evanston, IL: Northwestern University Press, 1968), p. 127; for the retrieval of essence and ideality, see pp. 107–121 and pp. 149–155, citation is p. 109. On the link with language, see esp. p. 117, pp. 125–127, and pp. 144–145.
148. Merleau-Ponty, *The Visible and the Invisible*, p. 111, also p. 152.
149. One should not underestimate the consensus between a great many of the contemporary thinkers here, see Levinas, *Otherwise Than Being*, p. 152. Heidegger takes a similar stance in *Introduction to Metaphysics*, trans. G. Fried and R. Polt (New Haven: Yale University Press, 2000), p. 7. Finally Merleau-Ponty, *Éloge de la philosophie et autres essais* (Paris: Gallimard, 1960), pp. 33–34.
150. Merleau-Ponty's thought on the matter seems not to have changed during his career; see *Signes*, p. 113, p. 115, pp. 120–121 and *Phénoménologie de la perception* (Paris: Gallimard, 1945), p. 210, p. 217, and p. 229.
151. Ignatius of Loyola, *Spiritual Exercises*, trans. E. Mullan, taken from the online Christian Classics Ethereal Library.

Chapter 3: Exercises in Religion I

1. Peter Sloterdijk, *You Must Change Your Life. On Anthropotechnics*, trans. W. Hoban (Cambridge, UK: Polity Press, 2013), p. 1. Hereafter abbreviated as *Life*.
2. Ibid., p. 132.
3. Sloterdijk, *God's Zeal. The Battle of the Three Monotheisms*, trans. W. Hoban (Cambridge, UK: Polity Press, 2009), p. 4.
4. Ibid., pp. 19–20.
5. Sloterdijk, *Life*, p. 1 and p. 3.
6. Sloterdijk, *God's Zeal*, pp. 13–15. Citation is p. 13.
7. Sloterdijk, *God's Zeal*, p. 4. Compare *Life*, p. 15.
8. Sloterdijk, *Life*, p. 14.
9. Ibid., p. 16.
10. Ibid., p. 8.

11. Ibid., p. 14.
12. Ibid., p. 14.
13. Ibid., p. 10.
14. Sloterdijk, *God's Zeal*, p. 19.
15. Ibid., p. 50.
16. Ibid., p. 34.
17. Ibid., pp. 56 and 55, respectively.
18. Ibid., p. 58.
19. Both citations ibid., pp. 61 and 62, respectively.
20. See for this my *Ontotheological Turnings?*, pp. 229ff.
21. Ibid., p. 69. For the question as to Christianity's inherent "ambivalence," see p. 59.
22. Ibid., p. 69.
23. Ibid., p. 83. Translation modified.
24. Ibid., p. 111.
25. On this very point, it seems in effect quite reasonable to follow Heidegger and try not to dream too prematurely about a postmetaphysical era, if at all. For Heidegger indeed, the foundation was indeed an "illusion" but, on the other hand, a "perhaps necessary" one at that. See Heidegger, *Introduction to Metaphysics*, p. 3. The remark on Nietzsche is inspired by Marion, who, in *The Visible and the Revealed*, trans. C. Gschwandtner (New York: Fordham University Press, 2008), pp. 52–55, argues that the "end of metaphysics" can legitimately be spoken of only *once* the foundation of all beings can be exposed to the question "why does there need to be a foundation of beings at all?"
26. Sloterdijk, *God's Zeal*, p. 93.
27. Ibid., pp. 92. Sloterdijk's italics.
28. Ibid., p. 93.
29. Our recurrent attempt to point to similarities between Sloterdijk and Derrida is by no means arbitrary. Although a detailed study of Derrida cannot be found in his works, the respective "contextualizations" in Sloterdijk's *Derrida: An Egyptian. On the Problem of the Jewish Pyramid* (Cambridge, UK: Polity Press, 2009) are a homage to Derrida by tracing his heritage and trying to "develop an image of the mountain range from which la montagne Derrida rises up as one of the highest peaks" (p. xiii). Also of note in this booklet is the idea of the *transportability* of the transcendent (in place of the rather static archive) and the comparison between the indeconstructible and the pyramid, whose "form is nothing other than the remainder of a construction that, following the plan of the architect, is built to look as it would after its own collapse" (p. 27).
30. Sloterdijk, *God's Zeal*, p. 95.
31. Ibid., p. 96.
32. See for this especially Lacoste's "L'intuition sacramentelle," in *Revue théologique de Louvain* 42 (2011): 496–525, a text contemporaneous with the publication of his *Être en danger* (Paris: Cerf, 2011).

33. Sloterdijk, *God's Zeal*, p. 97.
34. Heidegger, "The Word of Nietzsche: God is Dead," in *The Question Concerning Technology and Other Essays*, trans. W. Lovett (New York: Harper and Row, 1977), pp. 53–112, p. 61.
35. Sloterdijk, *God's Zeal*, p. 108 and p. 109, respectively.
36. Ibid., p. 108.
37. Ibid., p. 108.
38. Cf. ibid., p. 106.
39. Ibid., pp. 136–137 and p. 135, respectively.
40. Ibid., p. 111.
41. The phrase is repeated no fewer than three times in ibid., pp. 112–114.
42. Sloterdijk, "Luhmann. Anwalt des Teufels. Von der Erbsünde, dem Egoismus der Systeme und den neuen Ironien," in *Nicht gerettet. Versuche nach Heidegger* (Frankfürt a. M: Suhrkamp, 2001), pp. 82–141, p. 98.
43. Sloterdijk, *Rage and Time. A Psychopolitical Investigation*, trans. M. Wenning (New York: Columbia University Press, 2010), pp. 107–108.
44. See for this also Peter Fritz, "Capitalism—or Christianity. Creation and Incarnation in Jean-Luc Nancy," in *Political Theology* 15 (2014): 421–437.
45. Sloterdijk, *God's Zeal*, p. 115.
46. Ibid., p. 116.
47. Ibid., p. 116.

Chapter 4: Exercises in Religion II

1. Sloterdijk, *Bubbles. Spheres, vol. 1: Microspherology*, trans. W. Hoban (Los Angeles: Semiotexte, 2011), p. 27 and p. 630, respectively. With the theme of "das Ungeheure," the uncanny or in any case unusual, Sloterdijk is close to Heidegger. Important in this regard is Heidegger's contention in *Parmenides* (Frankfürt a. M: Klostermann, 1996), p. 151, "das Geheure selbst [. . .] ist das Ungeheure": the usual is what is unusual, like anxiety in *Being and Time* already showed nothing but the everydayness of being-in-a-world. For the English, see *Parmenides*, p. 102.
2. Sloterdijk, *Bubbles*, p. 46.
3. Reference is to Heidegger, *Einleitung in die Philosophie*, p. 334.
4. See for Sloterdijk's interpretation of Heidegger also the interviews in *Neither Sun nor Death*, trans. S. Corcoran (Los Angeles: Semiotexte: 2011), esp. pp. 174–176.
5. Sloterdijk, *Bubbles*, p. 54.
6. Ibid., 54.
7. All these quotes are Sloterdijk, *Globes, Spheres, vol. 2: Macrospherology*. I take and translate them from the Dutch, *Sferen*, trans. H. Driessen (Amsterdam: Boom, 2007), pp. 474–475.
8. Ibid., p. 447 and 462, respectively.
9. Ibid., p. 479.
10. Respectively, ibid., p. 475 and p. 484.

11. Sloterdijk, *Neither Sun nor Death*, p. 305.
12. Sloterdijk, *Globes*, in *Sferen*, p. 485.
13. Sloterdijk, Ibid., p. 485.
14. Sloterdijk, *Bubbles*, p. 54, trans. mod.
15. Sloterdijk, "Anwalt des Teufels," p. 101. Italics are mine.
16. Sloterdijk calls the egoism and individualism of our days "foam," like one can "foam with rage"; see his *Globes*, in *Sferen*, for instance, p. 490.
17. See especially "Anwalt des Teufels," pp. 101–102.
18. Sloterdijk, *Life*, p. 114. Compare *Globes* in *Sferen*, p. 423, where it is asked, "what will happen to the king in a time that knows not of any bubble and what will become of the bubble in a time without kings?"
19. Sloterdijk, *God's Zeal*, p. 148. See for this also Sloterdijk's *Kritiek van de cynische rede*, trans. T. Davids (Amsterdam: De Arbeiderspers, 1984), p. 459, which seemed to have reserved a similar role for religion: "religion [is also] a memory of the fact that there is more life in us than that which this life is able to realize. [This is why] it can liberate individuals [and] it can be the core of resistance against the powers that be." My translation.
20. Ibid., p. 159.
21. Ibid., pp. 140–141.
22. Ibid., p. 159 and p. 139 respectively. Translation modified considerably: the last sentence is even omitted in the English translation.
23. Sloterdijk, *Life*, pp. 6–7 and p. 15.
24. See for this "apocalyptic exhaustion," Sloterdijk, *Neither Sun nor Death*, p. 220: "I made an effort to invoke this era—*absolutely lost for us*—of the metaphysics of the globe, because I wanted to present [. . .] the situation that occurs *afterwards*." My emphasis.
25. Sloterdijk, *Life*, p. 68.
26. Ibid., p. 68.
27. Ibid., p. 71.
28. Ibid., p. 77.
29. Ibid., pp. 77–78.
30. Ibid., p. 82.
31. Ibid., p. 82.
32. Ibid., pp. 71–72.
33. The cravings for identity, so obvious in today's world, and the concomitant scare of everyone and everything that is other is for Sloterdijk, and no doubt rightly so, but a sign of laziness, see Ibid., pp. 199–200.
34. Ibid., p. 84.
35. See, for the athletic reduction of religion, especially ibid., p. 84, 90–91 and 117–119.
36. Cf. ibid., pp. 162ff. For Heidegger, see "Letter on Humanism," in *Basic Writings*, pp. 233–234.
37. Ibid., p. 164.
38. Ibid., p. 165.

39. Ibid., p. 177. We are close here, in our wariness of such apocalypticism, to Hans Achterhuis, "De utopie van Peter Sloterdijk: Regels voor het mensenpark," in *Tijdschrift voor filosofie* 64 (2002): 451–478, who notes that this theme of "drilling" is one of the continuing themes of Sloterdijk's work. But, whereas Sloterdijk in his cynical phase applauded any attempt to outwit such drills, the later work (and *Life* perhaps especially) focuses on ways to drill humanity into a co-immunity that prevails over the fate of the individual. Achterhuis rightly states that Sloterdijk never explains his change (p. 456) from an anarchist-cynic to a conservative and somewhat dictatorial philosopher-king. In this regard, this chapter might, if you will, be interpreted as "reading Sloterdijk against Sloterdijk," for it is yet to be seen whether a cynic philosopher who wants to be a philosopher-king is not a contradiction in terms.

40. Ibid., p. 166.

41. Ibid., p. 130.

42. Ibid., p. 247. This difference is central to Sloterdijk's *Eurotaoismus. Zur Kritik der politischen Kinetik* (Frankfurt a. Main: Suhrkamp, 1989), which can be read as Sloterdijk's "legitimacy of the modern age." Sloterdijk discusses here the deconstruction of the difference between the "onward" and "upward" through taking the escalator as a prime example: here the one advanced a bit farther is not necessarily "higher" (and vice versa).

43. Ibid., p. 253.

44. For what follows, *Life*, pp. 300–301. Citation is p. 301.

45. Ibid., p. 300.

46. Ibid., p. 301.

47. Ibid., p. 198.

48. Phenomenologically speaking, the problem can be formulated as follows: I am not able, as a phenomenologist, to speak of "life" in general without taking my own life into account. However, once I do so it becomes instantly problematic whether "my" life pertains (or not) to the problematic of the lives of others at all. The problem of phenomenology is therefore to know how to speak of "the" world from out of this small bit of world here in Belgium given, granted, and more or less familiar to me.

49. Ibid., p. 371.

50. Ibid., pp. 439–440.

51. See, for instance, Heidegger, *Being and Time*, p. 151.

52. This "horizontal transgression," dreading the standstill, is inspired by Michel Houellebecq, who has made meditations on mass tourism one of the recurring themes of his novels. He opines that rural France will never disappear, that is, not be replaced or recuperated by industry or cities, simply because it is this rural character that grants France "sufficient economic activity," through trips to pristine settings, in order to survive (post)modernity unscathed. If necessary, Houellebecq argues, France simply has to become "a brothel for tourists." See Houellebecq and Lévy, *Publieke vijanden* (Amsterdam: Arbeiderspers, 2009), pp. 130–132, translation

mine. Sloterdijk's conception of the "ontological tourism" of *Gelassenheit* is intriguing; see *Neither Sun nor Death*, pp. 346–348.

53. Respectively, Sloterdijk, *Life*, p. 437 and *Kansen in de gevarenzone. Kanttekeningen bij de variatie in spiritualiteit na de secularisatie*, trans. M. Wildschut (Kampen: Agora, 2003), p. 35.

54. This might again show Heidegger's diagnosis of (post)modernity, in which "quantity becomes a special kind of quality": the verticality of "the best" and "the higher" is substituted for the horizontal "more." Cf. Heidegger, "The Age of the World Picture," in *The Question Concerning Theology*, pp. 113–154, p. 135.

55. See Sloterdijk, *Neither Sun nor Death*, pp. 32–36.

56. Sloterdijk, *Life*, p. 216 and p. 305.

57. Ibid., p. 447.

58. Ibid., p. 441.

59. Sloterdijk, *Neither Sun nor Death*, p. 66.

60. See *Life*, p. 451 and *Neither Sun nor Death*, p. 71, respectively.

61. Sloterdijk, *Neither Sun nor Death*, p. 350.

62. Ibid., p. 318.

63. Sloterdijk, *Life*, p. 129.

64. Ibid., p. 409. But also bear in mind that such a severance of family ties is a common trait of, precisely, cynic philosophy.

Conclusion to Part 1

1. See for this the important passage in Derrida, *Margins of Philosophy*, pp. 134–135.

2. Heidegger, *Was ist Metaphysik?* (Frankfürt a. M: Klostermann, 1998), p. 21. My translation.

3. Heidegger, "The Word of Nietzsche," p. 69.

4. Cf. Heidegger, *Introduction to Metaphysics*, p. 3.

Chapter 5: In Defense of Deconstruction

1. Caputo, "On not Settling," p. 306 and 308, respectively. See also his "The Return of Anti-Religion," p. 38.

2. Ibid., pp. 307 and 310.

3. Nancy's "The Intruder," in Nancy, *Corpus*, trans. R. Rand (New York: Fordham University Press, 2008), pp. 161–170, can be read as a meditation on the auto-deconstruction of the identity of a subject, understood as a permanent and unchanging substrate beneath all perturbations and alterations of the outside world.

4. Caputo, "On Not Settling," p. 313.

5. Derrida, *On Touching*, p. 49. *Le toucher* (Paris: Galiléé, 2000) has "l'indéconstructible du christianisme," p. 63.

6. Caputo, "The Return of Anti-Religion," p. 61.
7. Ibid., p. 29.
8. Ibid., p. 61.
9. The reader is reminded that it is such a mode of procedure that Levinas denounced as "play," as an endless reversibility of "being" and "beings." *Otherwise Than Being* uses the example of "red reddens," pp. 38–39.
10. For Caputo, this contamination takes place in Neo-Platonism, to which, e.g., John Milbank wants to return and where Greek thought merges with biblical thinking. See for this especially *Prayers and Tears*, p. 25 and pp. 334–336, where Caputo intends to eradicate all "Hellenism" from his passionate account of faith. One will need to wonder whether this is desirable and possible at all: would not such an abandoning of "thought" end up in a "metaphysics without metaphysics," which, for Enlightened minds, might be too close to some sort of *Schwärmerei*?
11. Caputo, *Religion*, p. 59.
12. Ibid., p. 63.
13. Caputo, *Religion*, p. 64.
14. Ibid., p. 66.
15. See Caputo, *Philosophy and Theology* (Nashville: Abingdon Press, 2006), pp. 54–55.
16. Ibid., pp. 55–56.
17. Ibid., p. 57.
18. Ibid., p. 57.
19. Ibid., p. 57.
20. Caputo, "The Return of Anti-Religion," p. 32. Yet why would this generation forget that yesterday's hippies have become today's bankers?
21. Cf. Derrida, *Introduction to Husserl's Origin of Geometry*, p. 48.
22. Derrida, *On Touching*, p. 287.
23. Ibid., esp. pp. 232–237, on the "intertwining" of "flesh" (*Leib*) and "body" (*Körper*), disrupting the all too human interaction of the ego (and its "*corps-propre*") and the alter ego (and its "*corps propre*"), forcing us to think "an alterity [. . .] that is no longer necessarily and from the outset the locus of an alter ego" (237), but rather the muteness of matter that allows for no clear and distinct signification (but does allow Derrida, for instance, to move beyond anthropocentrism and to turn to the animal).
24. The phrase is the opening line of Caputo's "The Sense of God. A Theology of the Event with Special Reference to Christianity," in L. Boeve and C. Brabant (eds.), *Between Philosophy and Theology. Contemporary Interpretations of Christianity* (Aldershot: Ashgate, 2010), pp. 27–41.
25. Caputo here aligns himself with Derrida; see *Prayers and Tears*, p. 289: "the word 'theology' tends to have a strictly *onto*-theological sense for [Derrida]." Yet from *The Weakness of God. A Theology of the Event* (Bloomington: Indiana University Press, 2006) onward, Caputo seems to have realized that "religion without religion" needs to be accompanied by a "theology without theology"; see *The Weakness of God*, pp. 1–2 and the corresponding note on p. 301.
26. Caputo, "On Not Settling," p. 331.

27. Caputo, "The Return of Anti-Religion," p. 37.
28. Caputo, "On Not Settling," p. 275. See also Caputo's review of Marion's *In the Self's Place*, where he criticizes Marion's sharp distinction between love and hate (hate is but an absence of love): either you love the truth or you hate love as such. Caputo comments: "the limitation of this idea shows up in Augustine's episcopal preoccupations with "heretics," who obviously hate the truth of (Roman Catholic) love: "standing behind the erotic truth [. . .] lies the big stick of doctrinal rectitude and propositional truth [. . .]. Erotic truth has its police," online at *Notre Dame Philosophical Book Reviews* (2013/01/18).
29. Caputo, "On Not Settling," p. 301. See also Caputo's extensive confrontation with Marion in "Apostles of the Impossible. On God and the Gift in Derrida and Marion," in J. D. Caputo and M. Scanlon (eds.) *God, the Gift, and Postmodernism* (Bloomington, Indiana University Press, 1999), pp. 185–222. For a commentary, see my *Ontotheological Turnings?*, pp. 86ff.
30. Ibid., p. 272 and p. 273.
31. Cf. "On Not Settling," p. 303. Quote is p. 273. On this "historical approach" to ontotheology, see also my "Marion, Levinas, and Heidegger on the Question Concerning Ontotheology," in *Continental Philosophy Review* 43 (2010): 207–239.
32. Cf. Levinas, *Otherwise Than Being*, p. 80mod.
33. For an instructive introduction to this problem, see Maxime Doyon, *Die transzendentale Anspruch der Dekonstruktion. Zur Erneuerung des Begriffs "transzendental" bei Derrida* (Würzburg: Ergon Verlag, 2012), esp. pp. 135–163.
34. See especially Caputo, "The Return of Anti-Religion," pp. 75–84, where Caputo shows, mostly through citations of Derrida, that Hägglund short-circuits and abridges the "unconditional to-come" a bit too quickly.
35. Caputo, "The Return of Anti-Religion," pp. 55ff. on finite infinity and p. 79 for the quote.
36. Derrida, "Force of Law," p. 248.
37. Caputo "The Return of Anti-Religion," p. 72, also p. 121.
38. Derrida, "Linguistics and Grammatology," in *Of Grammatology*, pp. 27–73, p. 62. For Caputo's comments on this passage, see "The Return of Anti-Religion," pp. 54–55.
39. Derrida, *Adieu to Emmanuel Levinas*, trans. P.-A. Brault and M. Naas (Stanford: Stanford University Press, 1999), p. 76.
40. Someone should write a book titled "Deconstruction and Incarnation" soon. Cf. already in Derrida, *Introduction Husserl's Origin of Geometry*, p. 89, "the [. . .] necessity of *being incarnated* in a graphic sign is no longer simply extrinsic [. . .] in comparison with ideal Objectivity: it is the *sine qua non* condition of [its] completion."
41. Caputo, "The Return of Anti-Religion," p. 60.
42. Caputo, *Prayers and Tears*, p. 22.
43. For my take on Derrida's "Violence and Metaphysics" in relation to Levinas, see *Ontotheological Turnings?*, pp. 117ff. One might imagine a repetition of the theological debate between Barth and Rahner here, for, whereas the former pleas

for a *ganz andere Gott*, revealing himself of himself with no regard for the human condition, Rahner insists on a (transcendental) *Anknüpfungspunkt* with the human condition, for such revelation to be received at all. Revelation, for Rahner, occurs, if it occurs, "according to the mode of the perceiver," as Aquinas has it. Who would have thought, back in 1967, that Derrida would actually be siding with Aquinas here?

44. Caputo, "On Not Settling," p. 336.
45. Hägglund, *Radical Atheism*, p. 85.
46. Ibid., p. 123 and p. 88.
47. Ibid., p. 145.
48. Ibid., p. 93.
49. Ibid., p. 79.
50. Cf. ibid., p. 118. Caputo is right when he signals that Hägglund completely ignores the criticisms of such an Absolute internal to the Christian tradition. Yet it seems somewhat absurd to reproach an atheist for not being aware of the theological tradition. More important is that, "after" ontotheology, these indivisible Absolutes appear to be just that, just a *thought-experiment*, that is, with no real traction in existence-in-a-world. For a brilliant critique of such an Absolute—Hägglund would be surprised—see Leszek Kolakowski, *Metaphysical Horror* (Chicago: University of Chicago Press, 2001), p. 42, "the more unity, the more good [. . .]. Consequently, when good reaches the point of completeness, it loses any recognizable quality of goodness. [. . .]. Since the One remains unaffectable in its total unity, it seems to be severed for any reality other than itself. Life [. . .] involves differentiation and tension; *complete peace is achieved only through lifelessness*."
51. For this definition, see Derrida, *Rogues*, p. 123.
52. Hägglund, *Radical Atheism*, p. 86. The reader is reminded that this is, roughly, what my *Ontotheological Turnings?* advanced against Lacoste, (early) Levinas, and Marion, namely that that they project and posit a transcendence over and against an immanence supposedly devoid of such transcendence, which can then portrayed as a "prison" (Marion) or as "an egg in its shell" (Levinas).
53. See ibid., p. 31: "the ultratranscendental *description* of why we must be open for the other is conflated with an ethical *prescription* that we must be open to the other."
54. Ibid., p. 101.
55. One is reminded here of how Schürmann portrays the metaphysical referents of Cicero and Augustine, where all politics is to be measured respectively either against the ideal of "ancient Rome," the Rome of the ancestors (Cicero), or against the ideal of heavenly Jerusalem. See his *Broken Hegemonies*, pp. 200–238. In contemporary politics, something similar seems to occur in the repeated referral to the "Founding Fathers," who are supposed to have glimpsed the ideal of the nation-state *better* than we would do today.
56. Caputo, "The Return of Anti-Religion," e.g., p. 43 and 69.
57. Hägglund, *Radical Atheism*, p. 97 and p. 104, respectively.
58. Rubenstein, *Strange Wonder. The Closure of Metaphysics and the Beginning of Awe* (New York: Columbia University Press, 2006), pp. 145–147. Reference is to

Derrida's *Politics of Friendship*, trans. G. Collins (London: Verso, 1997), p. 69: "one must certainly know [. . .] knowledge is necessary if one is to assume responsibility, but the decisive moment of responsibility supposes a leap and free [oneself] of what is therefore heterogeneous to it, that is, knowledge."

59. Ibid., p. 177.
60. Caputo, "The Return of Anti-Religion," p. 57 and p. 70.
61. Heidegger, *Grundfragen der Philosophie* (Frankfürt a. Main, Klostermann, 1996), p. 166.
62. Hägglund, *Radical Atheism*, p. 104. It is true, Derrida does say that the relation between what is unconditional and conditional is one of indissociability and heterogeneity; see especially the "violent footnote" in *Rogues*, p. 172.
63. Derrida, *Adieu to Emmanuel Levinas*, pp. 116–117. See *À Dieu à Emmanuel Levinas* (Paris: Galilée, 1997), p. 201.
64. Cf. Derrida, *Àdieu.*, p. 138 and p. 146.
65. See already Caputo's, *Demythologizing Heidegger*, p. 199, "it is impossible for what is otherwise-than-Being to avoid being-otherwise." As I will show now, Levinas would be in complete agreement with this contention.
66. Levinas, *Otherwise Than Being*, p. 160.
67. Ibid., pp. 3–4. "The" otherwise than being? Levinas never uses the expression. Yet the whole problem might be restated in an abstract manner as the problem of just how this "infinition," this event, and its *modus irrealis* can just as well revert into a noun.
68. Ibid., p. 199n. 21.
69. Ibid., p. 199n. 21.
70. Cf. Levinas, *Totality and Infinity*, p. 41.
71. Derrida, *Adieu to Emmanuel Levinas*, p. 147n. 95.
72. Levinas, *Otherwise Than Being*, p. 8 and p. 125, respectively.
73. Ibid., p. 12 and p. 10, respectively. Italics are mine.
74. Ibid., p. 80.
75. Ibid., p. 95.
76. Ibid., pp. 151–152.
77. Ibid., p. 154.
78. Ibid., p. 156.
79. Ibid., p. 156.
80. Ibid., p. 70. Levinas's italics in the French text, see Levinas, *Autrement qu'être, où au-delà de l'essence* (The Hague: Nijhoff, 1974), p. 88.
81. Ibid., p. 154.
82. Levinas, *Otherwise Than Being*, p. 154 and Levinas, *Of God Who Comes to Mind*, trans. B. Bergo (Stanford: Stanford University Press, 1998), p. 108.
83. Marion, *Being Given*, p. 291.
84. Levinas, *Otherwise Than Being*, p. 199 n. 21.
85. Ibid., p. 78.
86. Ibid., p. 154/*Autrement qu'être*, p. 197. Confirmation for this interpretation in Levinas, *Otherwise Than Being*, p. 158: "the neighbor is [. . .] a face, at the

same time [*à la fois*] comparable and incomparable, a unique face and in relationship with faces"; for the French, see p. 201.

87. Ibid., p. 158, modified because the French was: "Il y a pesée, pensée, objectivation et, par là, *un arrêt* où se trahit ma relation anarchique à l'illéité"; see p. 201.

88. Levinas, *God, Death, and Time*, p. 203 and *Otherwise Than Being*, p. 199n. 21.

89. Levinas, *God, Death and Time*, pp. 203–204. The French again uses "un arrêt," a stop; see *Dieu, la mort et le temps* (Paris: Grasset, 1993), p. 233.

90. Hägglund, *Radical Atheism*, p. 92.

91. Derrida, "To Forgive," in J. Dooley, J. D. Caputo, and M. Scanlon (eds.), *Questioning God* (Bloomington: Indiana University Press, 2001), pp. 21–51, p. 28. For Caputo's discussion of this passage, see "The Return of Anti-Religion," p. 78.

92. Derrida, "Linguistics and Grammatology," in *Of Grammatology*, p. 61.

93. Levinas, *Otherwise Than Being*, p. 121. See Derrida's discussion in *Adieu to Emmanuel Levinas*, pp. 61–62 and p. 51.

94. Derrida, "Violence and Metaphysics," in *Writing and Difference*, p. 123.

95. Derrida, *Adieu*, p. 53. My italics.

96. Cf. Derrida, *Introduction to Husserl's Origin of Geometry*, p. 141.

97. Cf. "On Not Settling," pp. 352–353. Reference here is to Caputo's debate with James Olthuis, who proposed to start with "the with," from out of our being in concrete and factical beliefs, in order to come to a "with without with"; see Olthuis, "Testing the Heart of Khôra," in *Cross and Khôra*, pp. 174–185, p. 185.

98. See Caputo, "The Return of Anti-Religion," e.g., p. 55. For Derrida on empiricism, see "That Dangerous Supplement," in *Of Grammatology*, pp. 141–164, p. 162.

99. Caputo, "On Not Settling," p. 313.

100. Caputo, "The Return of Anti-Religion," pp. 79–80. My italics.

101. Ibid., p. 80.

102. Ibid. p. 88, p. 101, p. 107, and again p. 88.

103. Hägglund, *Radical Atheism*, p. 120. Hägglund is right, moreover, in insisting that even if Caputo is writing only a "poetics" (and not an ontology), this does not make an essential difference; see his "Radical Evil," p. 141. The problem (with the with) is in effect that whenever one would imagine God—for example—it might be that (with a certain Levinas) this imagining always and already occurs in an ontotheological way.

Chapter 6: Between Faith and Belief

1. Caputo, "On Not Settling," p. 337.
2. Ibid., p. 330.
3. Caputo, "The Sense of God," p. 36.

4. In this regard, nihilism resembles a sort of practical absolutization of contingency, different from the theoretical version one can detect in Milbank, who rejects contingency on entirely theoretical and rational grounds, forgetting that this move does not make things any less contingent, see John Milbank, "The Double Glory or Paradox versus Dialectics: On Not Quite Agreeing with Slavoj Žižek," in C. Davis (ed.), *The Monstrosity of Christ. Paradox or Dialectic?* (Cambridge: MIT Press, 2008), pp. 110–233, p. 114. Nihilism is, on the contrary, an embracing of contingency to such an extent that it knows nothing outside contingency and, in this sense, is taken as something absolute: if everything can always change in something else, one might just as well keep everything as it is. "It is as it is" both accepts and rejects contingency. Everything may change, yet one opts for not changing anything, because such change can only deliver "more of the same," for the results of change can indeed be changed in turn. This practical absolutization of contingency therefore is prone to confirm the status quo.

5. Both quotes, Caputo, *Religion*, p. 33. My italics.

6. See for this Caputo, "The Sense of God," p. 37n.6.

7. Caputo, *The Weakness of God*, p. 288.

8. See Geoffrey Bennington and Jacques Derrida, *Circumfession* (Chicago: University of Chicago Press, 1999), pp. 313–314. For Derrida, "the stabilized relation of destination," of a heaven, a classless society, and whatnot, is a "destinerrancy which was never my doing, nor to my taste." See for a commentary Caputo's *Prayers and Tears*, p. 306.

9. Derrida, "Confessions and 'Circumfession.' A Roundtable Discussion with Jacques Derrida," in J. D. Caputo and M. Scanlon (eds.), *Augustine and Postmodernism. Confessions and Circumfession* (Bloomington: Indiana University Press, 2005), pp. 28–49, p. 39.

10. Caputo, "Jacques Derrida (1930–2004)," in *Journal of Cultural and Religious Theory* 6 (2004): 6–9, p. 8. Last two italicizations are mine.

11. See Caputo, *Prayers and Tears*, p. 284.

12. Derrida, *Circumfession*, p. 188.

13. Ibid., p. 154.

14. See for this analysis Caputo, *Philosophy and Theology*, p. 64. My italics.

15. Caputo, *Religion*, p. 30.

16. Caputo, *Philosophy and Theology*, pp. 66–67.

17. Ibid., p. 67.

18. Ibid., p. 67. Italics are mine.

19. Derrida, *Of Hospitality. Anne Dufourmantelle Invites Jacques Derrida to Respond* (Stanford: Stanford University Press, 2000), p. 79.

20. See for such a line of reasoning Derrida, "How to Avoid Speaking: Denials," trans. K. Frieden, in S. Budick and W. Iser (eds.), *Languages of the Unsayable. The Play of Negativity in Literature and Literary Theory* (New York: Columbia University Press, 1989), pp. 3–70, pp. 25–26.

21. E.g., Levinas, *Otherwise Than Being*, p. 95, on the "faith of the coal-dealer" and *L'au-delà du verset. Lectures et discours talmudiques* (Paris: Minuit: 1982), p. 130.

22. Arto Paasilinna, *Wees genadig* (Amsterdam: Wereldbibliotheek, 2011), p. 18. My translation.

23. Derrida, *Circumfession*, p. 311.

24. See Caputo, "Shedding Tears Beyond Being. Derrida's Confession of Prayer," in J. D. Caputo and M. Scanlon (eds.), *Augustine and Postmodernism*, pp. 95–114, p. 102 and p. 105, respectively. Last quote is "On Not Settling," p. 397n.45.

25. Ibid., p. 102. One would be in need of a phenomenology of the fifty or so shades of gray between weak and strong theology or of the *gradations in transcendence* close to the ones Derrida detected in Levinas, see *Adieu to Emmanuel Levinas*, p. 41.

26. See Derrida, *Circumfession*, p. 117 and Caputo, *The Weakness of God*, p. xi.

27. Caputo, "Shedding Tears Beyond Being," p. 110.

28. Caputo, *Prayer and Tears*, p. 332.

29. Caputo, *Religion*, p. 31.

30. Caputo, *Philosophy and Theology*, p. 73.

31. Ibid., p. 35.

32. Caputo, *Religion*, p. 113.

33. Ibid., p. 117. Caputo's italics.

34. Ibid., p. 26. For a somewhat desperate attempt to show that love does actually proceed from God (with a fideism no longer recognizing itself as such), see Henri-Jérôme Gagey, *La vérité s'accomplit* (Paris: Bayard, 2009), pp. 251–276. One therefore still has to put fideism in its proper place. Lacoste, for instance, has written that fideism is partially right (*La phénoménalité de Dieu* (Paris: Cerf: 2008), p. 108): there simply are truths or insights that are proper to the believing mind, and for which the "eyes of faith" are needed "in order to see." One might, for example, interpret the immaculate conception as not entirely foreign to the human condition. If that had been the case, God could have just as well impregnated a man (the example, one recalls, is taken from Smith's *Speech and Theology*). The point here is that such an argument is valid only for those of us who still have a certain taste for theology and its arguments. This, however, does not mean that fideism is completely right: if this were the case, and the believer's interpretation of "what is there for all to see" is *just as good* as any other interpretation, faith is preparing its own downfall (simply because it is all too close to relativism), and it simply seems a matter of time before postmodern culture closes itself for the tiny bits of faith that remain there. What is more, this kind of fideism pertains to any human endeavor: for just as the believer knows and is "in the know" of truths that belong to its tradition and therefore "sees what is not available to sight" or "believes in order to see," so a cyclist know more and other things of his or her sport than an "outsider" or a simple supporter would.

35. I am happy to correct my *Ontotheological Turnings?* here, which relied too much on this distinction.

36. See first Caputo, *Prayers and Tears*, p. 140, and then "On Not Settling," p. 320–322; last quote is p. 322. The impulse "going on" in the traditions would then only be attested to *within* the traditions, and would contracted and determined

by all of these contingent configurations of the divine. But here is where Levinas and Schürmann haunt Caputo: what if this contraction is always and already done by a "natural ontotheologian"?

37. See Derrida's comment on this, in Caputo (ed.), *Deconstruction in A Nutshell*, p. 24.
38. Cf. Heidegger, *Being and Time*, p. 195.
39. Caputo, "Only as Hauntology," p. 112.
40. Cf. Caputo, "On Not Settling," p. 293, "deconstruction is faith" and p. 313, "deconstruction is love."
41. Caputo, *The Weakness of God*, p. 9.

Chapter 7: Between Strong and Weak Theology

1. Caputo, "On Not Settling," p. 286 and p. 293, respectively.
2. Caputo, *The Weakness of God*, p. 14.
3. Ibid., p. 1.
4. Ibid., p. 13 and p. 19 on Jesus as an anarchist.
5. Caputo, "The Sense of God," p. 38.
6. One should note, however, that Caputo somewhat conveniently leaves out those passages in which a certain power (*dunamis*) is ascribed to Jesus during his life that caused people to sense some sort of presence or anticipation of the Kingdom in the very person of Jesus. This presence obviously differs from the endless "anticipations" and "deconstructions" that Caputo sees as characteristic of the critique of idols. One can notice here, once again, Caputo's desire for a "pure" image of Jesus: his Jesus is one that in all domains has to be considered as the paradigm of powerlessness. This seems to be the reason why all instances of a power ascribed to Jesus, even the one of forgiving sinful behaviors (the capability that lies at the root of his conviction and crucifixion) goes, at least for Caputo, unnoticed. One should note just as well that this power (*exousia* and *dynamis*) does not primarily concern Jesus's supposed miracles (which are unbelievable in all senses of the word) but, more often than not, his words (e.g., Mt. 7, 28, Mk. 1, 22; Lk. 4, 31, 5, 24, and 10, 19). Something similar occurs in René Girard and his following, where Jesus is turned into the paradigm of nonviolence. Quite conveniently, one hears neither of God's wrath and the concomitant violence nor of Jesus's outbursts of rage, for instance, in the temple or against those of little faith (Mt. 14, 27–31).
7. See Caputo, *The Weakness of God*, passim.
8. Caputo, *Religion*, p. 138.
9. Caputo, "The Sense of God," p. 38. Citation is *Religion*, p. 123.
10. See Marion, *Dieu sans l'être. Hors Texte* (Paris: PUF, 2002), pp. 128–148. Citation is p. 135. Cf. *God without Being. Hors-Texte*, trans. T. A. Carlson (Chicago: University of Chicago Press, 1991), pp. 83–102, citation is p. 91. Marion's theology here coincides beautifully with his approach to ontotheology; see *The Visible and the Revealed*, p. 163n.5 on an ontology and ontotheology that never dared to think "the being as such," in its very *haeccitas*, that is, but rather subsumed this

being in a universal "essence" that would be common to all beings regardless of its singularity. Marion would, in effect, fully subscribe to Caputo's search for the singularity of all beings.

11. Marion, *Being Given*, p. 101, p. 108, p. 111, p. 115 and passim.

12. Martin Buber, *De weg van de mens*, trans. H. Korteweg (Utrecht: Klement, 1998), p. 18. My translation.

13. Marion, *God without Being*, p. 93. For Caputo's intriguing take on the *tohu vabohu*, as the undecidable material-maternal element within creation, see *The Weakness of God*, pp. 55–83.

14. Marion, *God without Being*, p. 101.

15. For Caputo's agreement with Marion, see *The Weakness of God*, esp. p. 35 and p. 47.

16. Ibid., p. 102.

17. Marion, *God without Being*, p. 110.

18. Marion, *Certitudes négatives* (Paris: Grasset, 2010), p. 106. My translation.

19. Caputo, *The Weakness of God*, p. 116.

20. Ibid., p. 121.

21. Ibid., p. 107.

22. Ibid., p. 216.

23. On this point, Caputo seems closer to Levinas than to Derrida when stating that "in Levinas, the notion of God functions as a kind of *ordo ordinans*, an overarching back-up or anchor"; *The Weakness of God*, p. 276.

24. See the discussion on "infinitude finitude" and "finite infinity" in Chapter 5.

25. Marion, *In the Self's Place*, p. 113. See also my "In (the) Place of the Self. A Critical Study of Jean-Luc Marion's "Au lieu de soi. L'approche de Saint Augustin," in *Modern Theology* 25 (2009): 661–686.

26. See, e.g., Caputo, "The Return of Anti-Religion," pp. 80–81.

27. Hägglund, "Radical Evil," p. 143.

28. Caputo, "On Not Settling," p. 333–334.

29. See Michel Houellebecq and Bernard-Henry Levy, *Publieke vijanden*, p. 143, where Houellebecq mentions a Jew named Lucas who on his deathbed got to hear, "tonight is the night that your life will be reclaimed."

30. See Marion, *God without Being*, pp. 95–101.

31. Milbank et al (eds.), *Radical Orthodoxy: A New Theology* (London: Routledge, 1999), p. 4.

32. Smith, *Introducing Radical Orthodoxy. Mapping a Post-Secular Theology* (Grand Rapids: Baker Academic, 2004), p. 189.

33. Marion, *The Idol and Distance*, p. 252.

34. Ibid., p. 42.

35. Marion, *God without Being*, p. 115.

36. Ibid., pp. 115–116.

37. Ibid., p. 38.

38. Ibid., p. 38.
39. Marion, *The Idol and Distance*, p. 225.
40. Respectively, ibid., p. 249, p. 253, p. 39, and p. 98.
41. Ibid., p. 225.
42. Ibid., p. 8.
43. Marion, *God without Being*, p. 21, for both quotes.
44. Cf. Marion, *The Idol and Distance*, p. 13.
45. Marion, "*Mihi magna quaestio factus sum.* The Privilege of Unknowing," in *Journal of Religion* 85 (2005): 1–24, pp. 11–14.
46. Ibid., p. 13.
47. One, of course, needs to recall Levinas here, but it is Nancy who has gone the furthest in identifying all thought of essence with evil. Evil lies, for Nancy, more in the seduction of one or the other essence (in racism, for instance) than in its deviation from the Good; see for Nancy *The Experience of Freedom*, pp. 121–142, esp. p. 128. However, from the fact that some essences are wrong, or bad even, it does not follow that all essence is evil. Therefore, one should patiently reconstruct what, if anything, is wrong with representations and conceptualizations.
48. Marion, *In the Self's Place*, pp. 254–255, and also p. 244.
49. Ibid., p. 23.
50. Marion, *God without Being*, p. 24.
51. Marion, *Being Given*, pp. 71–74.
52. Marion, *Being Given*, p. 13.
53. Ibid., p. 25.
54. Cf. ibid., p. 20, see *Étant donné. Essai d'une phénoménologie de la donation* (Paris: PUF, 1998), p. 32.
55. Cf. Marion, *Being Given*, p. 20.
56. Ibid., p. 21.
57. Marion, *Reduction and Givenness*, p. 32; *Réduction et donation. Recherches sur Husserl, Heidegger et la phénoménologie* (Paris: PUF, 1989), p. 52. Marion's italics.
58. Ibid., p. 32. For the French, p. 52.
59. Marion, *Being Given*, p. 52.
60. Ibid., p. 25. For the French, see p. 39. Marion's italics.
61. Ibid., p. 20.
62. Ibid., p. 20.
63. Ibid., p. 20.
64. Ibid., p. 69. For the French, see p. 101.
65. Ibid., p. 123, trans. mod. For the French, see p. 174.
66. Marion, "La transcendance par excellence," in *Le croire pour le voir. Réflexions diverses sur la rationalité de la révélation et l'irrationalité de quelques croyants* (Paris: Parole et Silence, 2010), pp. 167–175.
67. Marion, *The Idol and Distance*, p. 250 and p. 62.
68. Ibid., p. 176.
69. Marion, *God without Being*, p. 100.

70. Marion, *The Erotic Phenomenon*, trans. S. E. Lewis (Chicago: University of Chicago Press, 2007), p. 221. See on this "univocity of love," *In the Self's Place*, pp. 270–281 and also the illuminating account by Gschwandtner, *Reading Jean-Luc Marion. Exceeding Metaphysics* (Bloomington: Indiana University Press, 2007), pp. 106–137 and pp. 229–242.

71. Ibid., p. 95, p. 96, and p. 218 n. 73 (for God); p. 115, p. 123, and p. 125 (for the human being).

72. Ibid., pp. 87–88 and p. 115 (for God) and p. 119 (for the human being).

73. Ibid., p. 119.

74. Ibid., p. 116.

75. Cf. ibid., p. 3 and pp. 128–129.

76. Ibid., p. 134.

77. Ibid., p. 136.

78. Marion, *The Erotic Phenomenon*, pp. 19–37.

79. Marion, *In the Self's Place*, p. xv.

80. Marion, *God without Being*, p. 117 and *Being Given*, p. 305.

81. Marion, *Being Given*, p. 313mod.

82. I. Leask (ed.), "From Radical Hermeneutics to the Weakness of God. John D. Caputo in Dialogue with Mark Dooley," in *Cross and Khôra*, pp. 327–347, p. 333.

83. Caputo, "The Sense of God," p. 35.

84. Marion, *The Idol and Distance*, p. 144.

85. Marion, *God without Being*, p. 144.

86. Ibid., p. 193.

87. Cf. Marion, *Being Given*, p. 74.

88. I am deliberately playing here with, perhaps even aggravating somewhat, phenomenology's incarnational tendencies in the perils of translating Husserl's "*leibhaft da*," so astutely exposed by Derrida *On Touching*, pp. 235ff.

89. Marion, *Being Given*, pp. 306–307.

90. Ibid., p. 307.

91. Ibid., p. 215.

92. Ibid., p. 314.

93. See ibid., p. 309.: "Since its finitude essentially determines the gifted, it cannot by definition adequately receive the given such as it gives itself—namely without limit or reserve."

94. Marion, *In the Self's Place*, p. 185.

95. Marion, *Being Given*, p. 101.

96. Marion, *In the Self's Place*, pp. 113–137.

97. Marion, "La transcendance par excellence," p. 170.

98. Ibid., p. 171.

99. Perhaps theology, too, should do well in not accepting too easily Marion's dialectical dualism between love and hate, because separating so neatly between those who love and those who do not is to forget that Christ's advance was not

one toward "the healthy, who do not need a doctor, but towards the sick" (Cf. Mk 2:17), to those precisely who had not yet received God's grace. Ultimately, separating so exclusively between those who have seen, heard, and received and those who have not, might be to abandon and deny that it are precisely those who do not yet see who are to be preferred over those who are always on the verge of taking too much pride in their ability to see (Cf. John 20:29).

100. Marion, *Reduction and Givenness*, pp. 186–192.
101. Ibid., p. 191.

Conclusion to Part 2

1. It will become clear that, on this point, the point of a "different yes," I am closer to Derrida than to Caputo's "viens, oui, oui." For Derrida, see *On Touching*, p. 279.
2. Caputo, *Religion*, p. 125.
3. Ignace Verhack, *Wat bedoelen wij wanneer we God zeggen?* (Kalmthout: Pelckmans, 2011), pp. 158–161.
4. It is clear that for such a *religious resistance* a certain form of universality is needed, and an *exodus* out of the status quo of (postsecular) presuppositions, where everything depends on particular interpretations and contexts, is required. Such a hermeneutics is of course the starting point for a philosophy of finitude but can never be its conclusion: hermeneutics may not lose sight of the possibility that within all historical constructs something arises that is not dependent on human construction or machinations and, in this way, remains transcendent to finite and historical interpretation.
5. Derrida, "Force of Law," in *Acts of Religion*, pp. 230–298, p. 244.
6. Ibid., p. 251.
7. Ibid., p. 252, Derrida's italics.
8. Ibid., p. 257.
9. Derrida, "On Forgiveness. A Roundtable Discussion with Jacques Derrida," in J. D. Caputo and M. Scanlon (eds.), *Questioning God* (Bloomington: Indiana University Press, 2001), pp. 52–72, p. 69.
10. Rubenstein, *Strange Wonder*, p. 166. Citation is Derrida, *Aporias*, trans T. Dutoit (Stanford: Stanford University Press, 1993), p. 19.
11. Žižek, "Dialectical Clarity versus the Misty Conceit of Paradox," in *The Monstrosity of Christ*, p. 258.
12. Ibid., p. 258.
13. Here I am following Watkin's coinage in his *Phenomenology or Deconstruction? The Question of Ontology in Maurice Merleau-Ponty, Paul Ricoeur and Jean-Luc Nancy* (Edinburgh: Edinburgh University Press, 2009), p. 191.
14. Nancy, *The Inoperative Community*, trans. P. Connor (Minneapolis: University of Minneapolis Press, 2006), p. 66.
15. Watkin, *Phenomenology or Deconstruction?*, p. 192.

16. See my "Orthodoxy: Process nor Product. Truth and Its History," in L. Boeve et al. (ed.), *Orthodoxy: Process or Product?* (Leuven: Peeters, 2009), pp. 45–61, pp. 52ff.

17. See for this also Stephen Shakespeare, "The Word Became Machine: Derrida's Technology of Incarnation," in *Derrida Today* 6 (2013): 36–57.

Chapter 8: Ludwig Binswanger's Phenomenology of Love

1. "Brief von Binswanger and Richard Hönigswald, 6 February 1947," in M. Herzog (ed.), *Vorträge und Aufsätze: Ausgewählte Werke* 3 (Heidelberg: Asanger, 1994), p. 316. Hereafter AW.

2. Binswanger, "Über die daseinsanalytische Forschungsrichtung in der Psychiatrie," in *AW* 3 (Heidelberg: Asanger, 1994), pp. 231–257, p. 232.

3. Binswanger, *Grundformen*, p. 218, referencing *Being and Time*, p. 343.

4. Binswanger for instance regularly features in Merleau-Ponty's *Phenomenology of Perception*, and Levinas mentions him in *Otherwise than Being*, p. 119. For a historical introduction to Binswanger and his predecessors, see Phillippe Cabestan and Françoise Dastur (eds.), *Daseinsanalyse* (Paris: Vrin, 2011) and in English, Herbert Spiegelberg, *Phenomenology in Psychology and Psychiatry* (Evanston, IL: Northwestern University Press, 1972), pp. 193–232.

5. Consider, again, Nancy's statement about Heidegger's dismissal of "the They": "it is too contemptuous to represent humanity to oneself as though the immense majority of our peers [. . .] passed their lives [. . .] misunderstanding [. . .] the intractable real that is dying": see *Dis-Enclosure*, p. 102.

6. Merleau-Ponty, *Husserl at the Limits of Phenomenology* (Evanston, IL: Evanston University Press, 2002), p. 20.

7. See Nancy, *Being Singular Plural*, p. 31 and also p. 66. It is important to note that this insight is also fundamental to Levinas's thought; see for instance his *Totality and Infinity*, p. 100mod.: "the explanation of a thought can only happen among two."

8. Heidegger, *Contributions to Philosophy. From Enowning*, trans. P. Emad and K. Maly (Bloomington: Indiana University Press, 1999), p. 6.

9. Marion, *Being Given*, p. 6.

10. Levinas, *Entre Nous. Thinking-of-the-Other* (London: Continuum, 2006), p. 143.

11. Jill Robbins (ed.), *Is it Righteous To Be? Interviews with Emmanuel Levinas* (Stanford: Stanford University Press, 2001), pp. 211–212. Last italics are mine.

12. Levinas, *Ethics and Infinity. Conversations with Philippe Nemo* (Pittsburgh: Duquesne University Press, 1985), p. 88.

13. Levinas, *Difficile liberté* (Paris: Albin Michel, 1976), p. 20.

14. Levinas, *Otherwise Than Being*, pp. 143–144.

15. Levinas, *God, Death, and Time*, p. 193.

16. For the beginning of an answer, see my *Ontotheological Turnings?*, pp. 203–204.

17. Levinas, *L'au-delà du verset. Lectures et discours talmudiques* (Paris: Minuit, 1982), p. 134.

18. Levinas, *Of God Who Comes to Mind*, pp. 150–151. It might be no coincidence that one of the most important prayers in Catholicism starts with a greeting, "*Ave*" and "*Kaire*," as if Mary appears as soon as she is greeted.

19. One could point to similar thoughts in *Totality and Infinity* (but without the hyperbole proper to *Otherwise Than Being*); see p. 195: "the knowledge that absorbs the Other is forthwith situated within the discourse I address to him." One might argue that *Totality and Infinity* did not go far enough in thinking the-one-before-the-other, leaving too much space for the other and me to "go on with our business," whereas *Otherwise Than Being* did go too far, leaving no room at all for an ego doing anything whatsoever.

20. In the *Grundformen*, Binswanger regularly mentions that love is "beyond good and evil;" see p. 524. See for this also Mireille Coulomb's excellent *Phénoménologie du Nous et psychopathologie de l'isolement. La nostrité selon Ludwig Binswanger* (Paris: Vrin, 2009), pp. 78–79.

21. Coulomb, *Phénoménologie du Nous*, p. 228.

22. Ibid., p. 231.

23. Binswanger, *Grundformen*, p. 73, citing Hugo Von Hoffmannsthal, *Die Wege und die Begegnungen* (Leipzig: Reclam, 1931), p. 31. Binswanger considers this quote rather closely on the following pages, but the "borderlessness" of this greeting and enticement is mentioned already on p. 19 and p. 63. Other occurrences: p. 157 and p. 159.

24. For these quotes, see ibid., pp. 186–187.

25. Ibid., p. 230; see also p. 204.

26. All of this, of course, makes for the fact that many of Binswanger's distinctions could be patiently deconstructed by a somewhat Derridean spirit (as, for instance, the distinction between the ontological greeting and the embodied gaze), but perhaps it is time to ask, once and for all: *a quoi bon?*

27. Binswanger, *Grundformen*, p. 74.

28. Ibid., p. 197.

29. Ibid., p. 258.

30. Ibid., p. 56.

31. Ibid., p. 76.

32. Ibid., p. 46. For the "ekstasis" of love, see p. 61.

33. Ibid., p. 61. Binswanger's reference to Heidegger's care as "already being ahead of oneself" is deliberate, see Heidegger, *Being and Time*, p. 375.

34. See Levinas, *Totality and Infinity*, p. 291 and also p. 86.

35. Ibid., p. 18 and p. 68.

36. Ibid., p. 22.

37. Ibid., p. 112.

38. See, for all this, ibid., p. 19 and p. 37.

39. For Binswanger's thoughts on the hand, see ibid., pp. 254–256. Cf. also p. 459, "Das Sein der Liebe [ist] durchaus *dialektisch*." One might say that for Binswanger Hegel plays a role as important as Heidegger does.

40. For this androgyny, see p. 199 and p. 620. On this topic, Binswanger would be closer to Heidegger than to Derrida, because the latter reproached Heidegger's *Unterwegs zur Sprache* for esteeming the *Geschlecht* of humanity a tiny bit higher than the ambiguity that is inherent to the two *Geschlechter*. I would side with Heidegger here: it seems far more important to unite humanity than to focus on the most differing difference one can come up with. I boldly assume then, contra Derrida, that whereas all naming is a gathering (of differences), not all gathering is an inappropriate naming. For this, see *Unterwegs zur Sprache* (Pfüllingen: Neske, 1975), p. 50. For Derrida, *Psyche. Inventions of the Other* II, trans. P. Kamuf and E. Rottenberg (Stanford: Stanford University Press, 2008), pp. 7–62. For the *Heimat* without autochthony in Binswanger, see *Grundformen*, p. 20 n. 10 and 37.

41. For the spatiality of loving togetherness, see *Grundformen*, pp. 65–67.

42. I am combining two important passages of the *Grundformen* here; see p. 47 and p. 67.

43. Ibid., p. 43.

44. Ibid., p. 86.

45. Cf. Nancy, "Shattered love," in his *Finite Thinking* (Stanford: Stanford University Press, 2003), pp. 245–274, p. 245.

46. Nancy, "Shattered love," p. 250.

47. Ibid., p. 258.

48. Binswanger, *Grundformen*, p. 39; between brackets is a citation of p. 59. Binswanger's italics.

49. Ibid., p. 60. The reference is to Heidegger's account of Descartes's *Übersprung* (*Being and Time*, p. 128). See also Binswanger's bold remark late in the *Grundformen* that whoever has not understood Heidegger's critique of Descartes and Kant, and their outrageous attempts to "prove the existence of a world out there," will not understand the meaning of his book; cf. p. 487 n. 10.

50. See for what follows ibid., pp. 74–75.

51. Ibid., p. 74.

52. Ibid., p. 441.

53. Ibid., p. 75.

54. Ibid., p. 75.

55. Ibid., p. 107, "schaut Dasein [. . .] sich als Mitdasein an."

56. Ibid., p. 72.

57. Ibid., p. 33.

58. Ibid., p. 232.

59. It is good to be reminded here that this issues from a meditation of Binswanger on the romantic poet Elizabeth Barrett Browning's words "Yet still my heart goes to thee—ponder how—not as to a single good but to all my good."

Binswanger, significantly, prefers Rilke's translation: "nicht wie zu einem, nein, wie zu allem, was ich Güte heiße"; see *Grundformen*, p. 94.

60. Ibid., pp. 585–586.
61. Cf. Marion, *The Erotic Phenomenon*, pp. 67–97.
62. Heidegger, *Being and Time*, pp. 116–117.
63. For this, Binswanger, *Grundformen*, pp. 49–50.
64. Cf. ibid., pp. 135ff.
65. Ibid., pp. 136–137. First quote is an allusion to *Being and Time*, p. 354: Dasein "*is* the null basis of its own nullity."
66. Ibid., p. 137.
67. For instance, Levinas, *Entre nous*, p. 75.
68. Heidegger's best example of such a nullity and "Nicht-charakter" is still *Einleitung in die Philosophie*, pp. 330–336. Binswanger, however, bases himself on the then–already published "Vom Wesen des Grundes," in *Wegmarken* (Frankfürt a. M: Klostermann, 2004), pp. 123–177, esp. pp. 165–168.
69. See for this *Grundformen*, p. 139 and also p. 159, p. 193, and p. 442.
70. Ibid., p. 81, p. 102, and p. 502.
71. Ibid., p. 102.
72. Spiegelberg erroneously sees in this faith an entirely subjective belief; see Spiegelberg, *Phenomenology and Psychiatry*, p. 217.
73. Ibid., pp. 585ff and p. 102 on the double wonder. For Foucault, see his lengthy *Jugendschrift* introducing Binswanger's *Dream and Existence*, where the dream is interpreted as the unrestricted and unceasing experience of Dasein of its own *Da*: what remains, once the body sinks into its sleep, is the sheer ecstasy of one's *idios kosmos*: I—my imagination, that is—build a world of my own; see Michel Foucault, "Dream, Imagination, and Existence," in Binswanger, *Dream and Existence* (Atlantic Highlands, NJ: Humanities Press, 1993), pp. 31–80, pp. 59ff.
74. For this, see *Grundformen*, pp. 157–158.
75. Binswanger would correct Foucault when the latter states that the "imagination" is essentially "iconoclastic"—the fact that the image of the dream is always short-lived and succeeded by another image—because the imagination, beyond good and evil, realizes the unification of both deception and satisfaction through ultimately uniting possibility and actuality. See *Dream and Existence*, p. 72 (for Foucault) and pp. 81–83 for Binswanger on deception. For a similar critique of Foucault's interpretation, see Caroline Gros, *Ludwig Binswanger. Entre phénoménologie et psychiatrie* (Chatou: Éd. La Transparence, 2009), p. 250.
76. See *Grundformen*, p. 298: "in jener 'Einbildung' enthüllt sich nämlich ein anthropologischer Wesenszug."

Chapter 9: The "Ends" of Love

1. Ibid., p. 4. Indications of this can be found in the letters between Binswanger and Heidegger, in M. Herzog (ed.), *Vorträge und Aufsätze: Ausgewählte*

Werke, 3, pp. 339–348 and Heidegger's letters to Boss in the *Zollikon Seminars—Protocols—Conversations—Letters*, ed. M. Boss, trans. F. Mayr and R. Askay (Evanston, IL: Northwestern University Press, 2001).

2. Respectively, Gros, *Ludwig Binswanger*, p. 266 n. 3 and Coulomb, *Phénoménologie du Nous*, p. 141.

3. Binswanger, *Grundformen*, p. 131. See also p. 76.

4. Ibid., p. 85.

5. Jacob Needleman, *Being-in-the-World*, p. 26 and p. 125.

6. One obviously needs to think here of Lacoste trying to differentiate between Dasein and the human being first liturgically and later through his phenomenology of life but also of Marion, who tried to configure "there without being" phenomenologically in his *Reduction and Givenness*, pp. 198–200.

7. In fact, "it does not fail to lead to suicide," *Grundformen*, p. 402. On the difference with Heidegger's anxiety, see Binswanger's "Über die daseinsanalytische Forschungsrichtung in der Psychiatrie," pp. 246–248, where anxiety, for Binswanger, cannot entirely be separated from world. On the contrary, if experienced by a "healthy" Dasein, it cannot make for a complete collapse of one's world (Heidegger would agree) and always and already leaves Dasein "something to work with" to overcome its anxiety (Heidegger perhaps would not agree with this dialectical interpretation). Horror, for Binswanger, is an "intensified" anxiety.

8. Binswanger, *Grundformen*, p. 229.

9. This is as far as Binswanger's purported "anthropocentrism" goes—one should recall that Von Hoffmansthal, central to Binswanger's thesis, relates the revelation of the fullness of being to a "dog in the sun" as well as to "stones." For these views on the muteness of being, see *Grundformen*, p. 407: "the ground does not answer, but remains—enigmatic" and p. 442, for Binswanger's view on psychology as the science in which the being that is interrogated [*befragt*] answers to the interrogation. This is the play Dasein has with itself and ultimately, as will become obvious, "the conversation of humanity with itself"; Binswanger, "Über Sprache und Denken," in *Vorträge und Aufsätze*, pp. 275–290, p. 290.

10. Binswanger, *Grundformen*, p. 321.

11. Ibid., p. 407.

12. Ibid., pp. 367–368.

13. Ibid., pp. 24–25.

14. Ibid., p. 33.

15. Ibid., p. 76.

16. Ibid., p. 176.

17. Ibid., p. 176. These are the three *Stimmungen* Binswanger mentions of this dialectic.

18. Ibid., p. 453.i

19. For Dasein as a heart, see ibid., pp. 92–97 and p. 111 for the remark on the pulse.

20. Nancy, "Shattered Love," pp. 251–252.

21. References in Levinas to the descent of the divine are understandably scarce, but see *Les imprévus de l'histoire* (Montpellier: Fata Morgana, 1994), p. 179, "Dieu descend dans le visage de l'autre" and *Transcendance et intelligibilité* (Genève: Labor et Fides, 1997), p. 25.

22. For Dasein as a heart, see *Grundformen*, pp. 92–97 and p. 111 for the remark on the pulse.

23. Ibid., p. 397.

24. Cf. ibid., p. 143.

25. Ibid., p. 230.

26. Ibid., p. 586.

27. Ibid., p. 97.

28. Ibid., p. 75 n. 28.

29. For this example, see ibid., p. 75.

30. For this issue, see Edmund Husserl, *Cartesian Meditations. An Introduction to Phenomenology*, trans. D. Cairns (The Hague: Nijhoff, 1960), pp. 112–113. Compare with his *Ideas II*, trans. R. Rojcewicz and A. Schuwer (Dordrecht: Kluwer, 1989), p. 174: I see "the other's touching hand [, which] appresents to me his solipsistic view of this hand and then *also everything that must belong to it* in presentified co-presence." For a discussion, see also Coulomb, *Phénoménologie du Nous*, pp. 32–33.

31. See, for the abandonment of the reduction, ibid., pp. 589–599. In this regard, one might argue that the insertion of an abstract figuration of Binswanger's wife in the opening pages of the *Grundformen* is a well-founded philosophical decision by the editors; see p. 47. Heidegger, who does not seem to have *read* the *Grundformen* and seems thus to proceed rather ontically and inauthentically—from hearsay, that is—misses this point entirely when stating that Binswanger does not distinguish between "pure" phenomenology and "descriptive" phenomenology, a distinction that was already clear to Binswanger in 1922; see his "Über Phänomenologie," in *Vorträge und Aufsätze*, pp. 35–69, esp. pp. 52–53 and pp. 66–67. For Heidegger, see *Zollikon Seminars*, p. 192. Similarly, when Heidegger argues that Binswanger "confuses ontological insights with ontic matters" (p. 228) he misses that this back and forth between ontic insights and ontological matters is exactly Binswanger's point. For Lacoste on the irreducible, see his *La phénoménalité de Dieu*, pp. 55–86.

32. Ibid., p. 513. See for all this the—rather obscure—pp. 505–507 and p. 238 on the spontaneity of the choice.

33. See ibid., pp. 104–105 and p. 422.

34. Ibid., p. 132 and p. 238, referring the phrase to Goethe.

35. The expression is taken from Michael Schmidt, *Ekstatischen Transzendenz. Ludwig Binswangers Phänomenologie der Liebe und die Aufdeckung der sozialontologischen Defizite in Heideggers "Sein und Zeit"* (Würzburg: Königshauzen und Neumann, 2005), p. 119 and p. 234.

36. Binswanger, *Grundformen*, p. 193.

37. Ibid., p. 28.

38. Ibid., p. 247 and "Über Sprache und Denken," p. 290, respectively. Compare also his *Formen misglückten Daseins*, in *AW* 2 (Heidelberg: Asanger, 1992), pp. 263–264.

39. Binswanger, "Über psychotherapie," in *AW* 3, pp. 215–216.

40. See Binswanger, "L'appréhension héraclitéenne de l'homme," in *Introduction à l'analyse existentielle*, trans. J. Verdeaux and R. Kuhn (Paris: Minuit: 1971), pp. 159–198, p. 192.

41. Cf. ibid., p. 180 and *Dream and Existence*, p. 99, respectively. For an introduction to Binswanger's views on these syndromes, see "Extravagance (*Verstiegenheit*)," in Needleman, *Being-in-the-world*, pp. 342–349.

42. Binswanger, *Grundformen*, p. 569.

43. Binswanger, "Über die Daseinsanalytische Forschungsrichtung in der Psychiatrie," p. 236.

44. Elucidating in this regard is Needleman, *Being-in-the-World*, p. 75, "If knife is said to be symbol of phallus, understanding of the patient falls short if it is not further asked: what does the phallus mean to the individual." Throughout the *Grundformen*, Binswanger rejects intentionality as it would allow us to see and glimpse only objects; see p. 68, p. 157, and esp. p. 181. Binswanger's take on Husserl's *Logical Investigations* and Heidegger's *Being and Time* is helpful, pp. 636–637.

45. Cf. Christopher Fynsk, *Language and Relation . . . That There Is Language* (Stanford: Stanford University Press, 1996), pp. 95–96.

46. Binswanger, *Grundformen*, p. 638.

47. Coulomb, *Phénoménologie du Nous*, p. 192 tries to see in Binswanger's (in) famous turn to Husserl's transcendental intersubjectivity in his later works a *continuation* of the Heideggerian-inspired loving togetherness of the *Grundformen*, although it lacks "perhaps [. . .] a transcendental theory of "constituting togetherness." Coulomb argues against Theunissen's claim that Binswanger's "fall into transcendental philosophy [. . .] disturbs everything he had built up in the previous 650 pages"; see Michael Theunissen, *Der Andere. Studien zur Sozialontologie der Gegenwart* (Berlin: Walter de Gruyter, 1965), pp. 470–471, arguing that "*Duhaftigkeit*" and "*Wirheit*" are in the end inborn a priori features, i.e., apart from the world and present always and everywhere, thus "prescribing" for community "its being" from the outset. Theunissen neglects, however, the back and forth or the coming and the going, the "difference" between the very ontic you and the ontological "youness," so missing that it is only because of this very ontic longing that I know of ontological longing as much as it is because of this ontological longing that I long for you ontically. In short, Binswanger is much closer to Derrida's empirical-transcendental indications than to a straightforward transcendental philosophy of Kant, (early) Husserl, and the like.

48. Husserl, *Cartesian Meditations*, p. 129, on the "intentional communion." See also Coulomb, *Phénoménologie du Nous*, pp. 193ff.

49. Binswanger, *Grundformen*, p. 191.

50. Ibid., pp. 201ff.

51. Ibid., p. 203.
52. Ibid., p. 209 n. 6.
53. Cf. ibid., p. 210.
54. See ibid., p. 211, fate is "Ein-Bildung des Weltlaufs in die Heimat des Herzens." With this common fate of friends, one is reminded of one of Marion's beautiful statements, see *In Excess. Five Studies*, trans. R. Horner (New York: Fordham University Press, 2002), p. 123: "the measure of friendship always remains duration." Friendship, for Marion, shows itself in the history of responses of one *adonné* to the other.
55. Ibid., p. 219.
56. Ibid., p. 228.
57. Ibid., p. 228. Friendship here concerns "the entire array of human history" (cf. p. 223)—Binswanger names the authors he cites as "his friends"—as taking part in the "conversation" humanity has with (and about) itself, in which each one individually weaves a web, whereas the web as a whole remains one (the image is taken from Rudolph Hildebrand).
58. Ibid., p. 231. Note the brackets around "constitution."
59. Ibid., p. 222, "dem aus dem Miteinandersein verstandene Tod."
60. Ibid., p. 222.
61. E.g., ibid., p. 163.
62. Ibid., p. 153.
63. Ibid., pp. 152–153.
64. Ibid., p. 155.
65. Cf. Heidegger, *Being and Time*, p. 303.
66. Binswanger, *Grundformen*, p. 218.
67. Ibid., p. 218. But note the hesitation in Binswanger here compared to p. 114: "just as I cannot succeed in love from out of authentic existence, so love does not pass into "authentic wholeness" (in Heidegger's sense)." The hesitation might be explained by Binswanger's reluctance when it comes to the "feasibility" of such an authentic self, calling it toward the end of the book increasingly "a limit situation." See further below when I speak of the "Da" of Dasein as its body.
68. Ibid., p. 159.
69. Ibid., p. 166.
70. Ibid., p. 167.
71. Binswanger rarely and reluctantly speaks of grace but at times cannot avoid it: see ibid., pp. 136–137 and p. 143.
72. Ibid., p. 167. It is in sentences as these, where the very ontic you seems to be abandoned, that Theunissen's contention that there is a certain remnant of metaphysics, as "the subordination of the Faktum to the eidos" (*Der Andere*, p. 470) and the quest for a "purer love" than the one that can be bodily fulfilled if not consummated, seems justified. See, for a similar move in the *Grundformen*, p. 548. Yet the reverse tendency, pointing to the empirical as a proof for the transcendental, is present just as well, see p. 155. Would this not just be the risk of any empirical-transcendental phenomenology?

73. Ibid., p. 170.
74. Ibid., p. 222.
75. Cf. ibid., p. 115.
76. Ibid., p. 349. The German has: "fliegt [. . .] über Sein und Zeit hinaus . . ."
77. Ibid., p. 217.
78. See Cabestan and Dastur, *Daseinsanalyse*, p. 73.
79. Binswanger, *Grundformen*, p. 580.
80. Ibid., p. 581.
81. Ibid., p. 328.
82. Ibid., p. 271. It is to be noted that for Binswanger such a "Nehmen-bei Etwas" is one of the *Grundformen* of human existence (cf. p. 394).
83. Ibid., p. 280.
84. Ibid., p. 319.
85. Cf. ibid., p. 282.
86. Ibid., pp. 215–216. Binswanger is citing Löwith's *Das Individuum in der Rolle des Mitmenschen* (München: Wissenschaftliche Buchgesellschaft Darmstadt, 1928), p. 82.
87. The phrase is taken from Bradley Seidman, *Absent at the Creation. The Existential Psychiatry of Ludwig Binswanger* (New York: Libra Publishers, 1983), p. 19.
88. Binswanger, *Grundformen*, p. 216 and p. 231, respectively.
89. Ibid., p. 227.
90. Ibid., p. 237.
91. Cf. ibid., p. 241. Binswanger explains that the *dualis*, the between of beings that is the greeting of love, is not a limited pluralis, through which the event of being unfortunately and somewhat Platonically needs beings. Seen from the perspective of love, friendship and our dealings with world are indeed to be seen as a limitation of love; seen from the perspective of the world, it is a further unfolding of love. Whereas love cannot *not* shiver when it comes in the world, being-in-the-world in turn receives some warmth from its presencing.
92. Cf. ibid., p. 302.
93. Ibid., p. 401. Binswanger speaks beautifully of the "Einmaligkeit des Eine," cf. ibid., p. 345.
94. Ibid., p. 380 and p. 432.
95. It is the latter that shows why it is so important that your lover can "get along" with your friends and why soon after the loving relationship is established, this love undergoes the first test of meeting with friends.
96. Binswanger, *Grundformen*, p. 231.
97. Ibid., p. 408.
98. See Derrida, *On Touching*, p. 292 and also p. 66.
99. Binswanger, *Grundformen*, p. 442.
100. Ibid., pp. 430–431.
101. Ibid., p. 431.

102. See for this ibid., p. 407.
103. Ibid., p. 431.
104. Ibid., p. 431.
105. See ibid., e.g., p. 218.
106. Ibid., pp. 308–309.
107. Ibid., p. 309.
108. Ibid., p. 407, p. 425, p. 433, and p. 580.
109. See for this ibid., pp. 424–425.
110. Caputo points this out with extreme care in *Demythologizing Heidegger*, pp. 61–74.
111. For Heidegger, *Being and Time*, pp. 355–356. Binswanger comments in the *Grundformen*, p. 498.
112. Binswanger, *Grundformen*, p. 232.
113. Ibid., p. 231 and p. 505.
114. Ibid., p. 432.
115. Ibid., p. 432 and p. 433.
116. Ibid., p. 453.
117. Ibid., p. 435.
118. Ibid., p. 502 and p. 508, two similar quotes that I am combining here.

Chapter 10: From Love to Life (and Back Again)

1. Cf. Heidegger, *Zollikon Seminars*, p. 116.
2. Binswanger, *Grundformen*, p. 453 and p. 408.
3. Ibid., p. 444 and 554, respectively.
4. Ibid., p. 548. See on this "imaginative realization" also pp. 585–586.
5. Binswanger, *Grundformen*, p. 258.
6. Ibid., p. 241.
7. Ibid., p. 462.
8. The reader might wonder why Binswanger, and all this talk on love, speaks so little about sex. Binswanger indeed has the courtesy not to speak about sex too much—he leaves that to the psychoanalysts. For Binswanger, sex is to be conceived, quite traditionally, within the loving relationship, where sex "isolates the body" of the lover and makes it possible for both lovers to enjoy without any shame "what is most of the body about the body"—*das Leiblichste der Leibhaftigkeit*. See ibid., p. 336.
9. See for this Caputo's analysis in *Prayers and Tears*, p. 314. The quote within the quote is Derrida, *Memoirs of the Blind: The Self-Portrait and Other Ruins*, trans. P.-A. Brault and M. Naas (Chicago: University of Chicago Press, 1993), p. 5 as cited by Caputo.
10. Binswanger, *Grundformen*, p. 308, with reference to Heidegger *Being and Time*, p. 420.
11. For such "*Reifung*," see *Grundformen*, p. 432.

12. See Binswanger, *Henrik Ibsen und das Problem der Selbstrealisation in der Kunst* (Heidelberg: Verlag Lambert Schneider, 1949).

13. See, e.g., Heidegger, *The Fundamental Concepts of Metaphysics*, p. 13, "It will [. . .] become clear for the first time that philosophizing fundamentally belongs to each human being as something proper to them, that certain human beings merely can or must have the strange fate of being a spur for others, so that philosophizing awakens in them." One might wonder whether this is indeed what a philosopher must do: rather than awakening the Dasein in each of us, one longs for the time when philosophers aspired to communicate the good life (*eudaimonia*) for each and every one of us.

14. Binswanger, *Ibsen*, p. 55.

15. Sloterdijk, *Life*, p. 175.

16. Binswanger, *Ibsen*, p. 48.

17. Ibid., p. 56.

18. Ibid., p. 55, for the height of philosophy. But one must also ask what this "*und so weiter*" exactly means here; see p. 56 for the *Lebensrichtung*.

19. Sloterdijk, *Life*, p. 175.

20. Binswanger, *Ibsen*, p. 51.

21. See Jean-Marc Narbonne, *Levinas and the Greek Heritage* (Leuven: Peeters Press, 2006), p. 84.

22. Binswanger, *Ibsen*, p. 34.

23. Cf. ibid., p. 37.

24. Ibid., p. 21.

25. The distress and the doubt of the artist seem to be constantly present in Binswanger's works, see *Grundformen*, pp. 408–412 (on H. G. Wells), *Ibsen*, pp. 7–10, p. 22, and p. 76, and especially "Über den Satz von Hoffmannsthal: 'Was Geist ist, erfaßt nur der Bedrängte," in *Vorträge und Aufsatze*, pp. 265–273, which reads like a summary of the *Grundformen*.

26. Binswanger, "Über den Satz," p. 268.

27. Ibid., p. 269.

28. Ibid., p. 269.

29. Ibid., p. 270.

30. Ibid., p. 270.

31. Binswanger, *Ibsen*, pp. 43–44.

32. "Passion" is the term Binswanger uses for the artist, like Ibsen, who has found peace with and is at home in his art. Such "passion" arises out of love and is the "*liebende Hingabe*," the giving oneself over, to one's art, see ibid., p. 24. The *Grundformen* configure this moment as that instant through which the artist abandons his or her distress and "gathers everything in his or her power to complete the task that is conferred upon him or her," see *Grundformen*, p. 411. One might critique Binswanger here for a lack of compassion, though, as in the neoliberal society that is ours and in the hierarchical society that was his, fewer and fewer people have the possibility to lead a life in accordance with their passions.

33. Binswanger, *Ibsen*, p. 25.

34. Ibid., p. 38.
35. Ibid., p. 38.
36. Binswanger, *Grundformen*, p. 598, with reference to Dilthey's, *Der Aufbau der Geschichtliche Welt in den Geisteswissenschaften*, in B. Groethuysen (ed.), *Gesammelte Schriften*, *VII* (Göttingen: Vandenhoeck & Ruprecht, 1992), p. 290.
37. Binswanger, *Ibsen*, p. 44.
38. Ibid., p. 44.
39. Ibid., p. 44.
40. Ibid., p. 47.
41. See for this criticism Binswanger, *Grundformen*, pp. 613–614.

Conclusion to Part 3

1. Binswanger, *Grundformen*, p. 129. See also p. 132 and p. 149.
2. Binswanger here is close to Levinas's explanation of his method in *Totality and Infinity*, p. 173: "[t]he method practiced here does indeed consist in seeking the condition of empirical situations, but it leaves to the developments called empirical, in which the conditioning possibility is accomplished—it leaves to the *concretization*—an ontological role that specifies the meaning of the fundamental possibility, a meaning invisible in that condition."

General Conclusion

1. Binswanger, *Ibsen*, p. 44.
2. Cf. Marion, *The Reason of the Gift* (Charlottesville: University of Virginia Press, 2011), p. 46.
3. Coulomb, *Phénoménologie du Nous*, p. 164. Some indications of such a theory can be found in Nathalie Depraz, *Lucidité du corps. De l'empirisme transcendental en phénoménologie* (Dordrecht: Kluwer, 2001), pp. 205–227, although she seems to put too much stress on the empirical dimension of such a phenomenology, through which phenomenology might evaporate in sociology and become dependent entirely upon empirical studies of social behavior. Whereas for Depraz, the empirical is *constitutive* of the transcendental, for us the empirical remains mute and does not give any clear and distinct directions for the constitution of the transcendental.
4. Heidegger, "The Word of Nietzsche," p. 69.
5. In Nancy, the "being-with" of all beings leads to a community of humanity that shares only the sharing of being. Thus: not *what* we share in a particular culture (identity, family, nationality, etc.) but the sheer fact of sharing itself is what is important. Again: all naming is a gathering, but not all gathering need be a naming.
6. See my *An Introduction to Jean-Yves Lacoste* (Aldershot: Ashgate, 2012), p. 189.
7. Binswanger, *Grundformen*, p. 131.

8. Levinas, *Otherwise Than Being*, p. 194 n. 4 and n. 3, respectively.

9. Nancy, *Being Singular Plural*, p. 161.

10. See for this also Derrida, *On Touching*, p. 237, speaking of an "archifacticity" as "a place of alterity and heterogeneity that is not necessarily and foremost that of an *alter ego*," translation modified.

11. Ibid., p. 237.

12. Hägglund, *Radical Atheism*, p. 9 and p. 34. This, in fact, is already what my *Ontotheological Turnings?* argued for against Levinas's and Marion's version of the "without being," see p. 227, where it is said that "being presences through lacks, gaps and holes."

13. One should keep in mind that the concern for animals is the one thing that Caputo does not take from Derrida, and the sketch of the "animal needs" of Jesus (sleeping, eating, etc.) in his recent *The Insistence of God. A Theology of Perhaps* (Bloomington: Indiana University Press, 2013), e.g., p. 169 and p. 253 are too classically anthropocentric to convince: in Caputo, no cats regarding us (Derrida), no *Hunde unter dem Tisch* (Heidegger), and no dogs in the sun greeting us (Binswanger). See for Derrida on such privation, Leonard Lawlor, *This Is Not Sufficient. An Essay on Animality and Human Nature in Derrida* (New York: Columbia University Press, 2007).

14. Levinas, *Otherwise than Being*, p. 155.

15. Levinas, *Totality and Infinity*, p. 99.

16. Ibid., p. 153.

17. Ibid., p. 147.

18. Ibid., p. 96.

19. Ibid., p. 98. Note that the statements at the time of *Otherwise Than Being* are, for the most part, continuous to the account given in *Totality and Infinity*, for the Saying or the testimony is not to be taken as the "giving out of signs" or as "a simple transmission of a content or of a said," for speaking is not merely "a translating of thoughts into words," as if a transcendental ego (sender) would always already have chosen to say something (message) to the other, who would then in turn decipher the sign (receiver); see, respectively, Levinas, *Otherwise Than Being*, p. 49; *God, Death, and Time*, p. 151; and again *Otherwise Than Being*, p. 48.

20. Levinas, *Otherwise Than Being*, p. 140.

21. Ibid., p. 144.

22. Cf. ibid., p. 189 n. 21.

23. See, e.g., Heidegger, *On the Way to Language*, trans. P. D. Hert (Bloomington: Indiana University Press 1982), p. 62.

24. See Heidegger, *Parmenides*, p. 85, where Heidegger equates "*legein*" with the name "for Being itself."

25. Heidegger, *Plato's Sophist*, p. 408.

26. Ibid., pp. 411–422.

27. Ibid., p. 415mod. Again: the German has: "der 'logos' [. . .] hat zunächst vorgegeben eine unabgehobene Einheit eines Seienden," see Heidegger, *Platon: Sophistes* (Frankfürt a. M: Klostermann, 1992), p. 599.

28. Ibid., p. 415mod.; *Plato: Sophistes*, p. 600.
29. Ibid., pp. 416ff.
30. Cf. Levinas, *Totality and Infinity*, p. 139.
31. Levinas, *Otherwise Than Being*, p. 151.
32. See ibid., pp. 45–48, 150, 151 and also Levinas, *God, Death, and Time*, p. 191.
33. Heidegger, *Plato's Sophist*, p. 417.
34. Cf. Levinas, *Totality and Infinity*, p. 70 and pp. 175ff.
35. See also Scott M. Campbell, *The Early Heidegger's Philosophy of Life. Facticity, Being, and Language* (New York: Fordham University Press, 2012).
36. See for the "distortion" of truth through "the curial of the curia," Heidegger, *Parmenides*, pp. 45ff.
37. Heidegger, *The Phenomenology of Religious Life*, trans. M. Fritsch and J. A. Gosetti-Ferencei (Bloomington: Indiana University Press, 2010), p. 72; *Phänomenologie des Religiösen Lebens* (Fränkfurt a. M: Klostermann, 1995), p. 103, "kein Motiv zur Beunruhigung." One should, again, note the remarkable continuity in the use of this pair rest and unrest or certainty and uncertainty in Heidegger. In *Einführung in die Phänomenologische Forschung*, p. 224, "die Sorge der Beruhigung" is used to typify Descartes's evasion of all uncertainty to arrive at the (for Heidegger illusionary) *fundamentum inconcussum* of the ego. For its use in *Being and Time*, see p. 298, where "Beruhigung" is translated as "tranquillization."
38. Here I am portraying Heidegger, *The Phenomenology of Religious Life*, pp. 65–82.
39. On the concept of such an unredeemedness, see my *Ontotheological Turnings?*, pp. 229–238.
40. On this "liturgical unhappiness of conscience," Lacoste, *Experience and the Absolute. Disputed Questions on the Humanity of Man* (New York: Fordham University Press, 2004), pp. 66–70.

Bibliography

Abensour, Miguel, "Savage Democracy and 'Principle of Anarchy,' " in *Philosophy and Social Criticism* 28 (2002) 703–726.

Achterhuis, Hans, "De utopie van Peter Sloterdijk: Regels voor het mensenpark," in *Tijdschrift voor filosofie* 64 (2002) 451–478.

Binswanger, Ludwig, *Henrik Ibsen und das Problem der Selbstrealisation in der Kunst* (Heidelberg: Verlag Lambert Schneider, 1949).

———, "L'appréhension héraclitéenne de l'homme," in *Introduction à l'analyse existentielle*, trans. J. Verdeaux and R. Kuhn (Paris: Minuit: 1971), pp. 159–198.

———, "Formen misglückten Daseins," in M. Herzog (ed.) *Ausgewählte Werke* 1 (Heidelberg: Asanger, 1992), pp. 233–419.

———, "Grundformen und Erkenntnis des menschlichen Daseins," in M. Herzog and H. J. Braun (eds.), *Ausgewählte Werke* 2 (Heidelberg: Asanger Verlag, 1993).

———, *Dream and Existence* (Atlantic Highlands, NJ: Humanities Press, 1993).

———, "Über Phänomenologie," in M. Herzog (ed.), *Vorträge und Aufsätze: Ausgewählte Werke* 3 (Heidelberg: Asanger, 1994), pp. 35–69.

———, "Brief von Binswanger an Richard Hönigswald, 6 February 1947," in M. Herzog (ed.), *Vorträge und Aufsätze: Ausgewählte Werke* 3 (Heidelberg: Asanger, 1994), p. 316.

———, "Über psychotherapie," in M. Herzog (ed.), *Vorträge und Aufsätze: Ausgewählte Werke* 3 (Heidelberg: Asanger, 1994), pp. 205–230.

———, "Über die daseinsanalytische Forschungsrichtung in der Psychiatrie," in M. Herzog (ed.), *Vorträge und Aufsätze: Ausgewählte Werke* 3 (Heidelberg: Asanger, 1994), pp. 231–257.

———, "Über den Satz von Hoffmannsthal: 'Was Geist ist, erfaßt nur der Bedrängte,' " in M. Herzog (ed.), *Vorträge und Aufsätze: Ausgewählte Werke* 3 (Heidelberg: Asanger, 1994), pp. 265–273.

———, "Über Sprache und Denken," in M. Herzog (ed.), *Vorträge und Aufsätze: Ausgewählte Werke* 3 (Heidelberg: Asanger, 1994), pp. 275–290.

———, 'Über den Satz von Hoffmannsthal: 'Was Geist ist, erfaßt nur der Bedrängte,' in M. Herzog (ed.), *Vorträge und Aufsätze: Ausgewählte Werke* 3 (Heidelberg: Asanger, 1994), pp. 265–273.

Blumenberg, Hans, *The Legitimacy of the Modern Age*, trans. R. Wallace (Cambridge: MIT Press, 1985).
Buber, Martin, *De weg van de mens*, trans. H. Korteweg (Utrecht: Klement, 1998).
Cabestan, Phillip, and Françoise Dastur (eds.), *Daseinsanalyse* (Paris: Vrin, 2011).
Campbell, Scott M., *The Early Heidegger's Philosophy of Life. Facticity, Being, and Language* (New York: Fordham University Press, 2012).
Caputo, John D., *Demythologizing Heidegger* (Bloomington: Indiana University Press, 1993).
———, *Deconstruction in a Nutshell. A Conversation with Jacques Derrida* (New York: Fordham University Press, 1997).
———, *The Prayers and Tears of Jacques Derrida. Religion without Religion* (Bloomington: Indiana University Press, 1997).
———, "Apostles of the Impossible. On God and the Gift in Derrida and Marion," in J. D. Caputo and M. Scanlon (eds.), *God, the Gift, and Postmodernism* (Bloomington: Indiana University Press, 1999), pp. 185–222.
———, *On Religion* (London: Routledge, 2001).
———, "Jacques Derrida (1930–2004)," in *Journal of Cultural and Religious Theory* 6 (2004) 6–9.
———, and Scanlon Michael (eds.), *Augustine and Postmodernism. Confessions and Circumfession* (Bloomington: Indiana University Press, 2005).
———, "Shedding Tears Beyond Being. Derrida's Confession of Prayer," in J. D. Caputo and M. Scanlon (eds.), *Augustine and Postmodernism. Confessions and Circumfession* (Bloomington: Indiana University Press, 2005), pp. 95–114.
———, *The Weakness of God. A Theology of the Event* (Bloomington: Indiana University Press, 2006).
———, *Philosophy and Theology* (Nashville: Abingdon Press, 2006).
———, "Only as Hauntology Is Religion without Religion Possible. A Response to Hart," in M. Zlomislic and N. DeRoo (eds.), *Cross and Khôra. Deconstruction and Ethics in the Work of John D. Caputo* (Eugene, OR: Pickwick Publishers, 2010), pp. 109–117.
———, "The Chance of Love. A Response to Olthuis," in M. Zlomislic and N. DeRoo (eds.), *Cross and Khôra. Deconstruction and Ethics in the Work of John D. Caputo* (Eugene, OR: Pickwick Publishers, 2010), pp. 187–196.
———, "The Sense of God. A Theology of the Event with Special Reference to Christianity," in L. Boeve and C. Brabant (eds.), *Between Philosophy and Theology. Contemporary Interpretations of Christianity* (Aldershot: Ashgate, 2010), pp. 27–41.
———, "The Return of Anti-Religion: From Radical Atheism to Radical Theology," in *Journal of Cultural and Religious Theory* 11 (2011) 32–124.
———, "On Not Settling for an Abridged Edition of Postmodernism. Radical Hermeneutics as Radical Theology," in Aaron Simmons and Stephen Minister (eds.), *Reexamining Deconstruction and Determinate Religion. Toward a Religion with Religion* (Duquesne: Duquesne University Press, 2012), pp. 271–353.

———, review of *Difficult Atheism. Post-Theological Thinking in Alain Badiou, Jean-Luc Nancy and Quentin Meillassoux* by Christopher Watkin, *Notre Dame Philosophical Book Reviews* (2012/06/10).

———, review of *In the Self's Place: the Approach of Augustine* by Jean-Luc Marion, *Notre Dame Philosophical Book Reviews* (January 18, 2013).

———, *The Insistence of God. A Theology of Perhaps* (Bloomington: Indiana University Press, 2013).

Coulomb, Mireille, *Phénoménologie du Nous et psychopathologie de l'isolement. La nostrité selon Ludwig Binswanger* (Paris: Vrin, 2009).

Depraz, Natalie, *Lucidité du corps. De l'empirisme transcendantal en phénoménologie* (Dordrecht: Kluwer, 2001).

Derrida, Jacques, "Violence and Metaphysics. An Essay on the Thought of Emmanuel Levinas," in *Writing and Difference*, trans. A. Bass (Chicago: University of Chicago Press, 1978), pp. 79–153.

———, "Structure, Sign, and Play in the Discourse of the Human Sciences," in *Writing and Difference*, trans. A. Bass (Chicago: University of Chicago Press, 1978), pp. 278–293.

———, "Différance," in *Margins of Philosophy*, trans. A. Bass (Chicago: University of Chicago Press, 1982), pp. 1–28.

———, "The Ends of Man," in *Margins of Philosophy*, trans. A. Bass (Chicago: University of Chicago Press, 1982), pp. 109–136.

———, *Of Spirit. Heidegger and the Question*, trans. G. Bennington and R. Bowlby (Chicago: University of Chicago Press, 1989).

———, *Edmund Husserl's Origin of Geometry. An Introduction*, trans. J. P. Leavey (London: University of Nebraska Press, 1989).

———, "How to Avoid Speaking: Denials," trans. K. Frieden, in S. Budick and W. Iser (eds.), *Languages of the Unsayable. The Play of Negativity in Literature and Literary Theory* (New York: Columbia University Press, 1989), pp. 3–70.

———, *Aporias*, trans. T. Dutoit (Stanford: Stanford University Press, 1993).

———, *Àdieu à Emmanuel Levinas* (Paris: Galilée, 1996).

———, "History of the Lie. Prolegomena," in *Graduate Faculty Philosophy Journal* 19 (1997) 129–161.

———, *Politics of Friendship*, trans. G. Collins (London: Verso, 1997).

———, "Linguistics and Grammatology," in *Of Grammatology*, trans. G. Spivak (Baltimore: John Hopkins University Press, 1997), pp. 27–73.

———, "That Dangerous Supplement," in *Of Grammatology*, trans. G. Spivak (Baltimore: John Hopkins University Press, 1997), pp. 141–164.

———, *À Dieu to Emmanuel Levinas*, trans. P.-A. Brault and M. Naas (Stanford: Stanford University Press, 1999).

———, and Geoffrey Bennington, *Circumfession* (Chicago: University of Chicago Press, 1999).

———, *Of Hospitality. Anne Dufourmantelle Invites Jacques Derrida to Respond* (Stanford: Stanford University Press, 2000).

———, "To Forgive," in J. D. Caputo, and M. Scanlon (eds.), *Questioning God* (Bloomington: Indiana University Press, 2001), pp. 21–51.

———, "On Forgiveness. A Roundtable Discussion with Jacques Derrida," in J. D. Caputo and M. Scanlon (eds.), *Questioning God* (Bloomington: Indiana University Press, 2001), pp. 52–72.

———, "Faith and Knowledge. The Two Sources of 'Religion' at the Limits of Reason Alone," in J. Derrida, *Acts of Religion* (London: Routledge, 2002), pp. 42–101.

———, "Force of Law," in J. Derrida, *Acts of Religion* (London: Routledge, 2002), pp. 230–298.

———, *Le toucher-Jean-Luc Nancy* (Paris: Galilée, 2002).

———, *On Touching—Jean-Luc Nancy* (Stanford: Stanford University Press, 2005).

———, "Confessions and 'Circumfession.' A Roundtable Discussion with Jacques Derrida," in J. D. Caputo and M. Scanlon (eds.), *Augustine and Postmodernism. Confessions and Circumfession* (Bloomington: Indiana University Press, 2005), pp. 28–49.

———, *Rogues. Two Essays on Reason*, trans. P.-A. Brault and M. Baas (Stanford: Stanford University Press, 2005).

———, *L'animal que donc je suis* (Paris: Galilée, 2006).

———, *The Animal That Therefore I Am*, trans. M. Millet (New York: Fordham University Press, 2008).

———, *Psyche. Inventions of the Other II*, trans. P. Kamuf and E. Rottenberg (Stanford: Stanford: University Press, 2008).

Devisch, Ignaas, et al., *Re-treating Religion. Deconstructing Christianity with Jean-Luc Nancy* (New York: Fordham University Press, 2012).

Doyon, Maxime, *Die transzendentale Anspruch der Dekonstruktion. Zur Erneuerung des Begriffs "transzendental" bei Derrida* (Würzburg: Ergon Verlag, 2012).

Fabbri, Lorenzo, "Philosophy as Chance. An Interview with Jean-Luc Nancy," in *Critical Inquiry* 33 (2007) 427–440.

Foucault, Michel, "Dream, Imagination, and Existence," in Binswanger, *Dream and Existence* (Atlantic Highlands, NJ: Humanities Press, 1993), pp. 31–80.

Fynsk, Christopher, *Language and Relation . . . That There Is Language* (Stanford: Stanford University Press, 1996).

Gagey, Henri-Jérôme, *La vérité en procès* (Paris: Bayard, 2009).

Gasché, Rodolphe, "Hegemonic Fantasms," in *Research in Phenomenology* 35 (2005) 311–326.

Gros, Caroline, *Ludwig Binswanger. Entre phénoménologie et psychiatrie* (Chatou: Éd. La Transparence, 2009).

Gschwandtner, Christina, *Reading Jean-Luc Marion. Exceeding Metaphysics* (Bloomington: Indiana University Press, 2007).

———, *Postmodern Apologetics? Arguments for God in Contemporary Philosophy* (New York: Fordham University Press, 2013).

Hägglund, Martin, *Radical Atheism. Derrida and the Time of Life* (Stanford: Stanford University Press, 2008).
———, "The Challenge of Radical Atheism: A Response," in *The New Centennial Review* 9 (2009) 227–252.
———, "The Radical Evil of Deconstruction. A Reply to Caputo," in *Journal of Cultural and Religious Theory* 11 (2011) 126–150.
Hart, Kevin, "Without," in M. Zlomislic and N. DeRoo (eds.), *Cross and Khôra. Deconstruction and Ethics in the Work of John D. Caputo* (Eugene, OR: Pickwick Publishers, 2010), pp. 80–108.
Heidegger, Martin, *Being and Time*, trans. J. Macquarrie and E. Robinson (San Francisco: Harper and Row, 1962).
———, *Unterwegs zur Sprache* (Pfüllingen: Neske, 1975).
———, "The Word of Nietzsche. God Is Dead," in *The Question Concerning Technology and Other Essays*, trans. W. Lovitt (New York: Harper and Row, 1977), pp. 53–112.
———, "The Age of the World Picture," in *The Question Concerning Technology and Other Essays*, trans. W. Lovitt (New York: Harper and Row, 1977), pp. 114–154.
———, *On the Way to Language*, trans. P. D. Hert (Bloomington: Indiana University Press, 1982).
———, *Parmenides*, trans. A. Schuwer and R. Rojcewicz (Bloomington: Indiana University Press, 1992).
———, *Plato's Sophistes* (Frankfurt a. M.: Vittorio Klostermann, 1992).
———, "The Origin of the Work of Art," in *Basic Writings*, ed. D. F. Krell (London: Routledge, 1993), pp. 143–212.
———, "Letter on Humanism," in *Basic Writings*, ed. D. F. Krell (London: Routledge, 1993), pp. 213–265.
———, *Phänomenologie des Religiösen Lebens* (Fränkfurt a. M: Klostermann, 1995).
———, *The Fundamental Concepts of Metaphysics. World, Finitude. Solitude*, trans. W. McNeill and N. Walker (Bloomington: Indiana University Press, 1995).
———, *Grundfragen der Philosophie* (Frankfürt a. Main, Klostermann, 1996).
———, *Parmenides* (Frankfürt a. M: Klostermann, 1996).
———, *Plato's Sophist*, trans. R. Rojcewicz and A. Schuwer (Bloomington: Indiana University Press, 1997).
———, *Was ist Metaphysik?* (Frankfürt a. M: Klostermann, 1998).
———, *Contributions to Philosophy. From Enowning*, trans. P. Emad and K. Maly (Bloomington: Indiana University Press, 1999).
———, *Introduction to Metaphysics*, trans. G. Fried and R. Polt (New Haven: Yale University Press, 2000).
———, *Einleitung in die Philosophie* (Frankfürt a. M: Vittorio Klostermann, 2001).
———, *Zollikon Seminars. Protocols-Conversations-Letters*, trans. F. Mayr and R. Askay (Evanston, IL: Northwestern University Press, 2001).

———, "Der Ursprung des Kunstwerkes," in *Holzwege* (Frankfurt a. M: Vittorio Klostermann, 2003), pp. 7–74.

———, "Vom Wesen des Grundes," in *Wegmarken* (Frankfürt a. M: Klostermann, 2004), pp. 123–177.

———, *Einführung in die Phänomenologische Forschung* (Frankfürt a. Main: Klostermann, 2006).

———, *Phenomenology of Religious Life*, trans. M. Fritsch and J. A. Gosetti-Ferencei (Bloomington: Indiana University Press, 2010).

Heikkilä, Marta, *At the Limits of Presentation. Coming into Presence and Its Aesthetic Relevance in Jean-Luc Nancy's Philosophy* (Frankfurt: Peter Lang, 2008).

Husserl, Edmund, *Cartesian Meditations. An Introduction to Phenomenology*, trans. D. Cairns (The Hague: Nijhoff, 1960).

———, *Ideas Pertaining to A Pure Phenomenology and to a Phenomenological Philosophy II*, trans. R. Rojcewicz and A. Schuwer (Dordrecht: Kluwer, 1989).

Houellebecq, Michel, and Bernard-Henry Levy, *Publieke vijanden* (Amsterdam: Arbeiderspers, 2009).

James, Ian, *The Fragmentary Demand. An Introduction to the Philosophy of Jean-Luc Nancy* (Stanford: Stanford University Press, 2006).

Janicaud, Dominique, "Riveted to a Monstrous Site. Reiner Schürmann's Reading of Heidegger's Beiträge," in *Graduate Faculty Philosophy Journal* 19 (1997) 287–297.

Kolakowski, Leszek, *Metaphysical Horror* (Chicago: University of Chicago Press, 2001).

Lacoste, Jean-Yves, *Experience and the Absolute. Disputed Questions on the Humanity of Man*, trans. M. Raftery-Skehan (New York: Fordham University Press, 2004).

———, *La phénoménalité de Dieu. Neuf études* (Paris: Cerf, 2008).

———, *Être en danger* (Paris: Cerf, 2011).

———, "L'intuition sacramentelle," in *Revue théologique de Louvain* 42 (2011) 496–525.

Lawlor, Leonard, *This Is Not Sufficient. An Essay on Animality and Human Nature in Derrida* (New York: Columbia University Press, 2007).

Leask, Ian (ed.), "From Radical Hermeneutics to the Weakness of God. John D. Caputo in Dialogue with Mark Dooley," in M. Zlomislic and N. DeRoo (eds.), *Cross and Khôra. Deconstruction and Ethics in the Work of John D. Caputo* (Eugene, OR: Pickwick Publishers, 2010), pp. 327–347.

Levinas, Emmanuel, *Difficile liberté* (Paris: Michel Albin, 1976).

———, *L'au-delà du verset. Lectures et discours talmudiques* (Paris: Minuit: 1982).

———, *Ethics and Infinity. Conversations with Philippe Nemo* (Pittsburgh: Duquesne University Press, 1985).

———, *Time and the Other*, trans. R. A. Cohen (Pittsburgh: Duquesne University Press, 1987).

———, *Les imprévus de l'histoire* (Montpellier: Fata Morgana, 1994).

———, *Transcendance et intelligibilité* (Genève: Labor et Fides, 1997).

———, *Of God Who Comes to Mind*, trans. B. Bergo (Stanford: Stanford University Press, 1998).
———, *God, Death, and Time*, trans. B. Bergo (Stanford: Stanford University Press, 2000).
———, *Existence and Existents*, trans. A. Lingis (Pittsburgh: Duquesne University Press, 2001).
———, *Otherwise Than Being, or Beyond Essence*, trans. A. Lingis (Duquesne: Duquesne University Press, 2002).
———, *Totality and Infinity. An Essay on Exteriority*, trans A. Lingis (Pittsburgh: Duquesne University Press, 2002).
———, *Entre Nous. Thinking-of-the-Other* (London: Continuum, 2006).
Lilly, Reginald, "The Topology of Des hégémonies brisées," in *Research in Phenomenology* 28 (1998) 226–242.
Marion, Jean-Luc, *Réduction et donation. Recherches sur Husserl, Heidegger et la phénoménologie* (Paris: PUF, 1989).
———, *God without Being. Hors-Texte*, trans. T. A. Carlson (Chicago: University of Chicago Press, 1991).
———, *Étant donné. Essai d'une phénoménologie de la donation* (Paris: PUF, 1998).
———, *The Idol and Distance. Five Studies*, trans. T. A. Carlson (New York: Fordham University Press, 2001).
———, *Reduction and Givenness. Investigations of Husserl, Heidegger, and Phenomenology*, trans. T. A. Carlson (Evanston, IL: Northwestern University Press, 1998).
———, *Being Given. Toward a Phenomenology of Givenness*, trans. J. Kosky (Stanford: Stanford University Press, 2002).
———, *Dieu sans l'être. Hors Texte* (Paris: PUF, 2002).
———, *In Excess. Studies of Saturated Phenomena*, trans. R. Horner and V. Berraud (New York: Fordham University Press, 2002).
———, "Mihi magna quaestio factus sum. The Privilege of Unknowing," in *Journal of Religion* 85 (2005) 1–24.
———, *The Erotic Phenomenon*, trans. S. E. Lewis (Chicago: University of Chicago Press, 2007).
———, *The Visible and the Revealed*, trans. C. Gschwandtner (New York: Fordham University Press, 2008).
———, *Au lieu de soi. L'approach de Saint-Augustin* (Paris: PUF, 2008).
———, "La transcendance par excellence," in *Le croire pour le voir. Réflexions diverses sur la rationalité de la révélation et l'irrationalité de quelques croyants* (Paris: Parole et Silence, 2010), pp. 167–175.
———, *The Reason of the Gift* (Charlottesville: University of Virginia Press, 2011).
———, *In the Self's Place. The Approach of Saint Augustine*, trans. J. Kosky (Stanford: Stanford University Press, 2012).
Merleau-Ponty, Maurice, *Phénoménologie de la perception* (Paris: Gallimard, 1945).
———, *Signes* (Paris: Gallimard, 1960).
———, *Éloge de la philosophie et autres essais* (Paris: Gallimard, 1960).

———, *The Visible and the Invisible*, trans. A. Lingis (Evanston, IL: Northwestern University Press, 1968).
———, *Husserl at the Limits of Phenomenology* (Evanston, IL: Evanston University Press, 2002).
Milbank, John, "The Double Glory or Paradox versus Dialectics: On Not Quite Agreeing with Slavoj Žižek," in C. Davis (ed.), *The Monstrosity of Christ. Paradox or Dialectic?* (Cambridge: MIT Press, 2008), pp. 110–233.
———, et al. (eds.), *Radical Orthodoxy: A New Theology* (London: Routledge, 1999).
Naas, Michael, "An Atheism That (Dieu merci!) Still Leaves Something to Be Desired," in *The New Centennial Review* 9 (2009) 45–68.
———, *Miracle and Machine Jacques Derrida and the Two Sources of Religion, Science, and the Media* (New York: Fordham University Press, 2012).
Nancy, Jean-Luc, *The Experience of Freedom*, trans. B. McDonald (Stanford: Stanford University Press, 1993).
———, *The Gravity of Thought*, trans. F. Raffoul and G. Recco (Atlantic Highlands, NJ: Humanities Press, 1993).
———, *Le sens du monde* (Paris: Galilée, 1993).
———, *Être Singulier Pluriel* (Paris: Galilée, 1996).
———, *Des lieux divins, suivi du calcul du poète* (Mauvezin: T.E.R., 1997).
———, *Being Singular Plural*, trans. R. D. Richardson and A. E. O'Byrne (Stanford: Stanford University Press, 2000).
———, "L'éthique originaire de Heidegger," in *La pensée dérobée* (Paris: Galilée, 2001), pp. 85–113.
———, *La visitation (de la peinture chrétienne)* (Paris: Galilée, 2001).
———, *La création du monde ou la mondialisation* (Paris: Galilée, 2002).
———, "Shattered Love," in *A Finite Thinking* (Stanford: Stanford University Press, 2003), pp. 245–274.
———, "'Our World' An Interview," in *Angelaki* 8 (2003) 43–54.
———, *La communauté désœuvrée* (Paris: Christian Bourgois, 2004).
———, *La déclosion. Déconstruction du christianisme* (Paris: Galilée, 2005).
———, "Of Divine Places," in *The Inoperative Community*, trans. P. Connor et al. (Minneapolis: University of Minnesota Press, 2006), pp. 110–150.
———, *The Creation of the World or Globalization*, trans. F. Raffoul and D. Pettigrew (Albany: State University of New York Press, 2007).
———, "Hors tout," in D. Cohen-Levinas and B. Clément (eds.), *Emmanuel Levinas et les territoires de pensée* (Paris: PUF, 2007), pp. 382–392.
———, "The Intruder," in *Corpus*, trans. R. Rand and (New York: Fordham University Press, 2008), pp. 161–170.
———, "The Being-with of Being-there," in *Continental Philosophical Review* 41 (2008) 1–15.
———, *Dis-Enclosure. The Deconstruction of Christianity*, trans. B. Bergo, G. Malenfant, and M. B. Smith (New York: Fordham University Press, 2008).
———, *Noli me tangere. On the Raising of the Body*, trans. S. Clift, P.-A. Brault, and M. Naas (New York: Fordham University Press, 2008).

———, *Adoration. The Deconstruction of Christianity*, II, trans. J. McKeane (New York: Fordham University Press, 2013).
Narbonne, Jean-Marc, *Levinas and the Greek Heritage* (Leuven: Peeters Press, 2006).
Needleman, Jacob, *Being-in-the-World. Selected Papers of Ludwig Binswanger*, trans. and intro. J. Needleman (London: Basic Books, 1963).
Olthuis, James. "Testing the Heart of Khôra," in M. Zlomislic and N. DeRoo (eds.), *Cross and Khôra. Deconstruction and Ethics in the Work of John D. Caputo* (Eugene, OR: Pickwick Publishers, 2010), pp. 174–185.
Paasilinna, Arto, *Wees genadig* (Amsterdam: Wereldbibliotheek, 2011).
Raffoul, François, *A chaque fois mien. Heidegger et la question du sujet* (Paris: Galilée, 2004).
Robbins, Jill (ed.), *Is It Righteous To Be? Interviews with Emmanuel Levinas* (Stanford: Stanford University Press, 2001).
Rubenstein, Mary-Jane, *Strange Wonder. The Closure of Metaphysics and the Beginning of Awe* (New York: Columbia University Press, 2006).
Schmidt, Michael, *Ekstatischen Transzendenz. Ludwig Binswangers Phänomenologie der Liebe und die Aufdeckung der sozialontologischen Defizite in Heideggers "Sein und Zeit"* (Würzburg: Königshauzen und Neumann, 2005).
Schrijvers, Joeri, "A Phenomenology of Liturgy: Jean-Yves Lacoste, in *Heythrop Journal* 46 (2005) 314–333.
———, "Orthodoxy: Process Nor Product. Truth and Its History," in L. Boeve, M. Lamberigts, and T. Merrigan (eds.), *Orthodoxy: Process or Product?* (Leuven: Peeters, 2009), pp. 45–61.
———, "In (the) Place of the Self. A Critical Study of Jean-Luc Marion's 'Au lieu de soi. L'approche de Saint Augustin,'" in *Modern Theology* 25 (2009) 661–686.
———, "Marion, Levinas, and Heidegger on the Question Concerning Ontotheology," in *Continental Philosophy Review* 43 (2010) 207–239.
———, *Ontotheological Turnings? The Decentering of the Modern Subject in Recent French Phenomenology* (Albany: State University of New York Press, 2011).
———, *An Introduction to Jean-Yves Lacoste* (Aldershot: Ashgate, 2012).
Schürmann, Reiner, *Heidegger on Being and Acting. From Principles to Anarchy*, trans. C.-M. Gros (Bloomington: Indiana University Press, 1987).
———, *Broken Hegemonies*, trans. R. Lilly (Bloomington: Indiana University Press, 2003).
Seidman, Bradley, *Absent at the Creation. The Existential Psychiatry of Ludwig Binswanger* (New York: Libra Publishers, 1983).
Shakespeare, Stephen, "The Word Became Machine: Derrida's Technology of Incarnation," in *Derrida Today* 6 (2013) 36–57.
Sloterdijk, Peter, *Kritiek van de cynische rede*, trans. T. Davids (Amsterdam: De Arbeiderspers, 1984).
———, *Eurotaoismus. Zur Kritik der politischen Kinetik* (Frankfurt a. Main: Suhrkamp, 1989).
———, *Derrida: An Egyptian. On the Problem of the Jewish Pyramid*, trans. W. Hoban (Cambridge, UK: Polity Press, 2009).

———, "Luhmann. Anwalt des Teufels. Von der Erbsünde, dem Egoismus der Systeme und den neuen Ironien," in *Nicht gerettet. Versuche nach Heidegger* (Frankfürt a. M: Suhrkamp, 2001), pp. 82–141.

———, *Kansen in de gevarenzone. Kanttekeningen bij de variatie in spiritualiteit na de secularisatie*, trans. M. Wildschut (Kampen: Agora, 2003).

———, *Sferen*, trans. H. Driessen (Amsterdam: Boom, 2007).

———, *God's Zeal. The Battle of the Three Monotheismsi*, trans. W. Hoban (Cambridge, UK: Polity Press, 2009).

———, *Rage and Time. A Psychopolitical Investigation*, trans. M. Wenning (New York: Columbia University Press, 2010).

———, *Neither Sun Nor Death*, trans. S. Corcoran (Los Angeles: Semiotexte, 2011).

———, *Bubbles. Spheres*, vol. 1: Microspherology, trans. W. Hoban (Los Angeles: Semiotexte, 2011).

———, *You Must Change Your Life. On Anthropotechnics*, trans. W. Hoban (Cambridge, UK: Polity Press, 2013).

Smith, James K. A., *Speech and Theology. Language and the Logic of Incarnation* (London: Routledge, 2002).

———, *Introducing Radical Orthodoxy. Mapping a Post-Secular Theology* (Grand Rapids: Baker Academic, 2004).

Spiegelberg, Herbert, *Phenomenology in Psychology and Psychiatry* (Evanston, IL: Northwestern University Press, 1972).

Theunissen, Michael, *Der Andere. Studien zur Sozialontologie der Gegenwart* (Berlin: Walter de Gruyter, 1965).

Vahabzadeh, Peyman, review of *Broken Hegemonies* by Reiner Schürmann, in *Journal for Cultural and Religious Theory* 5 (2004) 51–56.

Verhack, Ignace, *Wat bedoelen wij wanneer we God zeggen?* (Kalmthout: Pelckmans, 2011).

Verter, Mitchell, "The Anarchism of the Other Person," in Nathan J. Jun and Shane Wahl (eds.), *New Perspectives on Anarchism* (Plymouth: Lexington Books, 2010), pp. 67–83.

Voti, Véronique-Marion, *Epochal Discordance. Hölderlin's Philosophy of Tragedy* (Albany: State University of New York Press, 2006).

Watkin, Christopher, *Phenomenology or Deconstruction? The Question of Ontology in Maurice Merleau-Ponty, Paul Ricoeur and Jean-Luc Nancy* (Edinburgh: Edinburgh University Press, 2009).

———, *Difficult Atheism. Post-Theological Thinking in Alain Badiou, Jean-Luc Nancy and Quentin Meillassoux* (Edinburgh: Edinburgh University Press, 2011).

Žižek, Slavoj, "Dialectical Clarity versus the Misty Conceit of Paradox," in C. Davis (ed.), *The Monstrosity of Christ. Paradox or Dialectic?* (Cambridge: MIT Press, 2009), pp. 234–306.

———, "The Fear of Four Words. A Modest Plea For the Hegelian Reading of Christianity," in C. Davis (ed.), *The Monstrosity of Christ. Paradox or Dialectic?* (Cambridge: MIT Press, 2009), pp. 24–109.

Index

Abensour, Miguel, 41, 323n64, 324n72
Achterhuis, Hans, 336n39
anarchy/ism, xiv, 30–43, 45, 117, 127, 158, 186–93, 204, 212, 300–302, 324n82, 325n90, 336n39, 345n4
animal/s, 19, 106, 112, 148, 230, 304, 319n49, 362n13
anthropocentrism, 34, 39–40, 51, 159, 304, 338n23, 354n9, 362n13
Arendt, Hannah, 31, 42, 45
atheism, xv, 1–2, 19, 59–60, 105, 122, 169–74, 177
  in Derrida, xiii, 171
  in Hägglund, 12, 15–16, 18, 146–51
authenticity/inauthenticity, 17, 32, 46, 50, 58, 256
  in Binswanger, 223, 233, 240–41, 257, 262, 265–67, 271–72, 278, 280–82, 357n67
  in Heidegger, 24–25, 264, 284, 303, 312, 326n19, 355n31
awe, 106, 152, 231, 242

Barth, Karl, 77, 339n43
Barthes, Roland, 71
Bataille, Georges, 66, 327n27
being in default, 303–305, 310–16
Binswanger, Ludwig, xi, xiii–xiv, xvi–xvii, 5–10, 20, 51, 103, 208, 209, 219, *223–297*, 299–301, 303–304, 311, 315
  on *Bedeutungsrichtung*, 278–84
  and Freud, 225, 257
  and Marion, 219, 234, 240, 268, 299–300, 357n54
  on proportionality, 236, 249, 281
  therapy/therapeutic practice, 230, 245, 256–57, 262, 267, 280–81
  transcendental turn in, 275–76
  See also authenticity/inauthenticity; Heidegger and; metaphysics and
Blanchot, Maurice, 67
Blumenberg, Hans, 58, 98, 103–104, 114, 328n19
Boss, Medard, 245–46, 267, 282
Brunner, Emil, 77
Buber, Martin, 188, 225, 250, 276, 346n12

capitalism, xi, 59, 71, 97, 112, 120–21, 127, 301
Caputo, John D., xii–xiv, xv, 2, 3, 7, 11–21, 85, 87, 94, 125, 126, 127, *133–211*, 215–16, 218–19, 279, 288, 295–96, 297, 299–300, 303, 315, 319n34, 359n110, 359n9, 362n13
  on (non)sovereign God, 178, 185–86, 188, 209, 300

375

Caputo, John D. *(continued)*
  on (un)conditionality, 167–69, 178–80, 219, 295–96, 300. *See also* Derrida on
  See also faith, finitude, event of world, Heidegger and; metaphysics and

christian reversal of values, 122, 127, 185–89, 206, 300, 315
Coulomb, Mireille, 258, 295, 351n20, 351n21, 354n2, 355n30, 356n47, 356n48, 361n3

decentering, 312
Depraz, Nathalie, 361n3
Derrida, Jacques, xii, iv, 3, 4, 6, 8, 15, 16–17, 30, 38, 40, 41–44, 45, 49, 51, 59, 61, 65, 67, 92, 94, 95, 108, 116, 123, 125, 133, 134, 141, 142, 145, 148, 149, 158, 160, 162, *165–85*, 192, 208, 216, 240, 253, 266, 272, 278–79, 286, 287, 297, 302, 306, 310, 311, 314, 315, 318n30, 319n33, 319n49, 319n51, 346n23
  critique of Nancy, 17, 57, 66, 72–82, 126, 135, 163
  on law/s, 211–15
  principle of philosophy, xvii, 269
  quasi-transcendental, xvi–xvii, 147, 163, 174, 295–96, 356n47
  salut sans salvation, 17, 18–21, 208, 291, 331n121
  sovereignty, xvi, 4, 14, 89–90, 93, 127, 143, 154, 298, 314. *See also* Sloterdijk on; Caputo on (non) sovereign God
  (un)conditional, xiii, 79, 123, 134–35, 142, 146, 150–53, 151–61, 165, 167–69, 171, 173–74, 192, 341n62
  See also Event of World; metaphysics and; phenomenology; transcendence; transcendental history (Heidegger) ontotheology; primacy of bad conscience

dialectic
  in Binswanger, xvii, 235, 237, 249, 254, 265, 283–84, 354n7, 354n17
  in Caputo, 190–92
  in Marion, 190–91, 203, 207, 348n99
  in Nancy, 241

Dilthey, Wilhelm, 257, 287–89, 361n36
Doyon, Maxime, 339n33

Eckhart, Meister, 44, 172
elementary faith, 3, 11–12, 18, 208, 254, 306, 318n29
  See also greeting
event of world, 18, 88, 106, 145, 180, 293, 300–302, 310, 313, 316
  in Binswanger, 283, 286, 292, 297, 315
  in Caputo, 13, 21, 133–34, 136, 144, 148, 162, 165–69, 178, 186, 190–91, 215
  in Derrida, 161, 330n89
  in Nancy, 51, 54, 64–65, 73, 302
  in Schürmann, 11, 33–38, 126, 297

Fabbri, Lorenzo, 324n 82
faith (and belief), xi, xii, xiv–xv, 18, 56, 77–78, 165, 182–83, 242, 287, 331n131
  in Binswanger, 242, 248, 254, 287, 353n72
  in Caputo, xv, 13–14, 21, 133, 142, 146, 161, 163, 174, 176, 182–83, 193, 206
  in Derrida, 173, 176, 183
  in Heidegger, 313
  in Nancy, 56, 71, 77–78, 80, 82

fanaticism/fundamentalism, 95, 128, 193, 249, 255, 271, 272, 285–86, 292

finitude, xi–xii, xvii, 1, 7, 9, 12, 13, 22, 88, 91, 161, 164, 194, 293, 295, 303, 305, 313, 314, 349n4
 in Binswanger, 10–11, 231–32, 248, 261, 287–89, 291
 in Caputo (finite infinity), 146–51, 154–55, 163, 191
 in Derrida, 159, 161
 in Hägglund (infinite finitude)12, 146–51
 in Heidegger, 25–26, 223, 312
 and Levinas, 155, 158, 161
 in Marion, 348n33
 in Schürmann, 31–32, 34, 44
 in Sloterdijk, 93–94
Foucault, Michel, 35, 242, 243, 353n73, 353n75
Freud, Sigmund
 See Binswanger and
Fritz, Peter, 334n44
Fynsk, Christopher, 356n45

Gagey, Henri-Jérôme, 344n34
Gasché, Rodolphe, 41, 44, 325n85
Gelassenheit (releasement), 37, 88, 125, 323n49, 337n52
Girard, René, 345n6
greeting (salutation), xiii, xvi–xvii, 6, 18, 20–21, 82, 179, 208, 226, 250–51, 311
 in Binswanger, 230–32, 291
 in Levinas, 227–29, 306
 in Nancy, 21, 51–53, 226–27
Granel, Gerhard, 67, 329n88, 330n93
Gros, Caroline, 353n75, 354n2
Gschwandtner, Christina, 22, 319n48, 348n70

Heidegger, Martin, xii, xiii, xiv, 4, 6, 16, 22–26, 29, 63, 65, 74, 125, 126, 152, 182–83, 226, 251, 276, 296, 298, 299, 302, 312–14, 320n51, 322n21, 360n13, 362n13, 362n24
 and Binswanger, 9, 11, 223–25, 233–37, 240–43, 245–49, 256–57, 261–62, 264–67, 271–72, 275, 277–82, 299, 303, 311, 350n40, 352n49, 355n31, 357n67
 and Caputo, 138, 145, 148, 168, 181, 192, 210, 216, 359n110
 and Derrida, 42–43, 73, 81, 125, 319n33
 failure of Dasein, 25–26, 257, 304, 311–12, 320n59
 fundamental uncertainty, xiv, 11, 94, 137, 148, 167, 169, 363n37
 and Levinas, 61, 155, 275, 303–10, 329n89, 332n142, 332n149
 and Nancy, 16, 48, 50–52, 53, 61, 64, 67, 278, 326n17, 350n5
 and Schürmann, 11, 29–38, 41, 45–46, 322n31
 and Sloterdijk, 83, 88, 91, 93–94, 102–103, 115–17, 120, 334n1
 transcendental history/icity, 66, 302, 319n51, 329n81
 See also Metaphysics and hermeneutics, 296, 349n4
Hägglund, Martin, xii–xiii, 1, 3, 11–18, 20, 22, 136, 141, 146–54, 159–63, 189, 191–92, 209, 303, 317n1, 317n14, 318n19, 319n40, 319n46, 339n34, 340n45, 340n52, 340n57, 341n62, 341n90, 341n103, 346n27, 362n12
Hart, Kevin, 13, 182, 318n16
Heikkila, Marta, 327n37
Husserl, Edmund, 76, 139, 159, 160, 199, 223, 240, 247, 253, 257, 258, 262, 293, 302, 306, 348n88, 355n30, 356n44, 356n47, 356n48
horror, 247, 261, 284, 353n7
Houellebecq, Michel, xvi, 83, 312, 336n52, 346n29
hubris, xi, xvii, 31, 37, 46, 153, 176, 226, 227, 267

incarnation, xiv, 6, 7, 8, 9, 20, 21, 26, 56, 63–66, 82, 134, 147, 154, 161, 168, 171, 182, 187, 201, 204, 209, 213, 215–19, 229, 231, 237, 240, 252, 268, 273, 291, 297, 299, 301, 304, 311, 330n96, 339n40, 348n88

indeconstructible, 161, 254, 292, 299
 in Caputo, 85, 300
 in Derrida, 134, 145–46, 337n5
 and Marion, 201
 in Nancy, 54–55, 66
 in Sloterdijk, 333n29

indifference, xv, 57, 89, 183, 185, 328n50 (to religion), 41 (to the other), 59–60, 89, 96, 108, 204, 207–209 (phenomenologically)

James, Ian, 327n35
Janicaud, Dominique, 42, 324n77

Kolakowski, Leszek, 340n50

Lacan, Jacques, 51
Lawlor, Leonard, 362n17
Lacoste, Jean-Yves, 301, 314, 333n32, 340n52, 344n34, 354n6, 355n31, 363n40
Levinas, Emmanuel, xiii, xiv, xvii, 2, 6, 7, 8, 12, 16, 18, 20, 30, 33, 34, 38–41, 45, 50–51, 59, 61, 79, 80–81, 86, 104, 107–108, 135, 145, 147–48, 150, 153–61, 162, 163, 165, 168, 175, 179, 180, 181, 185, 186, 187, 189, 192, 194, 210, 211, 2225, 227–30, 242, 247, 250–51, 264, 267, 269, 275, 276, 280, 282, 286, 292, 294, 295, 301, 303, 305–11, 319n47, 321n19, 321n20, 322n21, 323n55, 323n60, 327n27, 327n30, 329n89, 331n26, 331n141, 332n142, 338n9, 341n67, 342n86, 342n103, 343n21, 345n36, 346n23, 350n7, 355n21, 361n2, 362n19
 See also Heidegger and; metaphysics and
Loyola, Ignatius, 32, 332n151
Löwith, Karl, 4, 57, 85, 98, 265, 358n86
Lyotard, Jean-François, 53–54

Marion, Jean-Luc, xii, xv, 2, 4, 7, 16, 22, 33, 48, 57, 59, 60, 61, 87, 89, 96, 108, 144, 155, 157, 163, 183, *185–209*, 215, 217, 219, 226, 227, 251, 298, 309, 318n25, 321n19, 321n20, 322n21, 330n96, 333n25, 339n 28, 339n29, 340n52, 341n83, 345n10, 346n11–18, 346n25, 346n30, 346n33–37, 350n9, 353n; 61, 354n6, 361n2, 362n12. See also Binswanger and; metaphysics and; Nancy and
Merleau-Ponty, Maurice, 81–82, 216, 226, 250, 282, 327n27, 331n130, 332n147–49, 350n4, 350n6
metaphysics (ontotheology), xi–xii, 4–5, 14, 15, 33–35, 45, 46, 47, 75–82, 125–28, 144, 154, 298–99, 304–305, 320n52, 340n50, 345n36
 and Binswanger, 232, 241, 251–52, 304, 357n72
 and Caputo, 14, 16, 133, 136–37, 141, 152, 167, 189, 191, 215–16, 338n10, 342n103, 345n36
 and Derrida, xiv, 6, 8, 40, 42–43, 45, 73–81, 87, 150, 158–59, 161–62, 174–78, 216, 240, 250, 251–52, 315, 324n74, 338n25
 and Heidegger, 22, 43, 126–27, 177, 215–16, 298, 309, 320n52, 326n17, 333n25
 and Levinas, 38, 40, 154–59, 163, 175, 301
 and Marion, 144, 190, 195–98, 200, 345n10

and Nancy, 47–50, 54–58, 61, 67, 71, 73–81, 126, 217
and Schürmann, 31, 32, 34, 36–37, 43–44, 298, 340n55
and Sloterdijk, xv–xvi, 47, 87, 90–94, 98, 104, 105, 112–13, 115
See also natural metaphysician
Milbank, John, 59, 125, 144, 193, 214, 338n10, 343n4, 346n31
minimalistic universalism, 2–3, 6, 15, 111, 291, 300, 309, 311
Minister, Stephen, 3, 13, 317n2
muteness of being, xvii, 10–11, 35, 56, 64–66, 103–104, 122, 133, 218, 247, 270, 302, 304, 338n23, 354n9, 361n3

Naas, Michael, 3–4, 15, 18, 317n4, 318n23, 318n29
Nancy, Jean-Luc, xii, xiv, xv–xvii, 4, 6, 13, 16, 17, 20–21, 85, 88, 91, 94, 96, 97–98, 102–103, 121, 123, 125, 126, 128, 133–34, 135, 136, 146–47, 162, 180, 185, 191, 197, 217, 225–29, 250–51, 258, 268, 278, 292, 295, 297–98, 300, 302, 315, 318n27, 324n82, 337n3, 347n47, 350n5–7, 352n45–47, 354n20, 361n5, 362n9
and eclipse of essence, 66, 75–82, 126, 197
on love, 237–38
and Marion, 48, 61, 197, 217, 268
on unconditionality, 53, 66, 79
See also Derrida and; dialectic; Event of world; faith (and belief); greeting; Heidegger and; Metaphysics and
Narbonne, Jean-Marc, 282, 360n21
'natural metaphysician,' xv, 14, 15, 30, 31, 43–44, 45, 126–28, 154, 159, 162, 165, 174–78, 185, 189, 190, 193, 298–99

Needleman, Jacob, 246, 354n5, 356n41, 356n44
nihilism, 8, 18, 59, 69, 97, 140, 167, 185, 194–98, 207, 343n4
not quite non-christian culture, 17–18, 57, 60, 126, 170–71, 215–19

Olthuis, James, 342n97

phenomenology, xiii–xiv, 25, 34, 48, 76, 127, 141–42, 224, 226–27, 248, 250, 283, 285–86, 300, 302, 323n49, 336n48
in Binswanger, 254, 355n31
and Derrida, 76, 160–61, 293
empirical-transcendental, xvi–xvii, 3, 64, 182, 191, 219, 231–32, 240, 258, 268, 293–97, 355n31, 356n47, 357n72, 361n3
and Levinas, 157–61
and Marion, 199–201, 209
of the unapparent, 302
See also Derrida, quasi-transcendental
Pettigrew, David, 74, 327n35
Pirjeri, 175–76, 183, 215, 315
pluralism, 4, 84, 140–41, 217–18
politics of being, xiii, 4, 84, 95, 140–41, 153, 216, 218, 300
postsecularism, 2, 3–4, 5–11, 17, 60, 136, 140, 349n4
primacy of bad conscience, 303–16
in Binswanger, 304
in Caputo, 177
in Derrida, 167, 209–15, 286, 303–304
in Sloterdijk, 116–17
and theology, 314–15, 363n40

Raffoul, François, 25, 74, 320n60, 327n35
relativism, 60, 137, 140–41, 344
religious life (phenomenology of), xi, xiv–xv, 2, 6, 9, 15, 18–20, *21–28*, 116, 128, 177–78, 185, 208–209, 211, 282, 284–87, *293–317*, 349n4

religious life (phenomenology of) *(continued)*
  in Binswanger, 237–38, 251, 255, 265, 268, 275, 277, 282–87, 291, 299
  in Caputo, 87, 167, 178, 183, 185–89, 298–99
  in Derrida, 153–58
  in Heidegger, 22–26, 267, 312–16
  moments of, 22
  in Sloterdijk, xvi, 114–17, 120, 122
Rolland, Jacques, 41, 45, 324n73, 325n90
Rubenstein, Mary-Jane, 151–54, 159, 161, 340n58, 349n10

Sartre, Jean-Paul, 282, 327n27
secularization, 2–6, 10, 57–58, 98, 105, 247, 251
Schürmann, Reiner, xi, xii, xiv–xv, xvii, 4, 5, 11, 14, 15, 22, *29–46*, 53, 64, 106, 126, 127, 128, 133, 136, 150, 154, 165, 180, 193, 226, 283, 295, 297, 298, 300, 301, 305, 320n52, 325n4, 326n10, 329n74, 340n55, 345n36
  See also Event of world; finitude; Heidegger and; metaphysics and
Seidman, Bradley, 358n87
sex, 232, 252, 359n8
Schmidt, Michael, 355n35
Shakespeare, Stephen, 350n17
Simmons, Aaron, 3, 13, 22, 317n2
Sloterdijk, Peter, xii, xv–xvi, 2, 4–5, 47, 72, *83–129*, 183, 281–82, 291, 292, 295, 297, 298, 360n15, 360n19
  on sovereignty, 84, 92–93, 118–19, 120–22, 127

  See also finitude; Heidegger and; indeconstructible; metaphysics and; religious life
Smith, James K. A., 77, 194, 198, 331n134, 344n34, 346n32
Spiegelberg, Herbert, 350n4, 353n72

theology, 2, 4, 21, 57, 59–60, 65, 69, 72–73, 77–78, 96–98, 120, 122, 127–29, 136, 142–44, 149, 161, 167, 194, 196–99, 204, 206–207, 209, 215, 218, 268, 291n 312–16, 322n31, 338n25, 340n50, 344n34, 345n10, 348n99, 351n18
Theunissen, Michael, 275–76, 356n47, 356n72
transcendence, xi, xiv, 7, 34, 52–53, 58–59, 84, 129, 145, 147–48, 153–54, 155, 159, 194–95, 198–201, 208, 228–29, 237–38, 250–51, 257, 286, 295, 299, 339n43, 340n52, 344n25, 349n4

unredeemedness, 313–16

Vahabzadeh, Peyman, 31, 321n7
Verhack, Ignace, 211, 349n3
Verter, Mitchell, 325n90
Von Hoffmansthal, Hugo, xvii, 230, 241, 285, 351n23, 354n9
Voti, Véronique-Marion, 322n22

Watkin, Christopher, 1, 59, 217, 317n1, 328n48, 349n13, 349n15

Žižek, Slavoj, 215–16, 299, 349n11

www.ingramcontent.com/pod-product-compliance
Lightning Source LLC
Chambersburg PA
CBHW030125240426
43672CB00005B/27